...COUNTY PUBLIC LIBRARY
...N BRANCH LIBRARY
...ST WASHINGTON AVE.
...INTON, VA 24179

S0-AYA-382

Rumiko Takahashi

NO LONGER PROPERTY OF ROANOKE COUNTY LIBRARY

The spotlight on Rumiko Takahashi's career began in 1978 when she won an honorable mention in Shogakukan's annual New Comic Artist Contest for *Those Selfish Aliens*. Later that same year, her boy–meets–alien comedy series, *Urusei Yatsura*, was serialized in *Weekly Shonen Sunday*. This phenomenally successful manga series was adapted into anime format and spawned a TV series and half a dozen theatrical-release movies, all incredibly popular in their own right. Takahashi followed up the success of her debut series with one blockbuster hit after another—*Maison Ikkoku* ran from 1980 to 1987, *Ranma ½* from 1987 to 1996, and *Inuyasha* from 1996 to 2008. Other notable works include *Mermaid Saga*, *Rumic Theater*, and *One-Pound Gospel*.

Takahashi won the prestigious Shogakukan Manga Award twice in her career, once for *Urusei Yatsura* in 1981 and the second time for *Inuyasha* in 2002. A majority of the Takahashi canon has been adapted into other media such as anime, live-action TV series, and film. Takahashi's manga, as well as the other formats her work has been adapted into, have continued to delight generations of fans around the world. Distinguished by her wonderfully endearing characters, Takahashi's work adeptly incorporates a wide variety of elements such as comedy, romance, fantasy, and martial arts. While her series are difficult to pin down into one simple genre, the signature style she has created has come to be known as the "Rumic World." Rumiko Takahashi is an artist who truly represents the very best from the world of manga.

RIN-NE

VOLUME 6
Shonen Sunday Edition

STORY AND ART BY
RUMIKO TAKAHASHI

© 2009 Rumiko TAKAHASHI/Shogakukan
All rights reserved.
Original Japanese edition "KYOUKAI NO RINNE"
published by SHOGAKUKAN Inc.

Translation/Christine Dashiell
Touch-up Art & Lettering/Evan Waldinger
Design/Yukiko Whitley
Editor/Mike Montesa

The rights of the author(s) of the work(s) in this
publication to be so identified have been asserted in
accordance with the Copyright, Designs and Patents Act
1988. A CIP catalogue record for this book is available
from the British Library.

The stories, characters and incidents mentioned in
this publication are entirely fictional.

No portion of this book may be reproduced or
transmitted in any form or by any means without
written permission from the copyright holders.

Printed in the U.S.A.

Published by VIZ Media, LLC
P.O. Box 77010
San Francisco, CA 94107

10 9 8 7 6 5 4 3 2 1
First printing, July 2011

www.viz.com   WWW.SHONENSUNDAY.COM

PARENTAL ADVISORY
RIN-NE is rated T+ for Older Teen and is
recommended for ages 16 and up.
ratings.viz.com

0 1197 0650249 7

Story and Art by
Rumiko Takahashi

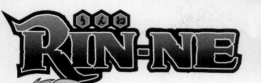

RIN-NE

りんね

Characters

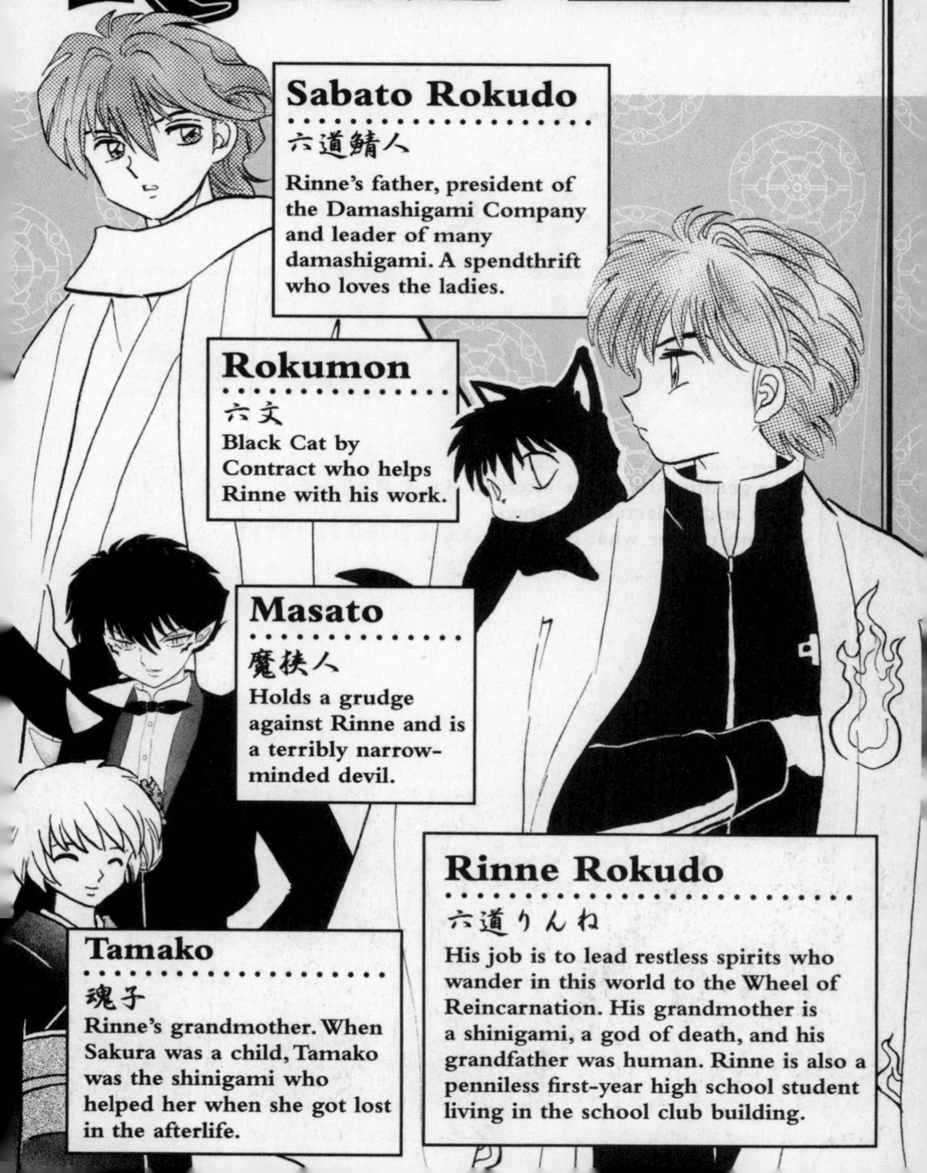

Sabato Rokudo

六道鯖人

Rinne's father, president of the Damashigami Company and leader of many damashigami. A spendthrift who loves the ladies.

Rokumon

六文

Black Cat by Contract who helps Rinne with his work.

Masato

魔狭人

Holds a grudge against Rinne and is a terribly narrow-minded devil.

Rinne Rokudo

六道りんね

His job is to lead restless spirits who wander in this world to the Wheel of Reincarnation. His grandmother is a shinigami, a god of death, and his grandfather was human. Rinne is also a penniless first-year high school student living in the school club building.

Tamako

魂子

Rinne's grandmother. When Sakura was a child, Tamako was the shinigami who helped her when she got lost in the afterlife.

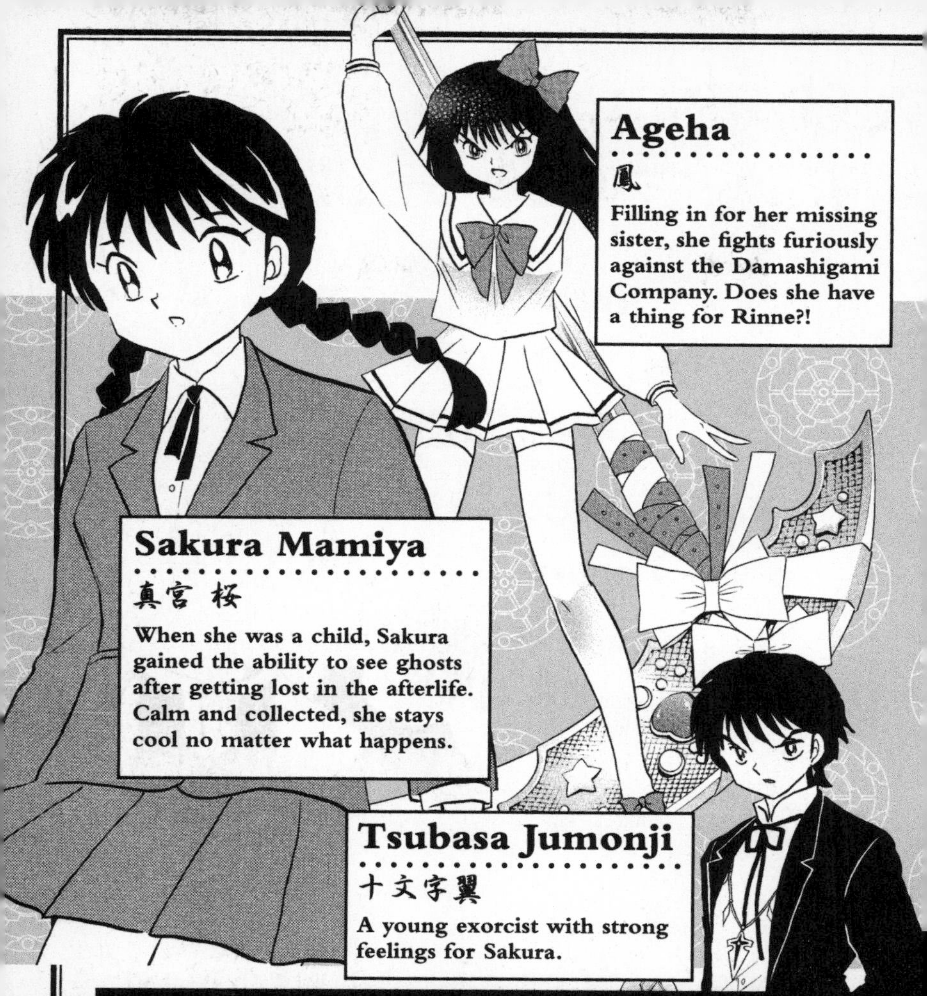

Ageha

鳳

Filling in for her missing sister, she fights furiously against the Damashigami Company. Does she have a thing for Rinne?!

Sakura Mamiya

真宮 桜

When she was a child, Sakura gained the ability to see ghosts after getting lost in the afterlife. Calm and collected, she stays cool no matter what happens.

Tsubasa Jumonji

十文字翼

A young exorcist with strong feelings for Sakura.

The Story So Far

Together, Sakura, the girl who can see ghosts, and Rinne the shinigami (sort of) spend their days helping spirits that can't pass on reach the afterlife, and deal with all kinds of strange phenomena at their school.

One day, Rinne's father Sabato appears and tries to force his son to take over the family business, the Damashigami Company. Rinne is able to fight off his father, but a young shinigami involved in the situation, Ageha, seems to have fallen in love with him. Sakura gets jealous, Jumonji cheers on Ageha, and Rinne's world is suddenly a lot more complicated.

RIN-NE

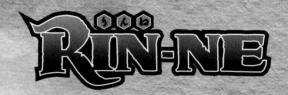

Contents

CHAPTER 49: THE POWER STONE'S CURSE

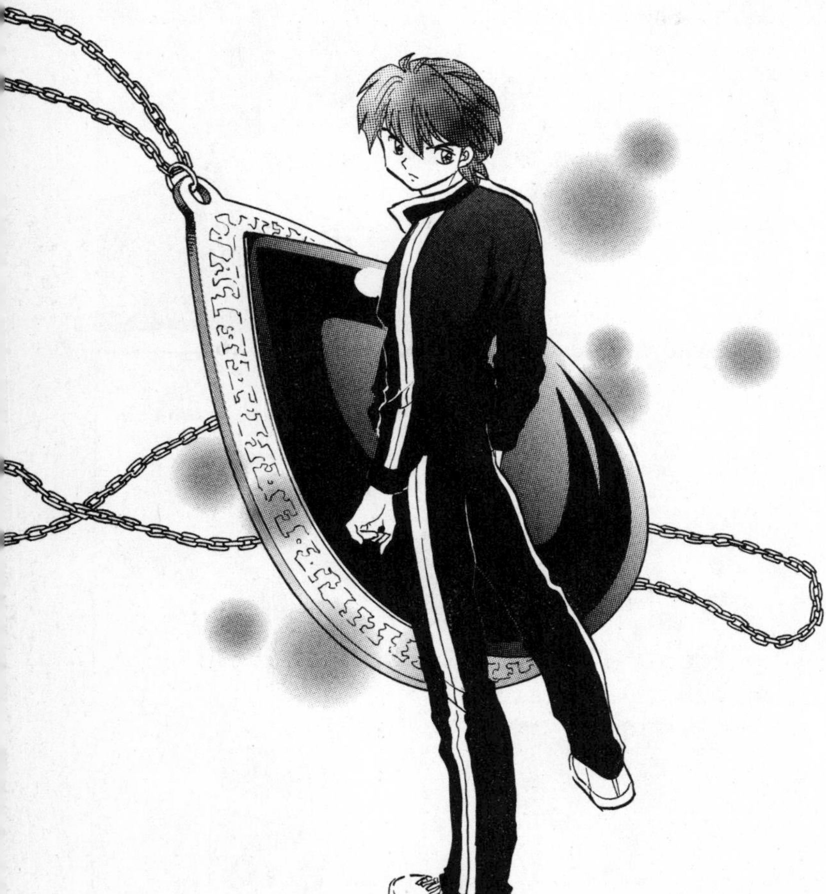

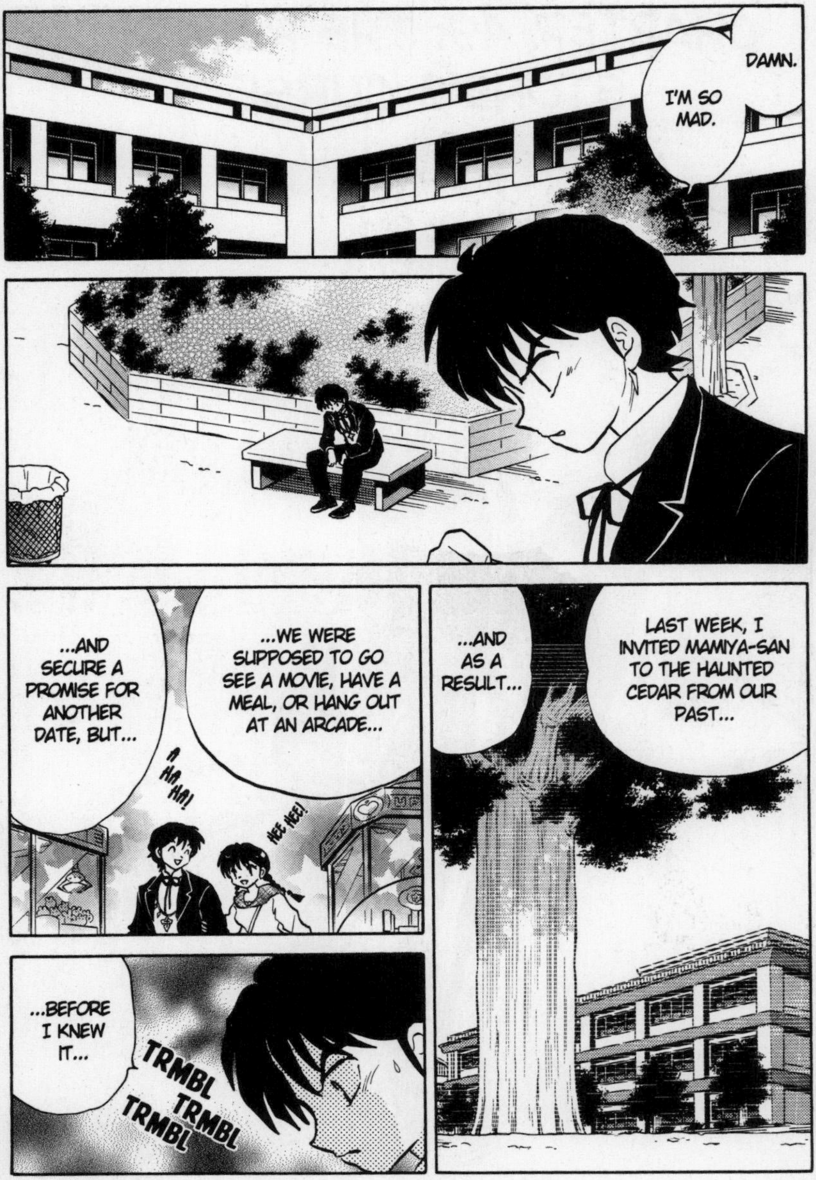
DAMN.
I'M SO MAD.
LAST WEEK, I INVITED MAMIYA-SAN TO THE HAUNTED CEDAR FROM OUR PAST...
...AND AS A RESULT...
...WE WERE SUPPOSED TO GO SEE A MOVIE, HAVE A MEAL, OR HANG OUT AT AN ARCADE...
...AND SECURE A PROMISE FOR ANOTHER DATE, BUT...
A HA HA!
HEE HEE!
...BEFORE I KNEW IT...
TRMBL TRMBL TRMBL

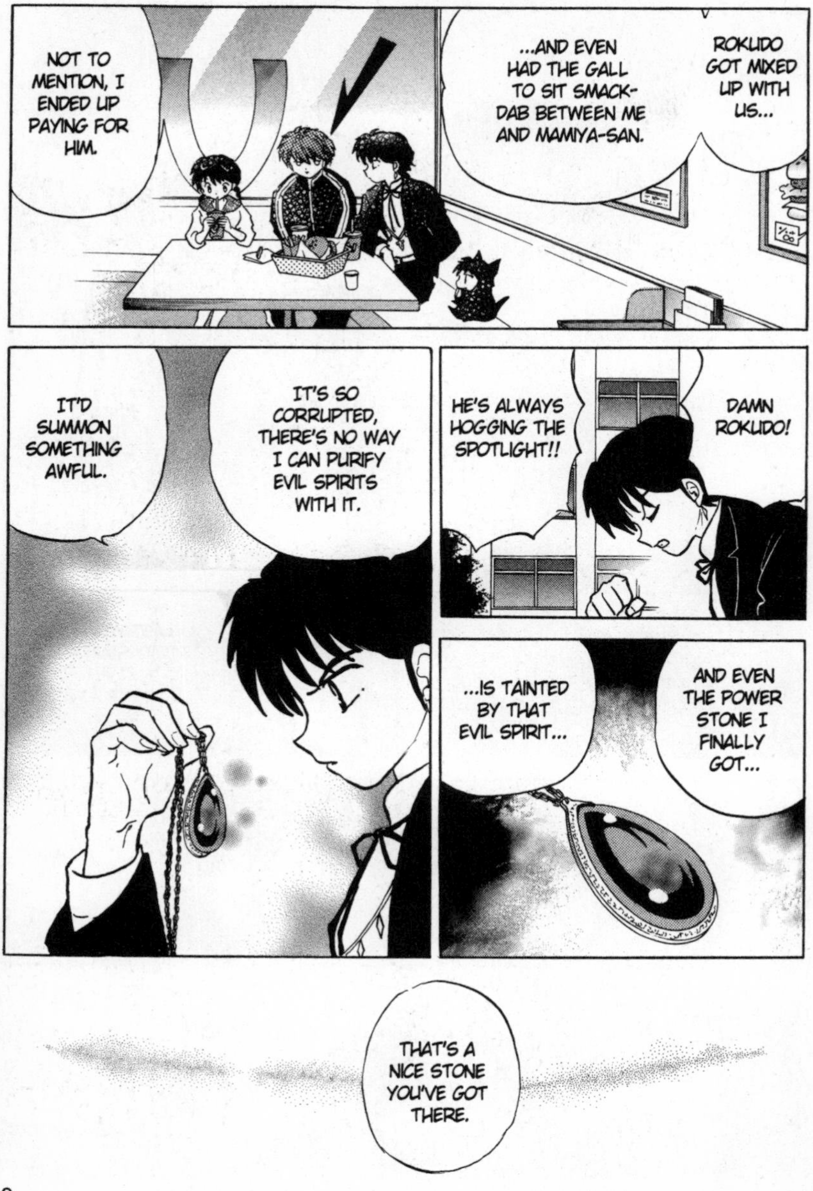
ROKUDO GOT MIXED UP WITH US...
...AND EVEN HAD THE GALL TO SIT SMACK-DAB BETWEEN ME AND MAMIYA-SAN.
NOT TO MENTION, I ENDED UP PAYING FOR HIM.
DAMN ROKUDO!
HE'S ALWAYS HOGGING THE SPOTLIGHT!!
AND EVEN THE POWER STONE I FINALLY GOT...
...IS TAINTED BY THAT EVIL SPIRIT...
IT'S SO CORRUPTED, THERE'S NO WAY I CAN PURIFY EVIL SPIRITS WITH IT.
IT'D SUMMON SOMETHING AWFUL.
THAT'S A NICE STONE YOU'VE GOT THERE.

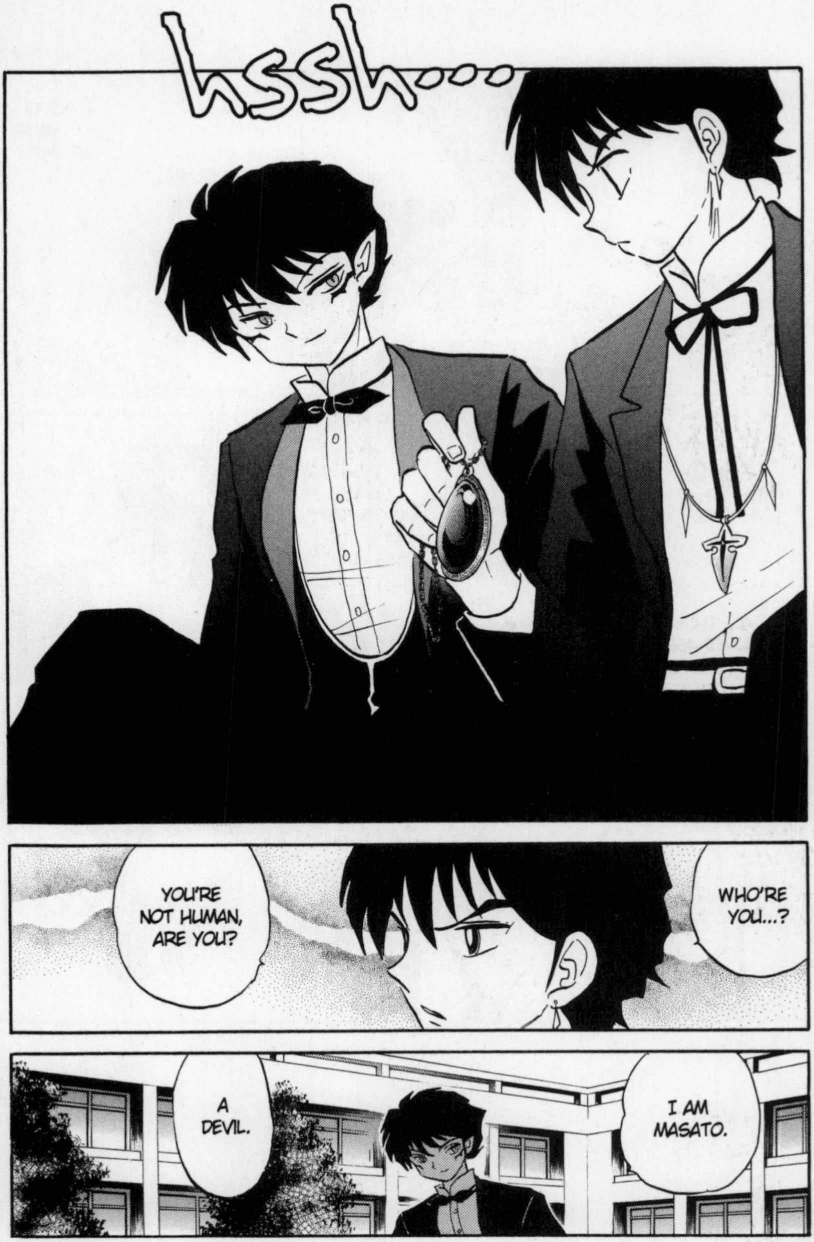
hssh...
WHO'RE YOU...?
YOU'RE NOT HUMAN, ARE YOU?
I AM MASATO.
A DEVIL.

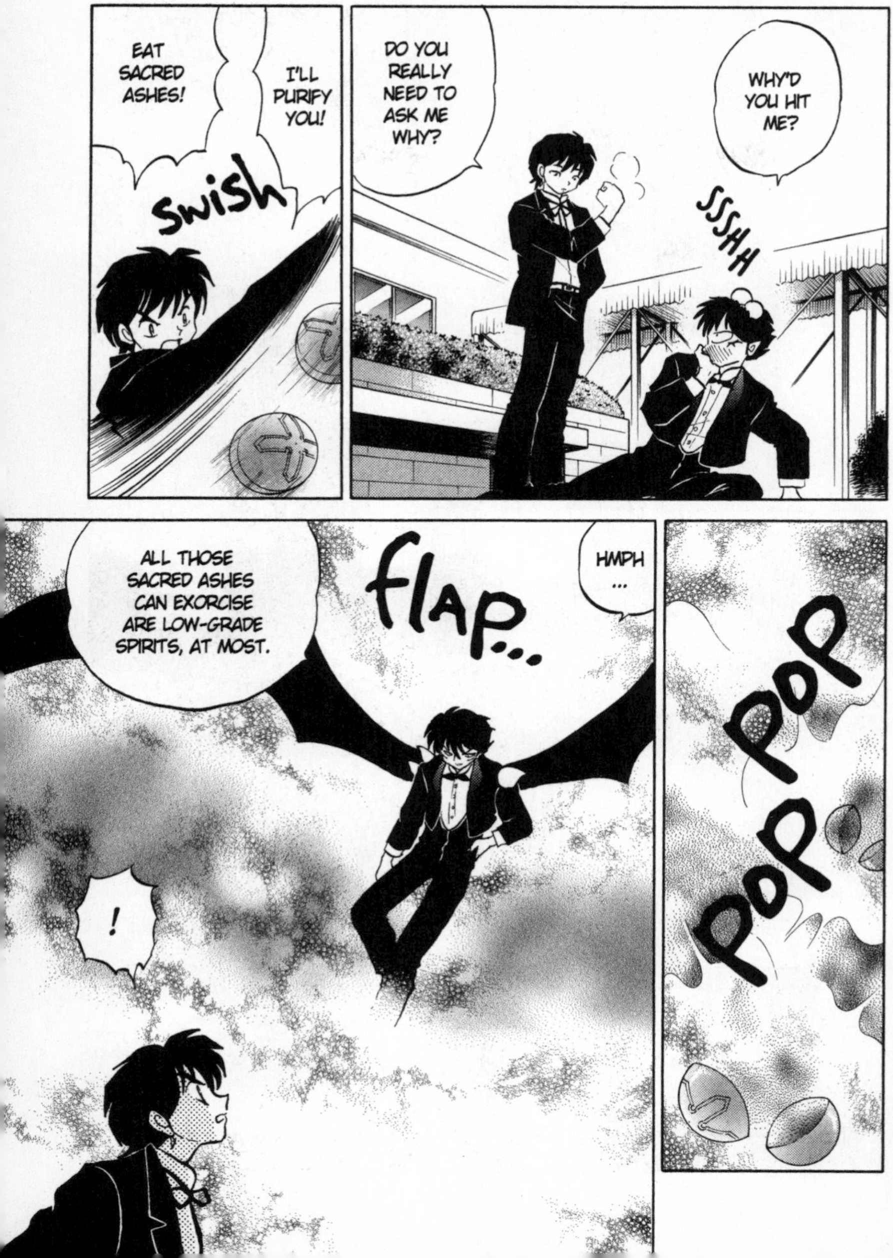
WHY'D YOU HIT ME?
SSSHH
DO YOU REALLY NEED TO ASK ME WHY?
I'LL PURIFY YOU!
EAT SACRED ASHES!
SWISH
POP POP
HMPH...
FLAP...
ALL THOSE SACRED ASHES CAN EXORCISE ARE LOW-GRADE SPIRITS, AT MOST.
!

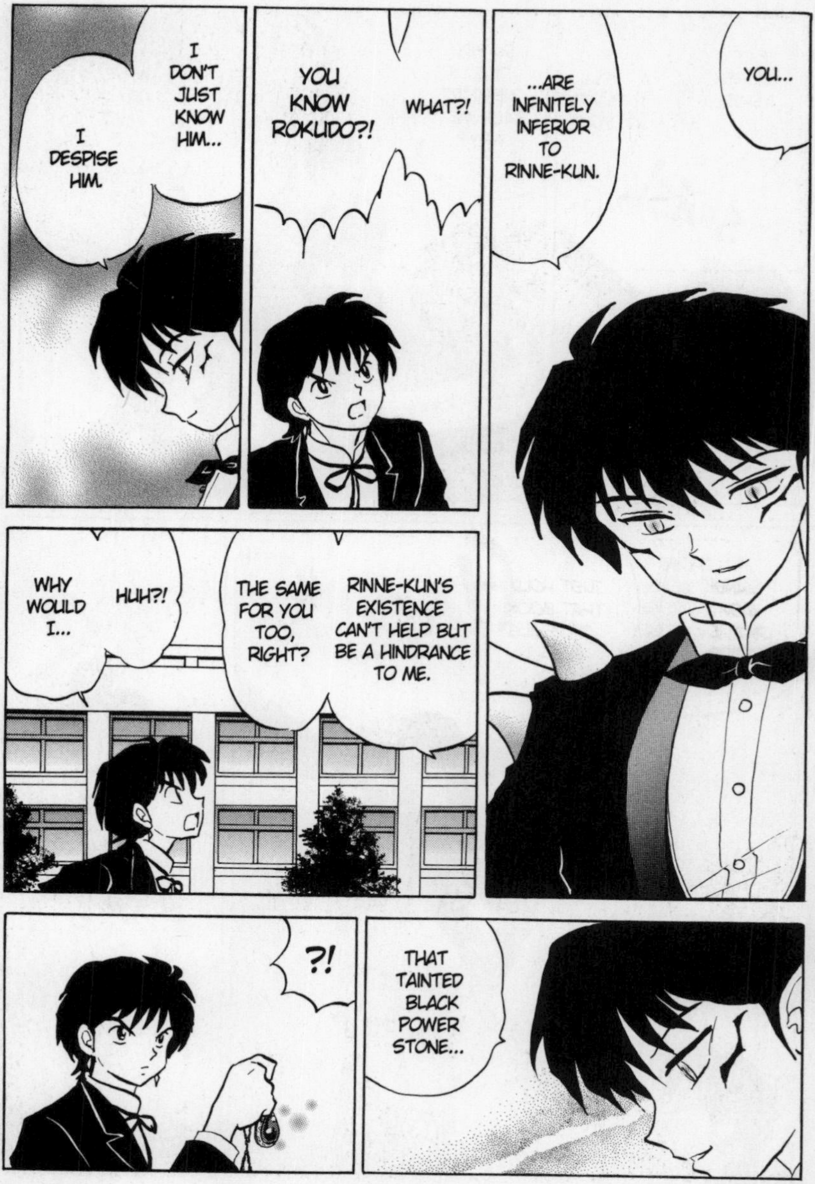
YOU...
...ARE INFINITELY INFERIOR TO RINNE-KUN.
WHAT?!
YOU KNOW ROKUDO?!
I DON'T JUST KNOW HIM...
I DESPISE HIM.
RINNE-KUN'S EXISTENCE CAN'T HELP BUT BE A HINDRANCE TO ME.
THE SAME FOR YOU TOO, RIGHT?
HUH?!
WHY WOULD I...
THAT TAINTED BLACK POWER STONE...
?!

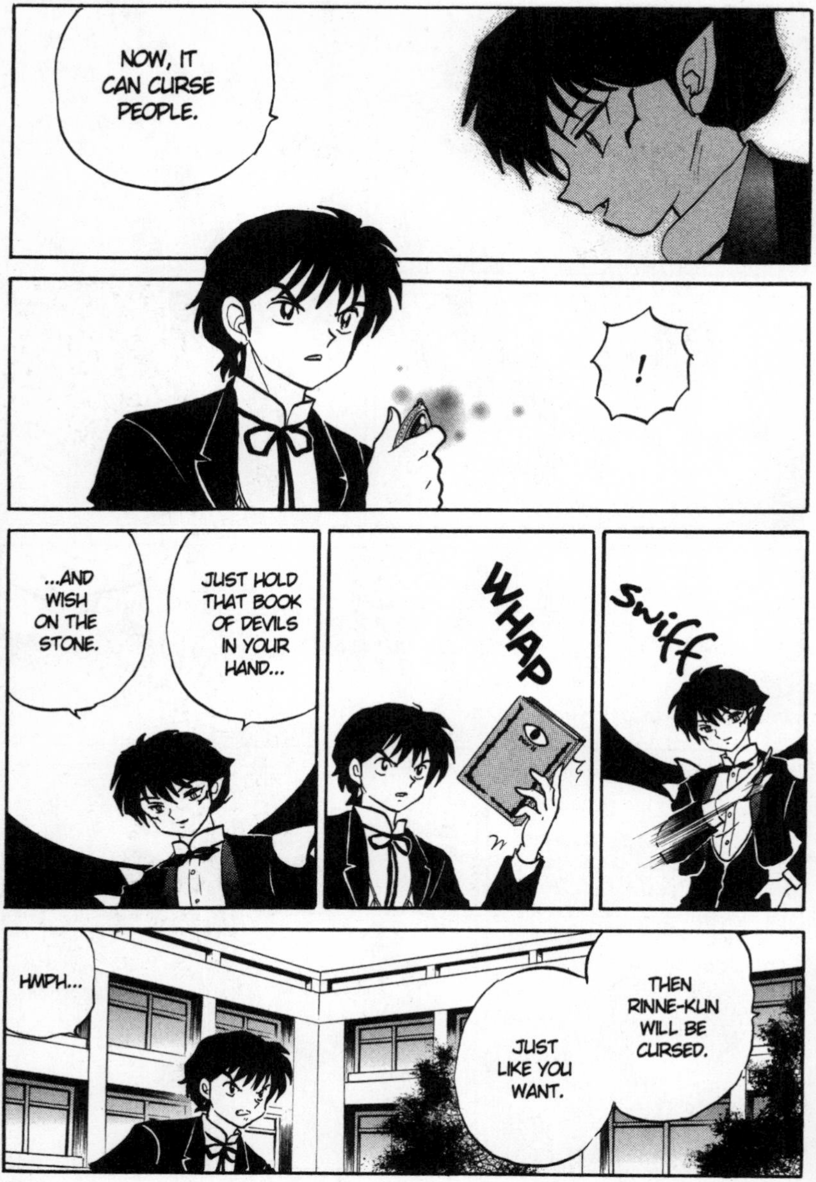
NOW, IT CAN CURSE PEOPLE.
!
Swiff
WHAP
JUST HOLD THAT BOOK OF DEVILS IN YOUR HAND...
...AND WISH ON THE STONE.
THEN RINNE-KUN WILL BE CURSED.
JUST LIKE YOU WANT.
HMPH...

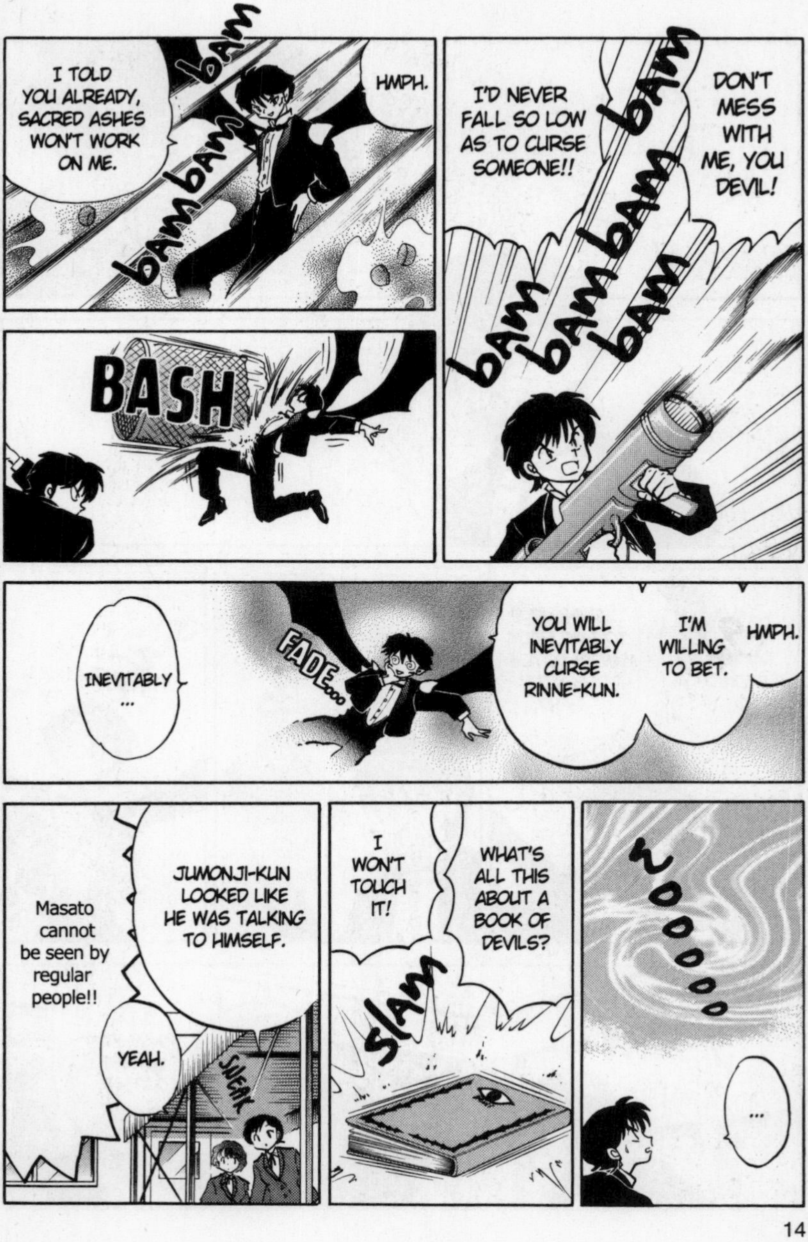
DON'T MESS WITH ME, YOU DEVIL!
I'D NEVER FALL SO LOW AS TO CURSE SOMEONE!!
bam bam bam bam bam bam bam
HMPH.
I TOLD YOU ALREADY, SACRED ASHES WON'T WORK ON ME.
bambam bam
BASH
HMPH.
I'M WILLING TO BET.
YOU WILL INEVITABLY CURSE RINNE-KUN.
FADE...
INEVITABLY ...
WOOOOOO
...
WHAT'S ALL THIS ABOUT A BOOK OF DEVILS?
I WON'T TOUCH IT!
SLAM
JUMONJI-KUN LOOKED LIKE HE WAS TALKING TO HIMSELF.
SNEAK
YEAH.
Masato cannot be seen by regular people!!

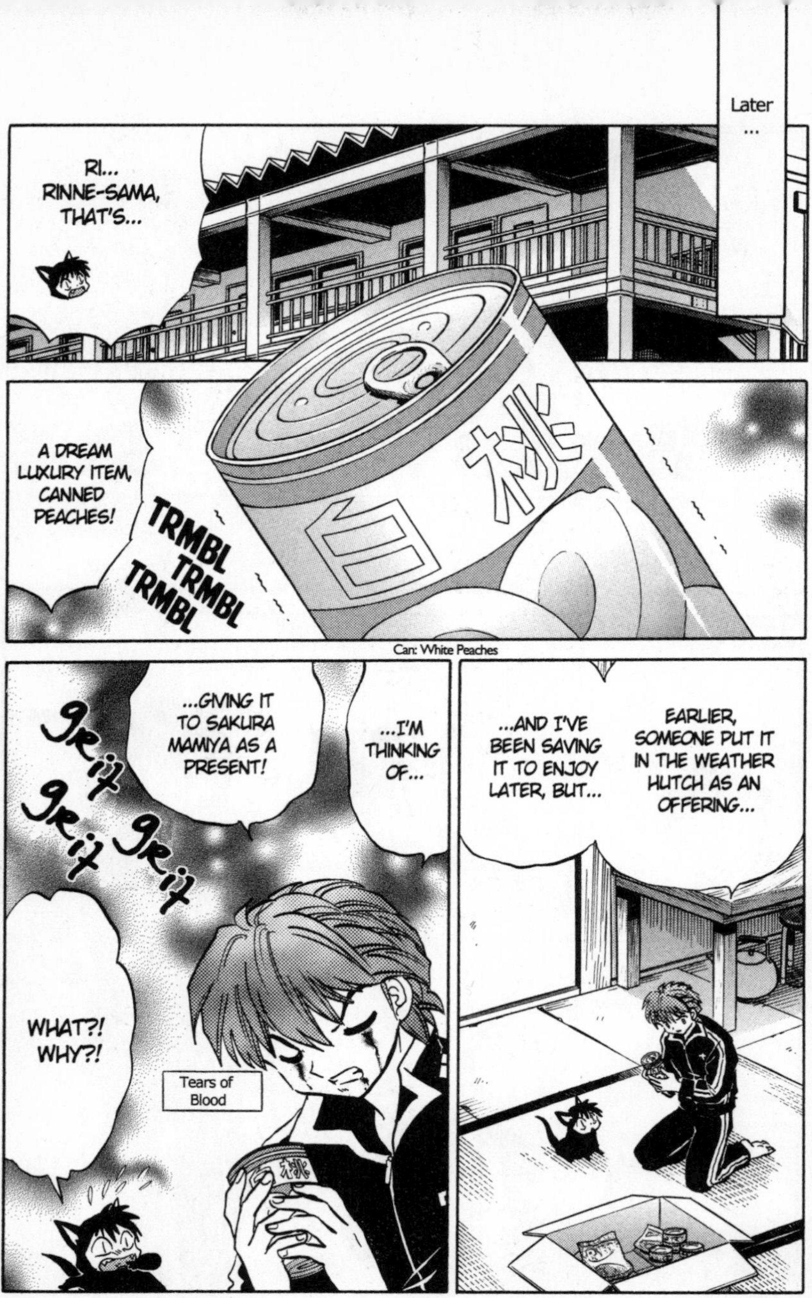

Later ...
RI... RINNE-SAMA, THAT'S...
A DREAM LUXURY ITEM, CANNED PEACHES!
TRMBL TRMBL TRMBL
Can: White Peaches
EARLIER, SOMEONE PUT IT IN THE WEATHER HUTCH AS AN OFFERING...
...AND I'VE BEEN SAVING IT TO ENJOY LATER, BUT...
...I'M THINKING OF...
...GIVING IT TO SAKURA MAMIYA AS A PRESENT!
grit grit grit
Tears of Blood
WHAT?! WHY?!

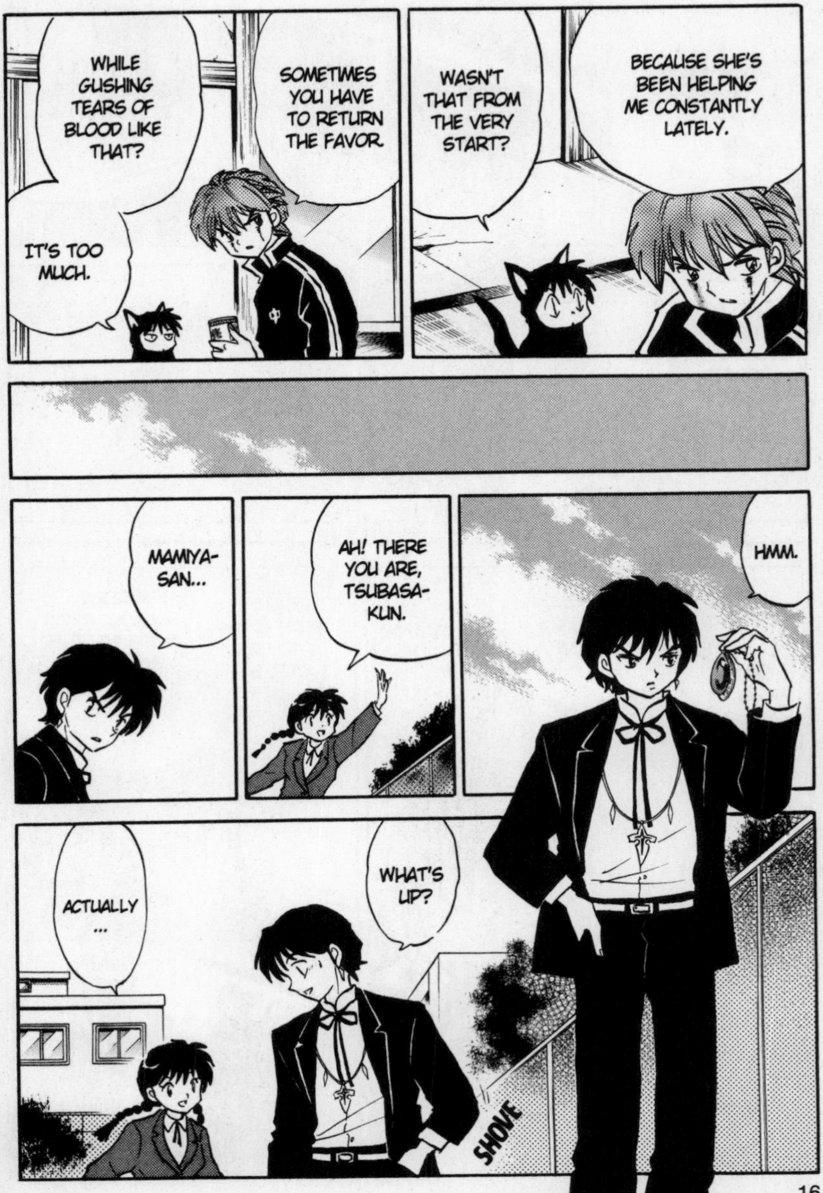
BECAUSE SHE'S BEEN HELPING ME CONSTANTLY LATELY.
WASN'T THAT FROM THE VERY START?
SOMETIMES YOU HAVE TO RETURN THE FAVOR.
WHILE GUSHING TEARS OF BLOOD LIKE THAT?
IT'S TOO MUCH.
HMM.
AH! THERE YOU ARE, TSUBASA-KUN.
MAMIYA-SAN...
WHAT'S UP?
ACTUALLY...
SHOVE

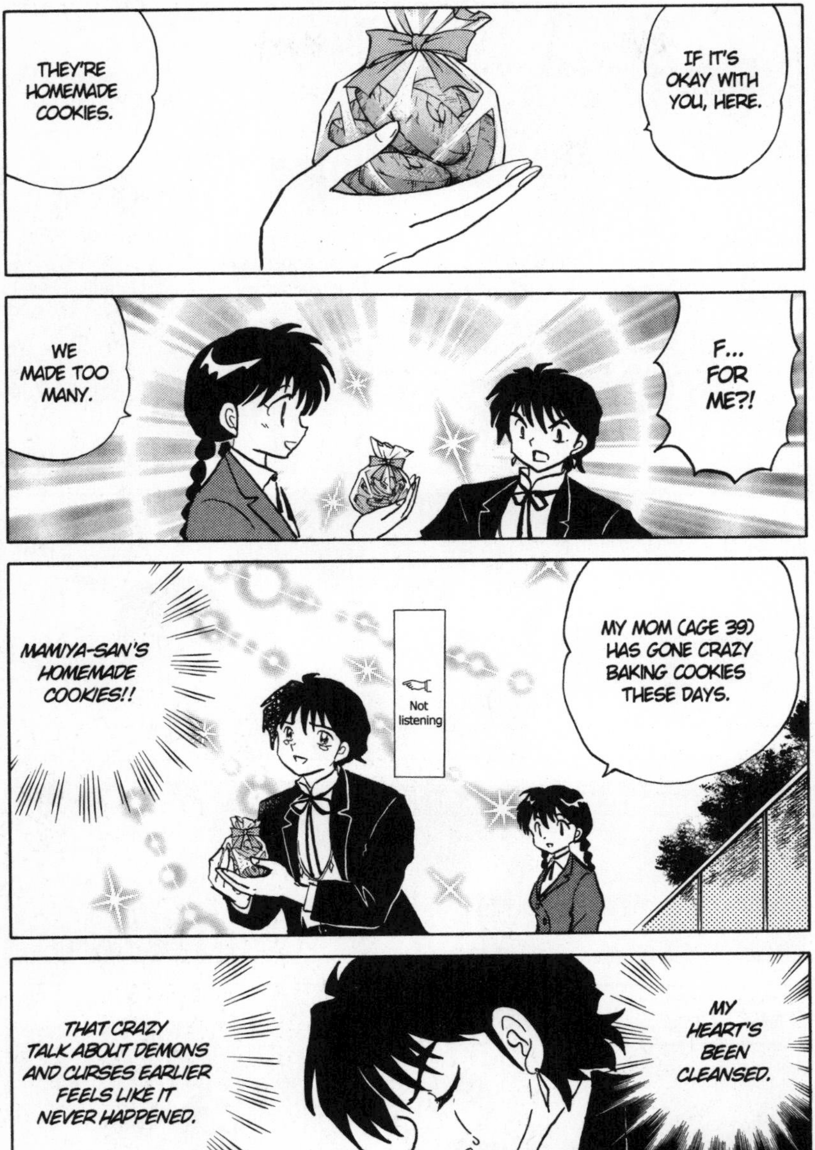
IF IT'S OKAY WITH YOU, HERE.
THEY'RE HOMEMADE COOKIES.
F... FOR ME?!
WE MADE TOO MANY.
MY MOM (AGE 39) HAS GONE CRAZY BAKING COOKIES THESE DAYS.
Not listening
MAMIYA-SAN'S HOMEMADE COOKIES!!
MY HEART'S BEEN CLEANSED.
THAT CRAZY TALK ABOUT DEMONS AND CURSES EARLIER FEELS LIKE IT NEVER HAPPENED.

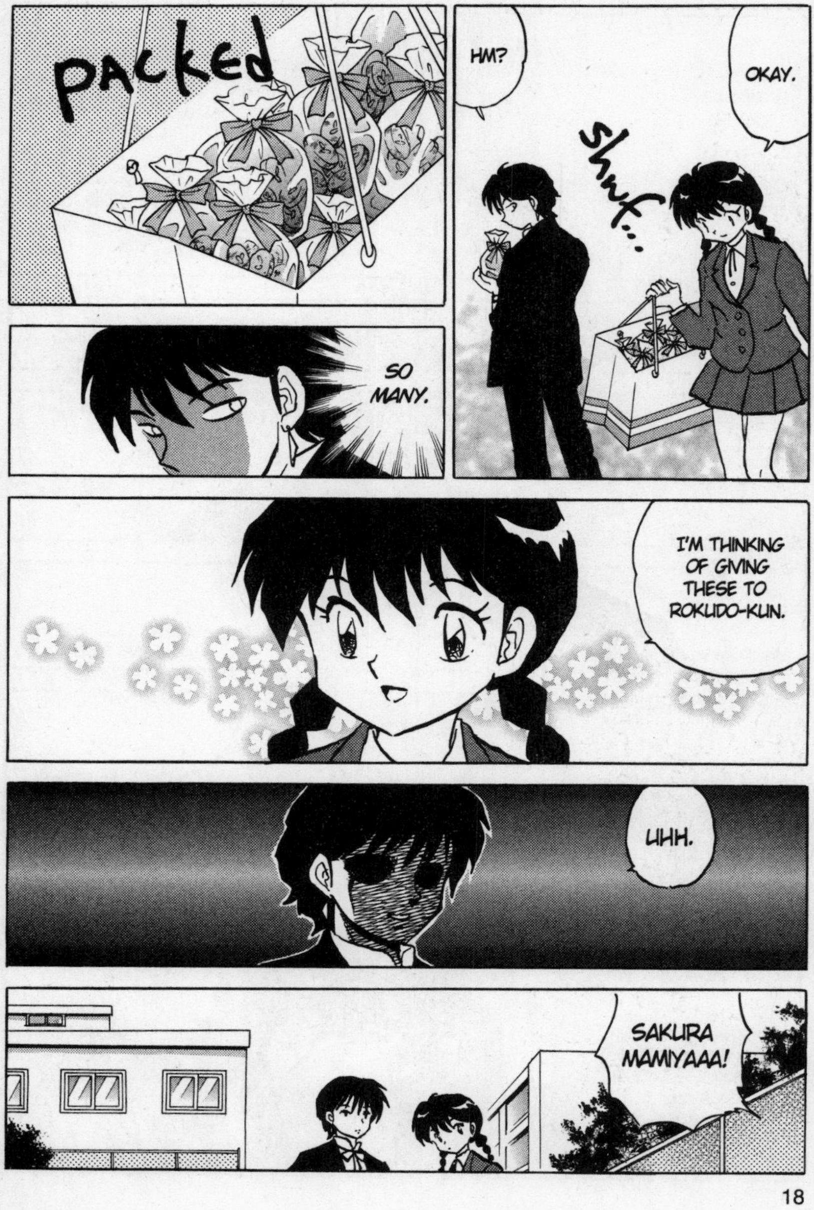
OKAY.
HM?
shuf...
packed
SO MANY.
I'M THINKING OF GIVING THESE TO ROKUDO-KUN.
UHH.
SAKURA MAMIYAAA!

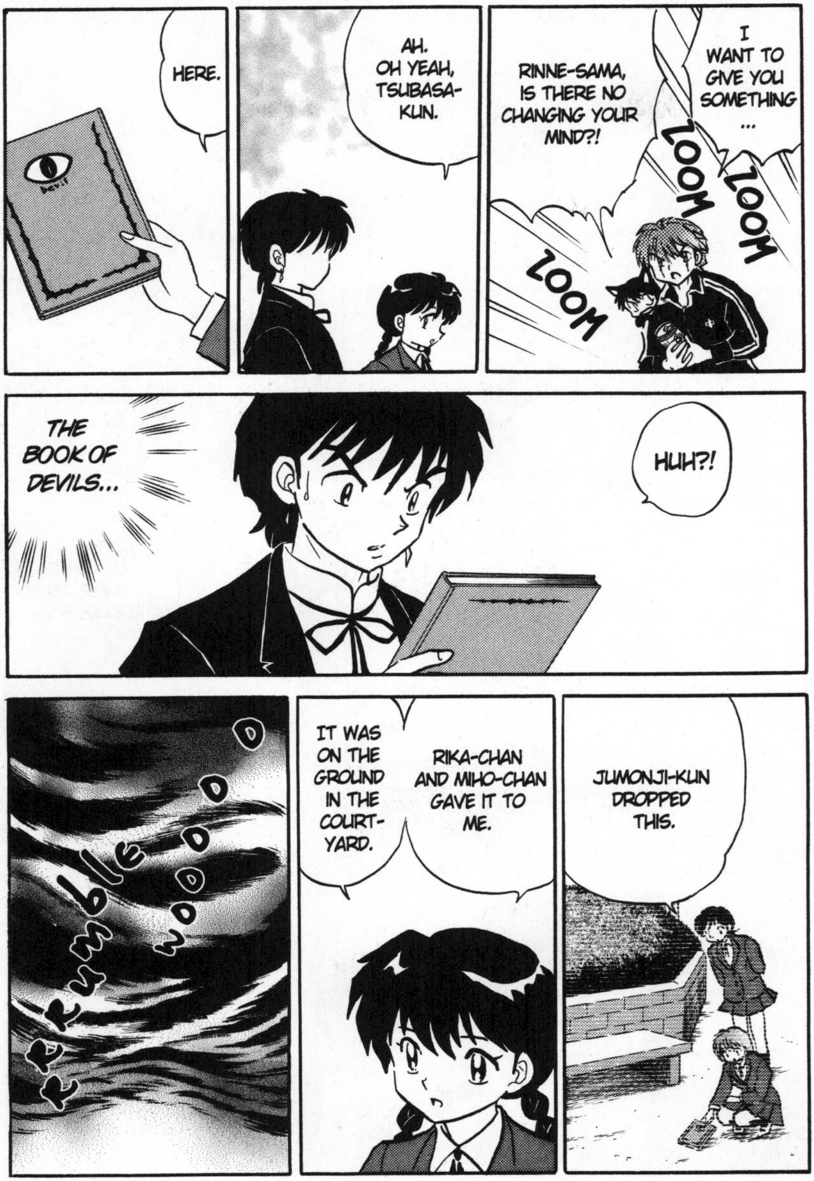
I WANT TO GIVE YOU SOMETHING ...
RINNE-SAMA, IS THERE NO CHANGING YOUR MIND?!
ZOOM
ZOOM
ZOOM
ZOOM
AH. OH YEAH, TSUBASA-KUN.
HERE.
HUH?!
THE BOOK OF DEVILS...
JUMONJI-KUN DROPPED THIS.
RIKA-CHAN AND MIHO-CHAN GAVE IT TO ME.
IT WAS ON THE GROUND IN THE COURTYARD.
RRumble
wooDDDD

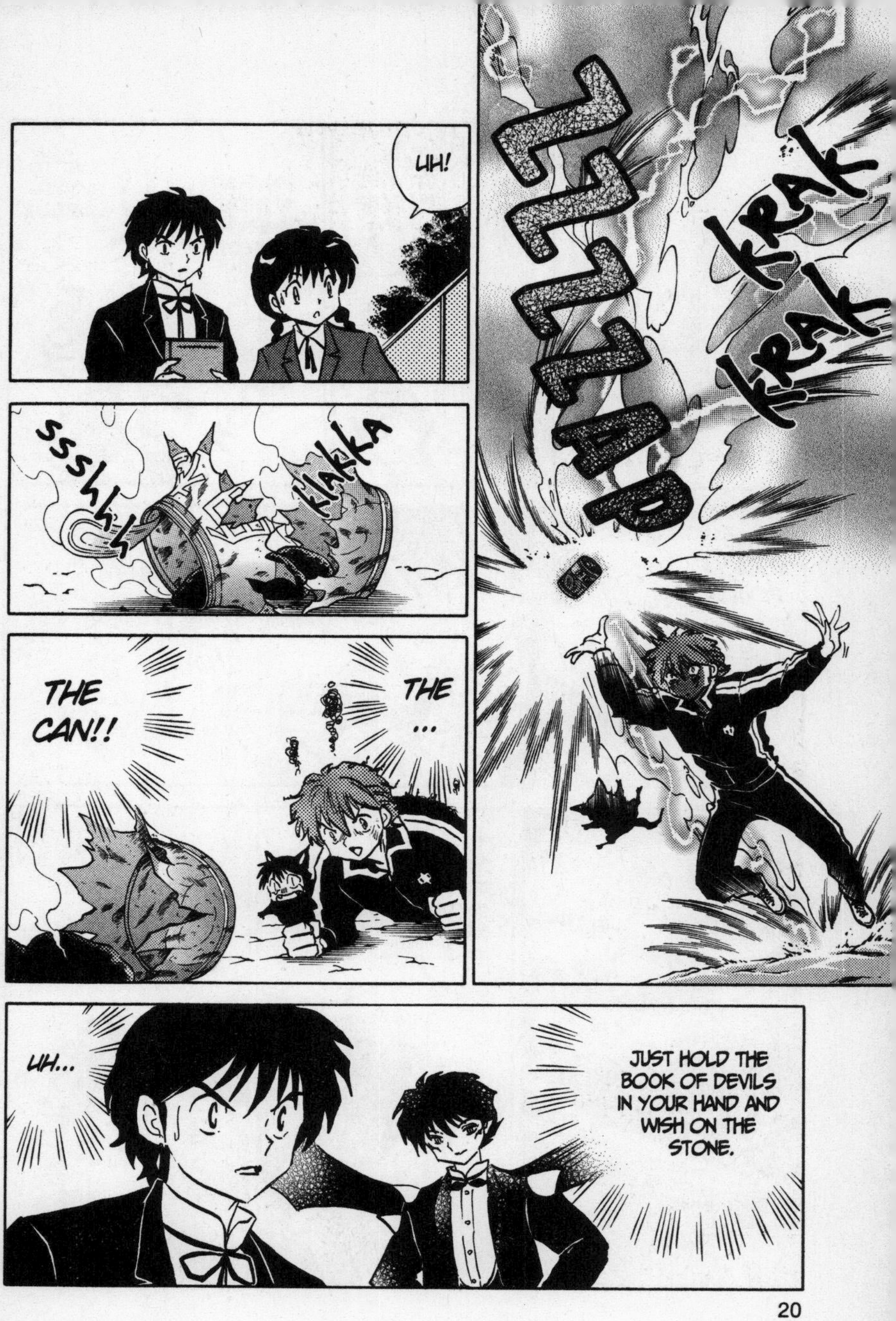
ZZZZAP
KRAK
KRAK
UH!
SSSHHHH
KLAKKA
THE ...
THE CAN!!
JUST HOLD THE BOOK OF DEVILS IN YOUR HAND AND WISH ON THE STONE.
UH...

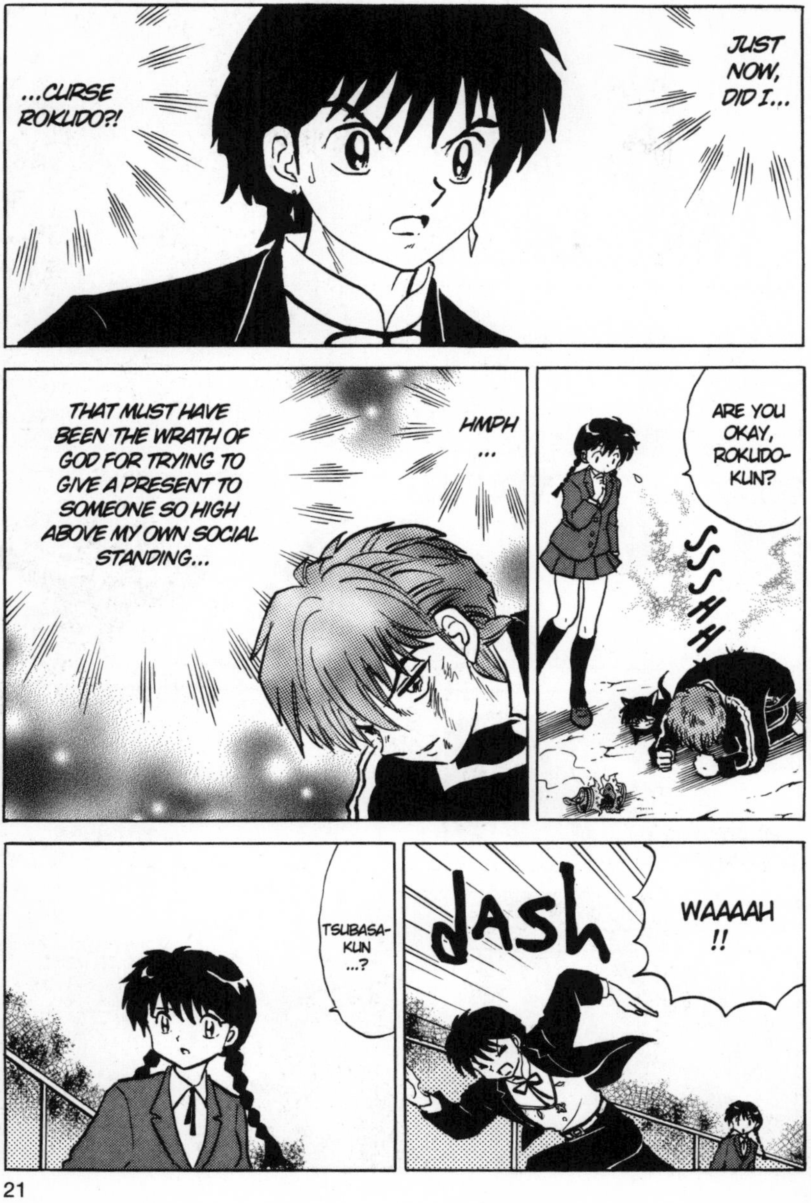
JUST NOW, DID I...
...CURSE ROKUDO?!
ARE YOU OKAY, ROKUDO-KUN?
SSSHHH
HMPH ...
THAT MUST HAVE BEEN THE WRATH OF GOD FOR TRYING TO GIVE A PRESENT TO SOMEONE SO HIGH ABOVE MY OWN SOCIAL STANDING...
WAAAAH !!
dash
TSUBASA-KUN ...?

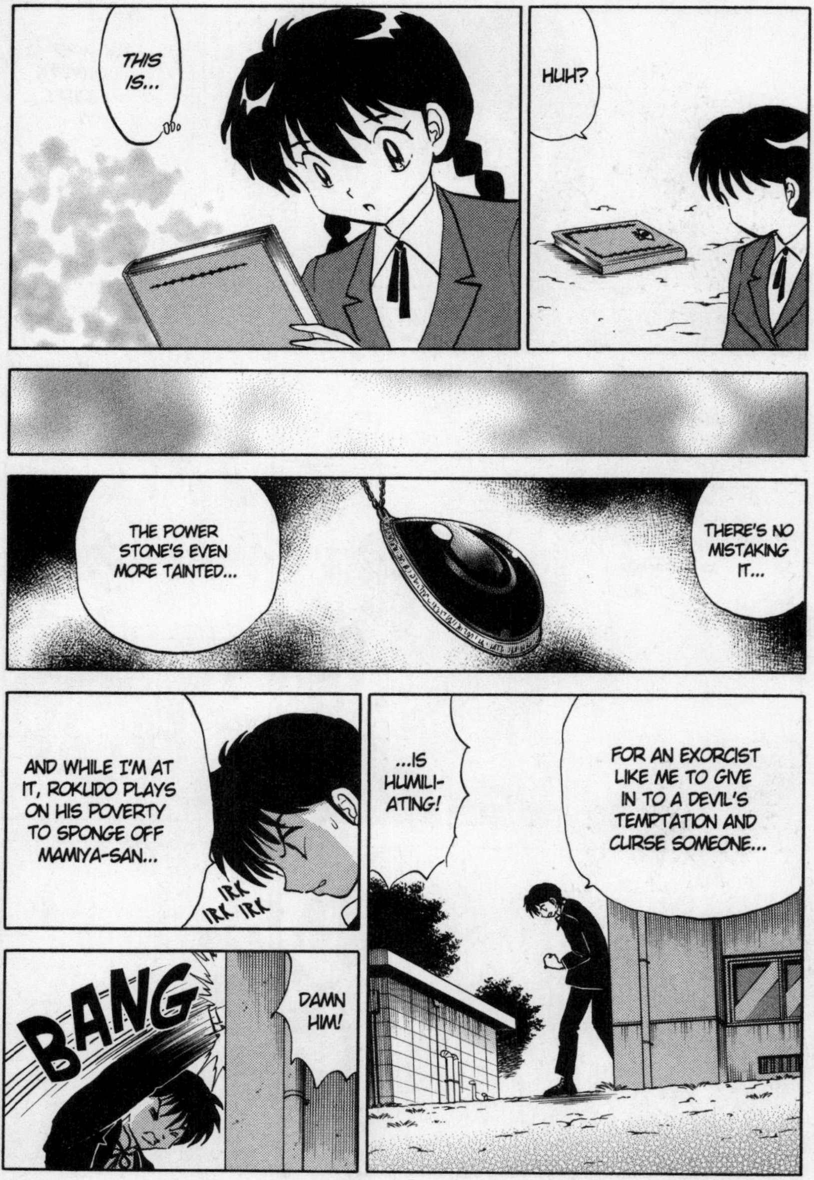
HUH?
THIS IS...
THERE'S NO MISTAKING IT...
THE POWER STONE'S EVEN MORE TAINTED...
FOR AN EXORCIST LIKE ME TO GIVE IN TO A DEVIL'S TEMPTATION AND CURSE SOMEONE...
...IS HUMILI-ATING!
AND WHILE I'M AT IT, ROKUDO PLAYS ON HIS POVERTY TO SPONGE OFF MAMIYA-SAN...
IRK IRK IRK
DAMN HIM!
BANG

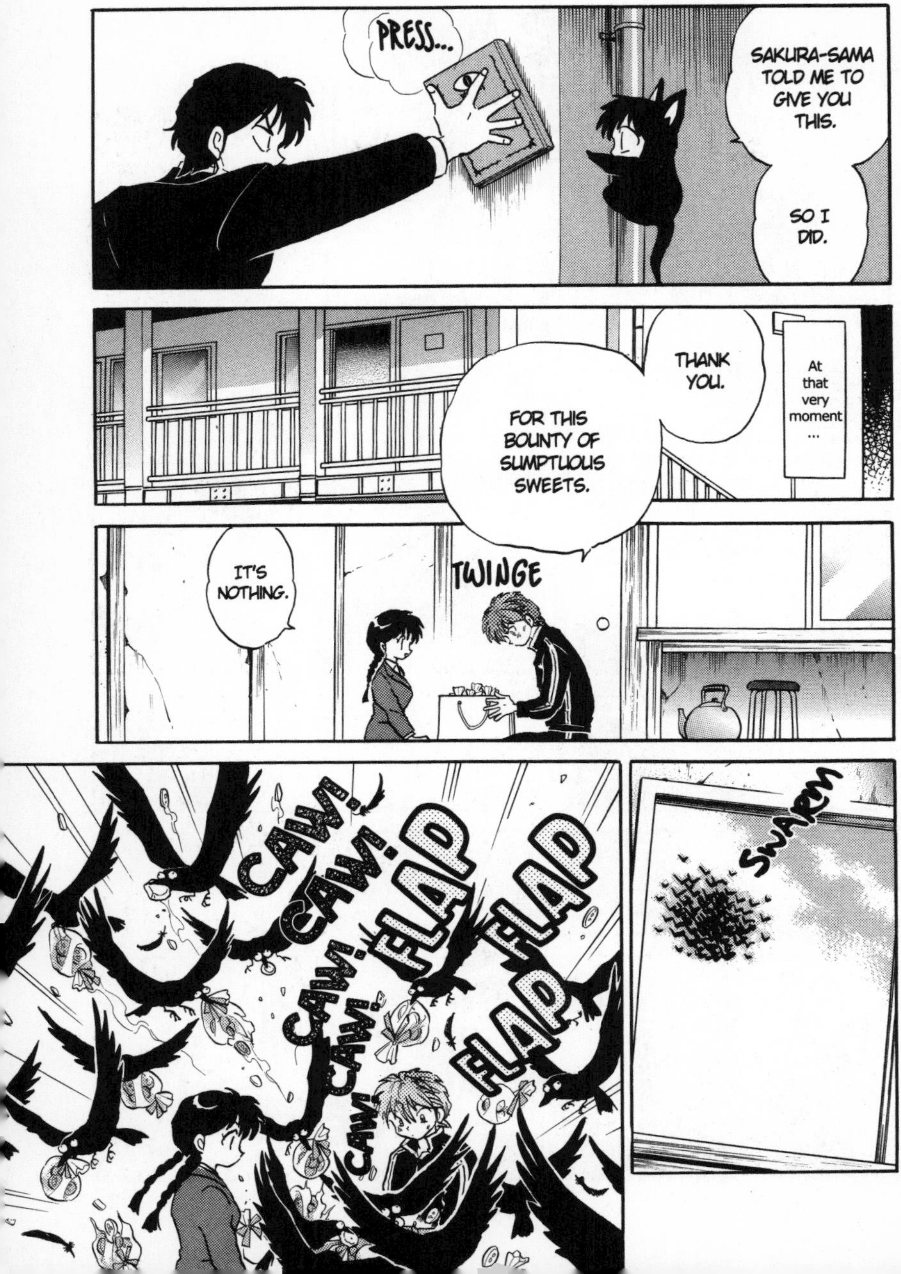
SAKURA-SAMA TOLD ME TO GIVE YOU THIS.
SO I DID.
PRESS...
At that very moment...
THANK YOU.
FOR THIS BOUNTY OF SUMPTUOUS SWEETS.
TWINGE
IT'S NOTHING.
SWARM
FLAP FLAP
FLAP FLAP
CAW! CAW!
CAW! CAW!
CAW!

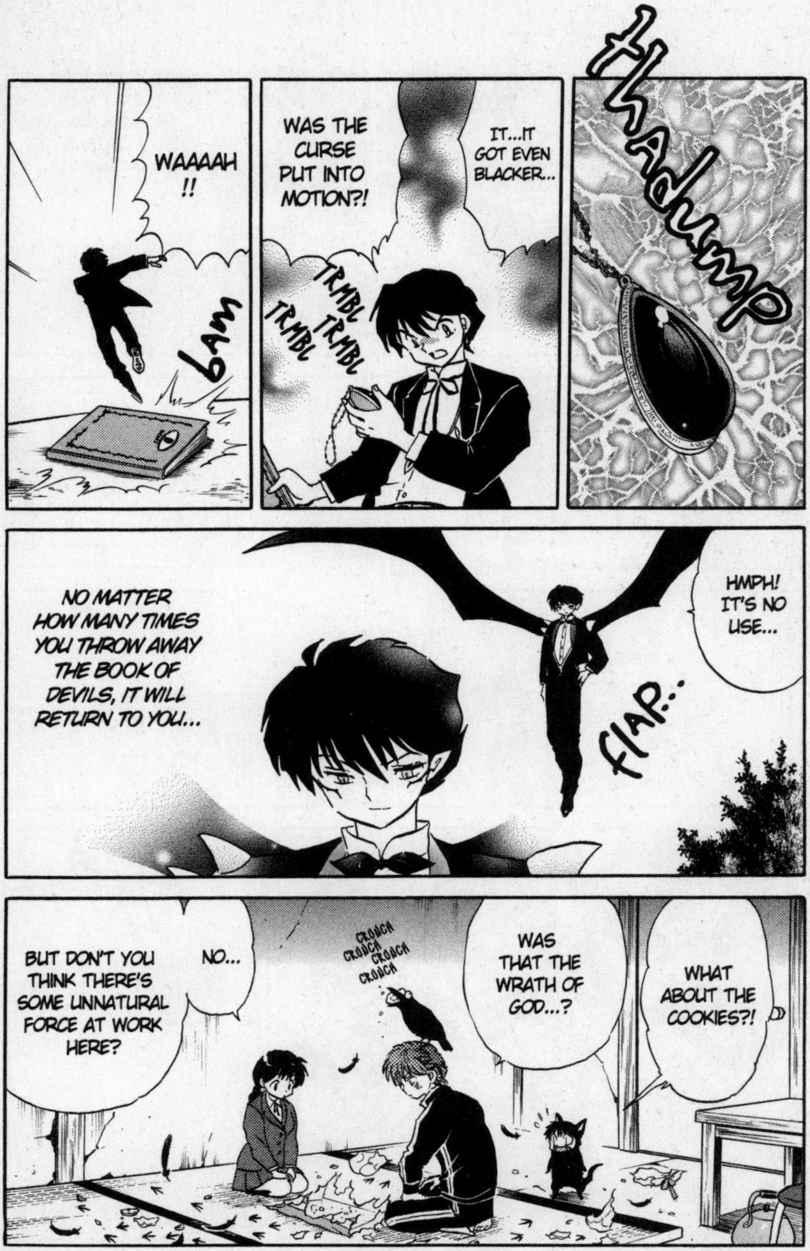
HADUMP
IT...IT GOT EVEN BLACKER...
WAS THE CURSE PUT INTO MOTION?!
TRMBL TRMBL TRMBL
WAAAAH !!
BAM
HMPH! IT'S NO USE...
FLAP...
NO MATTER HOW MANY TIMES YOU THROW AWAY THE BOOK OF DEVILS, IT WILL RETURN TO YOU...
WHAT ABOUT THE COOKIES?!
WAS THAT THE WRATH OF GOD...?
CRONCH CRONCH CRONCH CRONCH
NO...
BUT DON'T YOU THINK THERE'S SOME UNNATURAL FORCE AT WORK HERE?

CHAPTER 50: THE CHAIN OF NEGATIVITY

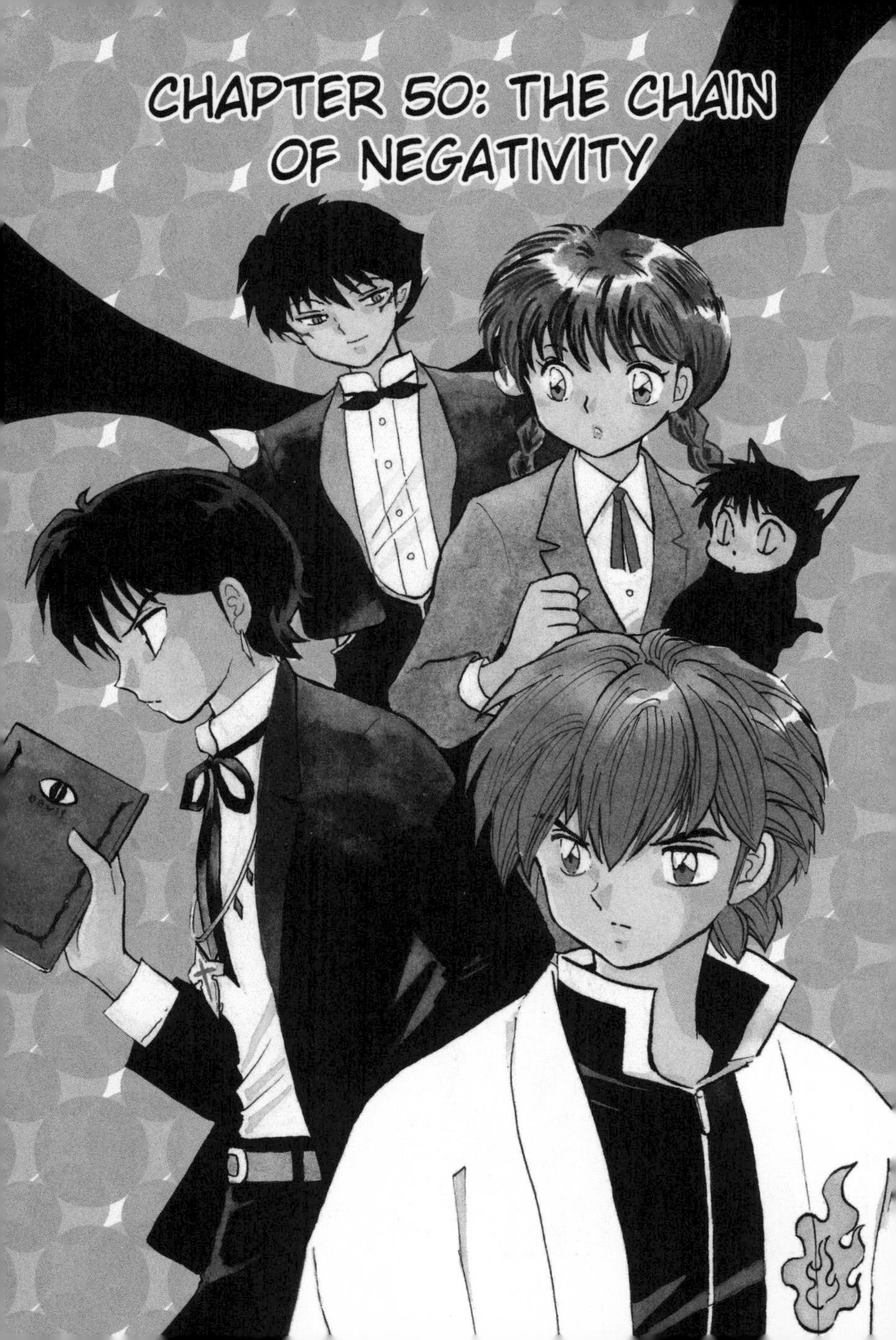

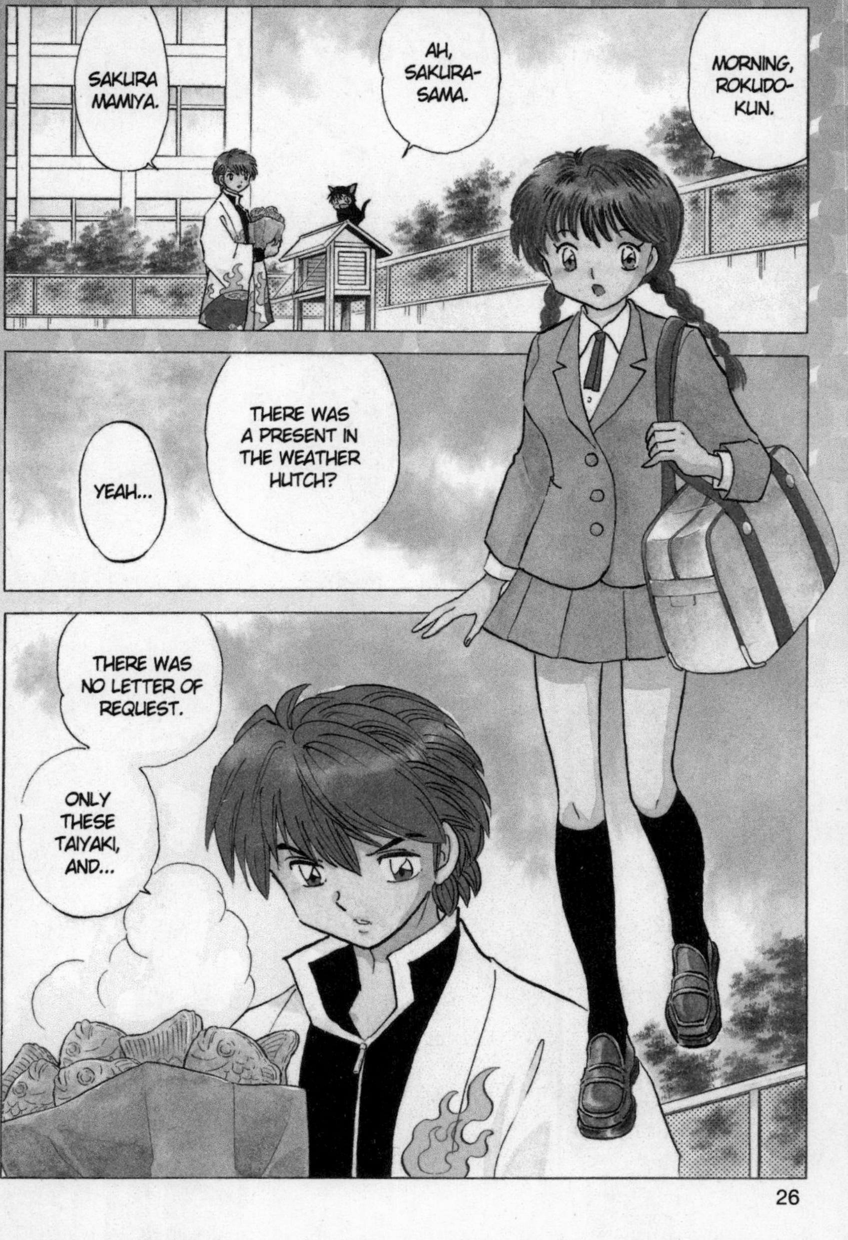
MORNING, ROKUDO-KUN.
AH, SAKURA-SAMA.
SAKURA MAMIYA.
THERE WAS A PRESENT IN THE WEATHER HUTCH?
YEAH...
THERE WAS NO LETTER OF REQUEST.
ONLY THESE TAIYAKI, AND...

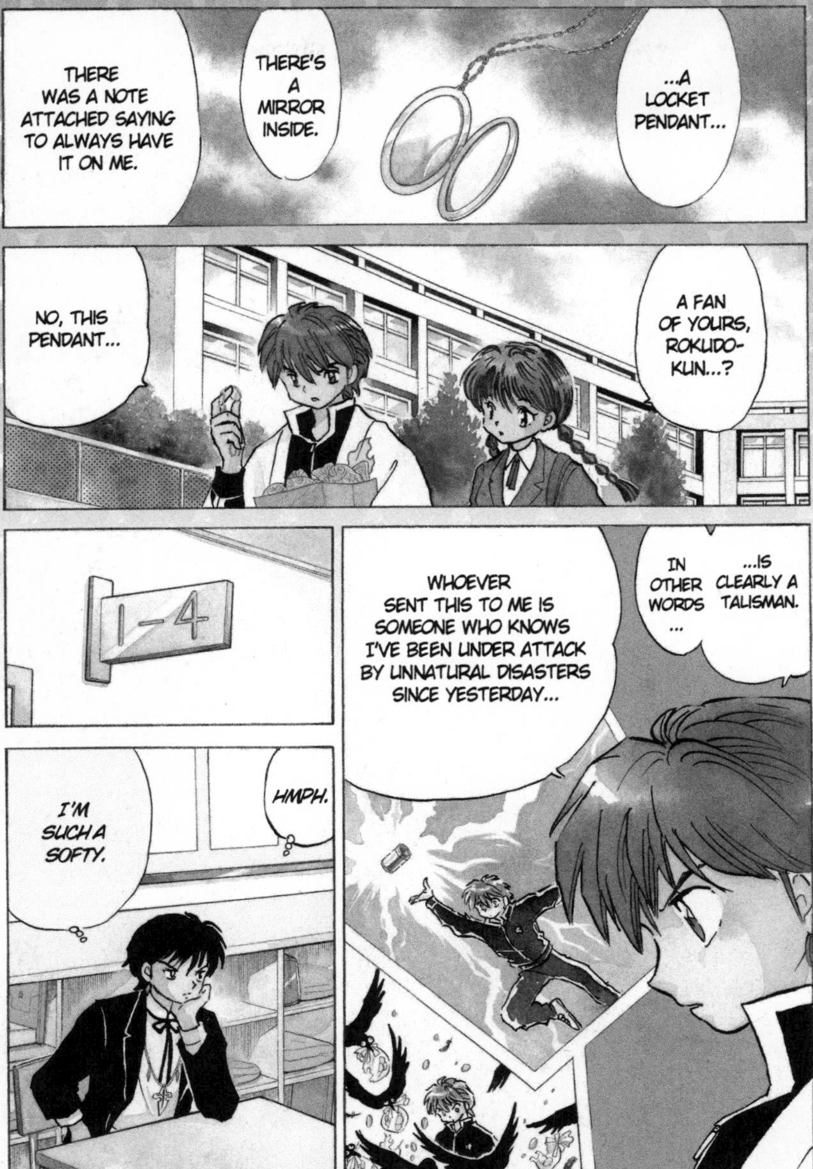
...A LOCKET PENDANT...
THERE'S A MIRROR INSIDE.
THERE WAS A NOTE ATTACHED SAYING TO ALWAYS HAVE IT ON ME.
A FAN OF YOURS, ROKUDO-KUN...?
NO, THIS PENDANT...
...IS CLEARLY A TALISMAN.
IN OTHER WORDS...
WHOEVER SENT THIS TO ME IS SOMEONE WHO KNOWS I'VE BEEN UNDER ATTACK BY UNNATURAL DISASTERS SINCE YESTERDAY...
1-4
HMPH.
I'M SUCH A SOFTY.

RIN-NE

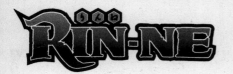

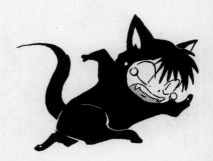

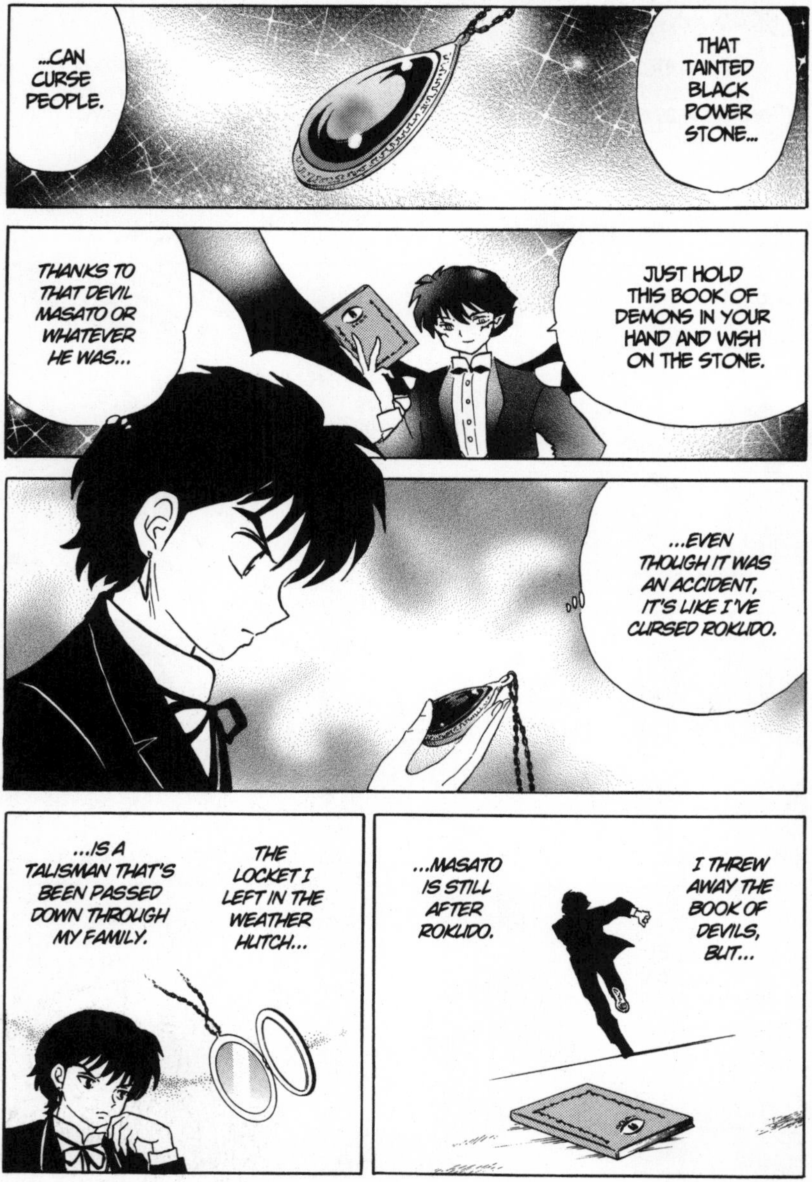
THAT TAINTED BLACK POWER STONE...
...CAN CURSE PEOPLE.
JUST HOLD THIS BOOK OF DEMONS IN YOUR HAND AND WISH ON THE STONE.
THANKS TO THAT DEVIL MASATO OR WHATEVER HE WAS...
...EVEN THOUGH IT WAS AN ACCIDENT, IT'S LIKE I'VE CURSED ROKUDO.
I THREW AWAY THE BOOK OF DEVILS, BUT...
...MASATO IS STILL AFTER ROKUDO.
THE LOCKET I LEFT IN THE WEATHER HUTCH...
...IS A TALISMAN THAT'S BEEN PASSED DOWN THROUGH MY FAMILY.

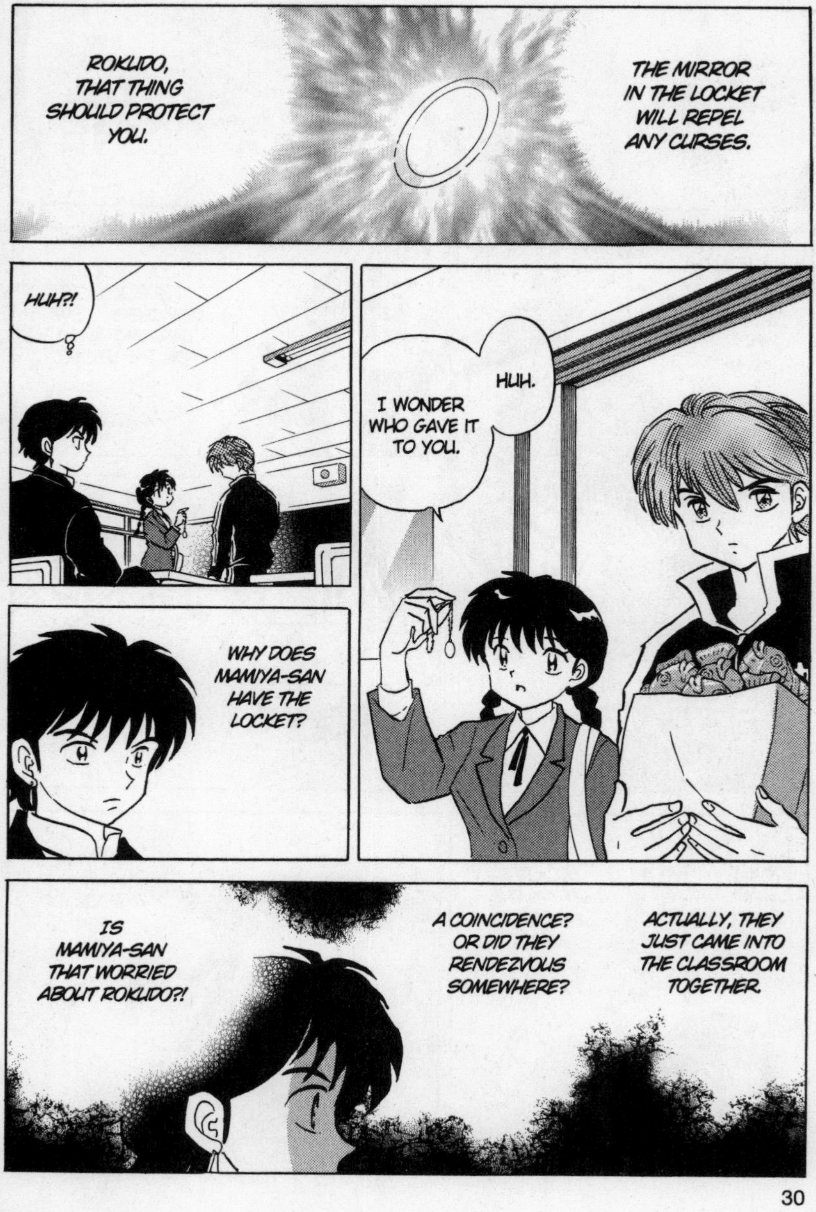
THE MIRROR IN THE LOCKET WILL REPEL ANY CURSES.
ROKUDO, THAT THING SHOULD PROTECT YOU.
HUH.
I WONDER WHO GAVE IT TO YOU.
HUH?!
WHY DOES MAMIYA-SAN HAVE THE LOCKET?
ACTUALLY, THEY JUST CAME INTO THE CLASSROOM TOGETHER.
A COINCIDENCE? OR DID THEY RENDEZVOUS SOMEWHERE?
IS MAMIYA-SAN THAT WORRIED ABOUT ROKUDO?!

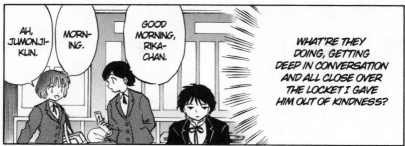

WHAT'RE THEY DOING, GETTING DEEP IN CONVERSATION AND ALL CLOSE OVER THE LOCKET I GAVE HIM OUT OF KINDNESS?
GOOD MORNING, RIKA-CHAN.
MORN-ING.
AH, JUMONJI-KUN.
THIS IS YOURS, RIGHT, JUMONJI-KUN?
YOU DROPPED IT.
JAB
HMPH...FOR A SECOND I THOUGHT I OWED ROKUDO AN APOLOGY, BUT...
...I WAS AN IDIOT.
SLAM
ssshhh
Rumble Rumble Rumble
WAH!
A SUDDEN DOWN-POUR!
SSSSHHHHH

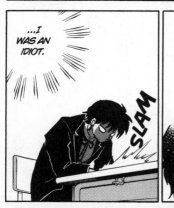

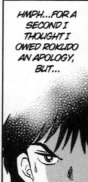

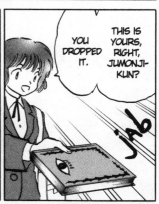

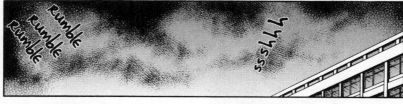

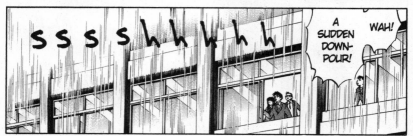

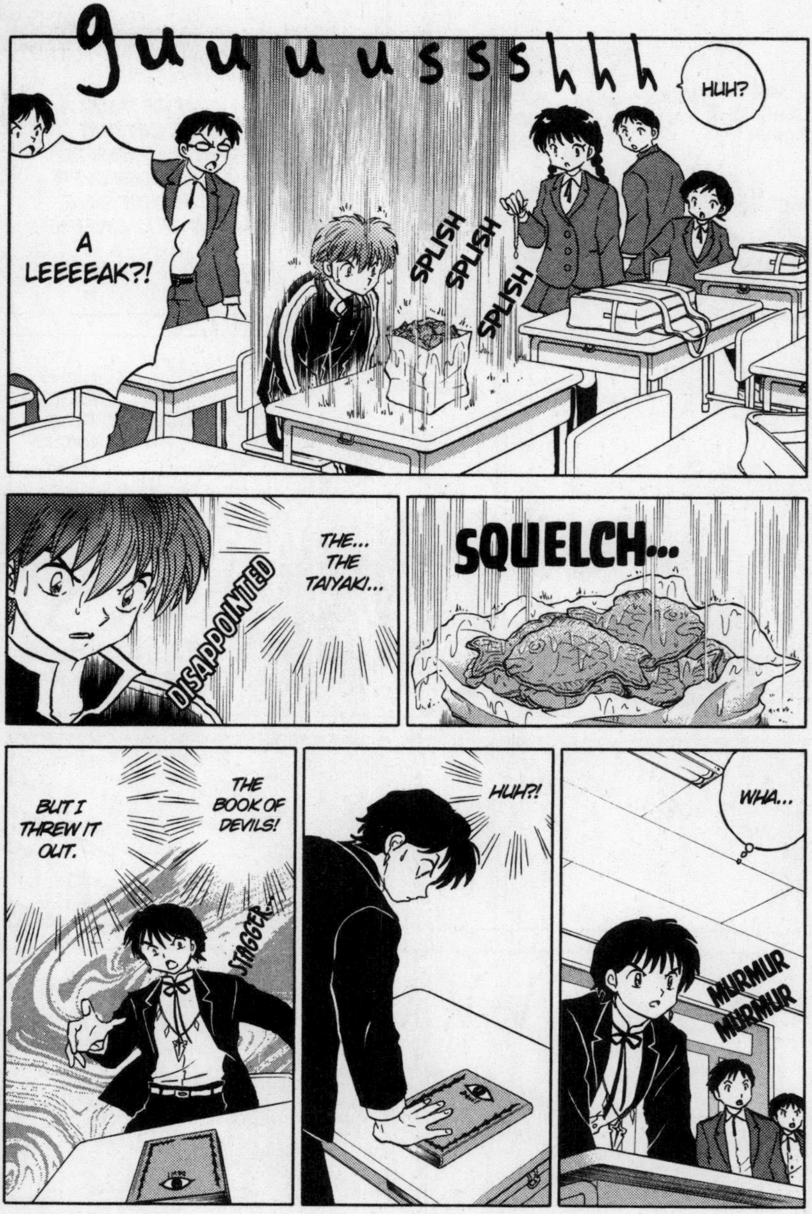
guuuussshhh
HUH?
SPLISH SPLISH SPLISH
A LEEEEAK?!
SQUELCH...
THE... THE TAIYAKI...
DISAPPOINTED
WHA...
MURMUR MURMUR
HUH?!
THE BOOK OF DEVILS!
BUT I THREW IT OUT.
STAGGER...

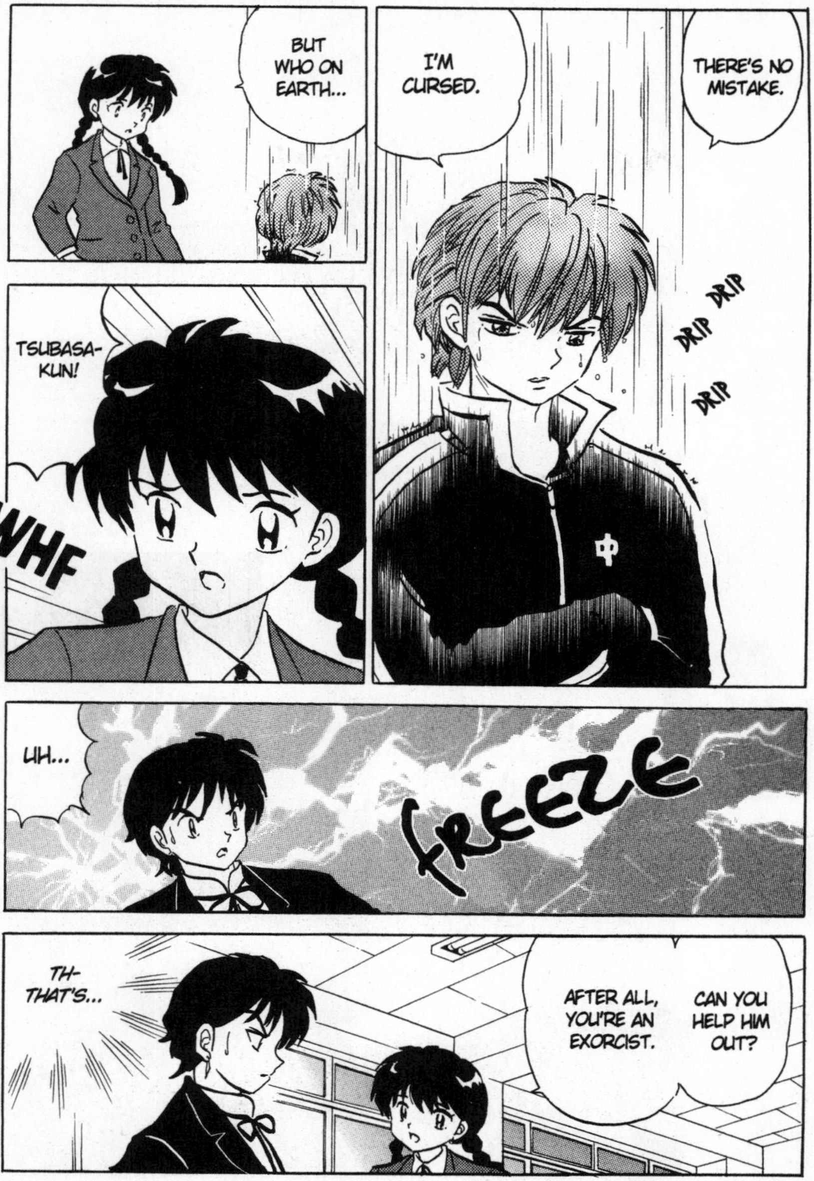
THERE'S NO MISTAKE.
I'M CURSED.
DRIP DRIP
DRIP
BUT WHO ON EARTH...
TSUBASA-KUN!
WHF
FREEZE
UH...
CAN YOU HELP HIM OUT?
AFTER ALL, YOU'RE AN EXORCIST.
TH-THAT'S...

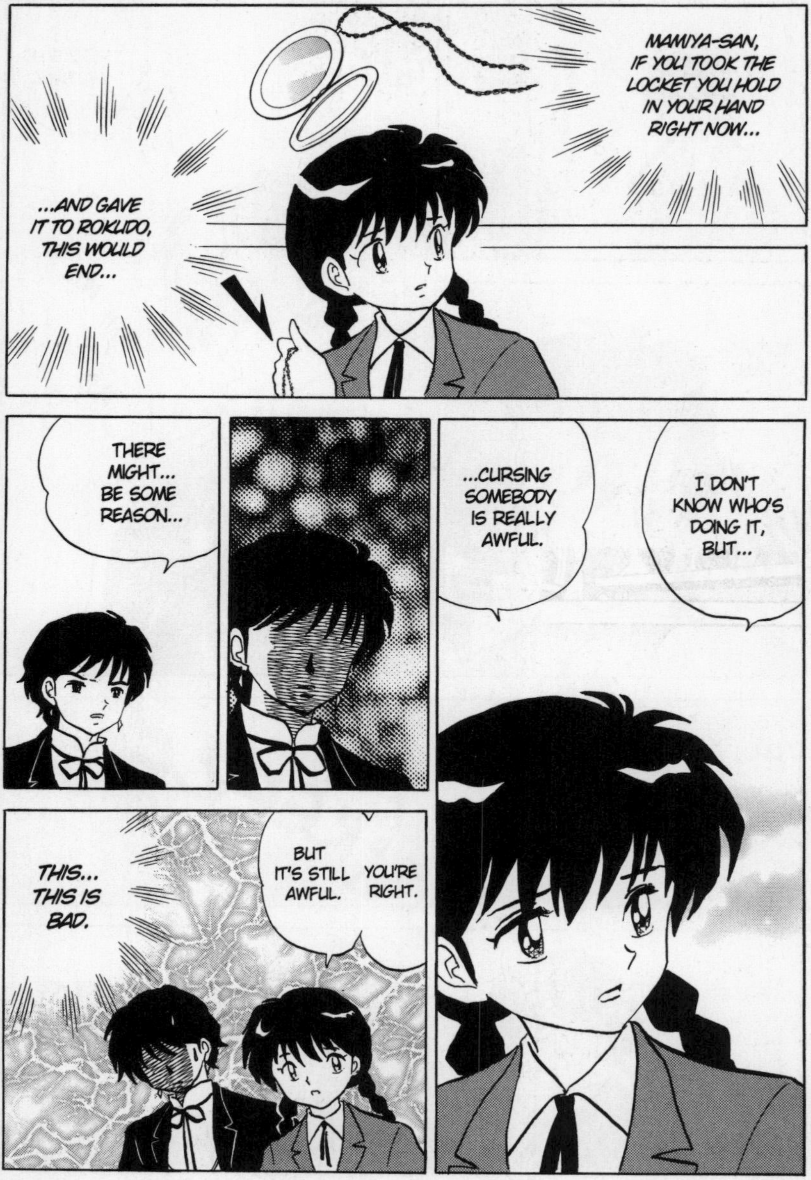
MAMIYA-SAN, IF YOU TOOK THE LOCKET YOU HOLD IN YOUR HAND RIGHT NOW...
...AND GAVE IT TO ROKUDO, THIS WOULD END...
I DON'T KNOW WHO'S DOING IT, BUT...
...CURSING SOMEBODY IS REALLY AWFUL.
THERE MIGHT... BE SOME REASON...
YOU'RE RIGHT.
BUT IT'S STILL AWFUL.
THIS... THIS IS BAD.

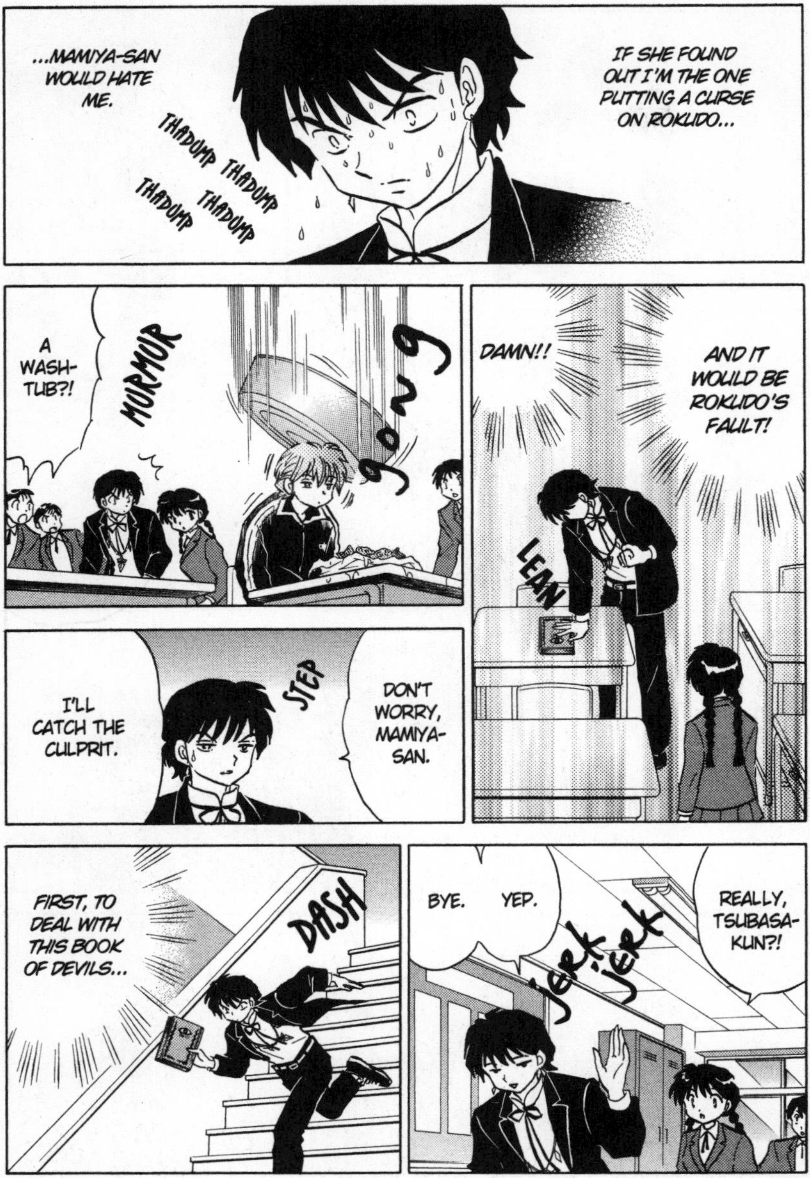
IF SHE FOUND OUT I'M THE ONE PUTTING A CURSE ON ROKUDO...
...MAMIYA-SAN WOULD HATE ME.
THADUMP THADUMP
THADUMP THADUMP
AND IT WOULD BE ROKUDO'S FAULT!
DAMN!!
LEAN
GONG
MURMUR
A WASH-TUB?!
DON'T WORRY, MAMIYA-SAN.
STEP
I'LL CATCH THE CULPRIT.
REALLY, TSUBASA-KUN?!
JERK JERK
YEP.
BYE.
DASH
FIRST, TO DEAL WITH THIS BOOK OF DEVILS...

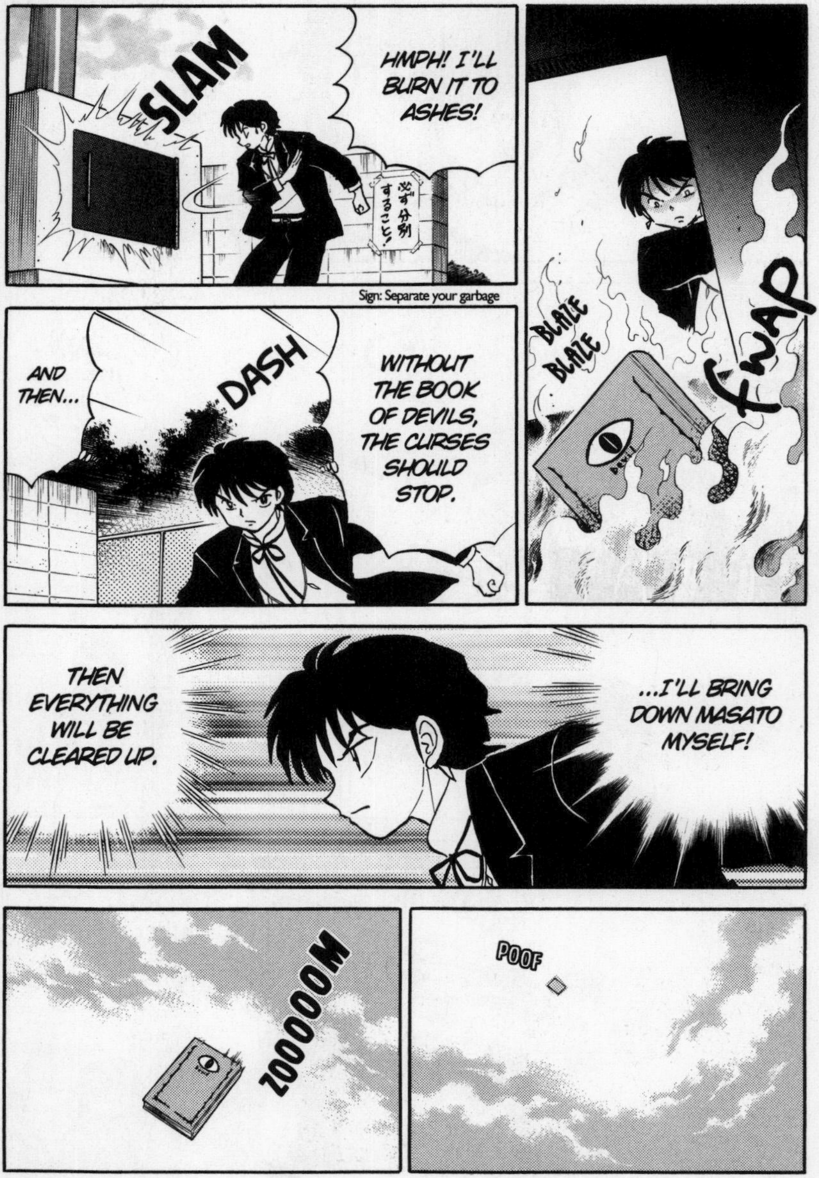
BLAZE BLAZE
FWAP
HMPH! I'LL BURN IT TO ASHES!
SLAM
必ず分別すること!
Sign: Separate your garbage
WITHOUT THE BOOK OF DEVILS, THE CURSES SHOULD STOP.
DASH
AND THEN...
...I'LL BRING DOWN MASATO MYSELF!
THEN EVERYTHING WILL BE CLEARED UP.
POOF
ZOOOOOM

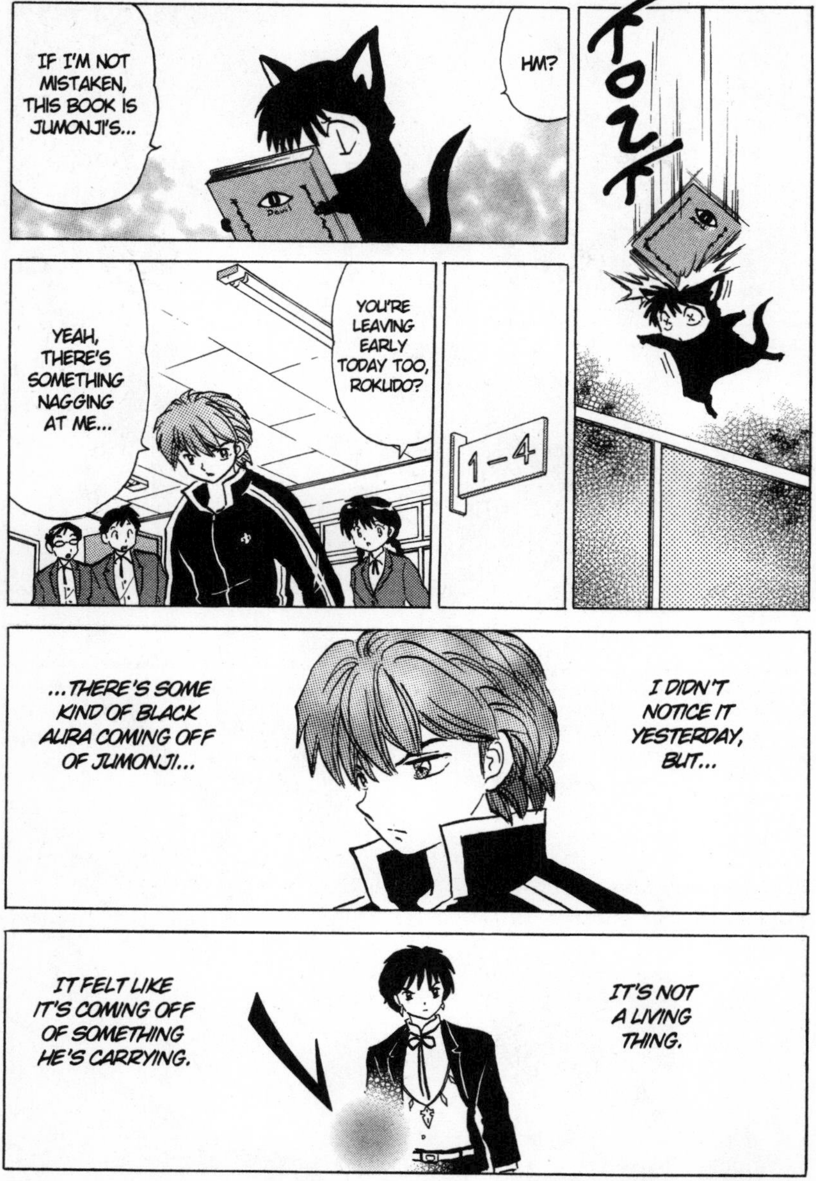
TONK
HM?
IF I'M NOT MISTAKEN, THIS BOOK IS JUMONJI'S...
1-4
YOU'RE LEAVING EARLY TODAY TOO, ROKUDO?
YEAH, THERE'S SOMETHING NAGGING AT ME...
I DIDN'T NOTICE IT YESTERDAY, BUT...
...THERE'S SOME KIND OF BLACK AURA COMING OFF OF JUMONJI...
IT'S NOT A LIVING THING.
IT FELT LIKE IT'S COMING OFF OF SOMETHING HE'S CARRYING.

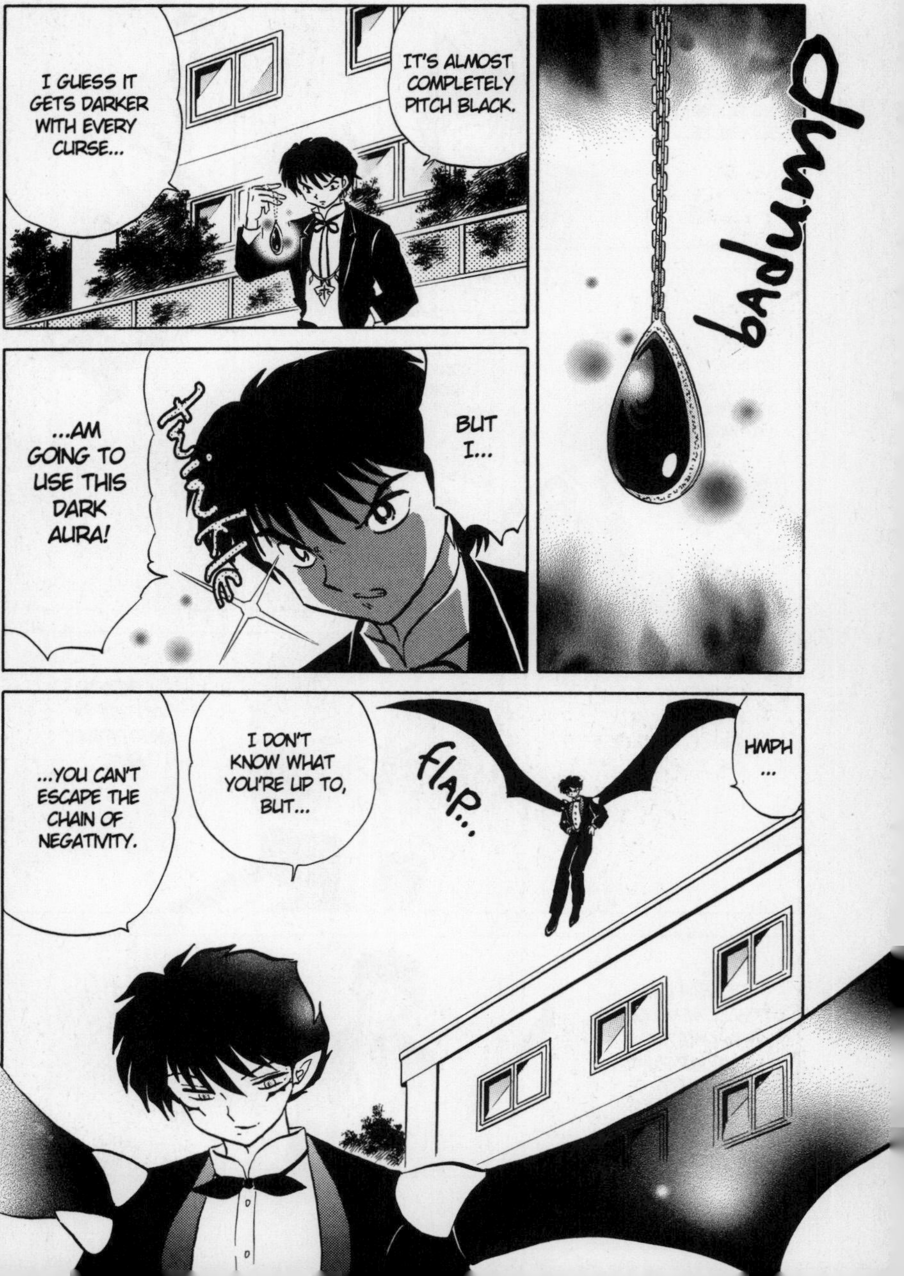
badump
IT'S ALMOST COMPLETELY PITCH BLACK.
I GUESS IT GETS DARKER WITH EVERY CURSE...
BUT I...
...AM GOING TO USE THIS DARK AURA!
HMPH ...
flap...
I DON'T KNOW WHAT YOU'RE UP TO, BUT...
...YOU CAN'T ESCAPE THE CHAIN OF NEGATIVITY.

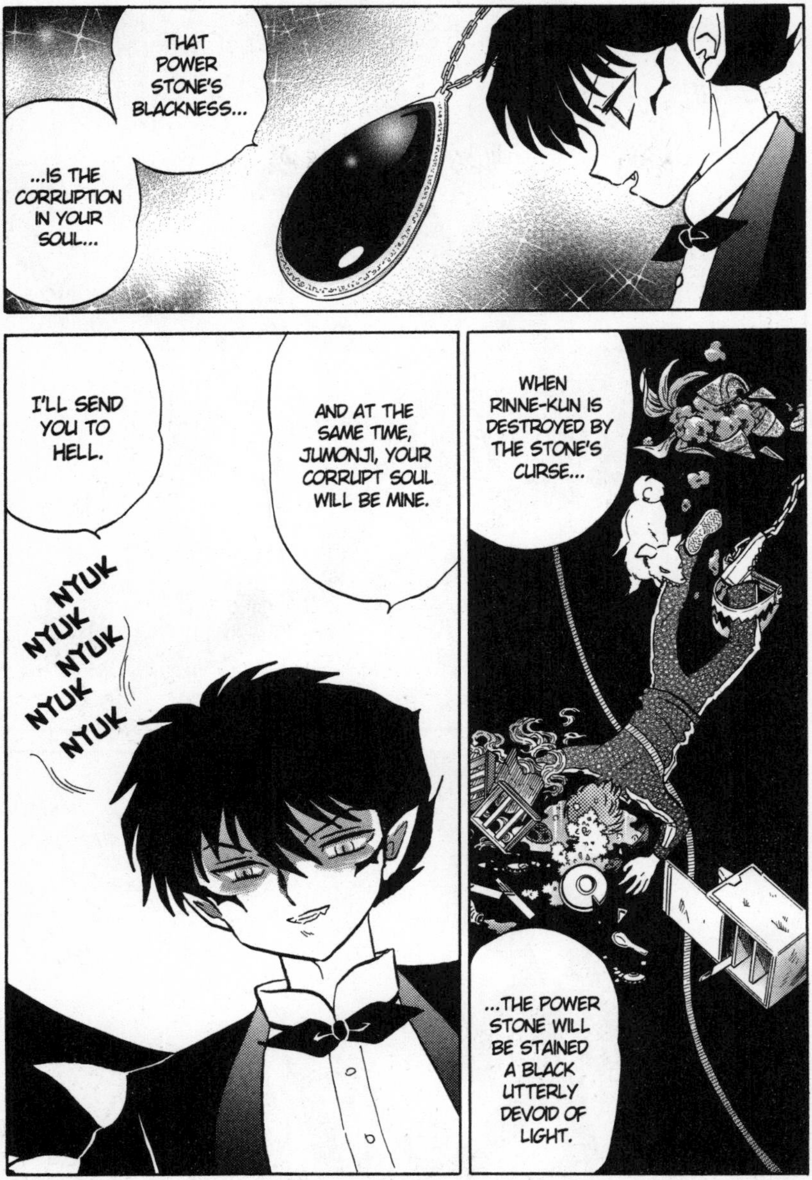
THAT POWER STONE'S BLACKNESS...
...IS THE CORRUPTION IN YOUR SOUL...
WHEN RINNE-KUN IS DESTROYED BY THE STONE'S CURSE...
...THE POWER STONE WILL BE STAINED A BLACK UTTERLY DEVOID OF LIGHT.
AND AT THE SAME TIME, JUMONJI, YOUR CORRUPT SOUL WILL BE MINE.
I'LL SEND YOU TO HELL.
NYUK NYUK NYUK NYUK NYUK

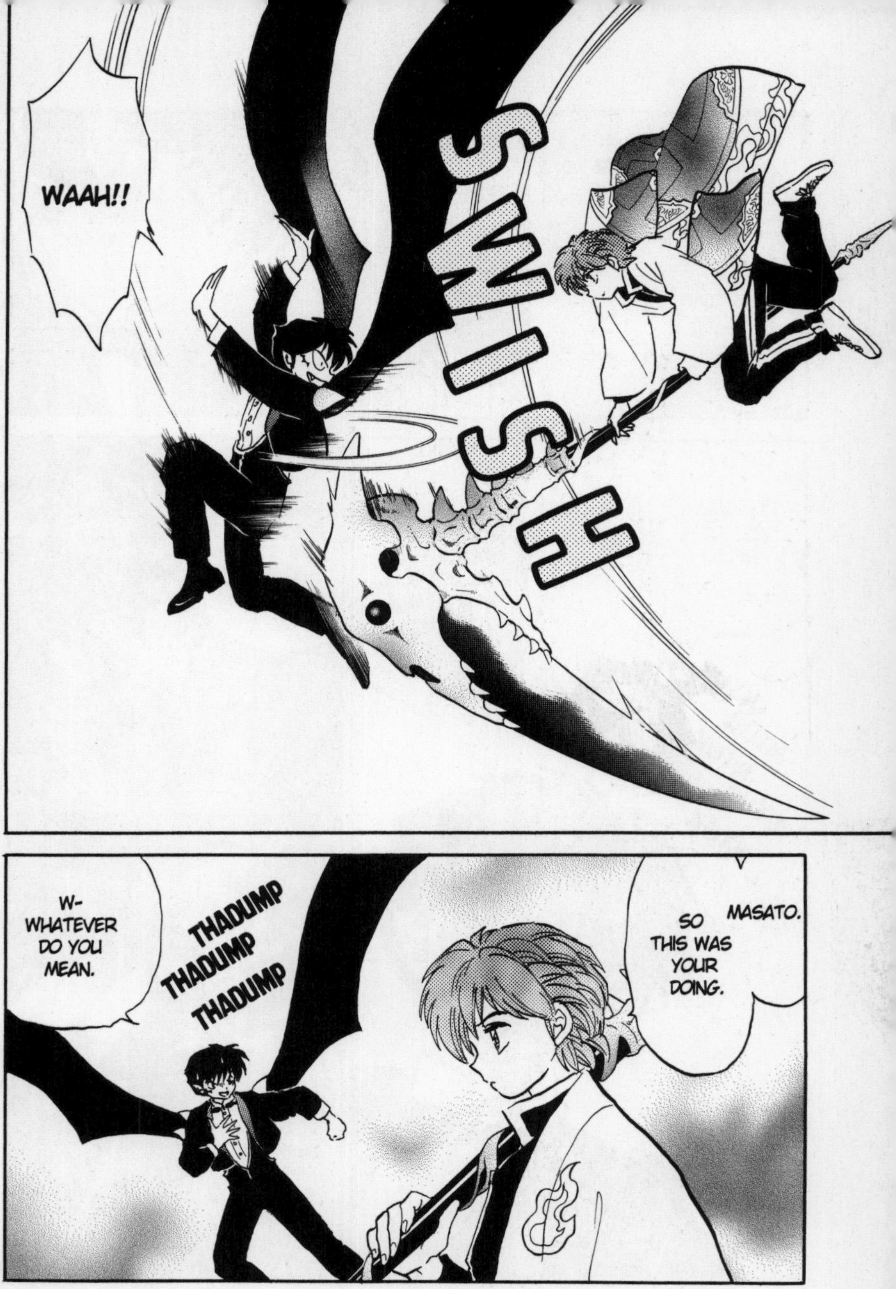
SWISH
WAAH!!
MASATO.
SO THIS WAS YOUR DOING.
THADUMP THADUMP THADUMP
W- WHATEVER DO YOU MEAN.

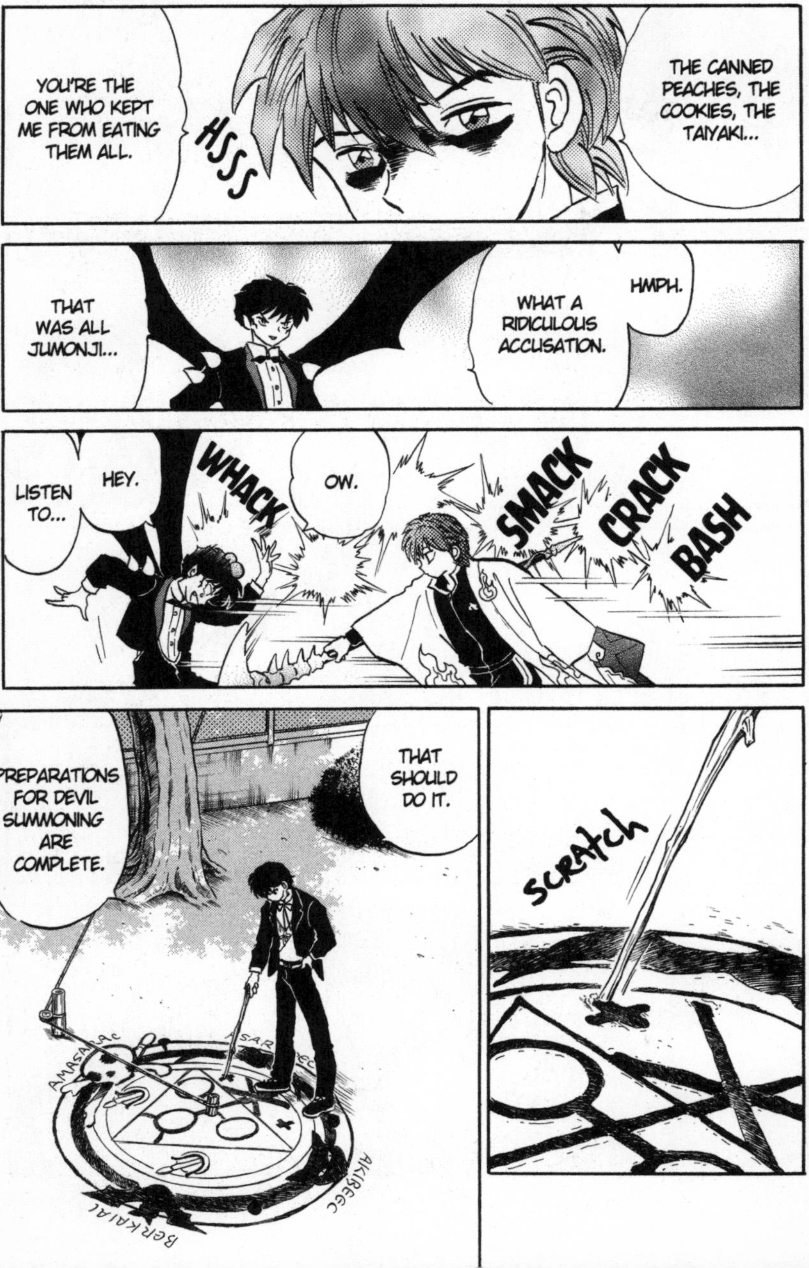
THE CANNED PEACHES, THE COOKIES, THE TAIYAKI...
HSSS
YOU'RE THE ONE WHO KEPT ME FROM EATING THEM ALL.
HMPH.
WHAT A RIDICULOUS ACCUSATION.
THAT WAS ALL JUMONJI...
BASH
CRACK
SMACK
OW.
WHACK
HEY.
LISTEN TO...
SCRATCH
THAT SHOULD DO IT.
PREPARATIONS FOR DEVIL SUMMONING ARE COMPLETE.
AMASARAC
BERKAIAL

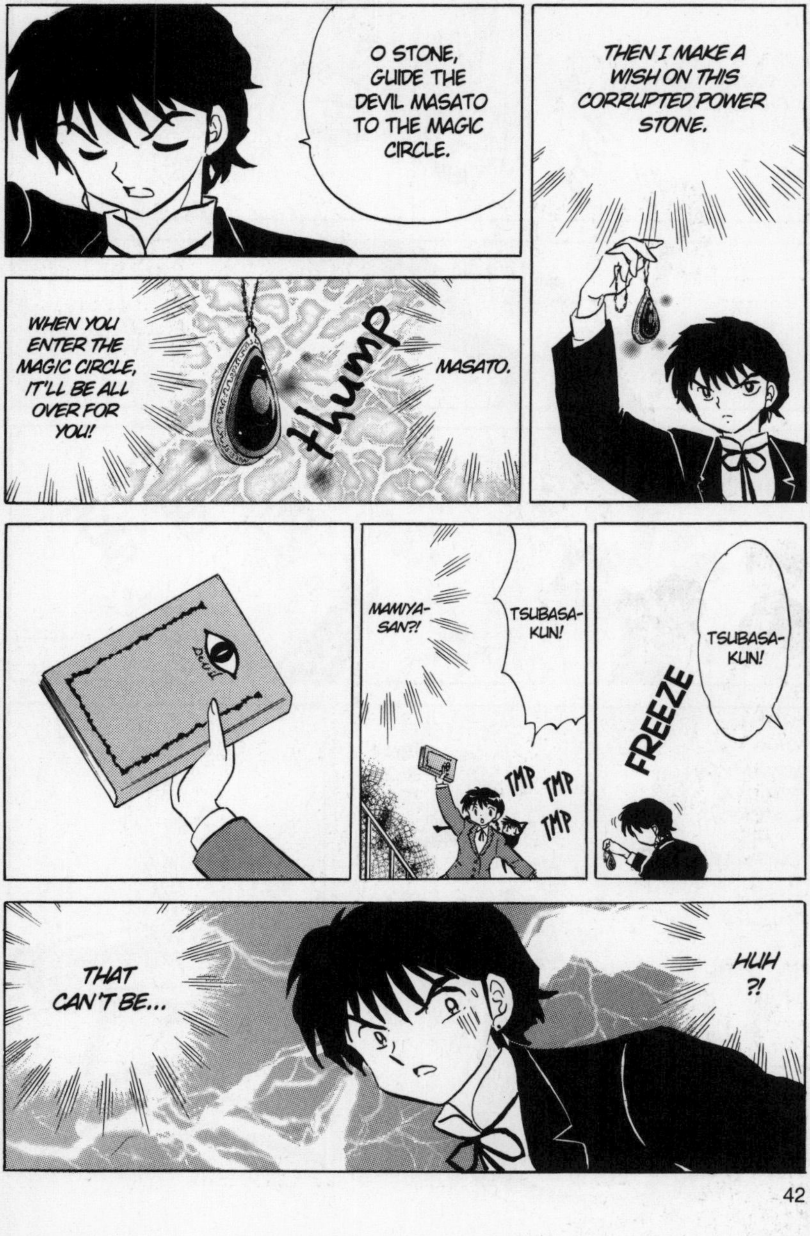
THEN I MAKE A WISH ON THIS CORRUPTED POWER STONE.
O STONE, GUIDE THE DEVIL MASATO TO THE MAGIC CIRCLE.
MASATO.
THUMP
WHEN YOU ENTER THE MAGIC CIRCLE, IT'LL BE ALL OVER FOR YOU!
TSUBASA-KUN!
FREEZE
TSUBASA-KUN!
MAMIYA-SAN?!
TMP TMP TMP
Devil
HUH ?!
THAT CAN'T BE...

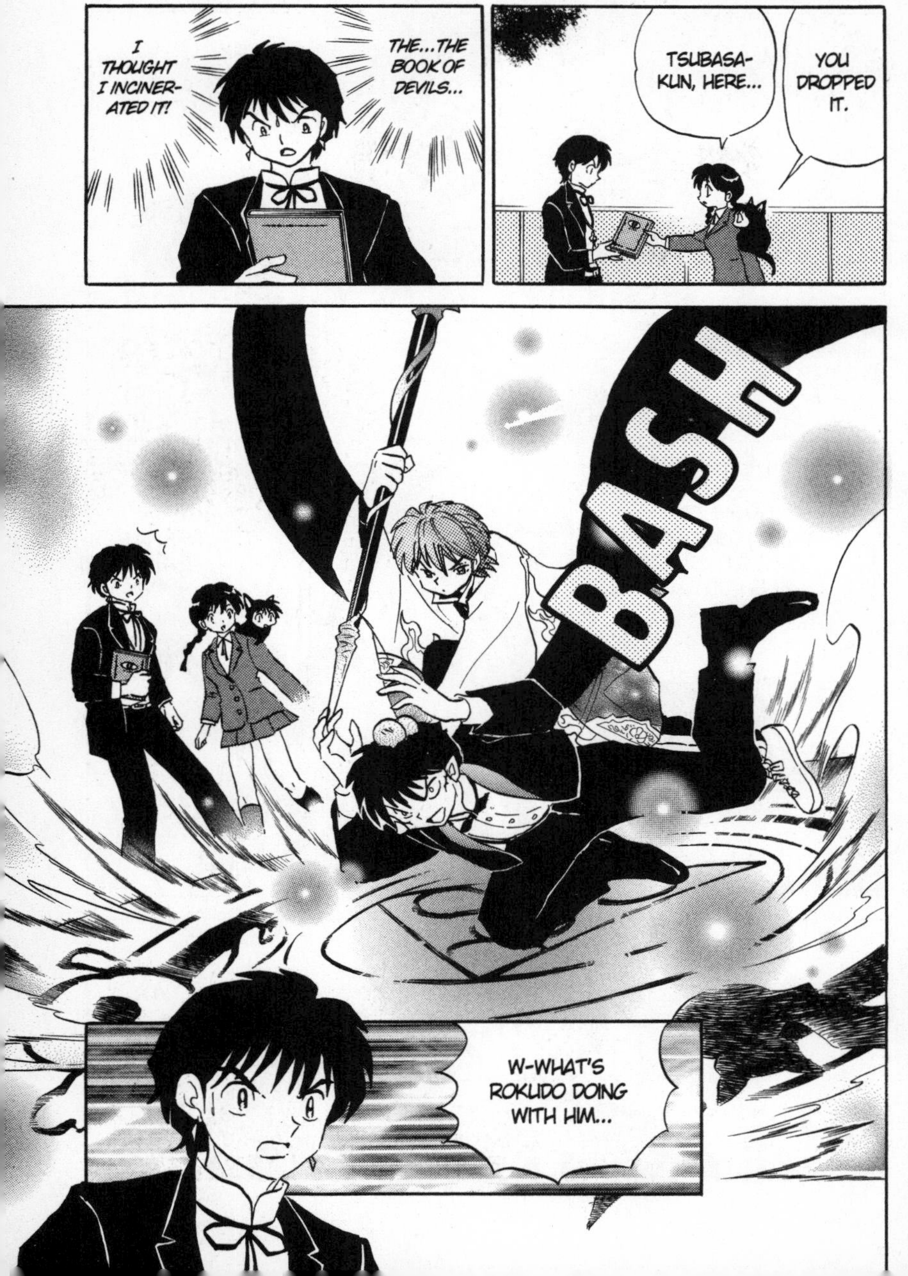
TSUBASA-KUN, HERE...
YOU DROPPED IT.
THE...THE BOOK OF DEVILS...
I THOUGHT I INCINERATED IT!
BASH
W-WHAT'S ROKUDO DOING WITH HIM...

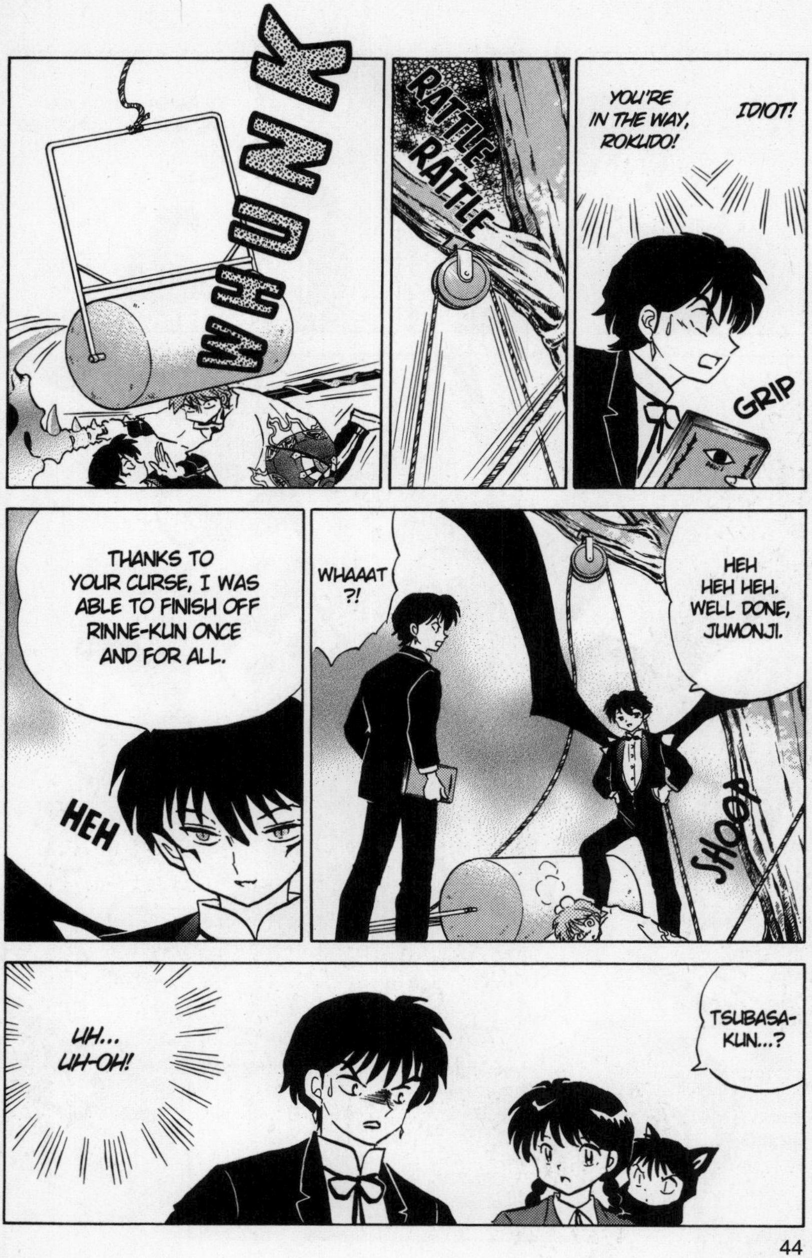
IDIOT!
YOU'RE IN THE WAY, ROKUDO!
GRIP
RATTLE RATTLE
WHUNK
HEH HEH HEH. WELL DONE, JUMONJI.
SHOOP
WHAAAT ?!
THANKS TO YOUR CURSE, I WAS ABLE TO FINISH OFF RINNE-KUN ONCE AND FOR ALL.
HEH
TSUBASA-KUN...?
UH... UH-OH!

CHAPTER 51: SPIRITS

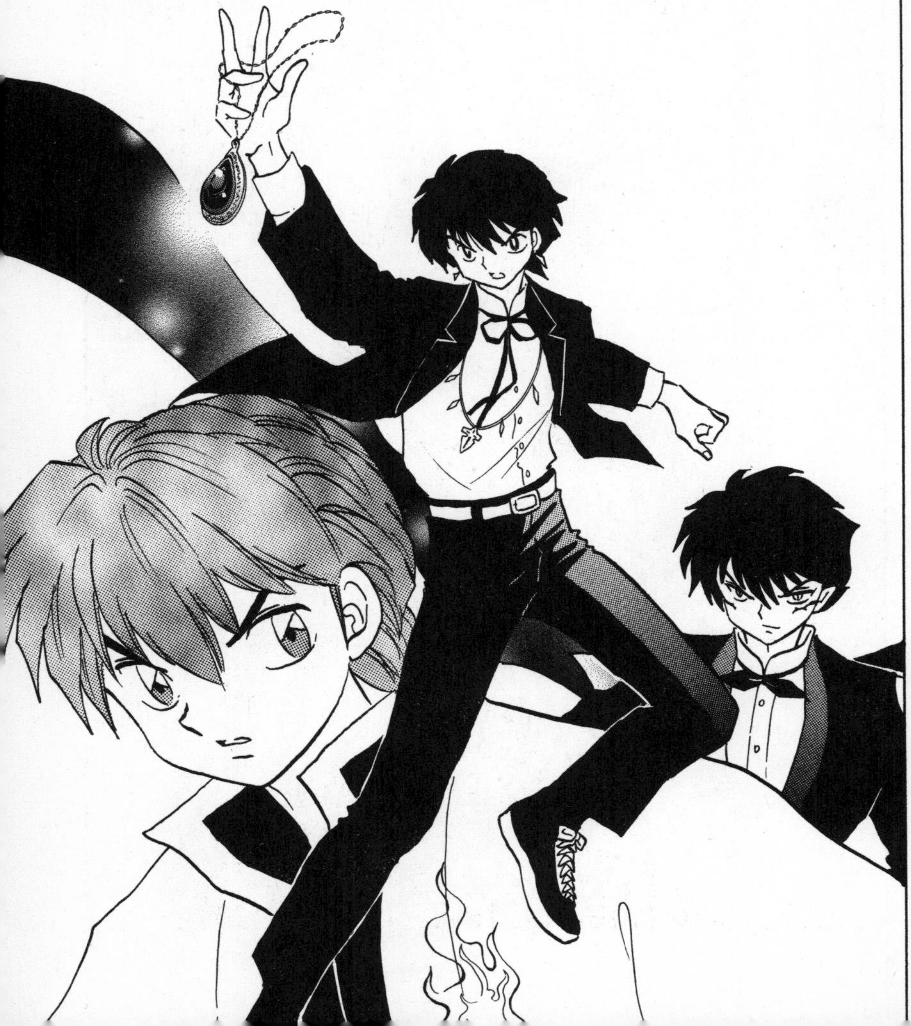

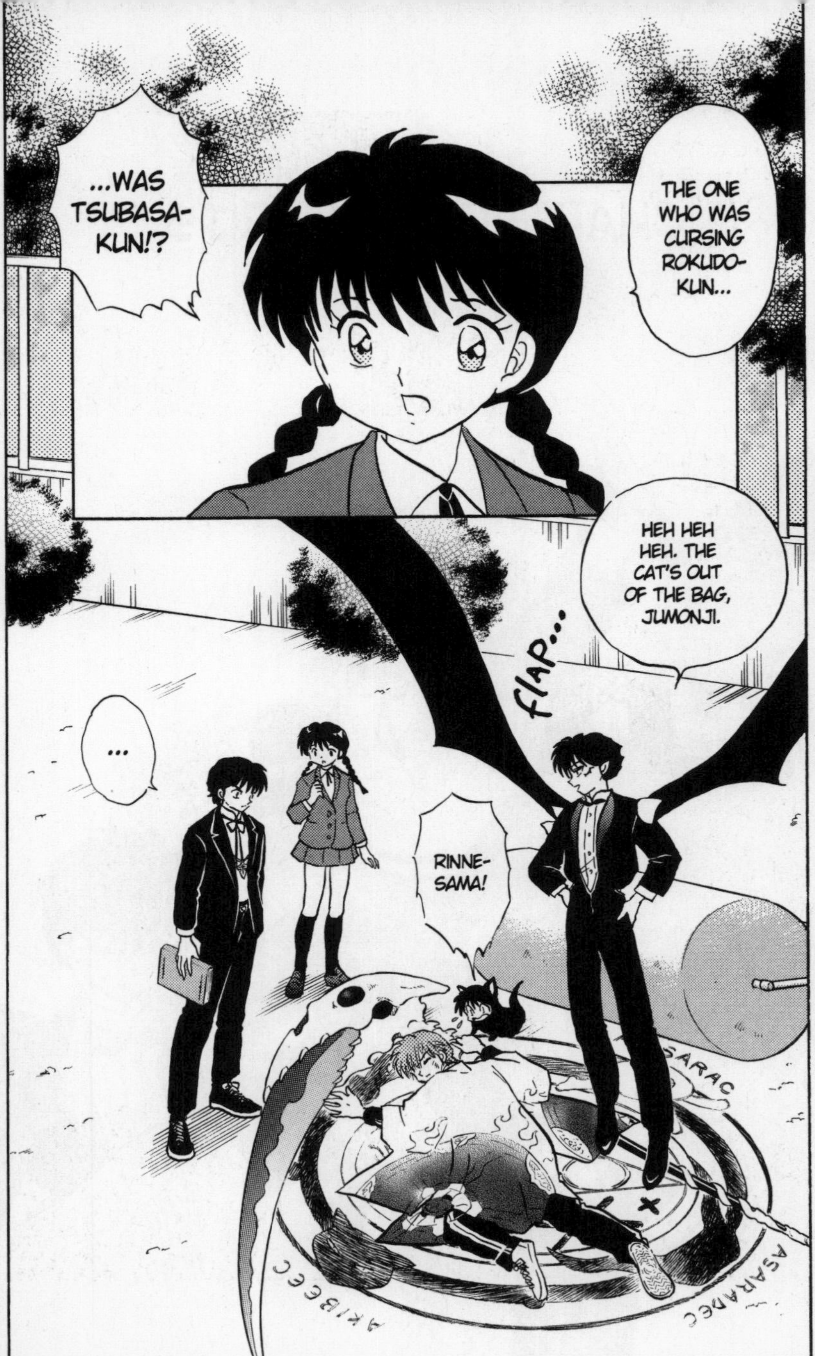
THE ONE WHO WAS CURSING ROKUDO-KUN...
...WAS TSUBASA-KUN!?
HEH HEH HEH. THE CAT'S OUT OF THE BAG, JUMONJI.
flap...
RINNE-SAMA!
...
ASARAC
ASARADEC
AKIBEEC

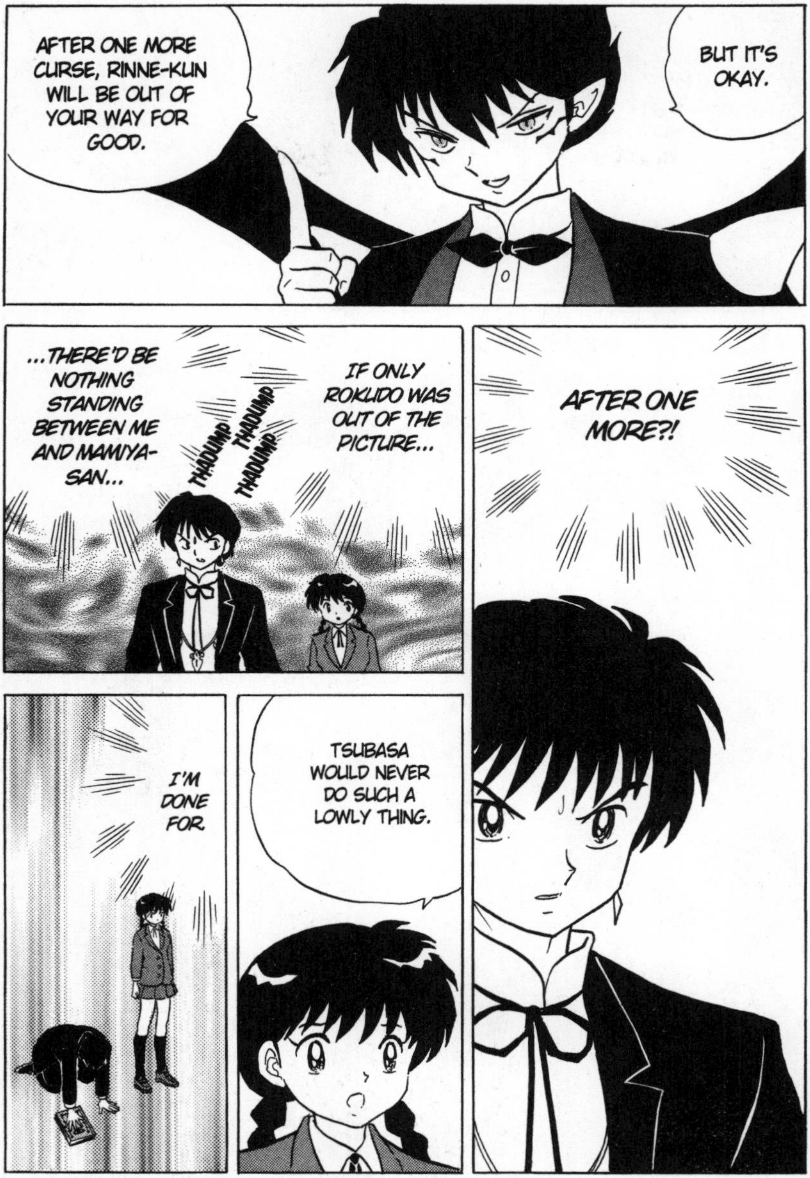
BUT IT'S OKAY.
AFTER ONE MORE CURSE, RINNE-KUN WILL BE OUT OF YOUR WAY FOR GOOD.
AFTER ONE MORE?!
IF ONLY ROKUDO WAS OUT OF THE PICTURE...
THADUMP THADUMP
...THERE'D BE NOTHING STANDING BETWEEN ME AND MAMIYA-SAN...
TSUBASA WOULD NEVER DO SUCH A LOWLY THING.
I'M DONE FOR.

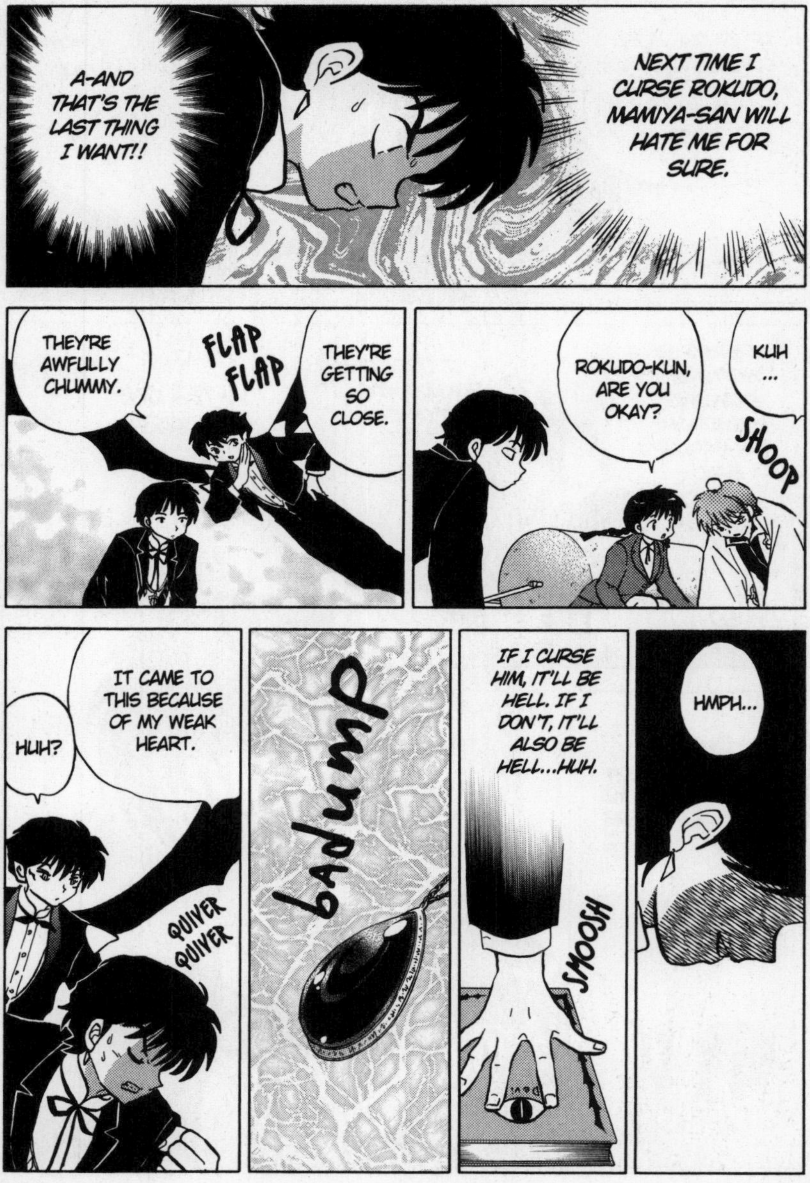
NEXT TIME I CURSE ROKUDO, MAMIYA-SAN WILL HATE ME FOR SURE.
A-AND THAT'S THE LAST THING I WANT!!
KUH ...
ROKUDO-KUN, ARE YOU OKAY?
SHOOP
THEY'RE GETTING SO CLOSE.
FLAP FLAP
THEY'RE AWFULLY CHUMMY.
HMPH...
IF I CURSE HIM, IT'LL BE HELL. IF I DON'T, IT'LL ALSO BE HELL...HUH.
SMOOSH
badump
IT CAME TO THIS BECAUSE OF MY WEAK HEART.
HUH?
QUIVER QUIVER

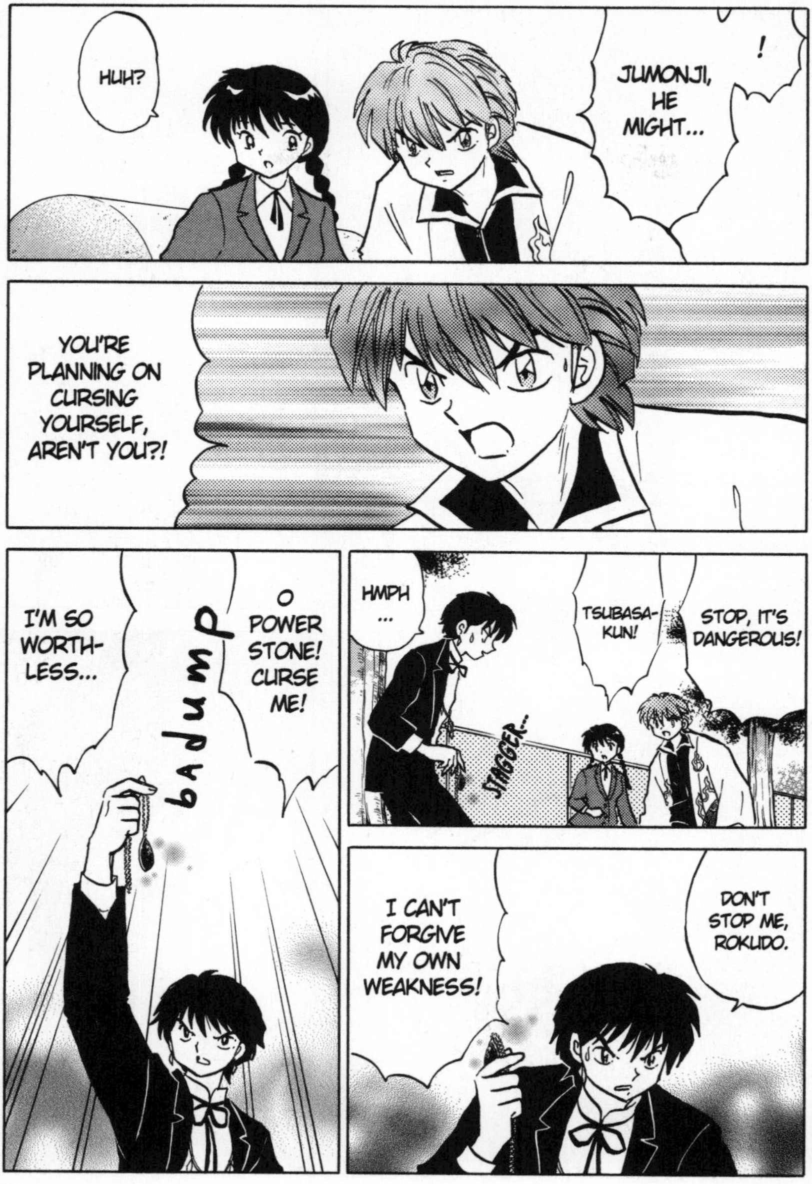
!
JUMONJI, HE MIGHT...
HUH?
YOU'RE PLANNING ON CURSING YOURSELF, AREN'T YOU?!
STOP, IT'S DANGEROUS!
TSUBASA-KUN!
HMPH ...
STAGGER...
DON'T STOP ME, ROKUDO.
I CAN'T FORGIVE MY OWN WEAKNESS!
O POWER STONE! CURSE ME!
badump
I'M SO WORTH-LESS...

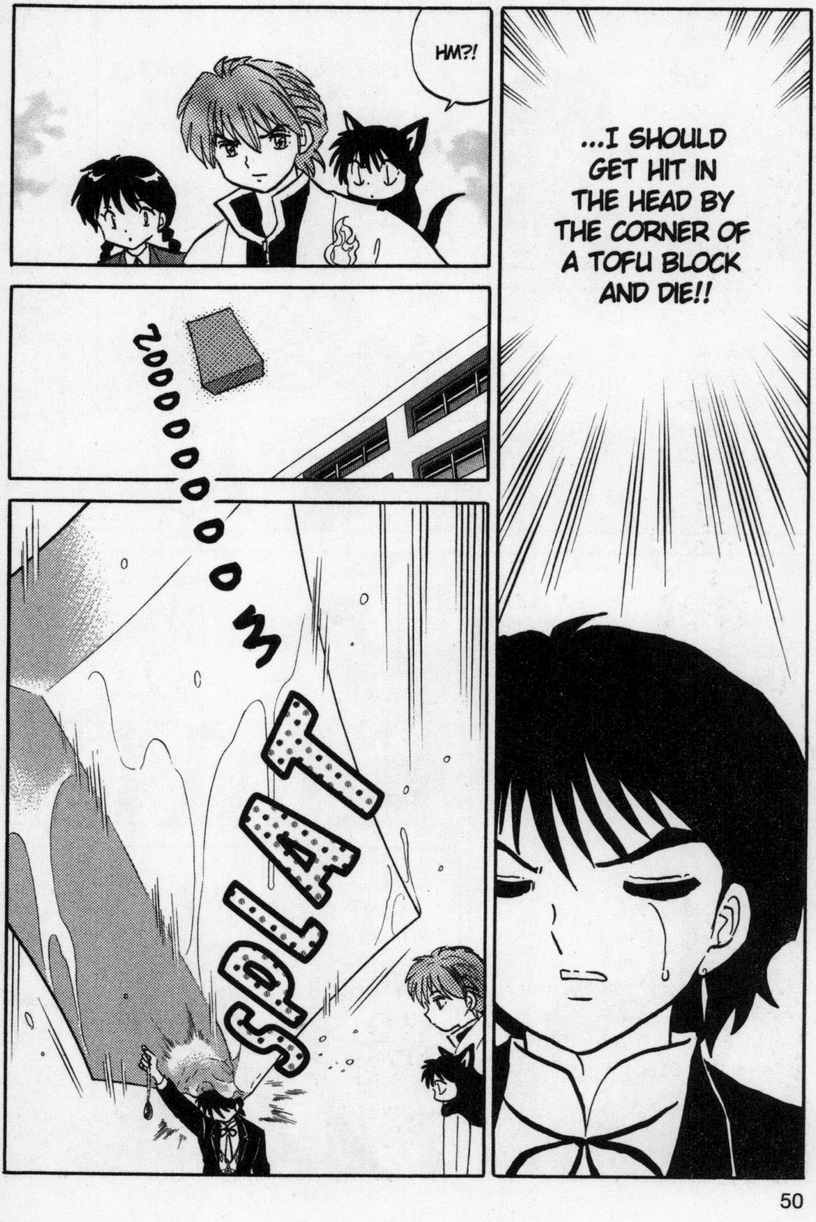

...I SHOULD GET HIT IN THE HEAD BY THE CORNER OF A TOFU BLOCK AND DIE!!
HM?!
ZOOOOOOOOOOOM
SPLAT

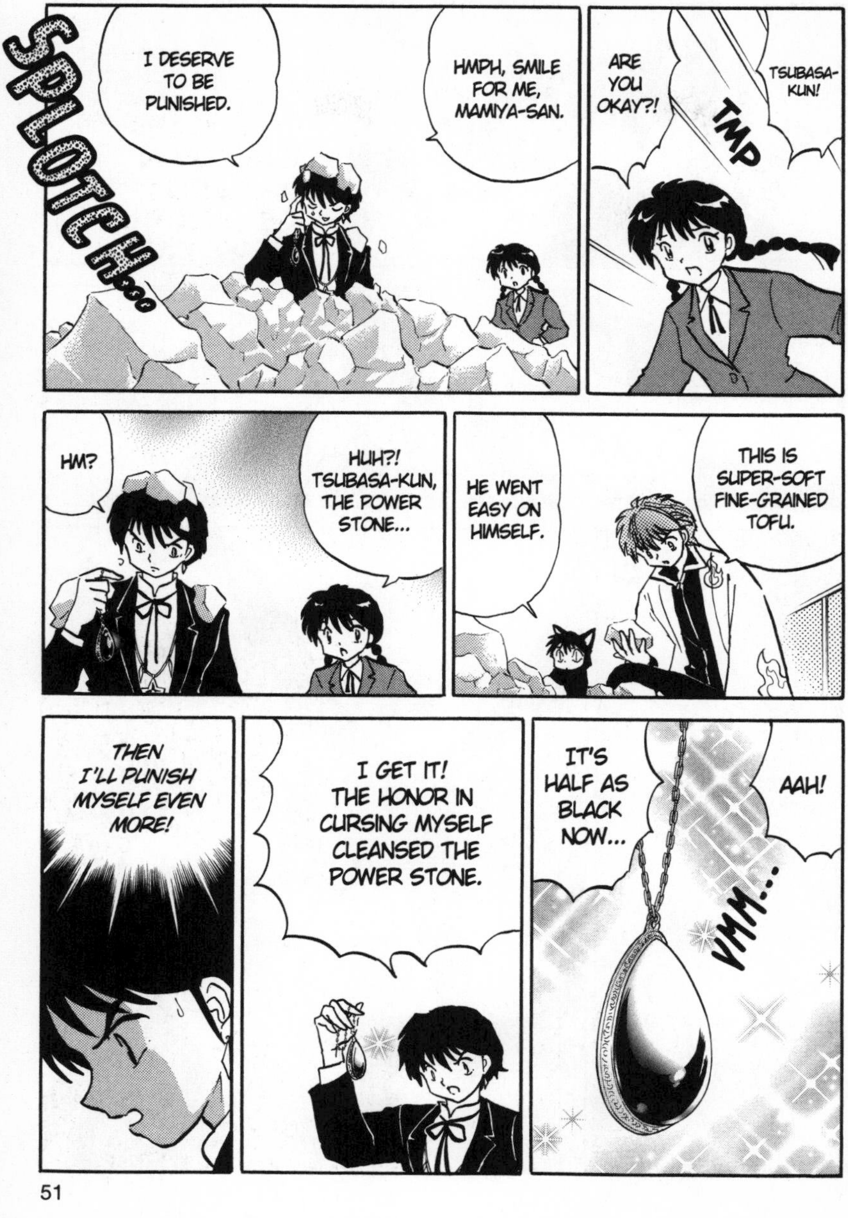
TSUBASA-KUN!
ARE YOU OKAY?!
TMP
HMPH, SMILE FOR ME, MAMIYA-SAN.
I DESERVE TO BE PUNISHED.
SPLOTCH...
THIS IS SUPER-SOFT FINE-GRAINED TOFU.
HE WENT EASY ON HIMSELF.
HUH?! TSUBASA-KUN, THE POWER STONE...
HM?
AAH!
IT'S HALF AS BLACK NOW...
VMM...
I GET IT! THE HONOR IN CURSING MYSELF CLEANSED THE POWER STONE.
THEN I'LL PUNISH MYSELF EVEN MORE!

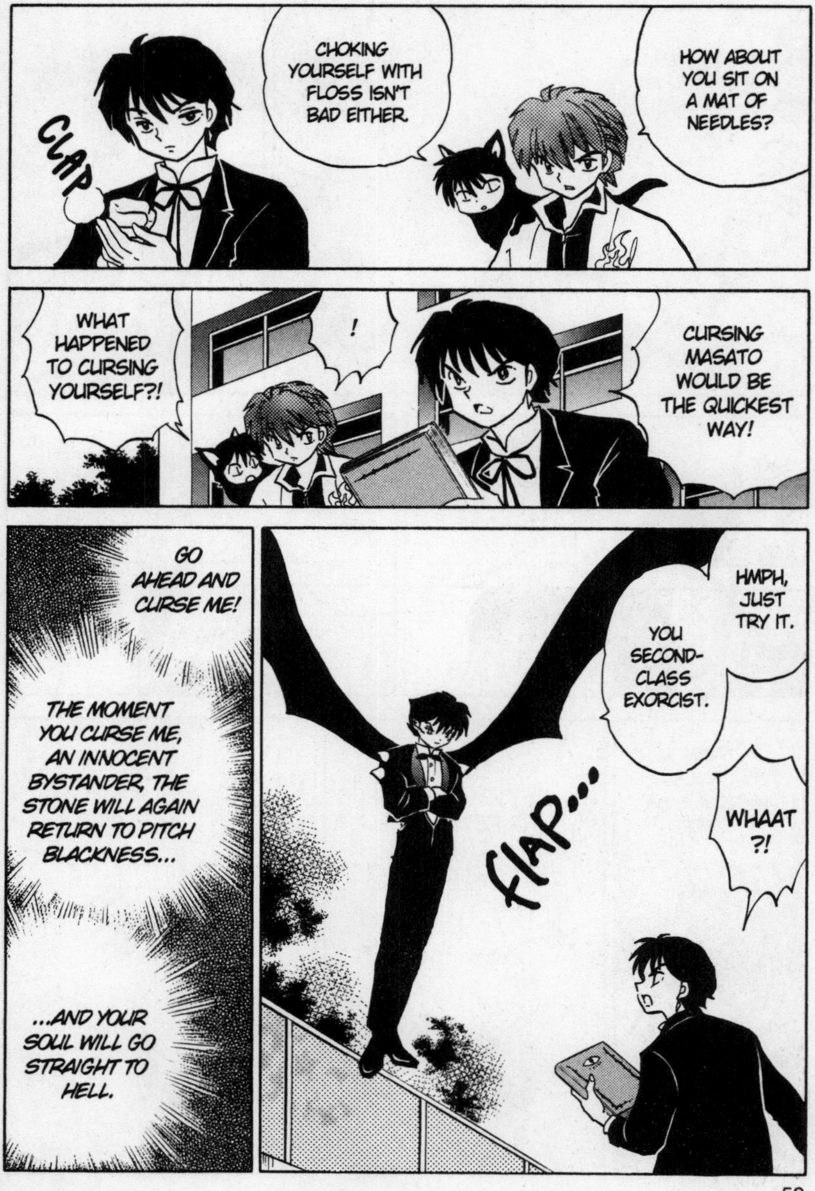
HOW ABOUT YOU SIT ON A MAT OF NEEDLES?
CHOKING YOURSELF WITH FLOSS ISN'T BAD EITHER.
CLAP
CURSING MASATO WOULD BE THE QUICKEST WAY!
!
WHAT HAPPENED TO CURSING YOURSELF?!
HMPH, JUST TRY IT.
YOU SECOND-CLASS EXORCIST.
FLAP...
WHAAT ?!
GO AHEAD AND CURSE ME!
THE MOMENT YOU CURSE ME, AN INNOCENT BYSTANDER, THE STONE WILL AGAIN RETURN TO PITCH BLACKNESS...
...AND YOUR SOUL WILL GO STRAIGHT TO HELL.

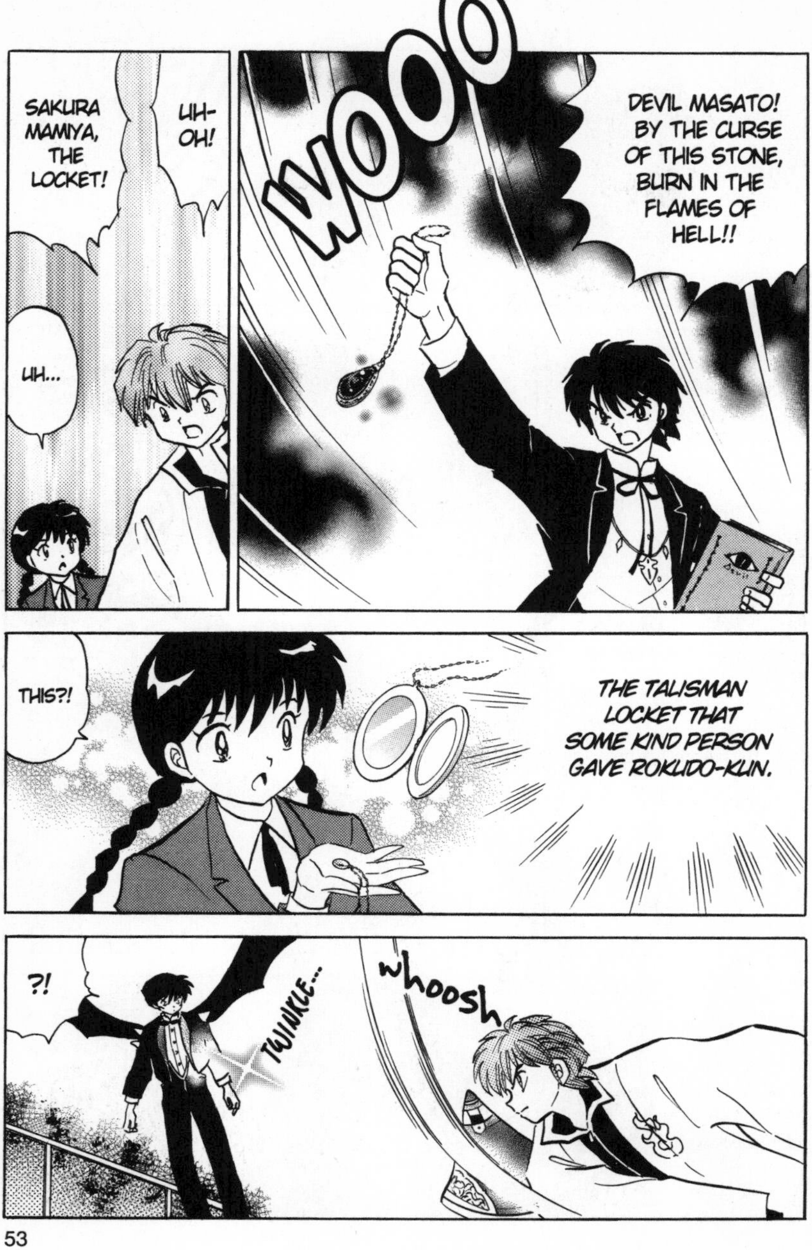
WOOO
DEVIL MASATO! BY THE CURSE OF THIS STONE, BURN IN THE FLAMES OF HELL!!
UH-OH!
SAKURA MAMIYA, THE LOCKET!
UH...
THE TALISMAN LOCKET THAT SOME KIND PERSON GAVE ROKUDO-KUN.
THIS?!
whoosh
TWINKLE...
?!

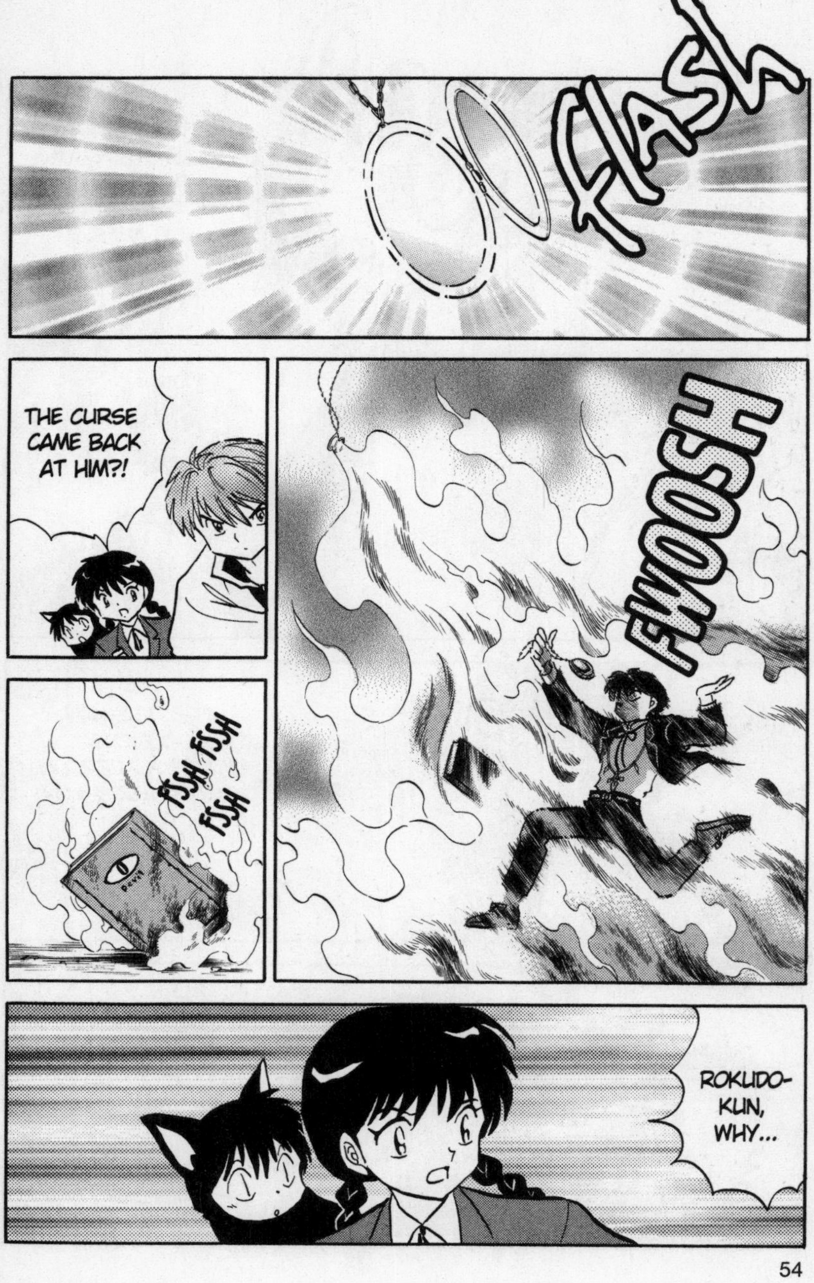
FLASH
FWOOSH
THE CURSE CAME BACK AT HIM?!
FSSH FSSH FSSH
ROKUDO-KUN, WHY...

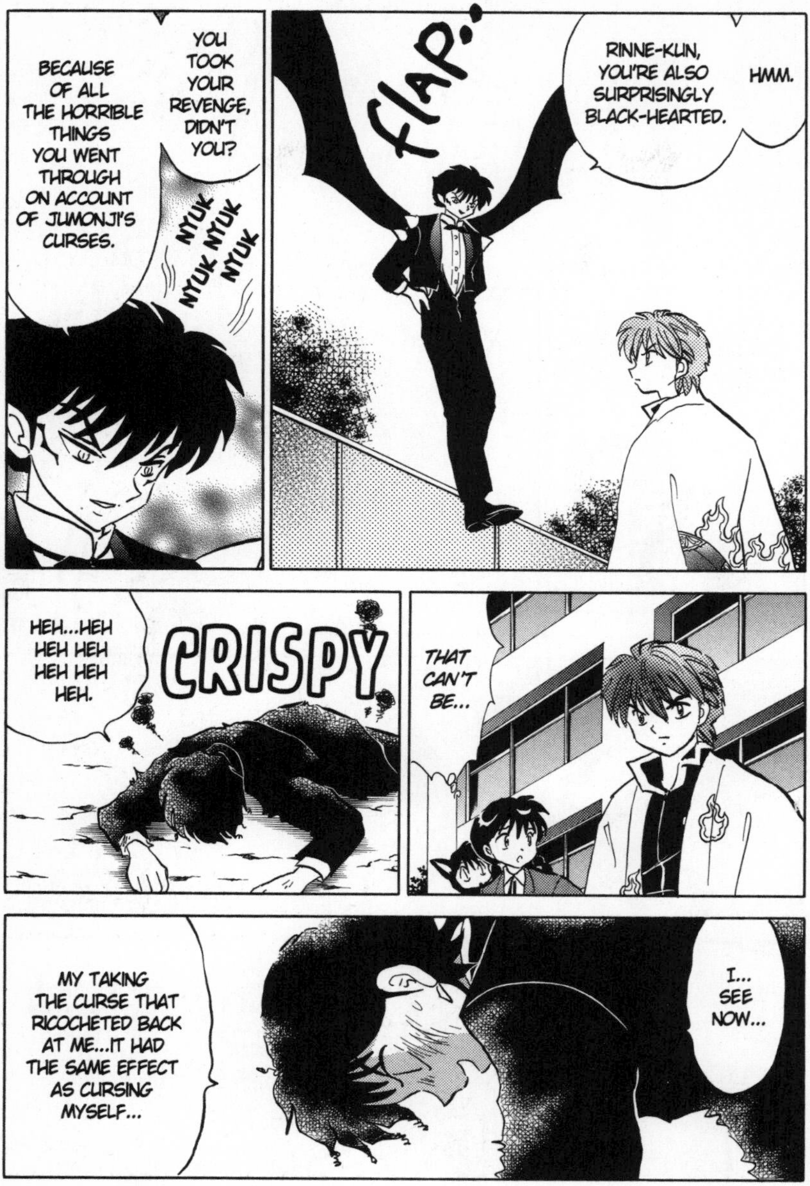
HMM.
RINNE-KUN, YOU'RE ALSO SURPRISINGLY BLACK-HEARTED.
FLAP...
YOU TOOK YOUR REVENGE, DIDN'T YOU?
BECAUSE OF ALL THE HORRIBLE THINGS YOU WENT THROUGH ON ACCOUNT OF JUMONJI'S CURSES.
NYUK NYUK NYUK NYUK
THAT CAN'T BE...
CRISPY
HEH...HEH HEH HEH HEH HEH HEH.
I... SEE NOW...
MY TAKING THE CURSE THAT RICOCHETED BACK AT ME...IT HAD THE SAME EFFECT AS CURSING MYSELF...

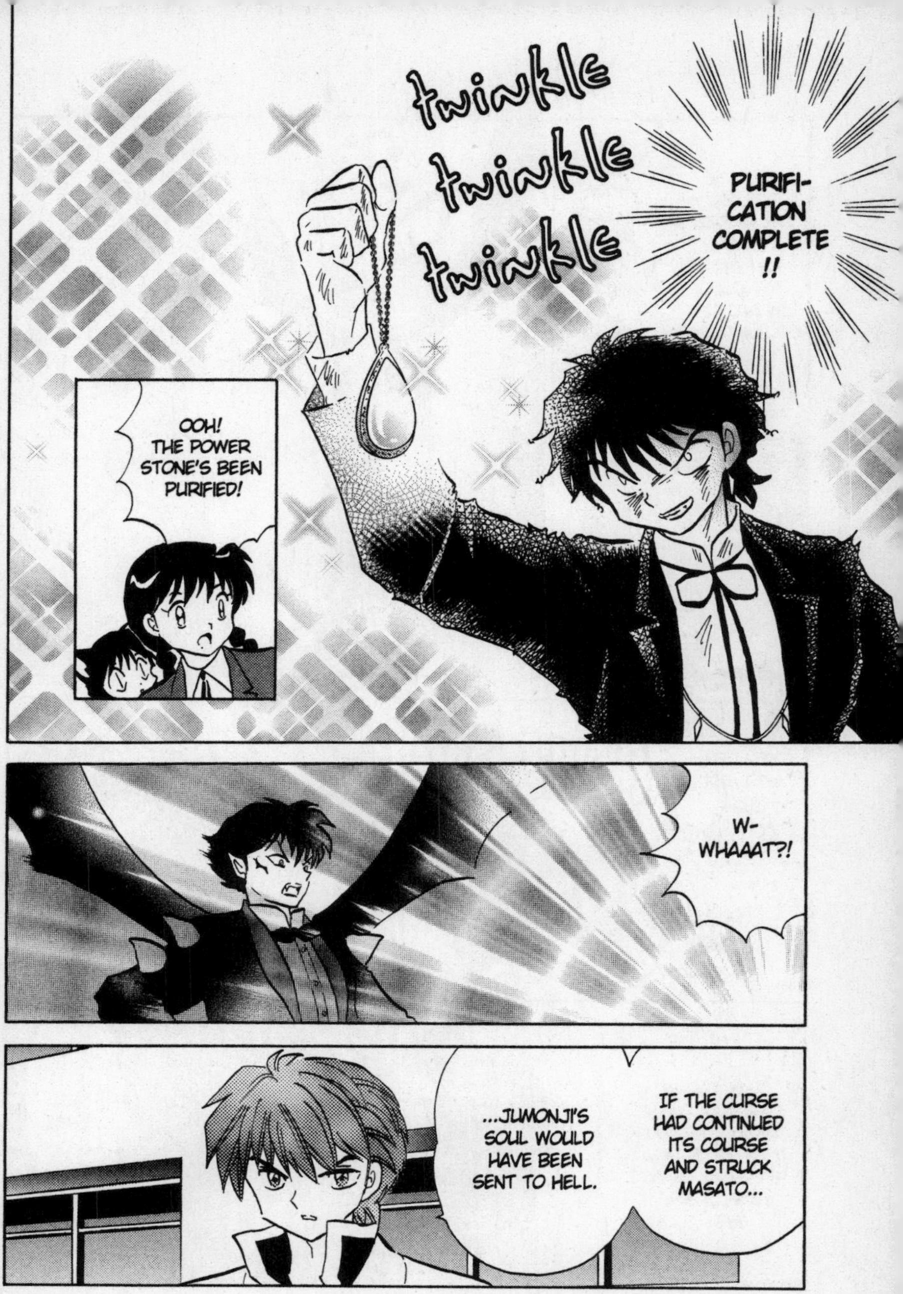
PURIFI-CATION COMPLETE !!
twinkle twinkle twinkle
OOH! THE POWER STONE'S BEEN PURIFIED!
W-WHAAAT?!
IF THE CURSE HAD CONTINUED ITS COURSE AND STRUCK MASATO...
...JUMONJI'S SOUL WOULD HAVE BEEN SENT TO HELL.

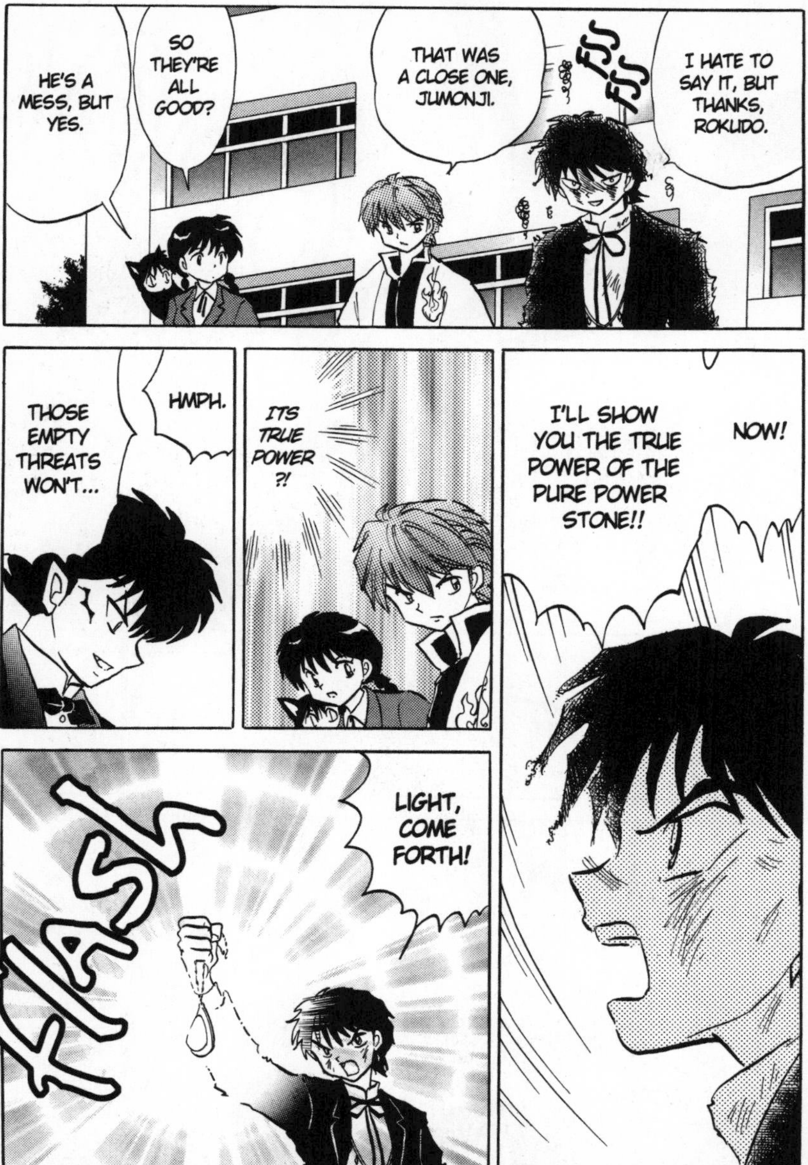
I HATE TO SAY IT, BUT THANKS, ROKUDO.
FJJ FJJ
THAT WAS A CLOSE ONE, JUMONJI.
SO THEY'RE ALL GOOD?
HE'S A MESS, BUT YES.
NOW!
I'LL SHOW YOU THE TRUE POWER OF THE PURE POWER STONE!!
ITS TRUE POWER?!
HMPH.
THOSE EMPTY THREATS WON'T...
LIGHT, COME FORTH!
FLASH

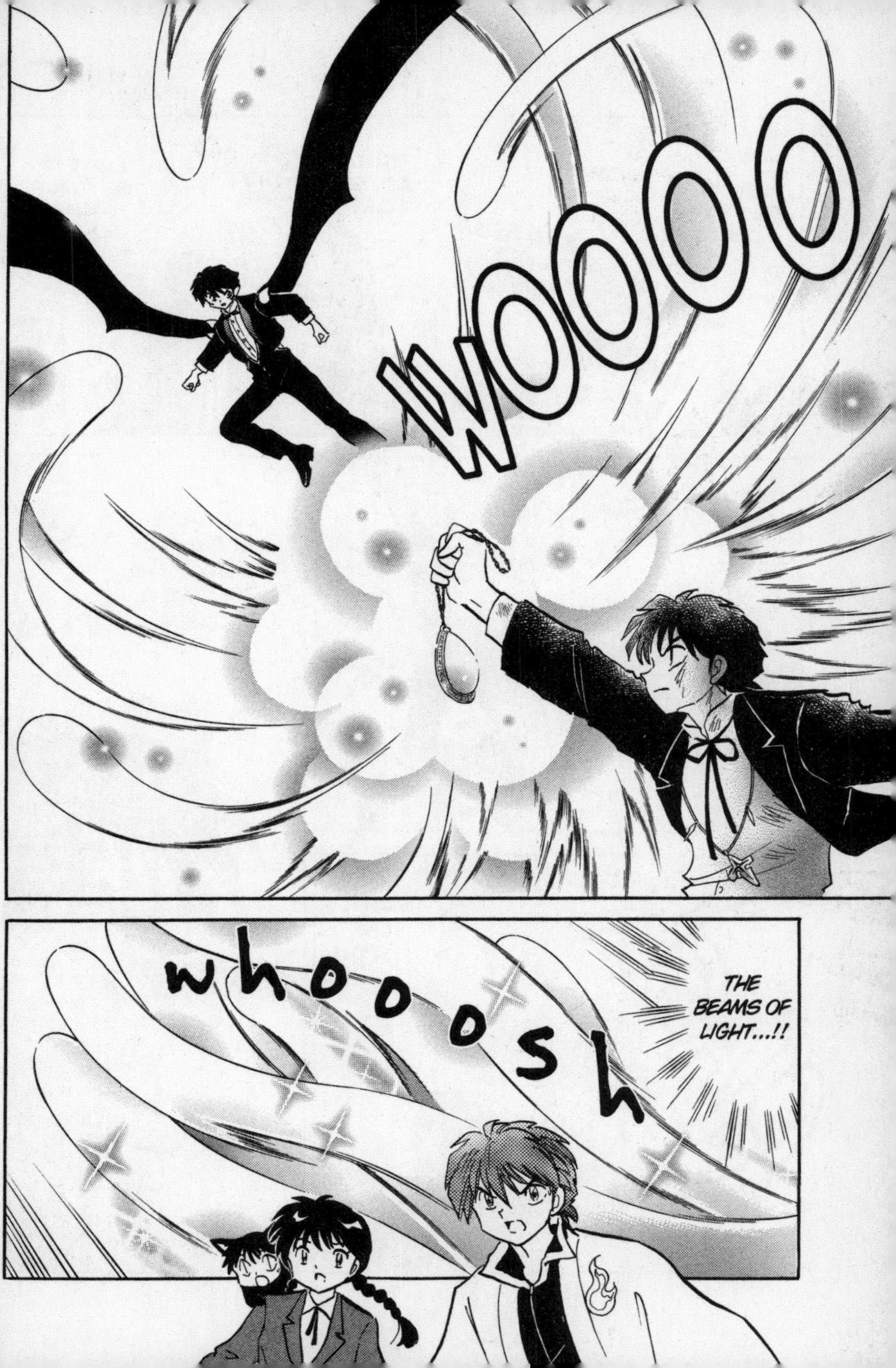
WOOOO
whooosh
THE BEAMS OF LIGHT...!!

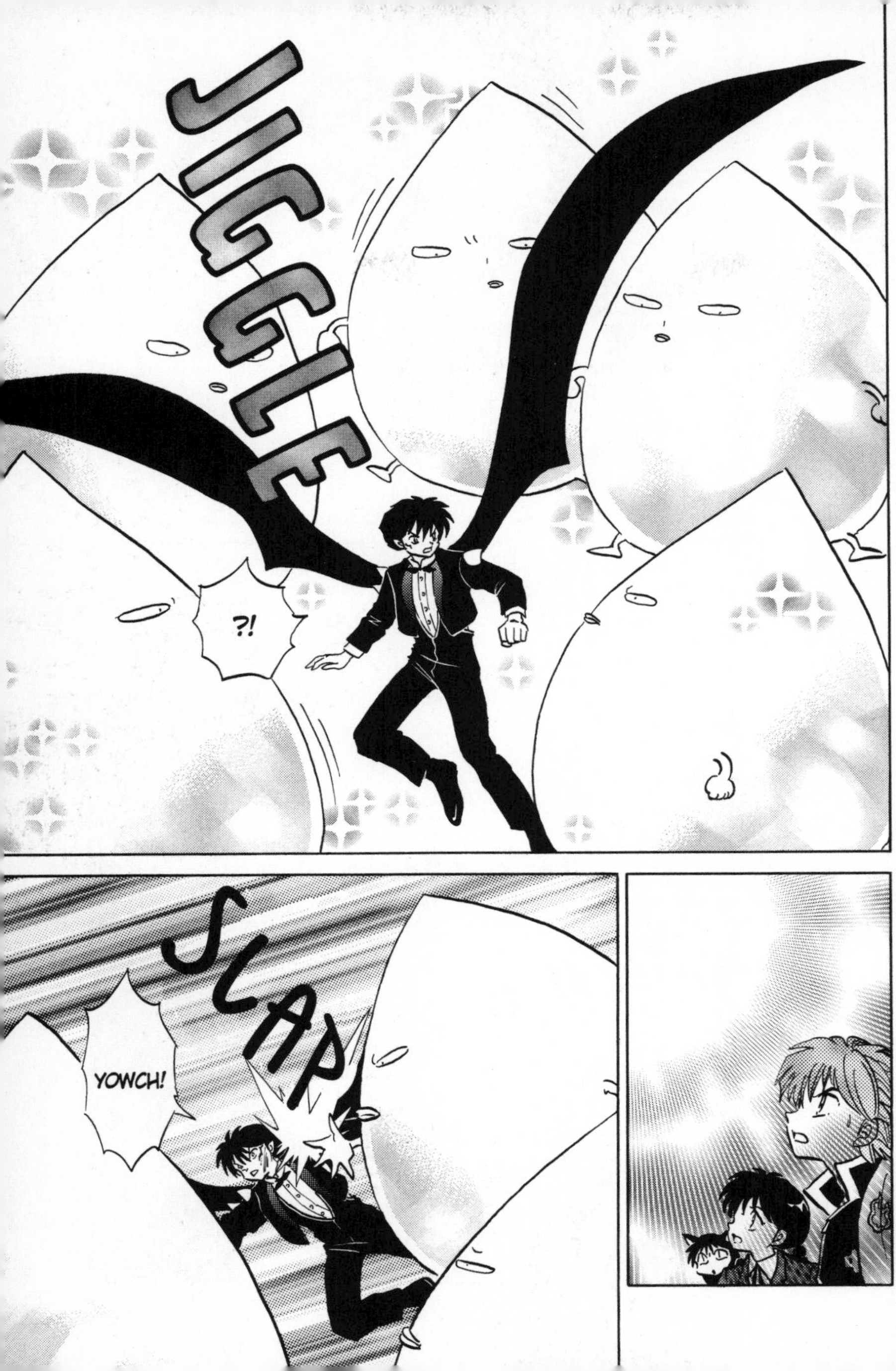
JIGGLE
?!
SLAP
YOWCH!

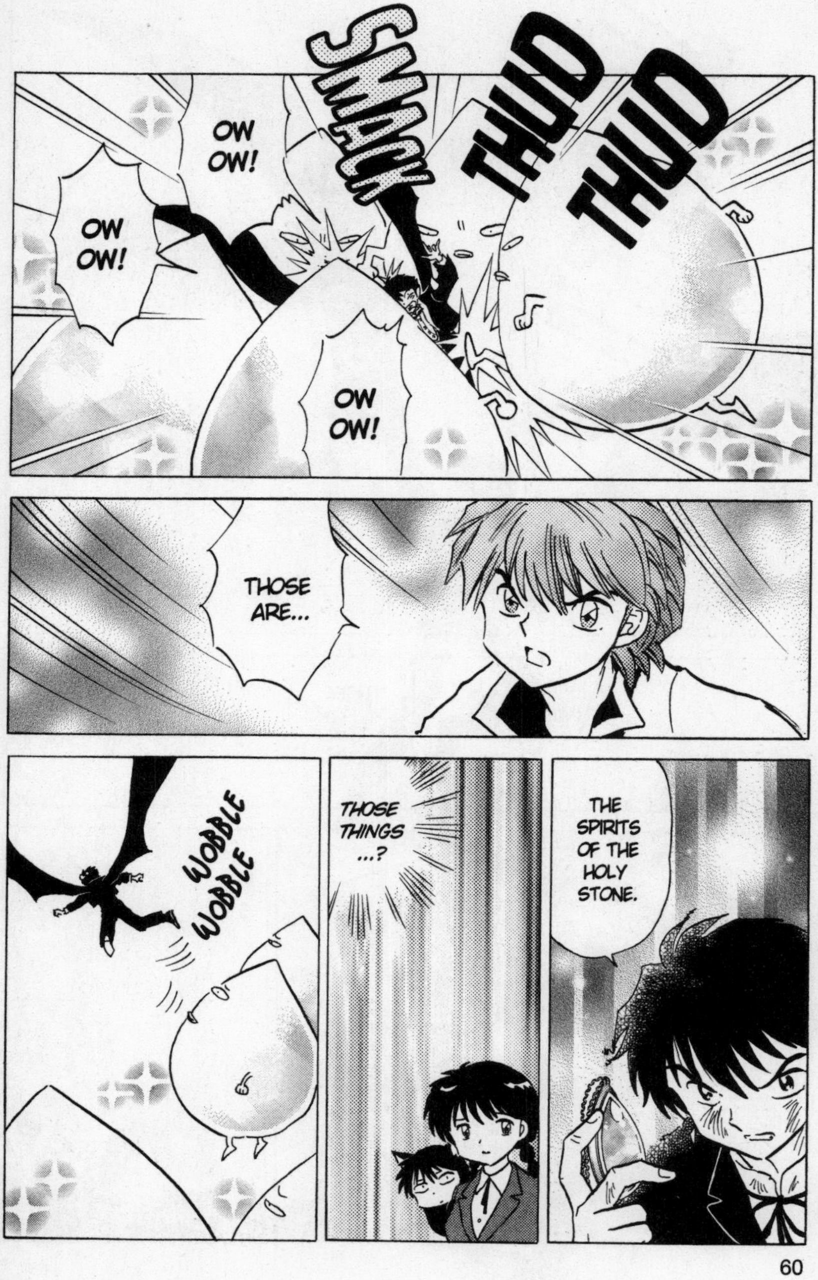
THUD THUD
SMACK
OW OW!
OW OW!
OW OW!
THOSE ARE...
THE SPIRITS OF THE HOLY STONE.
THOSE THINGS ...?
WOBBLE WOBBLE

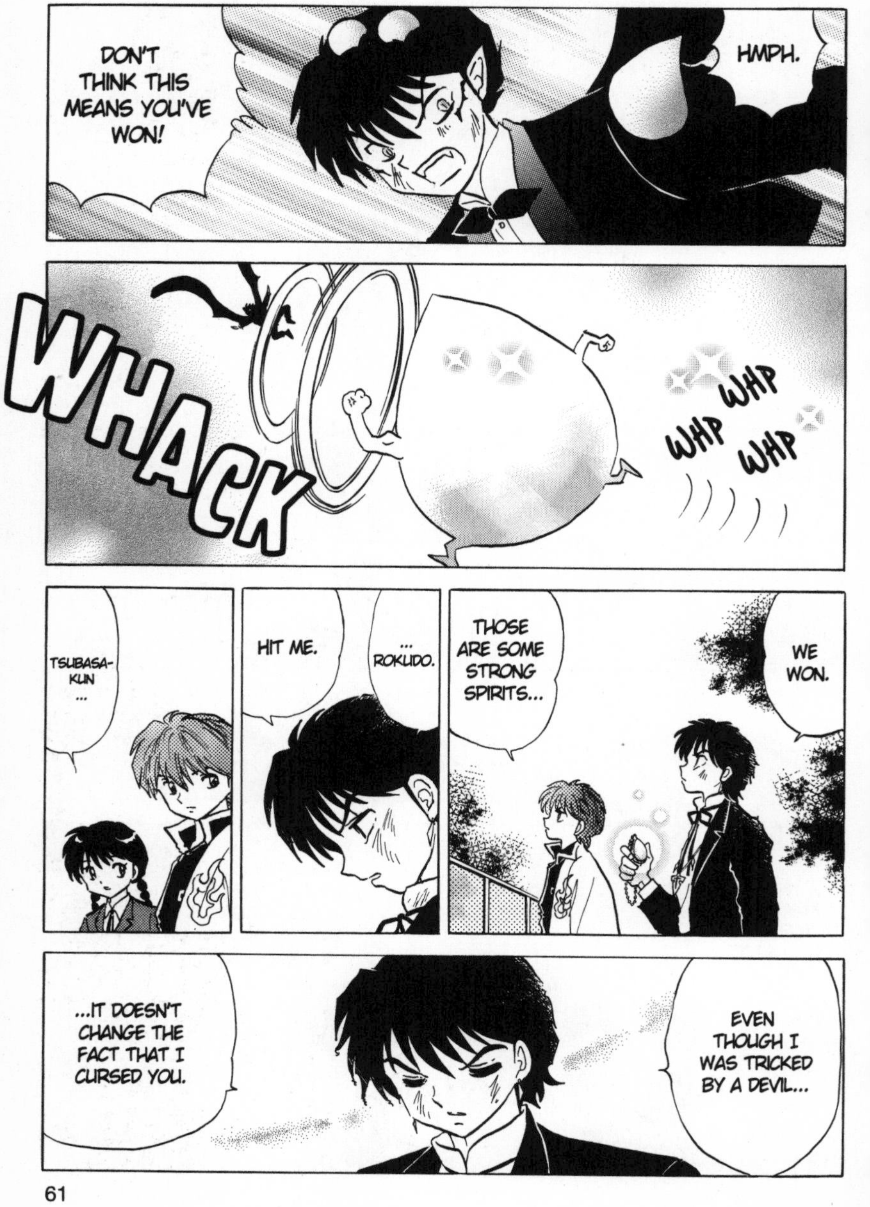
HMPH.
DON'T THINK THIS MEANS YOU'VE WON!
WHP WHP WHP WHP
WHACK
WE WON.
THOSE ARE SOME STRONG SPIRITS...
... ROKUDO.
HIT ME.
TSUBASA-KUN ...
EVEN THOUGH I WAS TRICKED BY A DEVIL...
...IT DOESN'T CHANGE THE FACT THAT I CURSED YOU.

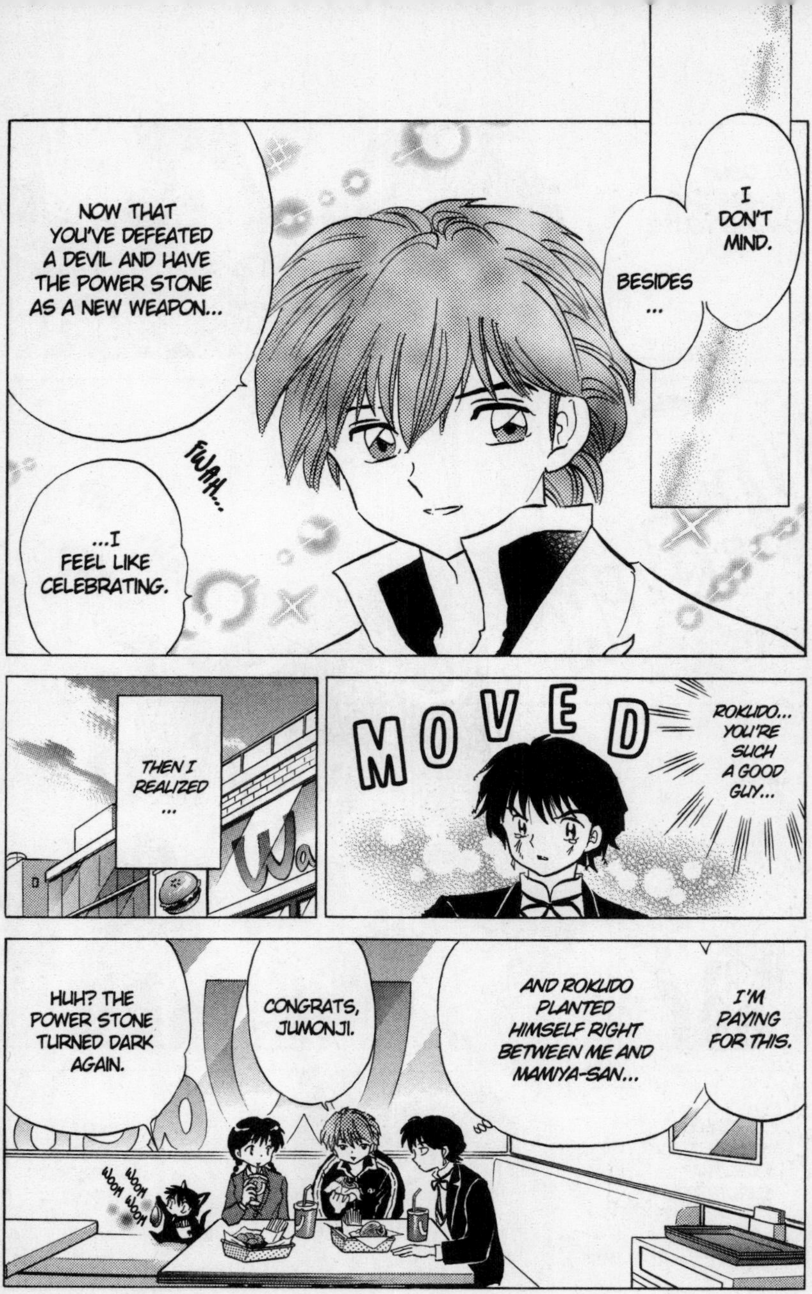
I DON'T MIND.
BESIDES...
NOW THAT YOU'VE DEFEATED A DEVIL AND HAVE THE POWER STONE AS A NEW WEAPON...
FWAH...
...I FEEL LIKE CELEBRATING.
MOVED
ROKUDO... YOU'RE SUCH A GOOD GUY...
THEN I REALIZED...
I'M PAYING FOR THIS.
AND ROKUDO PLANTED HIMSELF RIGHT BETWEEN ME AND MAMIYA-SAN...
CONGRATS, JUMONJI.
HUH? THE POWER STONE TURNED DARK AGAIN.
WOOM WOOM
WOOM WOOM

CHAPTER 52: THE LOOK-ALIKE GHOST

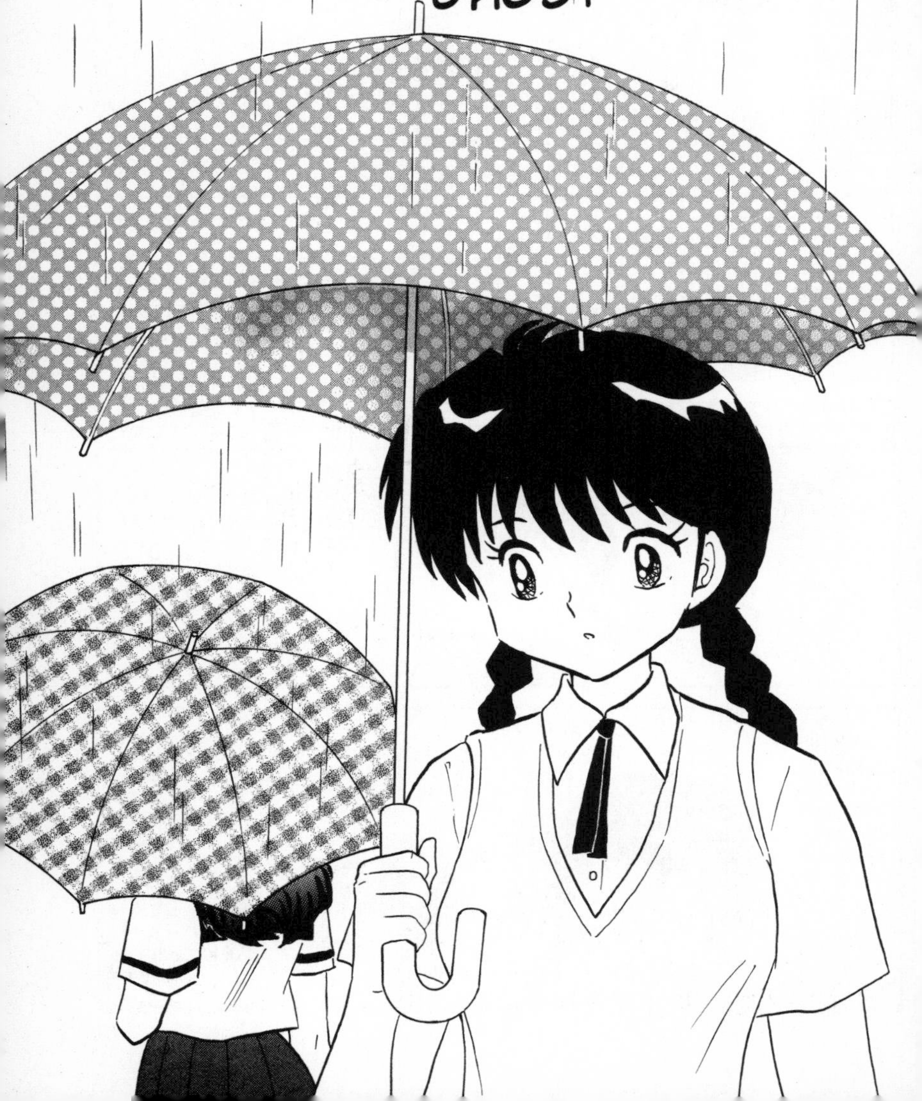

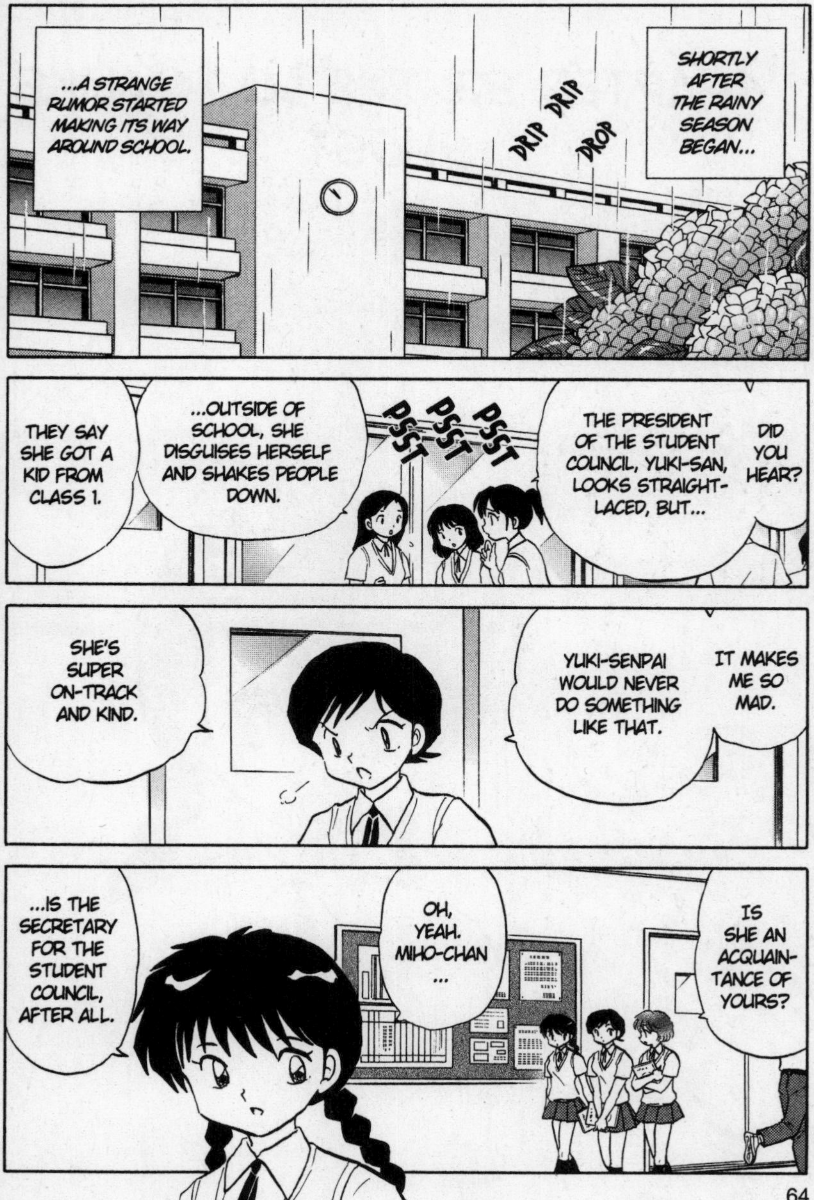
SHORTLY AFTER THE RAINY SEASON BEGAN...
DRIP DRIP DROP
...A STRANGE RUMOR STARTED MAKING ITS WAY AROUND SCHOOL.
DID YOU HEAR?
THE PRESIDENT OF THE STUDENT COUNCIL, YUKI-SAN, LOOKS STRAIGHT-LACED, BUT...
PSST PSST PSST
...OUTSIDE OF SCHOOL, SHE DISGUISES HERSELF AND SHAKES PEOPLE DOWN.
THEY SAY SHE GOT A KID FROM CLASS 1.
IT MAKES ME SO MAD.
YUKI-SENPAI WOULD NEVER DO SOMETHING LIKE THAT.
SHE'S SUPER ON-TRACK AND KIND.
IS SHE AN ACQUAINTANCE OF YOURS?
OH, YEAH. MIHO-CHAN ...
...IS THE SECRETARY FOR THE STUDENT COUNCIL, AFTER ALL.

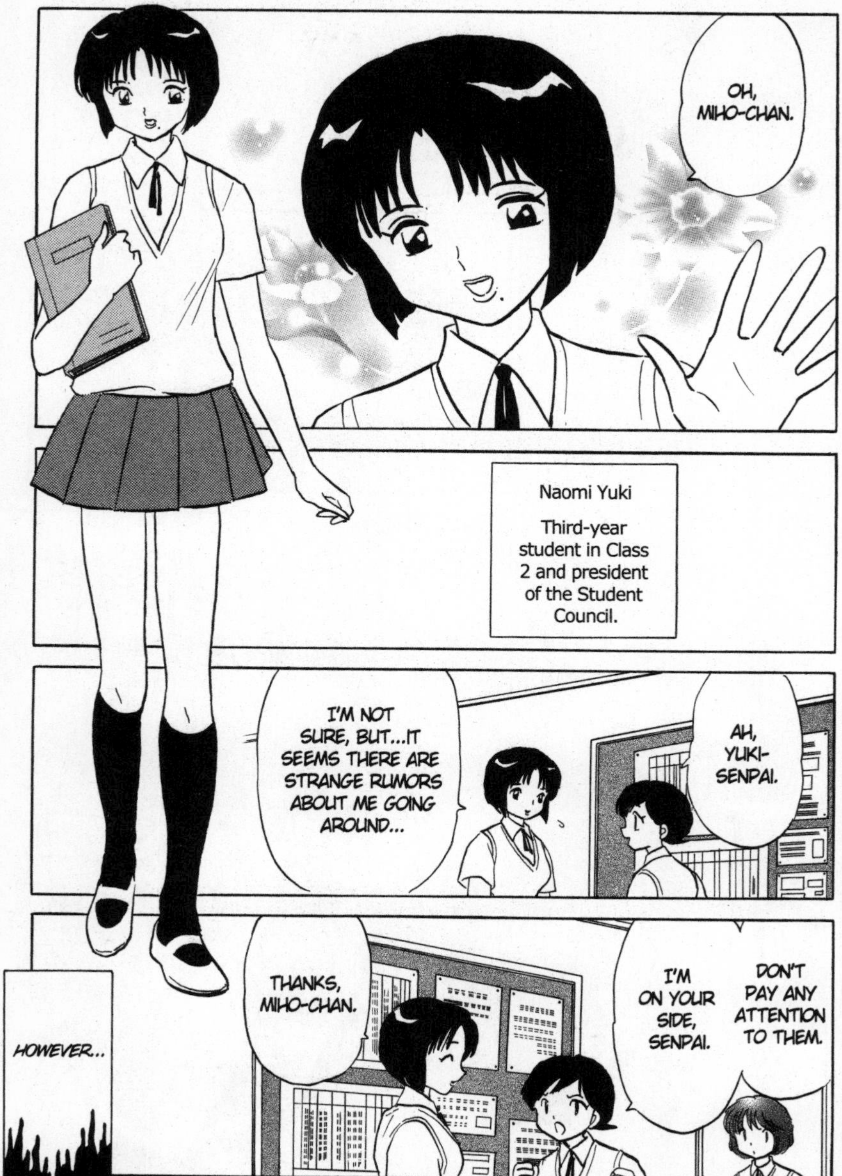
OH, MIHO-CHAN.
Naomi Yuki
Third-year student in Class 2 and president of the Student Council.
AH, YUKI-SENPAI.
I'M NOT SURE, BUT...IT SEEMS THERE ARE STRANGE RUMORS ABOUT ME GOING AROUND...
DON'T PAY ANY ATTENTION TO THEM.
I'M ON YOUR SIDE, SENPAI.
THANKS, MIHO-CHAN.
HOWEVER...

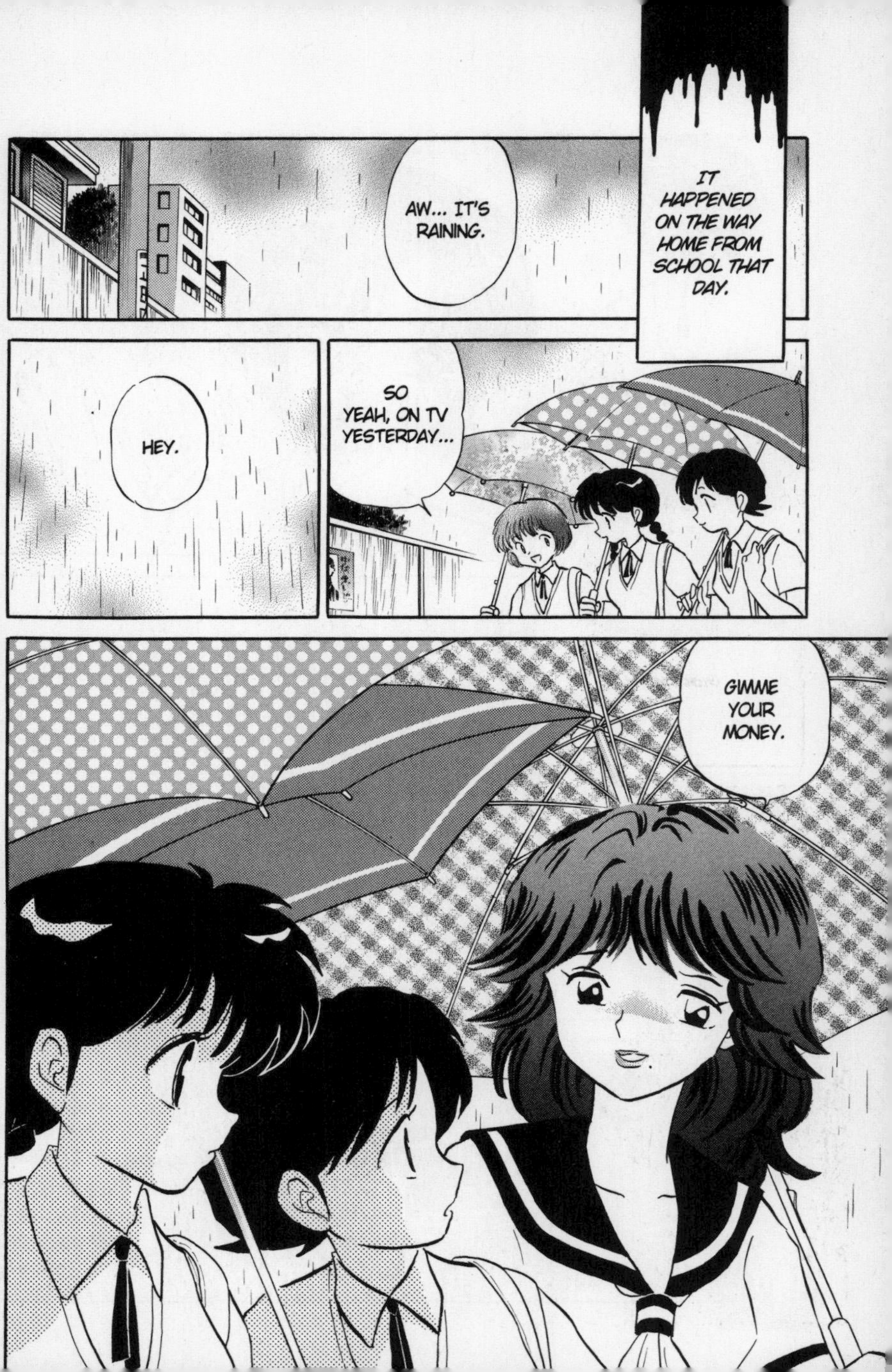
IT HAPPENED ON THE WAY HOME FROM SCHOOL THAT DAY.
AW... IT'S RAINING.
SO YEAH, ON TV YESTERDAY...
HEY.
GIMME YOUR MONEY.

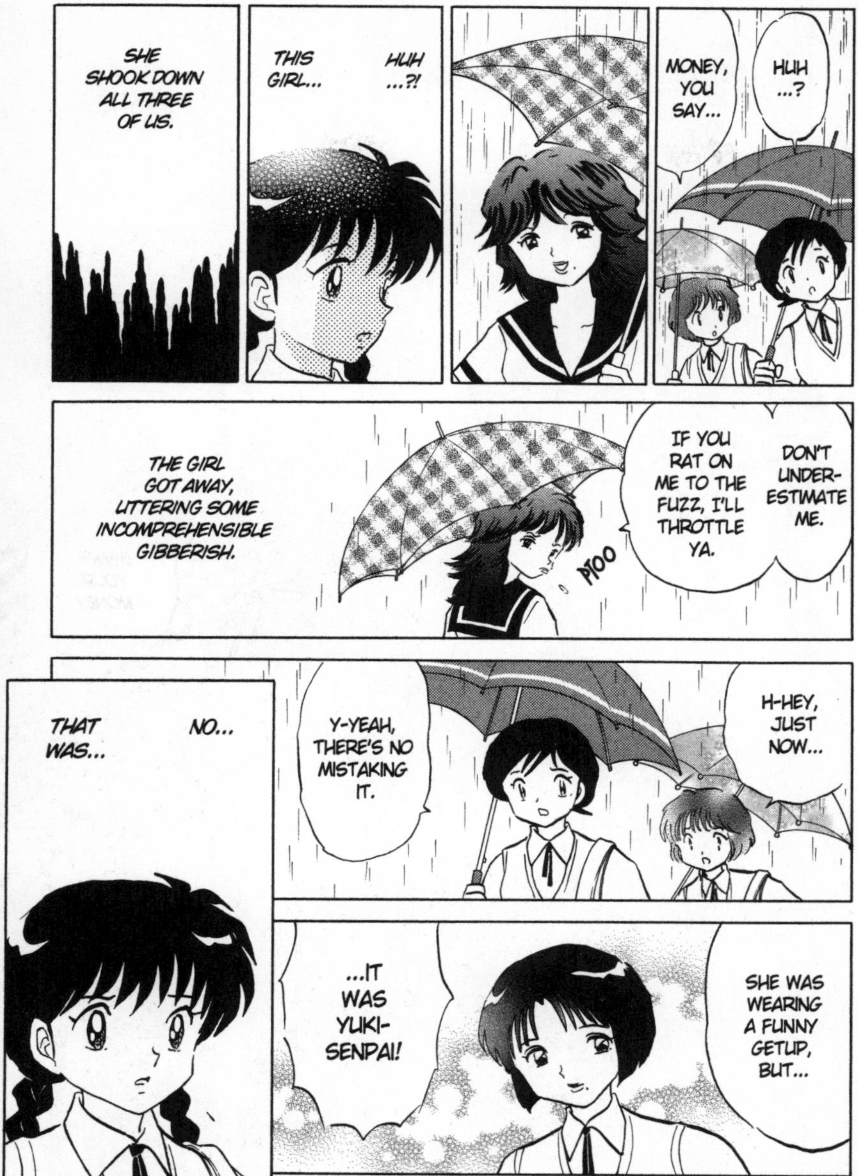
HUH ...?
MONEY, YOU SAY...
HUH ...?!
THIS GIRL...
SHE SHOOK DOWN ALL THREE OF US.
DON'T UNDERESTIMATE ME.
IF YOU RAT ON ME TO THE FUZZ, I'LL THROTTLE YA.
PTOO
THE GIRL GOT AWAY, UTTERING SOME INCOMPREHENSIBLE GIBBERISH.
H-HEY, JUST NOW...
Y-YEAH, THERE'S NO MISTAKING IT.
SHE WAS WEARING A FUNNY GETUP, BUT...
...IT WAS YUKI-SENPAI!
NO...
THAT WAS...

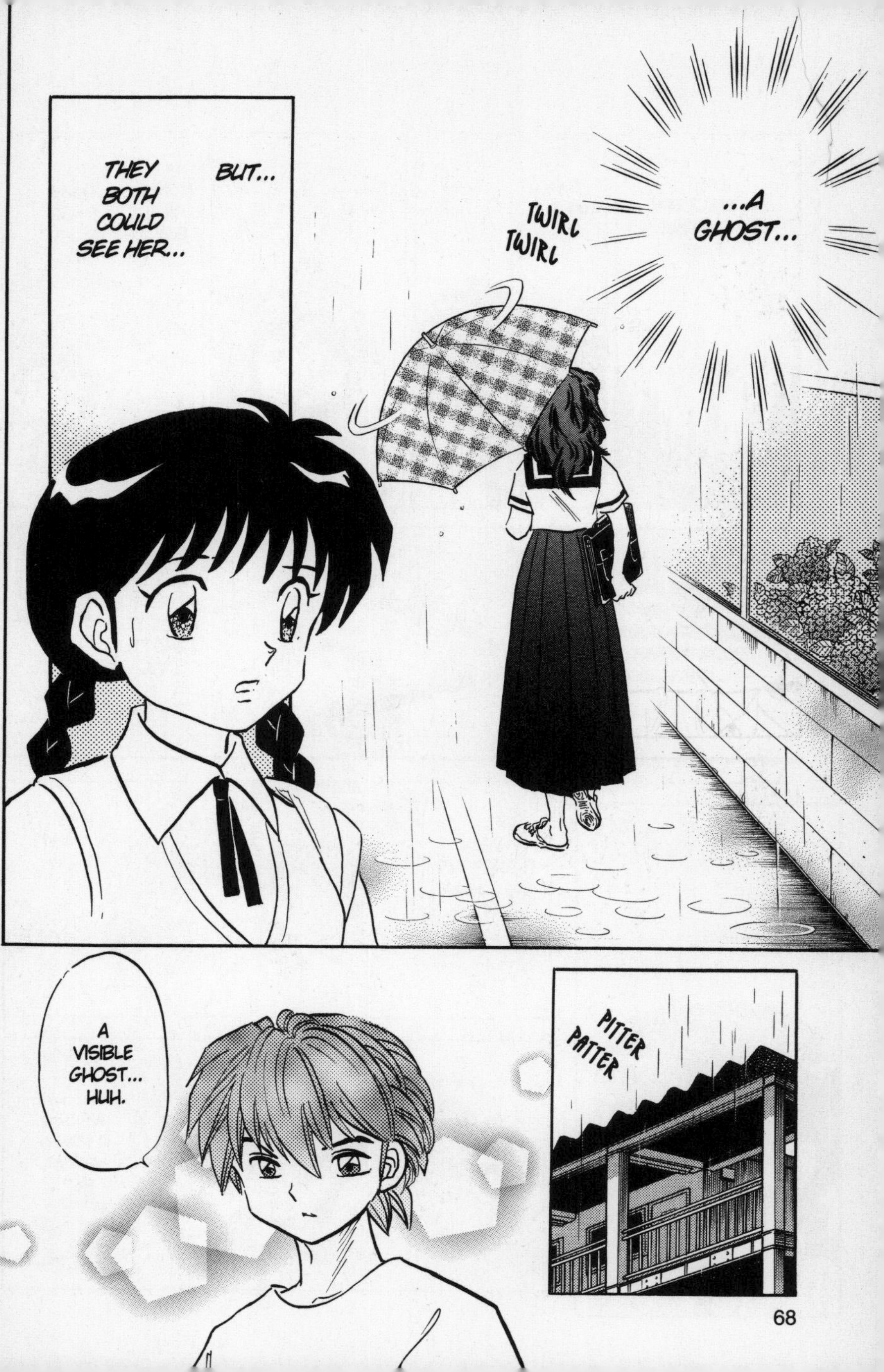
...A GHOST...
TWIRL TWIRL
BUT...
THEY BOTH COULD SEE HER...
PITTER PATTER
A VISIBLE GHOST... HUH.

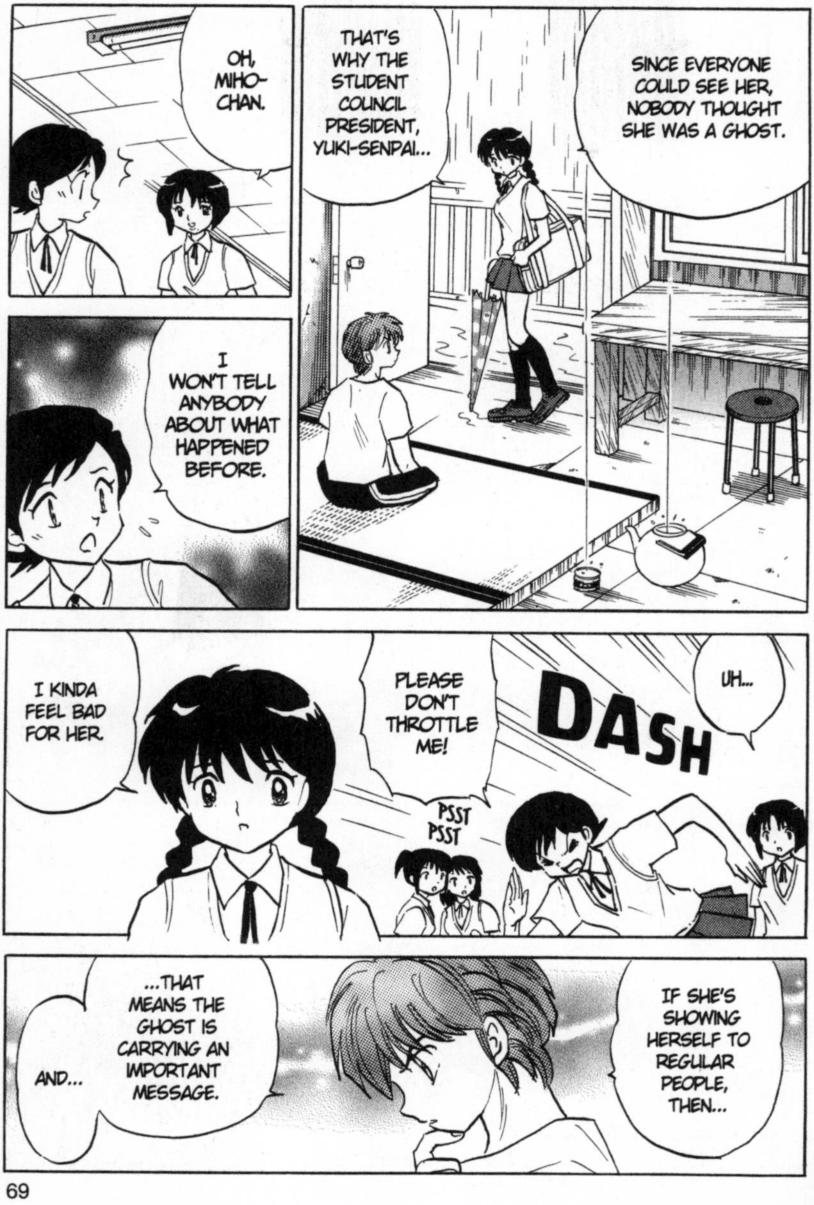

SINCE EVERYONE COULD SEE HER, NOBODY THOUGHT SHE WAS A GHOST.
THAT'S WHY THE STUDENT COUNCIL PRESIDENT, YUKI-SENPAI...
OH, MIHO-CHAN.
I WON'T TELL ANYBODY ABOUT WHAT HAPPENED BEFORE.
UH...
DASH
PLEASE DON'T THROTTLE ME!
PSST PSST
I KINDA FEEL BAD FOR HER.
IF SHE'S SHOWING HERSELF TO REGULAR PEOPLE, THEN...
...THAT MEANS THE GHOST IS CARRYING AN IMPORTANT MESSAGE.
AND...

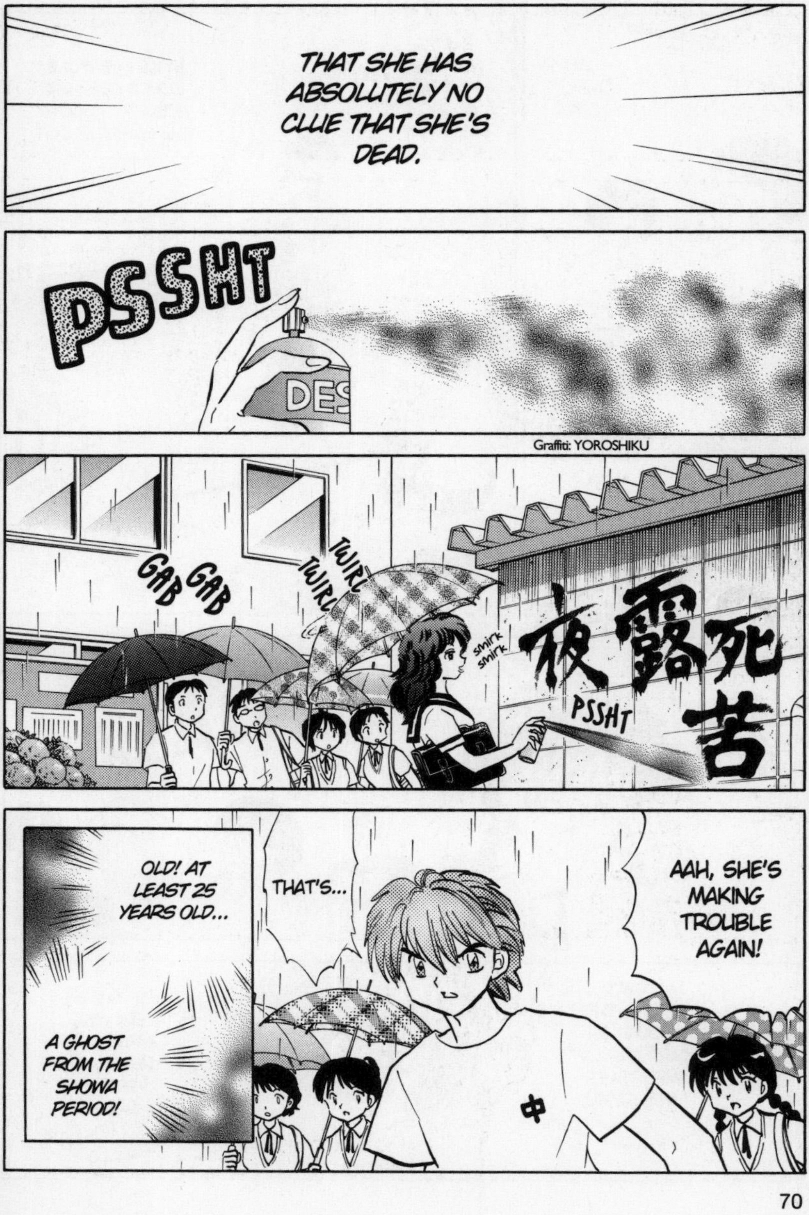
THAT SHE HAS ABSOLUTELY NO CLUE THAT SHE'S DEAD.
PSSHT
DES
Graffiti: YOROSHIKU
夜露死苦
PSSHT
smirk smirk
TWIRL TWIRL
GAB GAB
AAH, SHE'S MAKING TROUBLE AGAIN!
THAT'S...
OLD! AT LEAST 25 YEARS OLD...
A GHOST FROM THE SHOWA PERIOD!
中

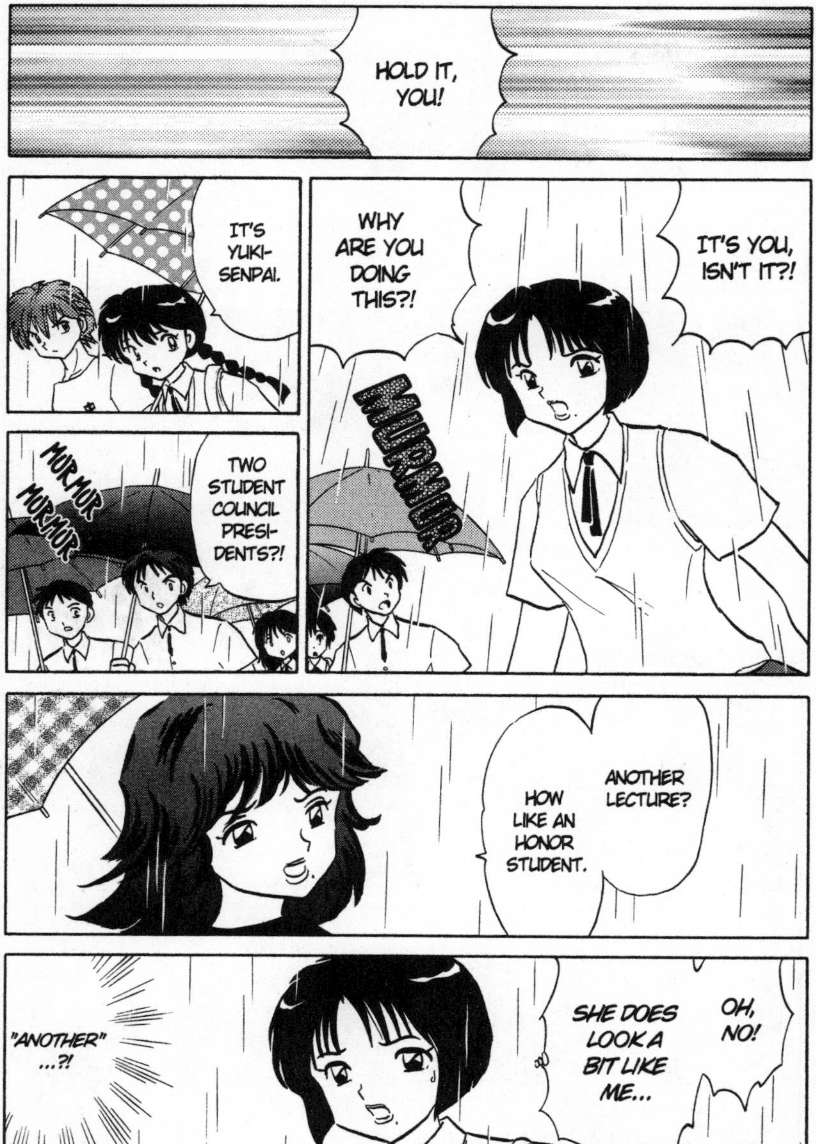
HOLD IT, YOU!
IT'S YOU, ISN'T IT?!
WHY ARE YOU DOING THIS?!
MURMUR
IT'S YUKI-SENPAI.
TWO STUDENT COUNCIL PRESIDENTS?!
MUR MUR MUR MUR
ANOTHER LECTURE?
HOW LIKE AN HONOR STUDENT.
OH, NO!
SHE DOES LOOK A BIT LIKE ME...
"ANOTHER" ...?!

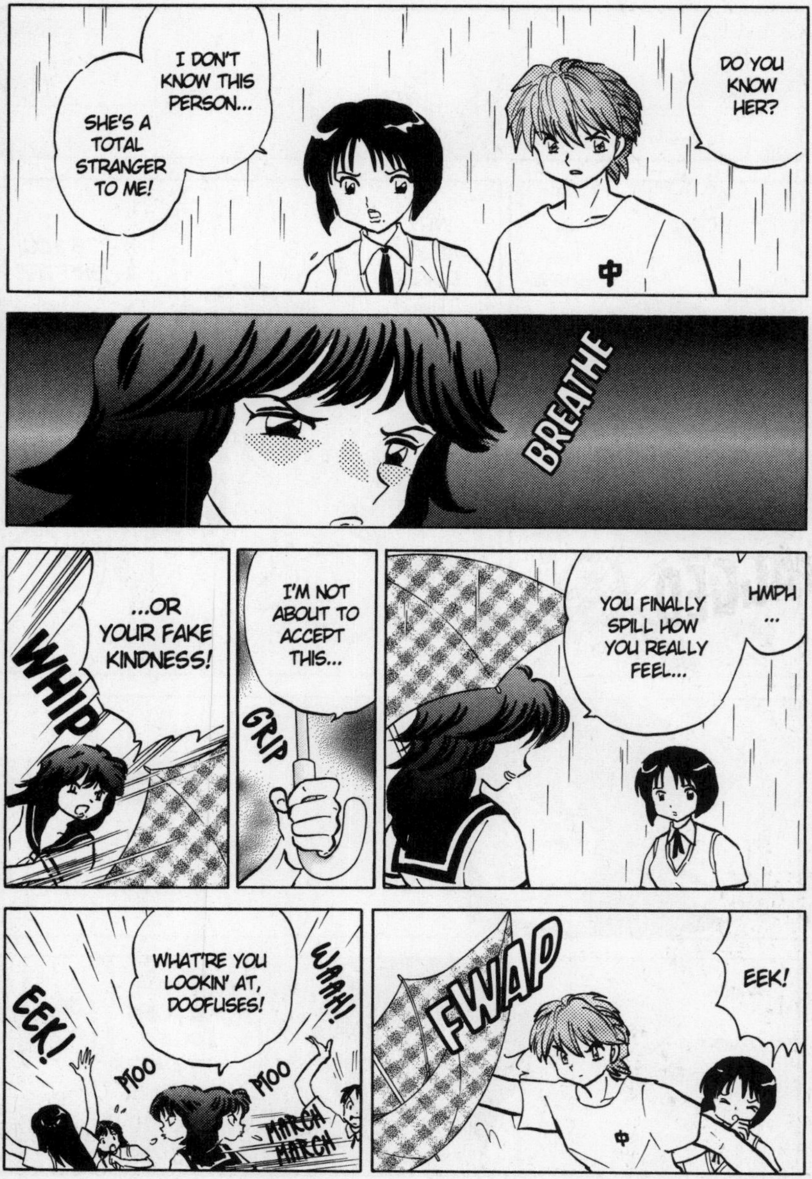
DO YOU KNOW HER?
I DON'T KNOW THIS PERSON...
SHE'S A TOTAL STRANGER TO ME!
BREATHE
HMPH ...
YOU FINALLY SPILL HOW YOU REALLY FEEL...
I'M NOT ABOUT TO ACCEPT THIS...
GRIP
...OR YOUR FAKE KINDNESS!
WHIP
EEK!
FWAP
WAAAH!
WHAT'RE YOU LOOKIN' AT, DOOFUSES!
PTOO
MARCH MARCH
PTOO
EEK!

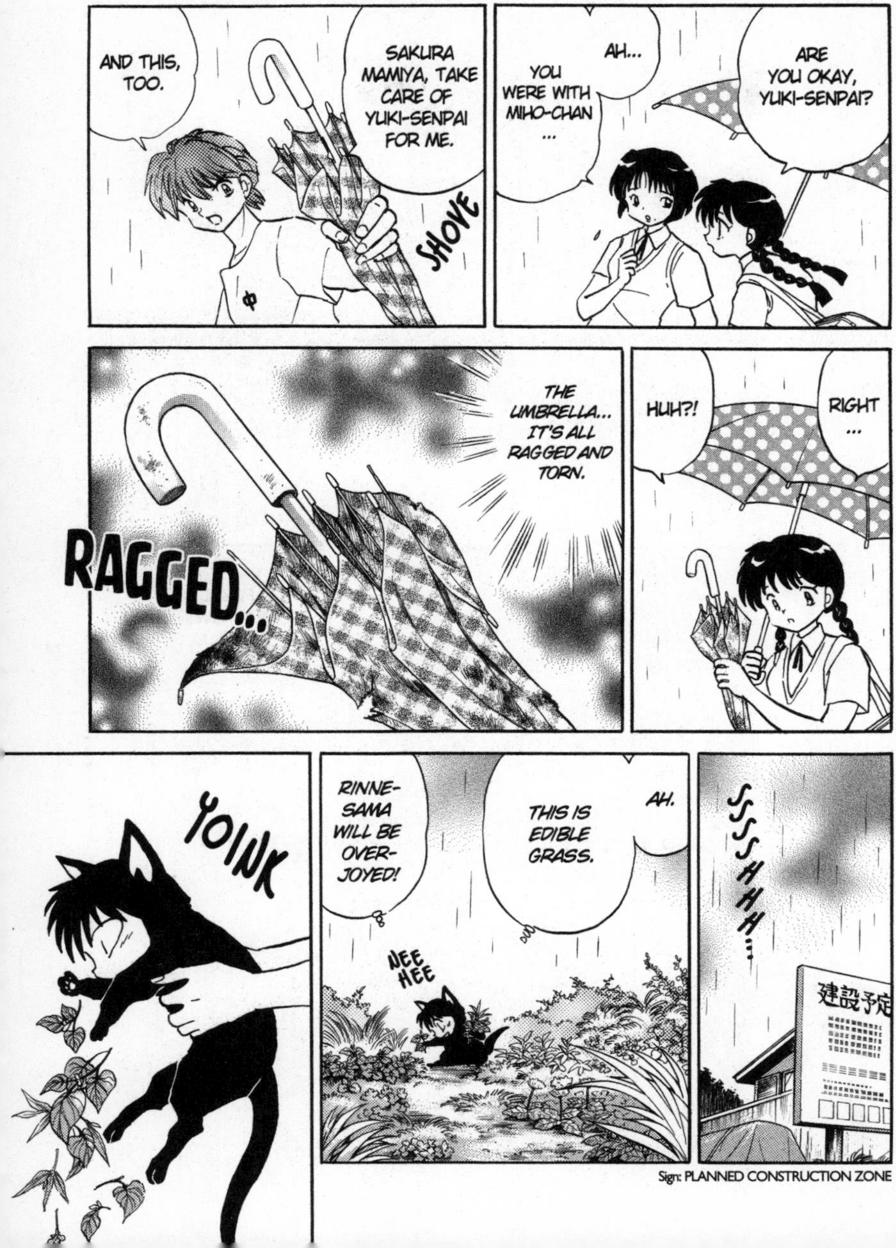
ARE YOU OKAY, YUKI-SENPAI?
AH...
YOU WERE WITH MIHO-CHAN ...
SAKURA MAMIYA, TAKE CARE OF YUKI-SENPAI FOR ME.
SHOVE
AND THIS, TOO.
RIGHT ...
HUH?!
THE UMBRELLA... IT'S ALL RAGGED AND TORN.
RAGGED...
SSSHHHH...
建設予定
AH.
THIS IS EDIBLE GRASS.
RINNE-SAMA WILL BE OVER-JOYED!
NEE HEE
YOINK

Sign: PLANNED CONSTRUCTION ZONE

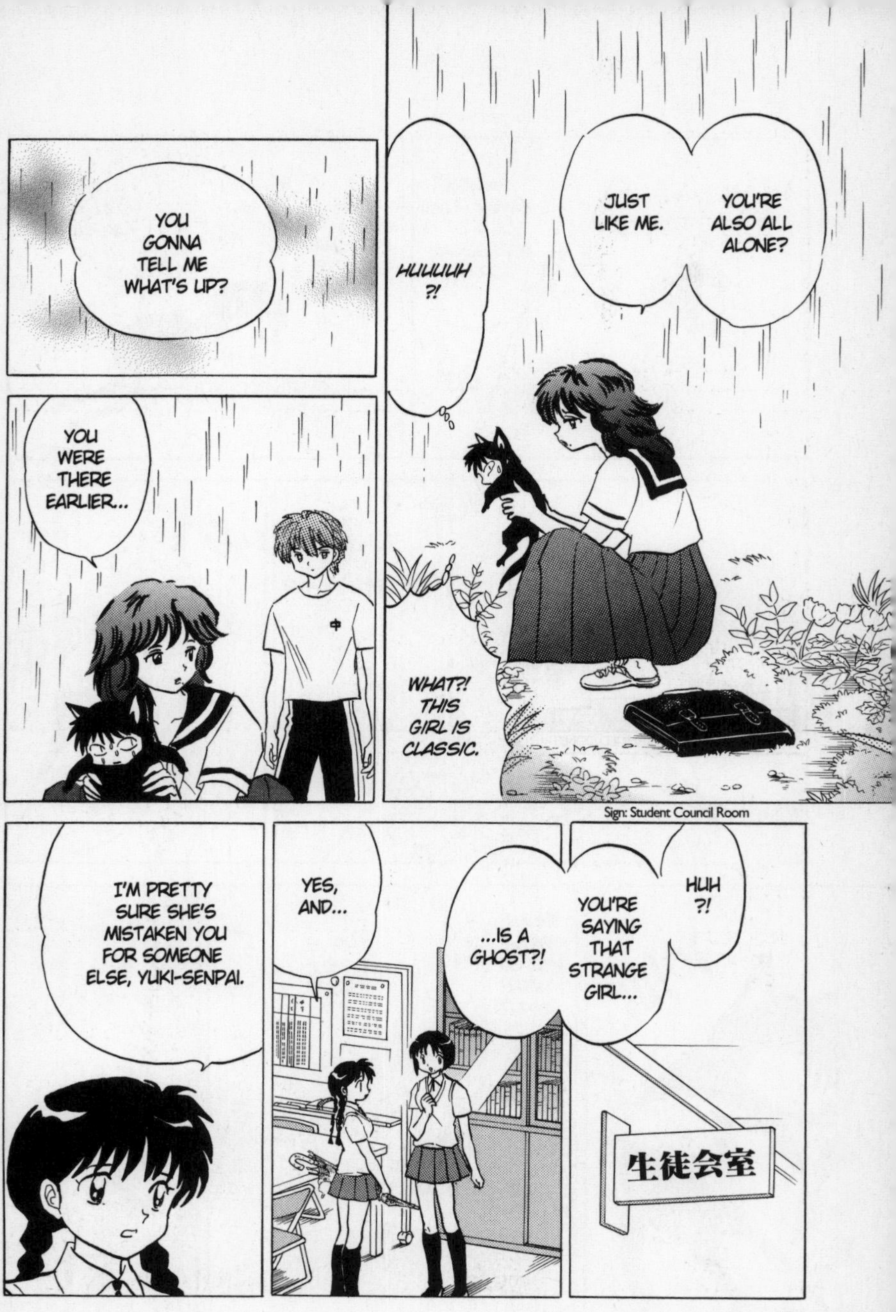
YOU'RE ALSO ALL ALONE?
JUST LIKE ME.
HUUUUH ?!
WHAT?! THIS GIRL IS CLASSIC.
YOU GONNA TELL ME WHAT'S UP?
YOU WERE THERE EARLIER...
Sign: Student Council Room
HUH ?!
YOU'RE SAYING THAT STRANGE GIRL...
...IS A GHOST?!
生徒会室
YES, AND...
I'M PRETTY SURE SHE'S MISTAKEN YOU FOR SOMEONE ELSE, YUKI-SENPAI.

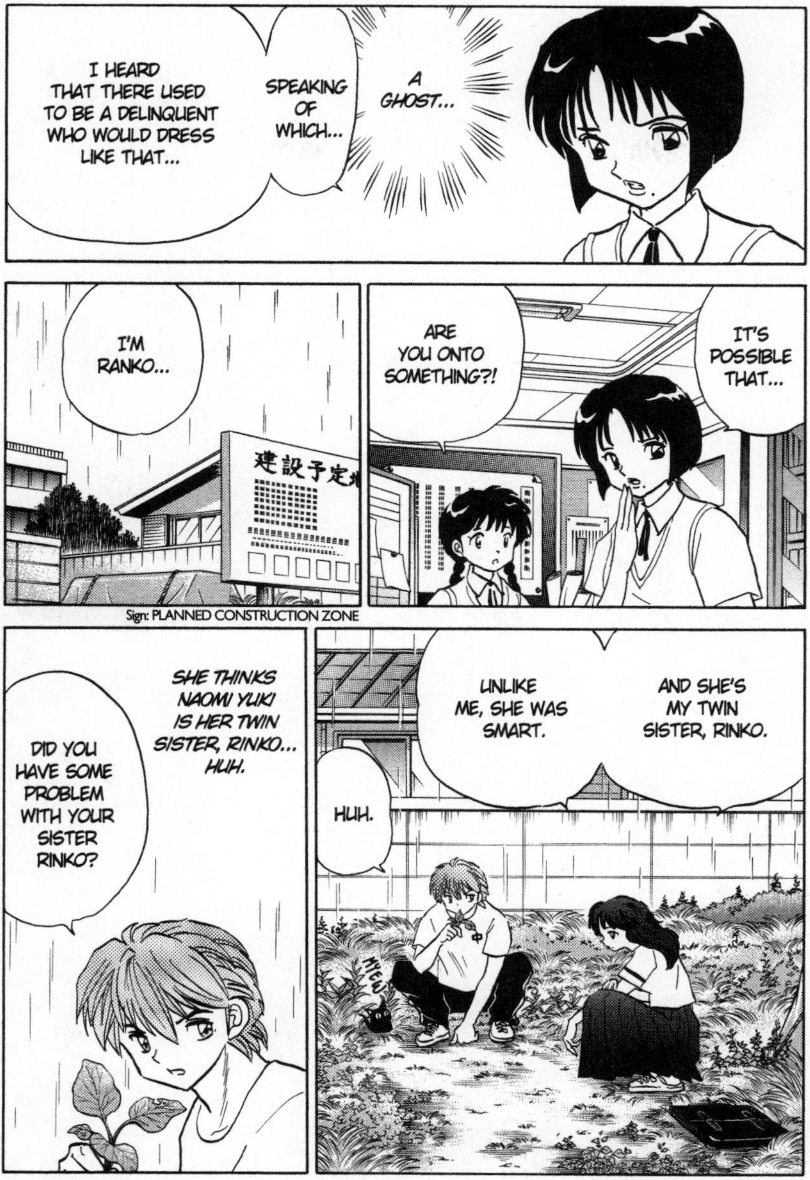
A GHOST...
SPEAKING OF WHICH...
I HEARD THAT THERE USED TO BE A DELINQUENT WHO WOULD DRESS LIKE THAT...
IT'S POSSIBLE THAT...
ARE YOU ONTO SOMETHING?!
I'M RANKO...
建設予定地
AND SHE'S MY TWIN SISTER, RINKO.
UNLIKE ME, SHE WAS SMART.
HUH.
MYEW
SHE THINKS NAOMI YUKI IS HER TWIN SISTER, RINKO... HUH.
DID YOU HAVE SOME PROBLEM WITH YOUR SISTER RINKO?
Sign: PLANNED CONSTRUCTION ZONE

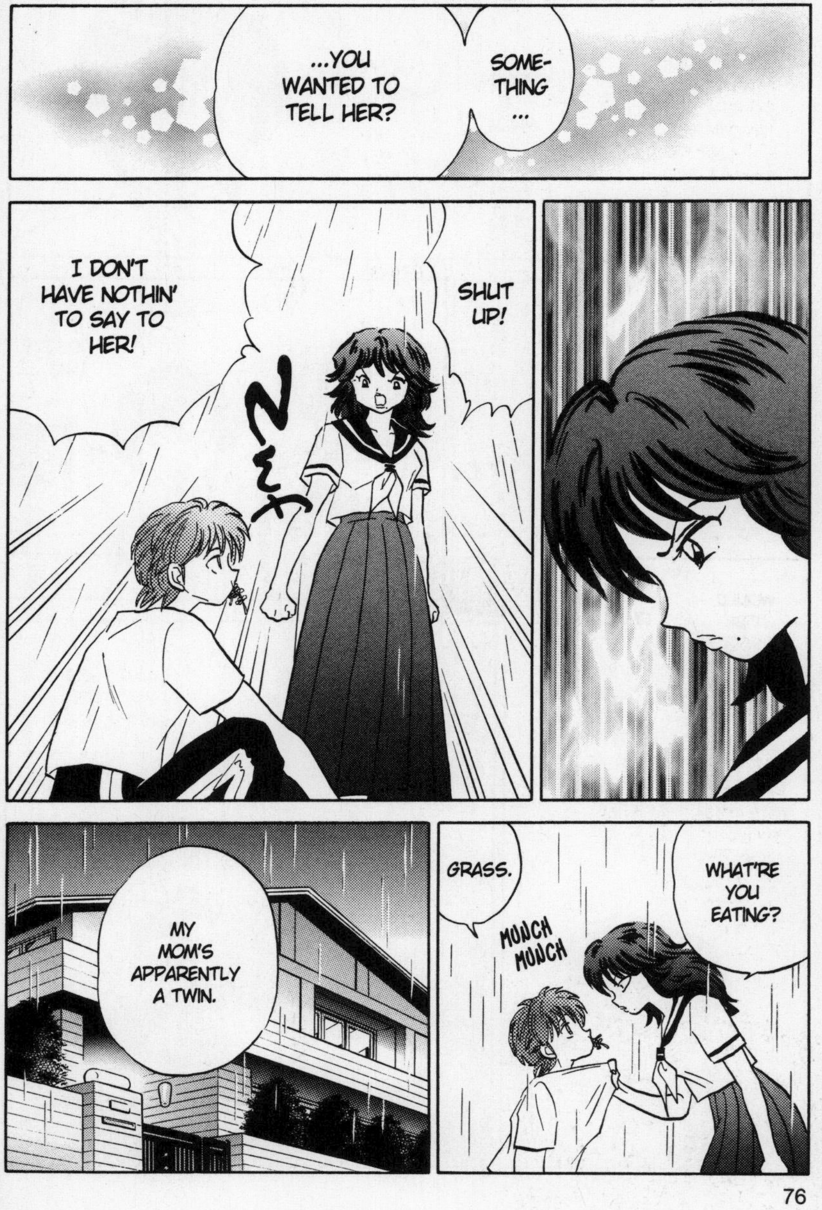
SOME-THING ...
...YOU WANTED TO TELL HER?
SHUT UP!
I DON'T HAVE NOTHIN' TO SAY TO HER!
WHAT'RE YOU EATING?
GRASS.
MONCH MONCH
MY MOM'S APPARENTLY A TWIN.

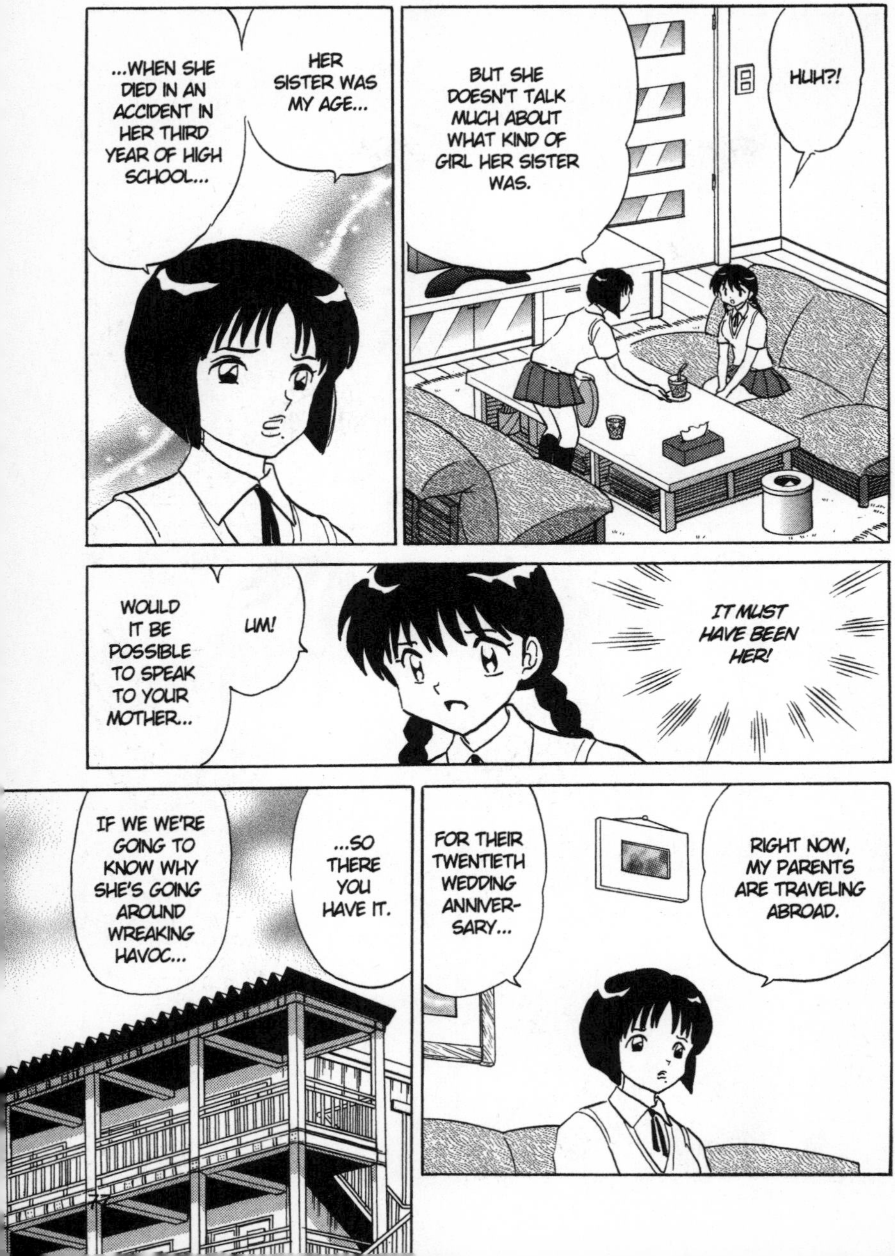
HUH?!
BUT SHE DOESN'T TALK MUCH ABOUT WHAT KIND OF GIRL HER SISTER WAS.
HER SISTER WAS MY AGE...
...WHEN SHE DIED IN AN ACCIDENT IN HER THIRD YEAR OF HIGH SCHOOL...
IT MUST HAVE BEEN HER!
UM!
WOULD IT BE POSSIBLE TO SPEAK TO YOUR MOTHER...
RIGHT NOW, MY PARENTS ARE TRAVELING ABROAD.
FOR THEIR TWENTIETH WEDDING ANNIVER-SARY...
...SO THERE YOU HAVE IT.
IF WE WE'RE GOING TO KNOW WHY SHE'S GOING AROUND WREAKING HAVOC...

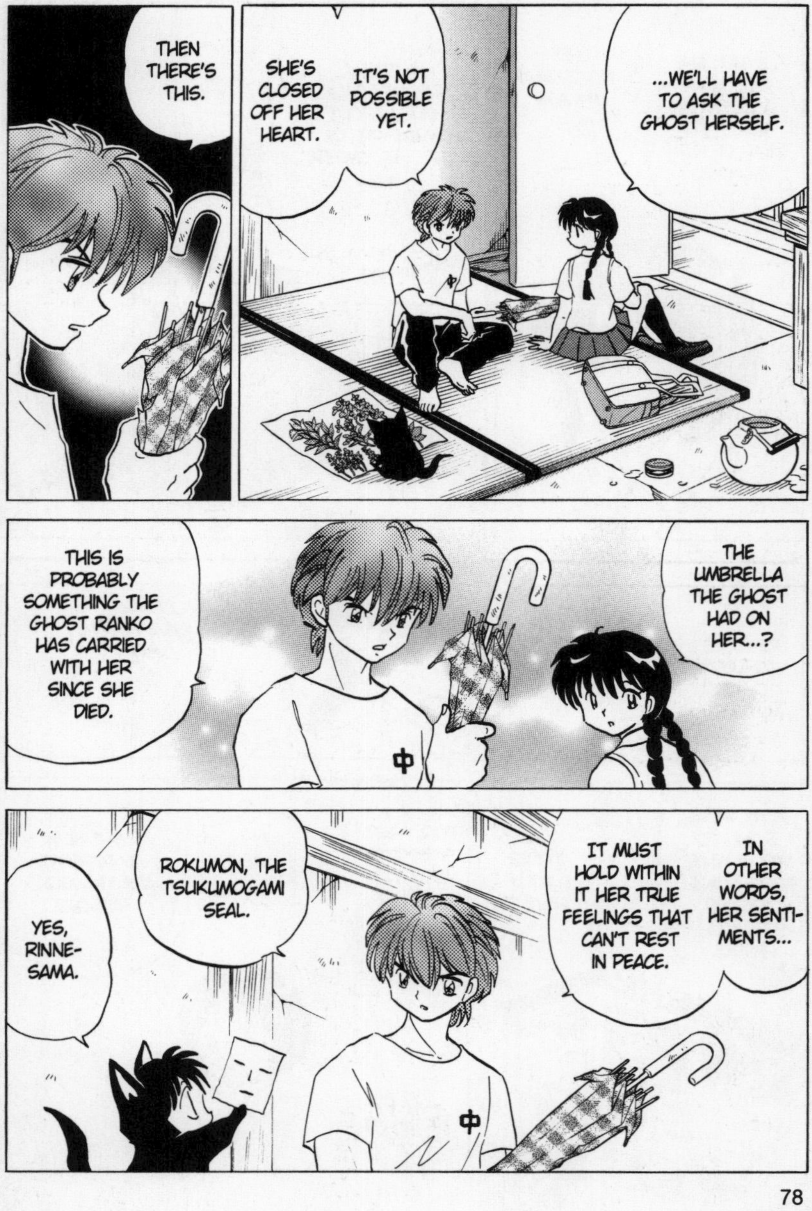
...WE'LL HAVE TO ASK THE GHOST HERSELF.
IT'S NOT POSSIBLE YET.
SHE'S CLOSED OFF HER HEART.
THEN THERE'S THIS.
THE UMBRELLA THE GHOST HAD ON HER...?
THIS IS PROBABLY SOMETHING THE GHOST RANKO HAS CARRIED WITH HER SINCE SHE DIED.
IN OTHER WORDS, HER SENTIMENTS...
IT MUST HOLD WITHIN IT HER TRUE FEELINGS THAT CAN'T REST IN PEACE.
ROKUMON, THE TSUKUMOGAMI SEAL.
YES, RINNE-SAMA.

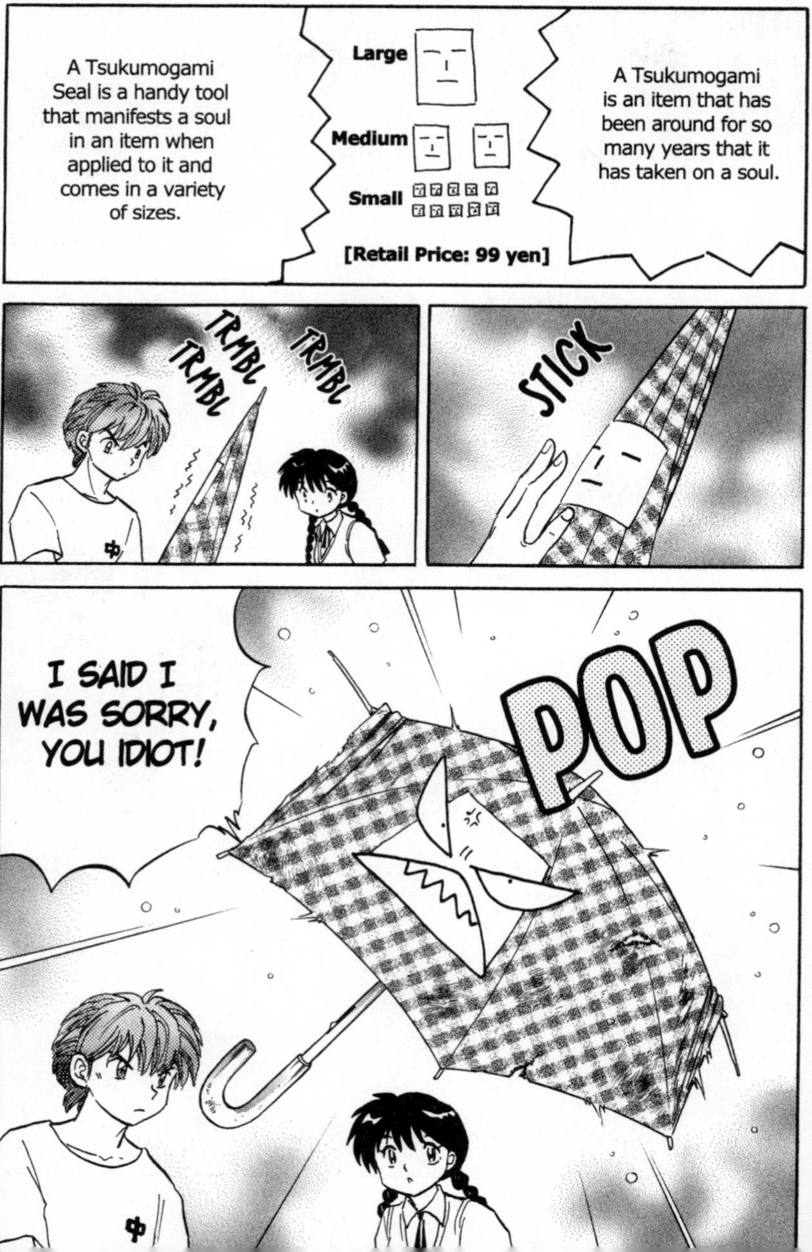
A Tsukumogami is an item that has been around for so many years that it has taken on a soul.
Large
Medium
Small
[Retail Price: 99 yen]
A Tsukumogami Seal is a handy tool that manifests a soul in an item when applied to it and comes in a variety of sizes.
STICK
TRMBL
TRMBL
TRMBL
POP
I SAID I WAS SORRY, YOU IDIOT!

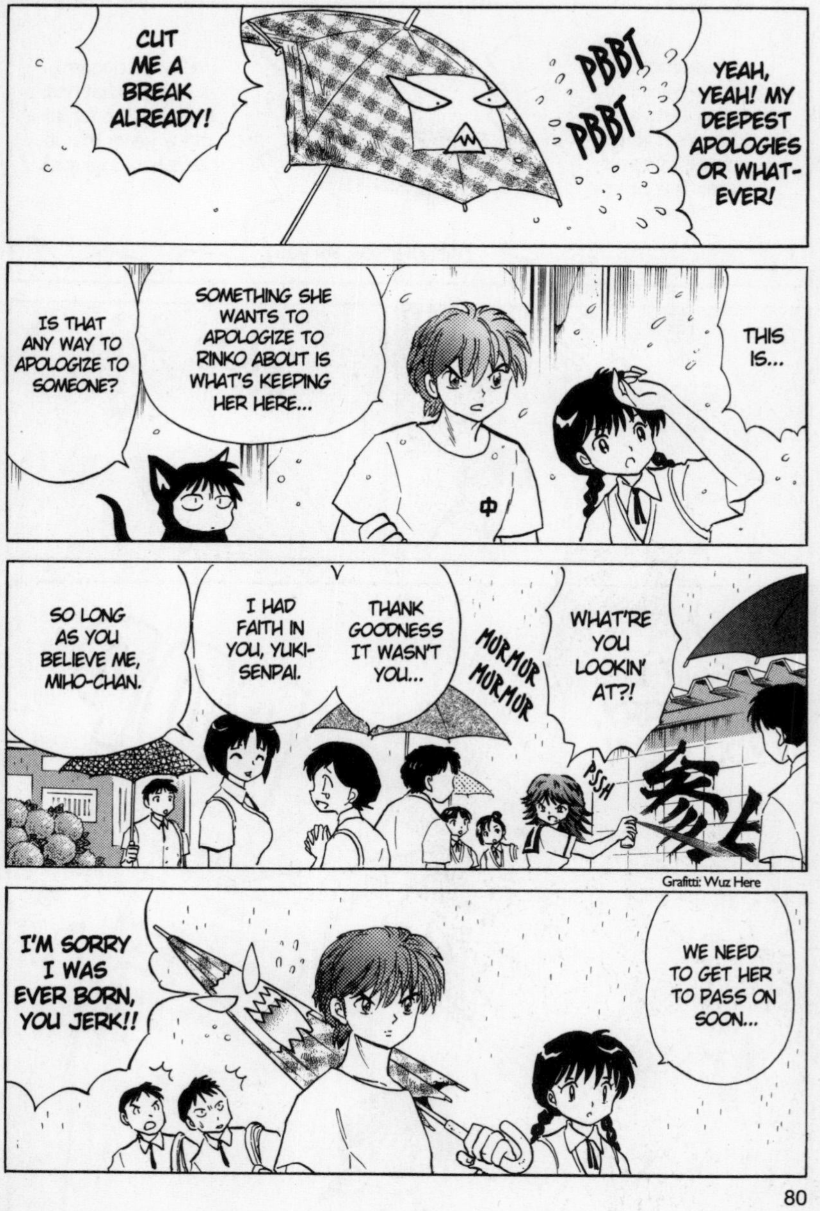
YEAH, YEAH! MY DEEPEST APOLOGIES OR WHAT-EVER!
PBBT PBBT
CUT ME A BREAK ALREADY!
THIS IS...
SOMETHING SHE WANTS TO APOLOGIZE TO RINKO ABOUT IS WHAT'S KEEPING HER HERE...
IS THAT ANY WAY TO APOLOGIZE TO SOMEONE?
WHAT'RE YOU LOOKIN' AT?!
PSSH
MURMUR MURMUR
THANK GOODNESS IT WASN'T YOU...
I HAD FAITH IN YOU, YUKI-SENPAI.
SO LONG AS YOU BELIEVE ME, MIHO-CHAN.
Grafitti: Wuz Here
WE NEED TO GET HER TO PASS ON SOON...
I'M SORRY I WAS EVER BORN, YOU JERK!!

CHAPTER 53: LOVE SONG

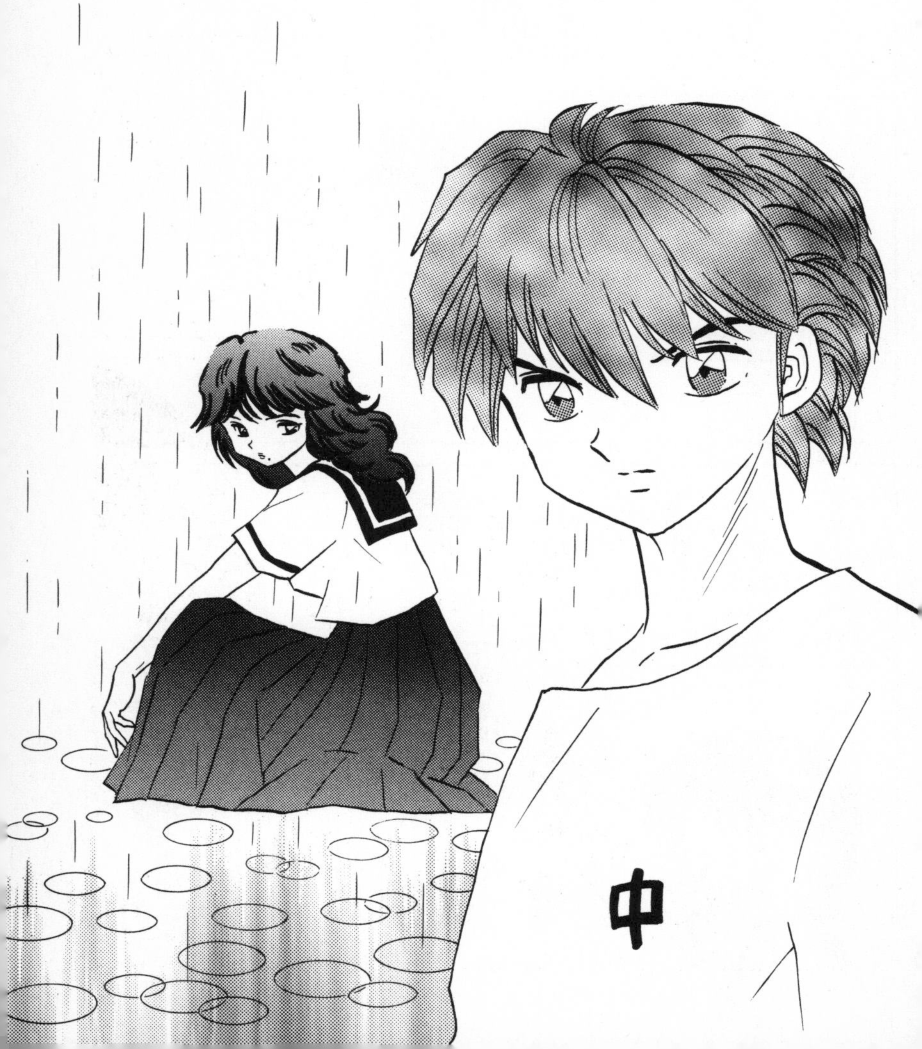
中

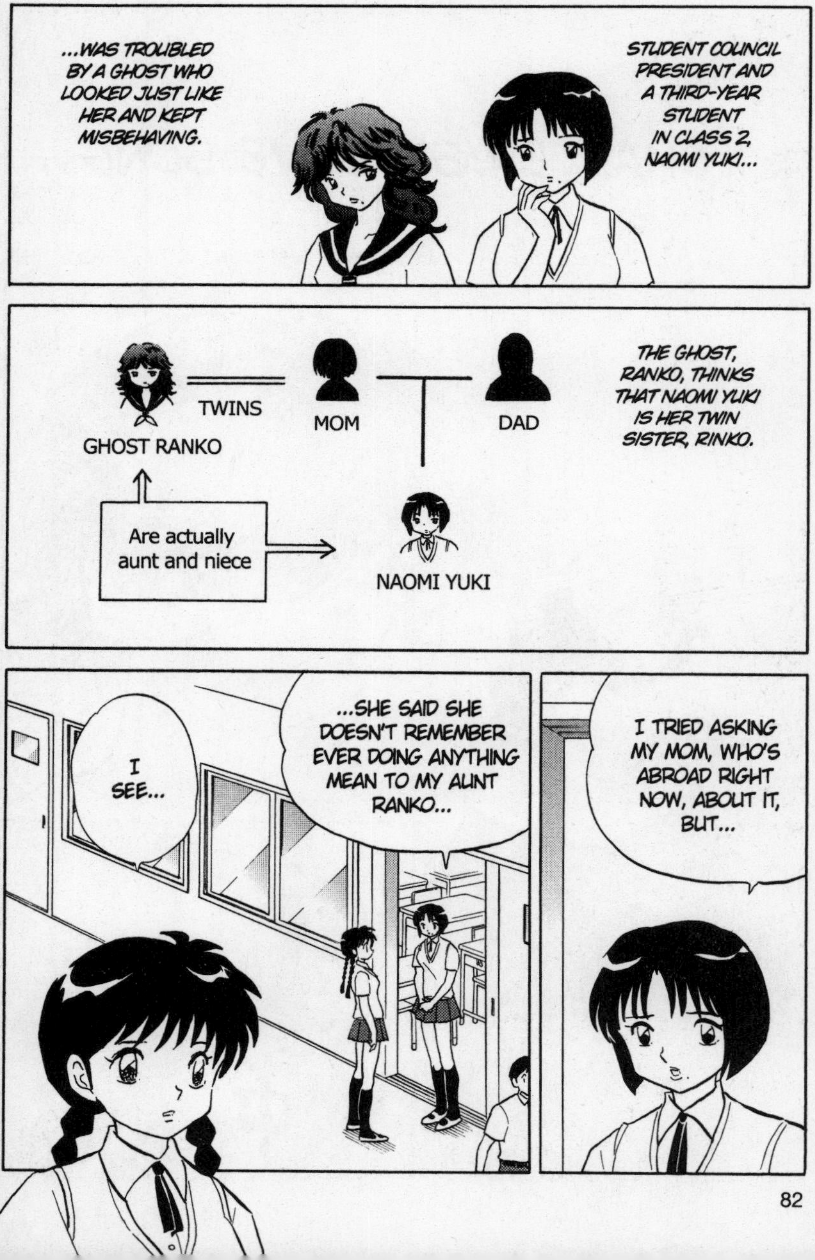

STUDENT COUNCIL PRESIDENT AND A THIRD-YEAR STUDENT IN CLASS 2, NAOMI YUKI...
...WAS TROUBLED BY A GHOST WHO LOOKED JUST LIKE HER AND KEPT MISBEHAVING.
THE GHOST, RANKO, THINKS THAT NAOMI YUKI IS HER TWIN SISTER, RINKO.
DAD
MOM
TWINS
GHOST RANKO
Are actually aunt and niece
NAOMI YUKI
I TRIED ASKING MY MOM, WHO'S ABROAD RIGHT NOW, ABOUT IT, BUT...
...SHE SAID SHE DOESN'T REMEMBER EVER DOING ANYTHING MEAN TO MY AUNT RANKO...
I SEE...

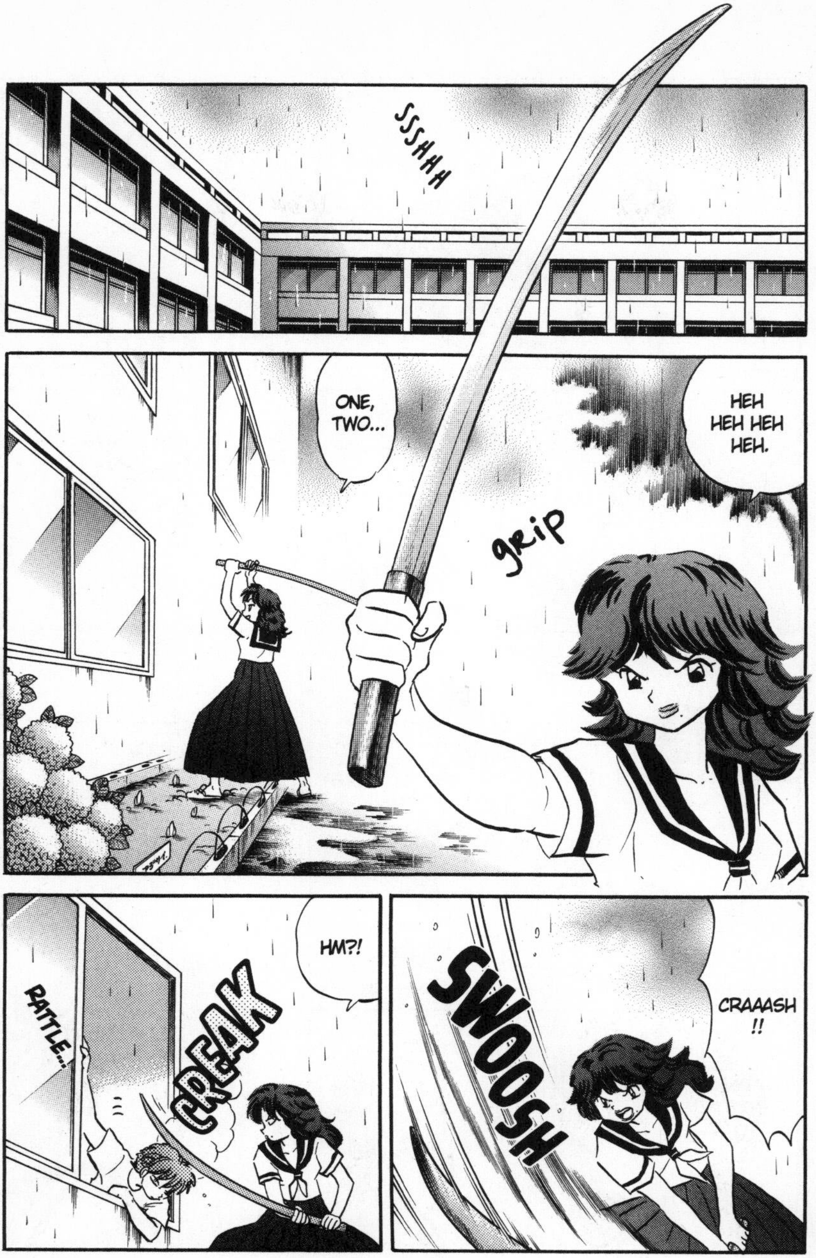

SSSHHH
HEH HEH HEH HEH.
ONE, TWO...
grip
SWOOSH
CRAAASH !!
HM?!
CREAK
RATTLE...

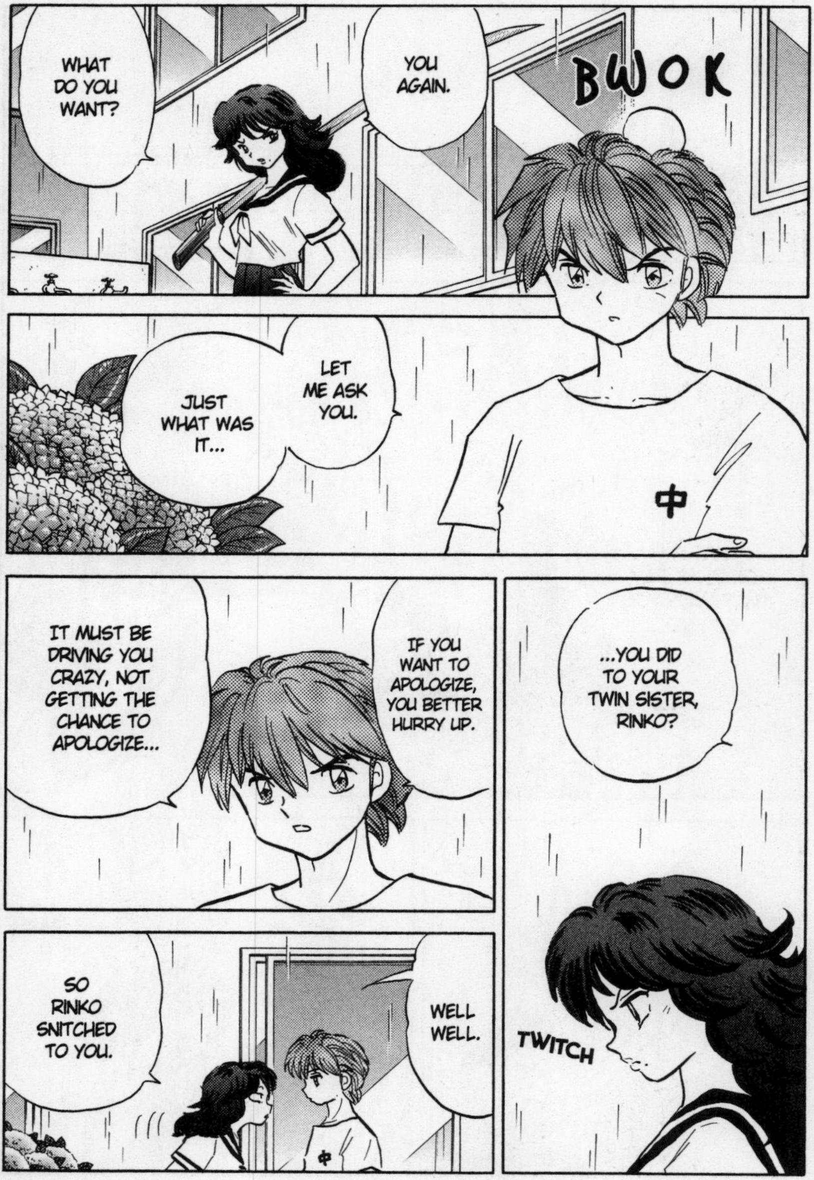
BWOK
YOU AGAIN.
WHAT DO YOU WANT?
LET ME ASK YOU.
JUST WHAT WAS IT...
...YOU DID TO YOUR TWIN SISTER, RINKO?
TWITCH
IF YOU WANT TO APOLOGIZE, YOU BETTER HURRY UP.
IT MUST BE DRIVING YOU CRAZY, NOT GETTING THE CHANCE TO APOLOGIZE...
WELL WELL.
SO RINKO SNITCHED TO YOU.

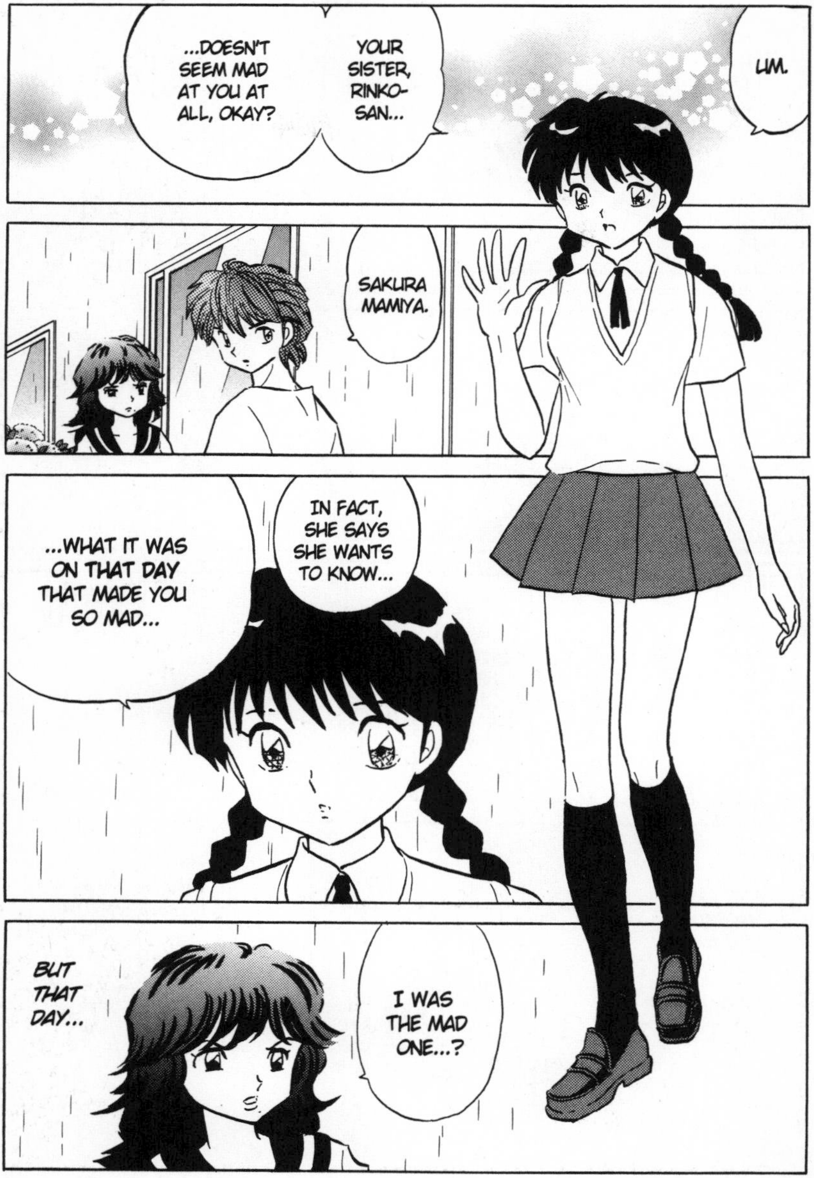
UM.
YOUR SISTER, RINKO-SAN...
...DOESN'T SEEM MAD AT YOU AT ALL, OKAY?
SAKURA MAMIYA.
IN FACT, SHE SAYS SHE WANTS TO KNOW...
...WHAT IT WAS ON THAT DAY THAT MADE YOU SO MAD...
I WAS THE MAD ONE...?
BUT THAT DAY...

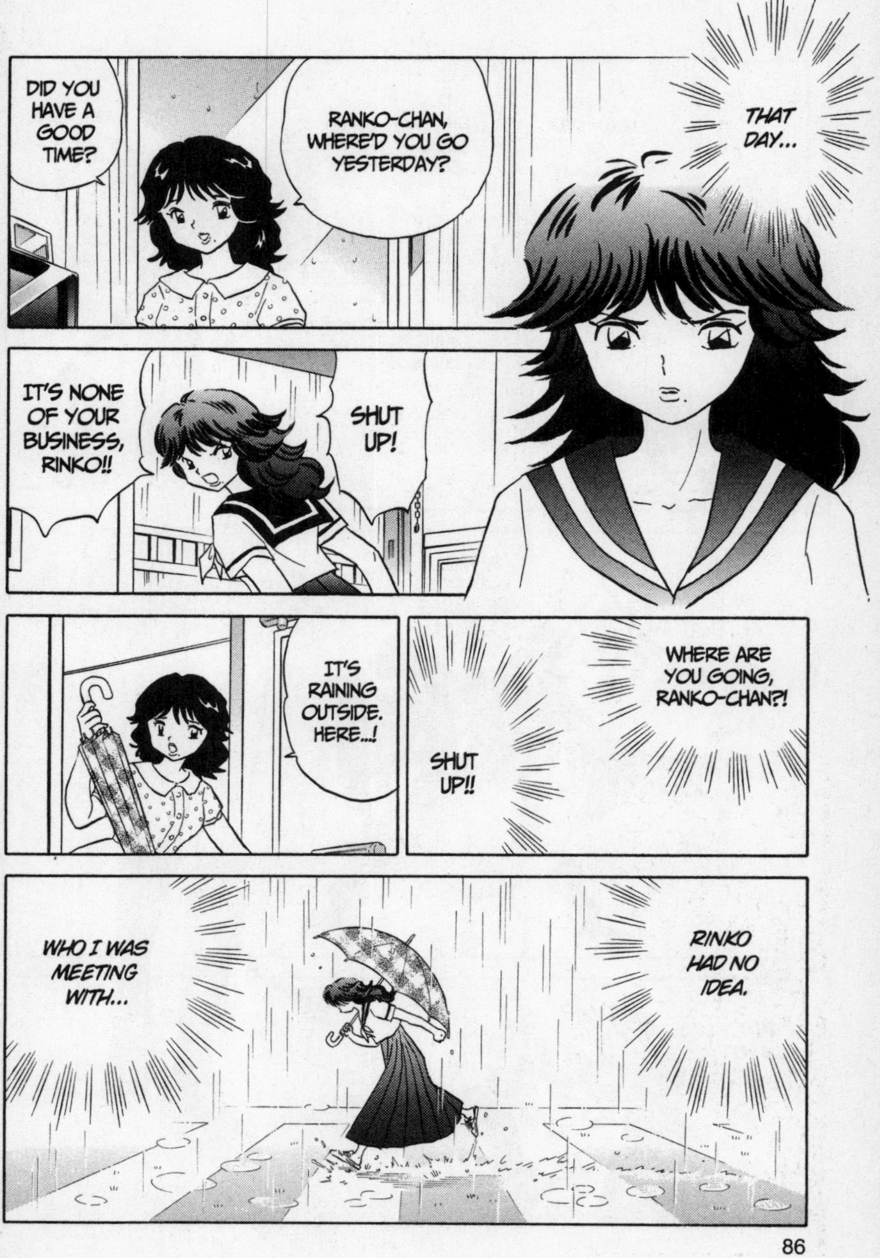
THAT DAY...
RANKO-CHAN, WHERE'D YOU GO YESTERDAY?
DID YOU HAVE A GOOD TIME?
SHUT UP!
IT'S NONE OF YOUR BUSINESS, RINKO!!
WHERE ARE YOU GOING, RANKO-CHAN?!
SHUT UP!!
IT'S RAINING OUTSIDE. HERE...!
RINKO HAD NO IDEA.
WHO I WAS MEETING WITH...

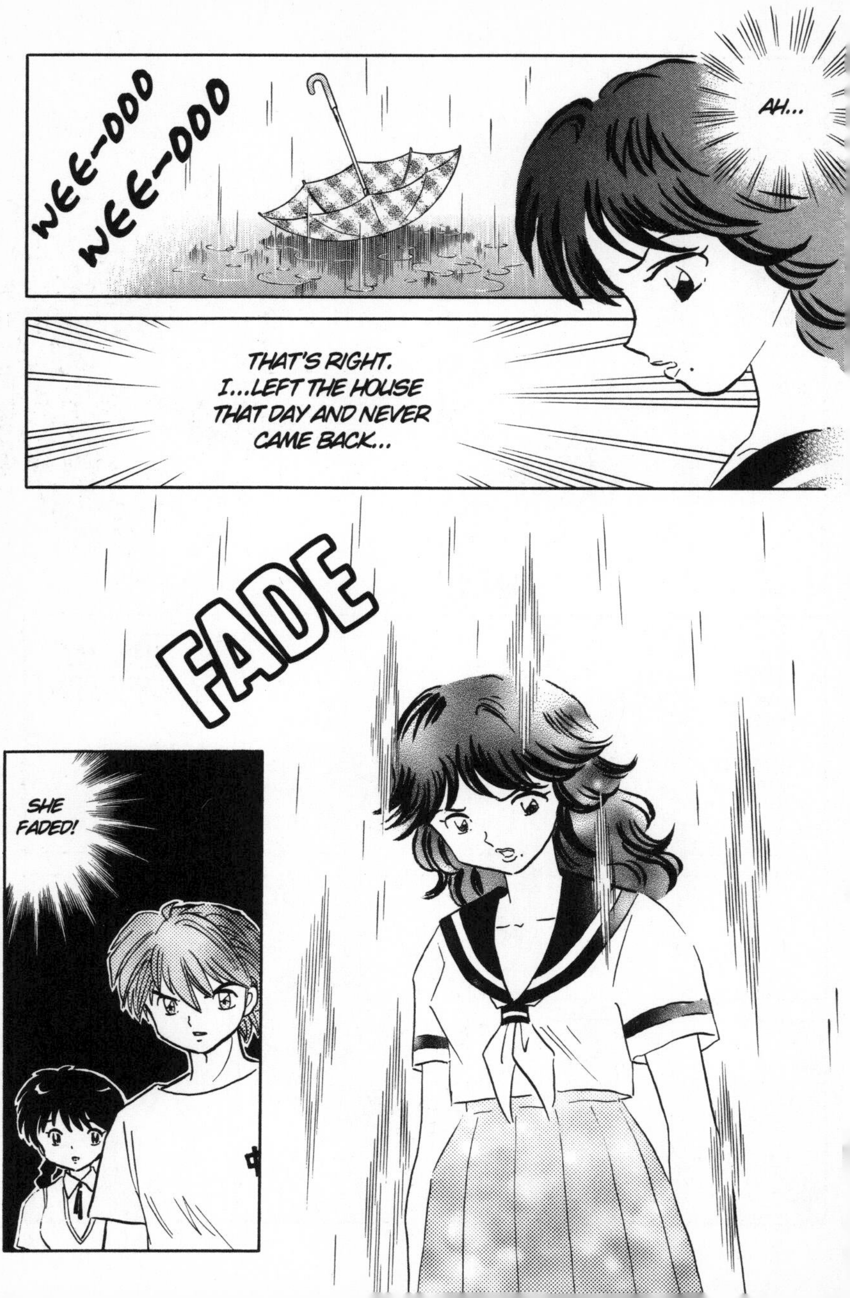
AH...
WEE-OOO
WEE-OOO
THAT'S RIGHT.
I...LEFT THE HOUSE
THAT DAY AND NEVER
CAME BACK...
FADE
SHE
FADED!

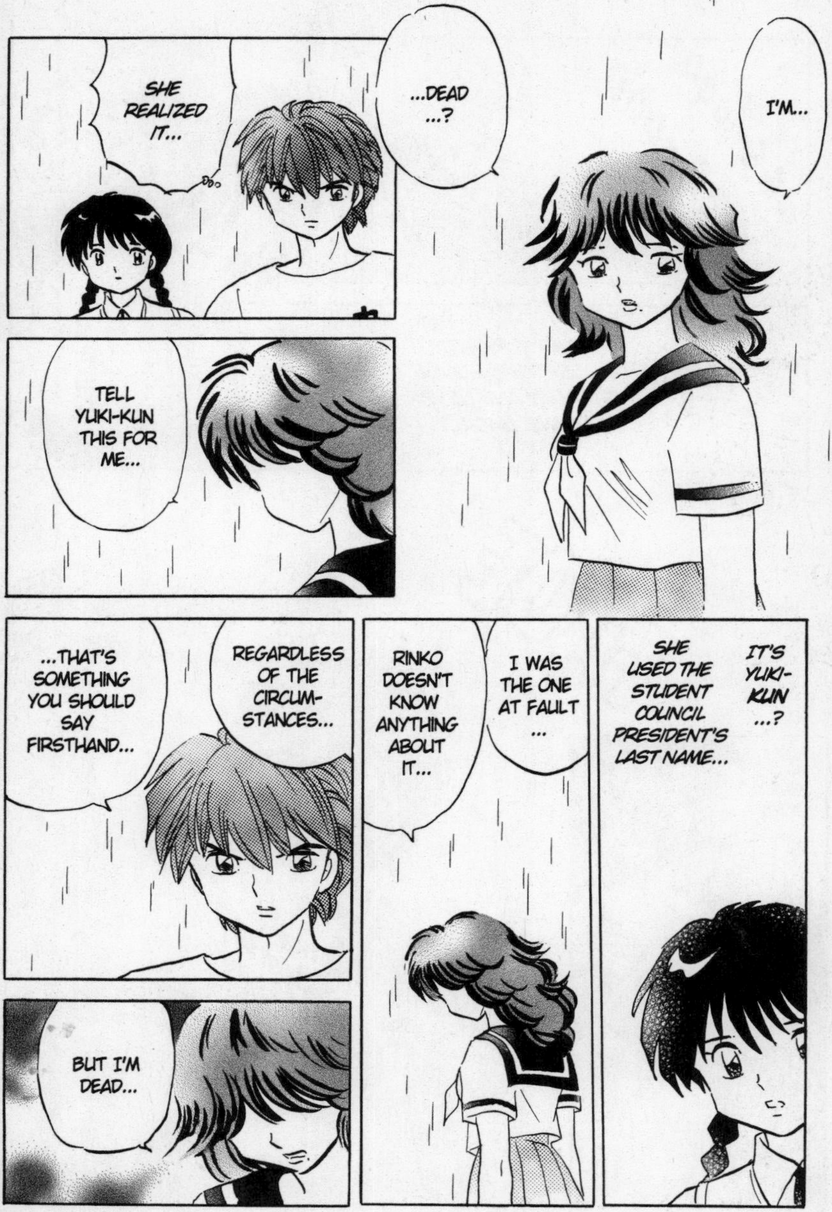
I'M...
...DEAD ...?
SHE REALIZED IT...
TELL YUKI-KUN THIS FOR ME...
IT'S YUKI-KUN ...?
SHE USED THE STUDENT COUNCIL PRESIDENT'S LAST NAME...
I WAS THE ONE AT FAULT ...
RINKO DOESN'T KNOW ANYTHING ABOUT IT...
REGARDLESS OF THE CIRCUM-STANCES...
...THAT'S SOMETHING YOU SHOULD SAY FIRSTHAND...
BUT I'M DEAD...

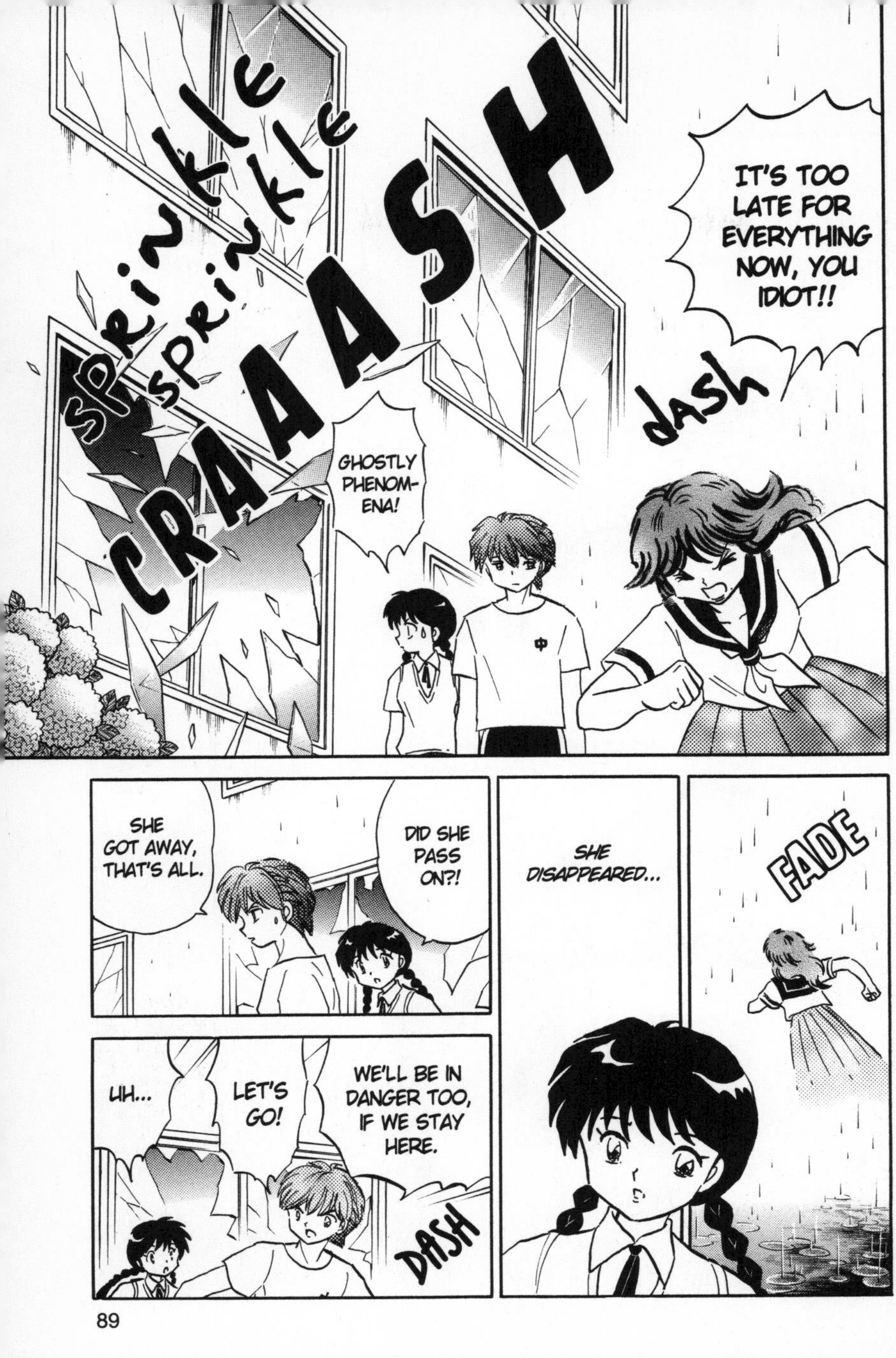
IT'S TOO LATE FOR EVERYTHING NOW, YOU IDIOT!!
dash
CRAAASH
SPRINKLE
SPRINKLE
GHOSTLY PHENOM-ENA!
FADE
SHE DISAPPEARED...
DID SHE PASS ON?!
SHE GOT AWAY, THAT'S ALL.
WE'LL BE IN DANGER TOO, IF WE STAY HERE.
DASH
LET'S GO!
UH...

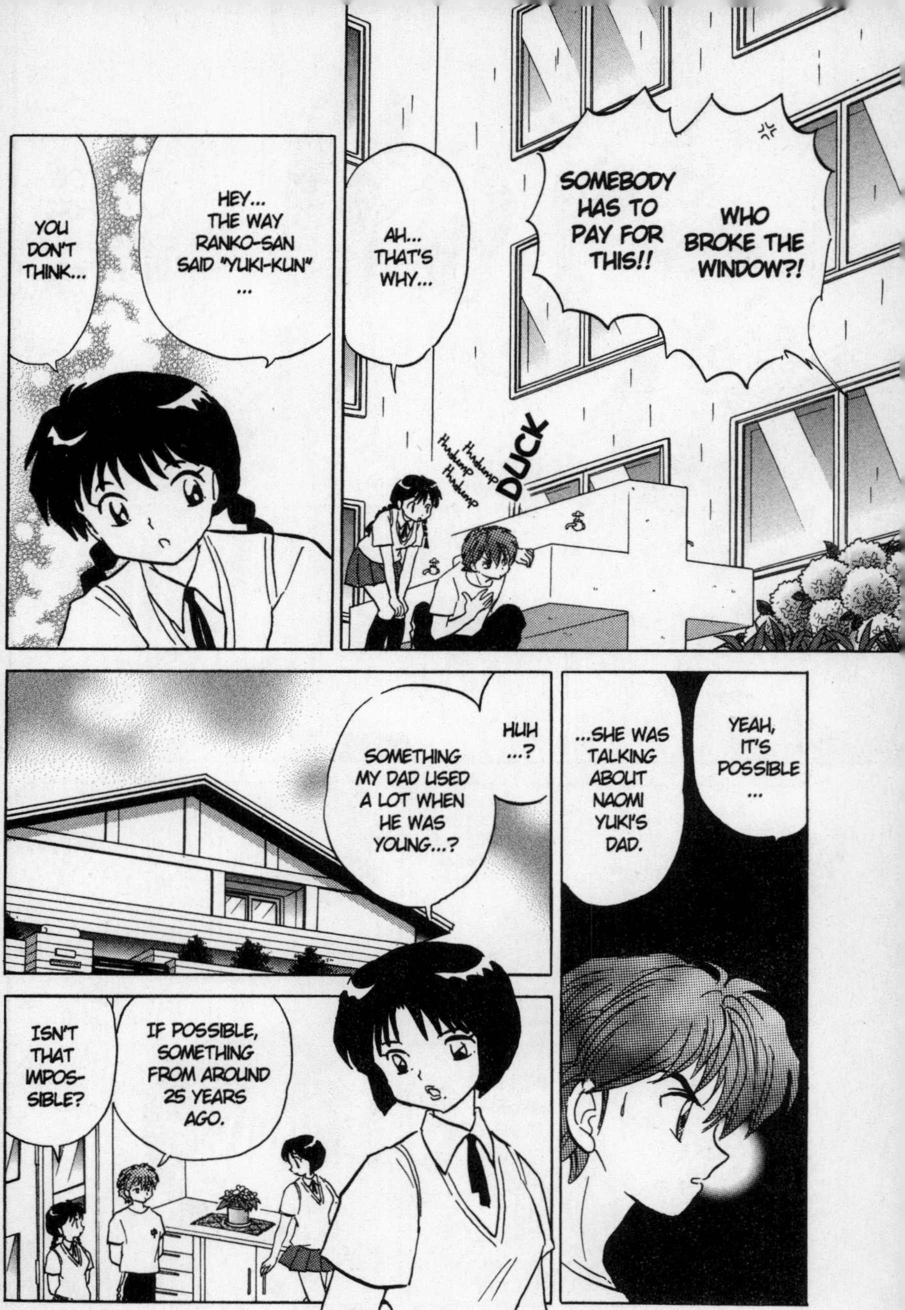
WHO BROKE THE WINDOW?!
SOMEBODY HAS TO PAY FOR THIS!!
DUCK
AH... THAT'S WHY...
HEY... THE WAY RANKO-SAN SAID "YUKI-KUN" ...
YOU DON'T THINK...
YEAH, IT'S POSSIBLE ...
...SHE WAS TALKING ABOUT NAOMI YUKI'S DAD.
HUH ...?
SOMETHING MY DAD USED A LOT WHEN HE WAS YOUNG...?
IF POSSIBLE, SOMETHING FROM AROUND 25 YEARS AGO.
ISN'T THAT IMPOSSIBLE?

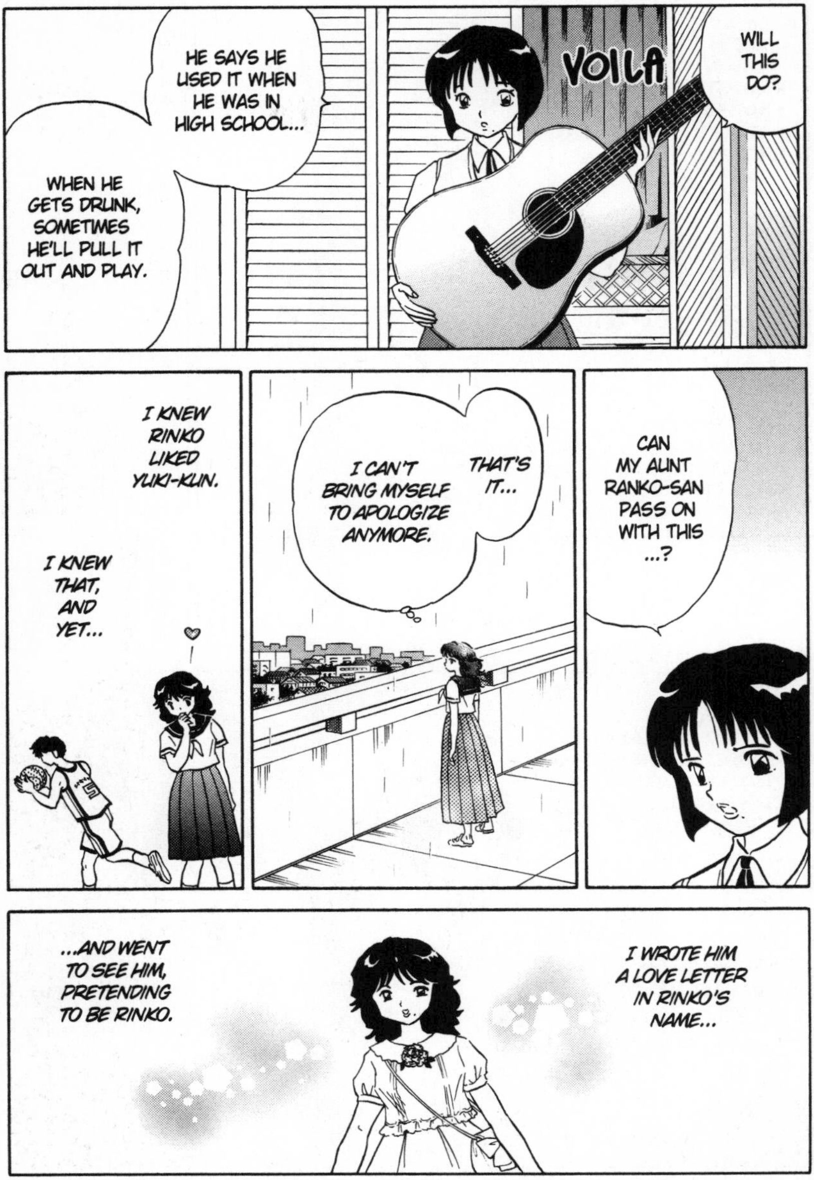
WILL THIS DO?
VOILA
HE SAYS HE USED IT WHEN HE WAS IN HIGH SCHOOL...
WHEN HE GETS DRUNK, SOMETIMES HE'LL PULL IT OUT AND PLAY.
CAN MY AUNT RANKO-SAN PASS ON WITH THIS ...?
THAT'S IT...
I CAN'T BRING MYSELF TO APOLOGIZE ANYMORE.
I KNEW RINKO LIKED YUKI-KUN.
I KNEW THAT, AND YET...
I WROTE HIM A LOVE LETTER IN RINKO'S NAME...
...AND WENT TO SEE HIM, PRETENDING TO BE RINKO.

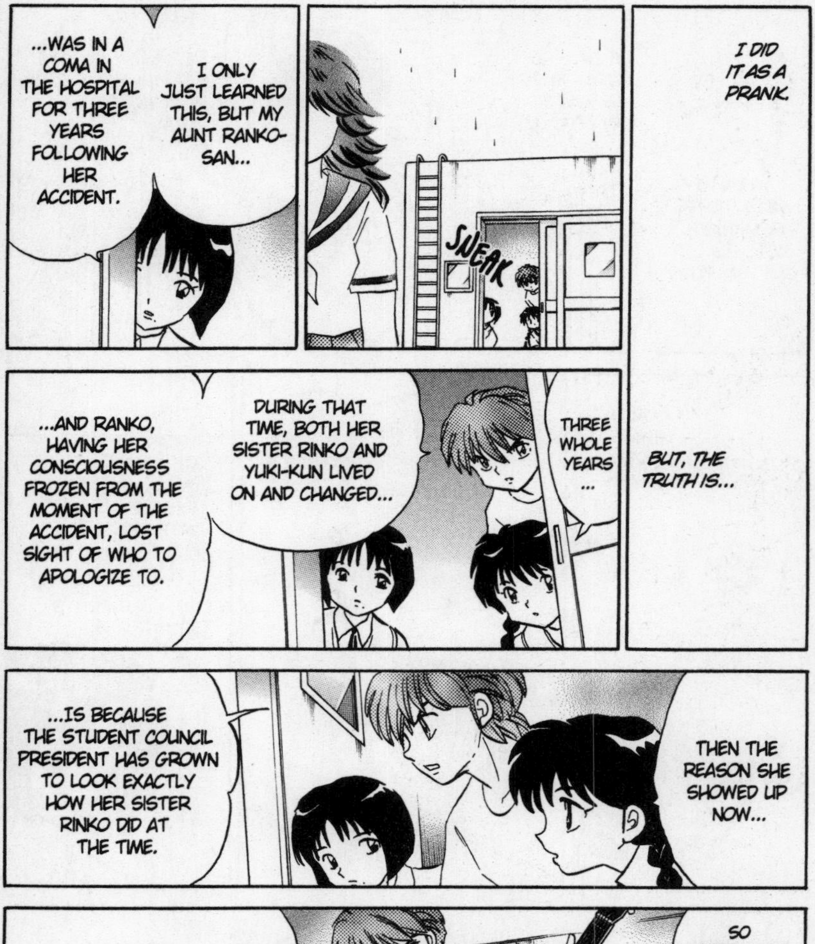
I DID IT AS A PRANK.
BUT, THE TRUTH IS...
SWEAK
I ONLY JUST LEARNED THIS, BUT MY AUNT RANKO-SAN...
...WAS IN A COMA IN THE HOSPITAL FOR THREE YEARS FOLLOWING HER ACCIDENT.
THREE WHOLE YEARS ...
DURING THAT TIME, BOTH HER SISTER RINKO AND YUKI-KUN LIVED ON AND CHANGED...
...AND RANKO, HAVING HER CONSCIOUSNESS FROZEN FROM THE MOMENT OF THE ACCIDENT, LOST SIGHT OF WHO TO APOLOGIZE TO.
THEN THE REASON SHE SHOWED UP NOW...
...IS BECAUSE THE STUDENT COUNCIL PRESIDENT HAS GROWN TO LOOK EXACTLY HOW HER SISTER RINKO DID AT THE TIME.
SO WE'RE GOING TO NEED THE OTHER PERSON INVOLVED IN THIS...
...YUKI-KUN, TO SHOW UP AND REENACT WHAT HAPPENED 25 YEARS AGO.

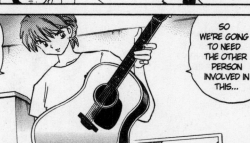

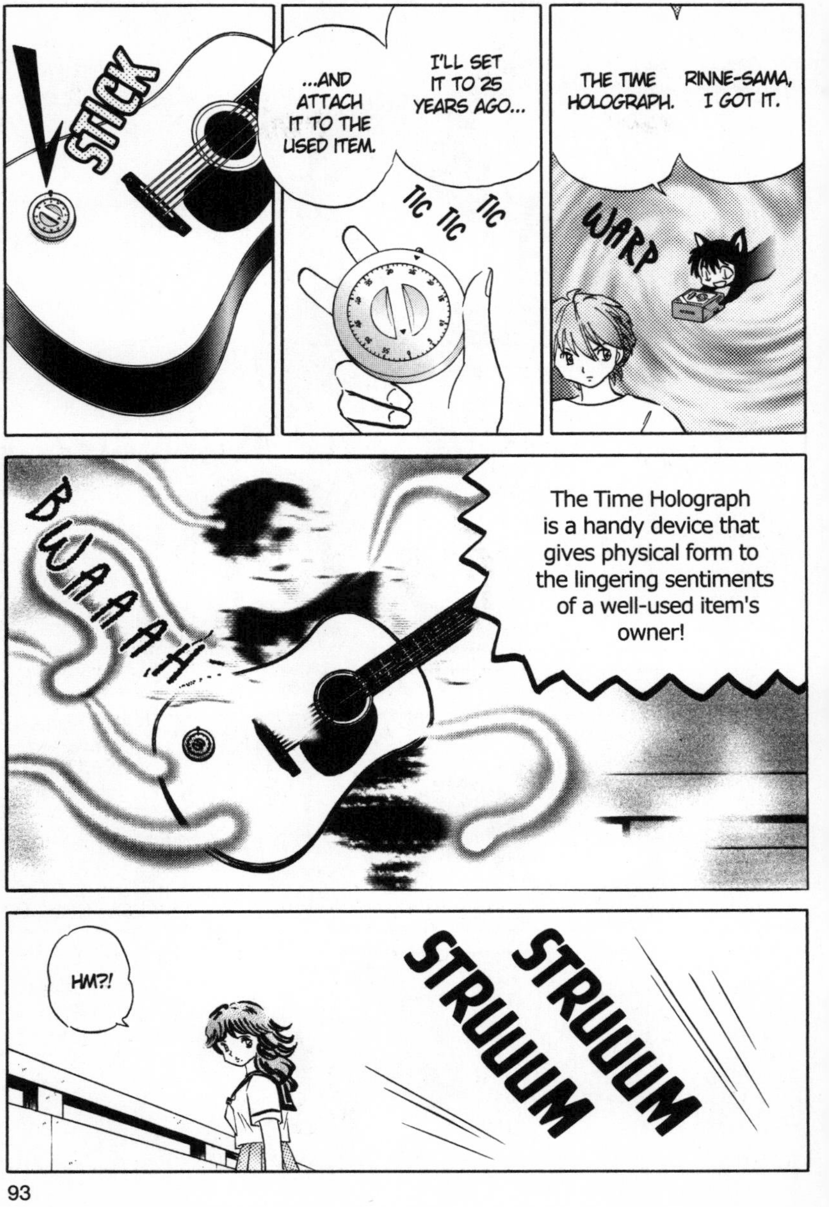
RINNE-SAMA, I GOT IT.
THE TIME HOLOGRAPH.
WARP
I'LL SET IT TO 25 YEARS AGO...
...AND ATTACH IT TO THE USED ITEM.
TIC TIC TIC
STICK
The Time Holograph is a handy device that gives physical form to the lingering sentiments of a well-used item's owner!
BWAAAH...
STRUUUM
STRUUUM
HM?!

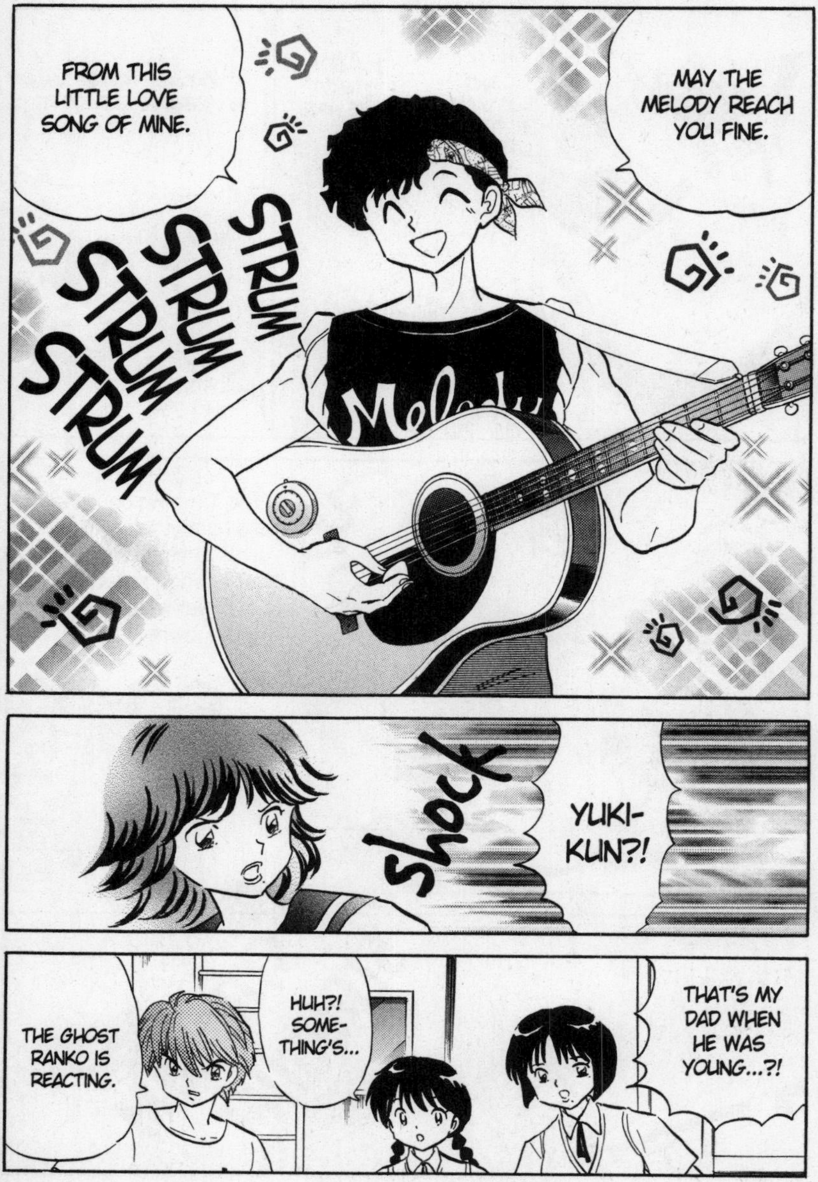
MAY THE MELODY REACH YOU FINE.
FROM THIS LITTLE LOVE SONG OF MINE.
STRUM STRUM STRUM STRUM
YUKI-KUN?!
shock
THAT'S MY DAD WHEN HE WAS YOUNG...?!
HUH?! SOME-THING'S...
THE GHOST RANKO IS REACTING.

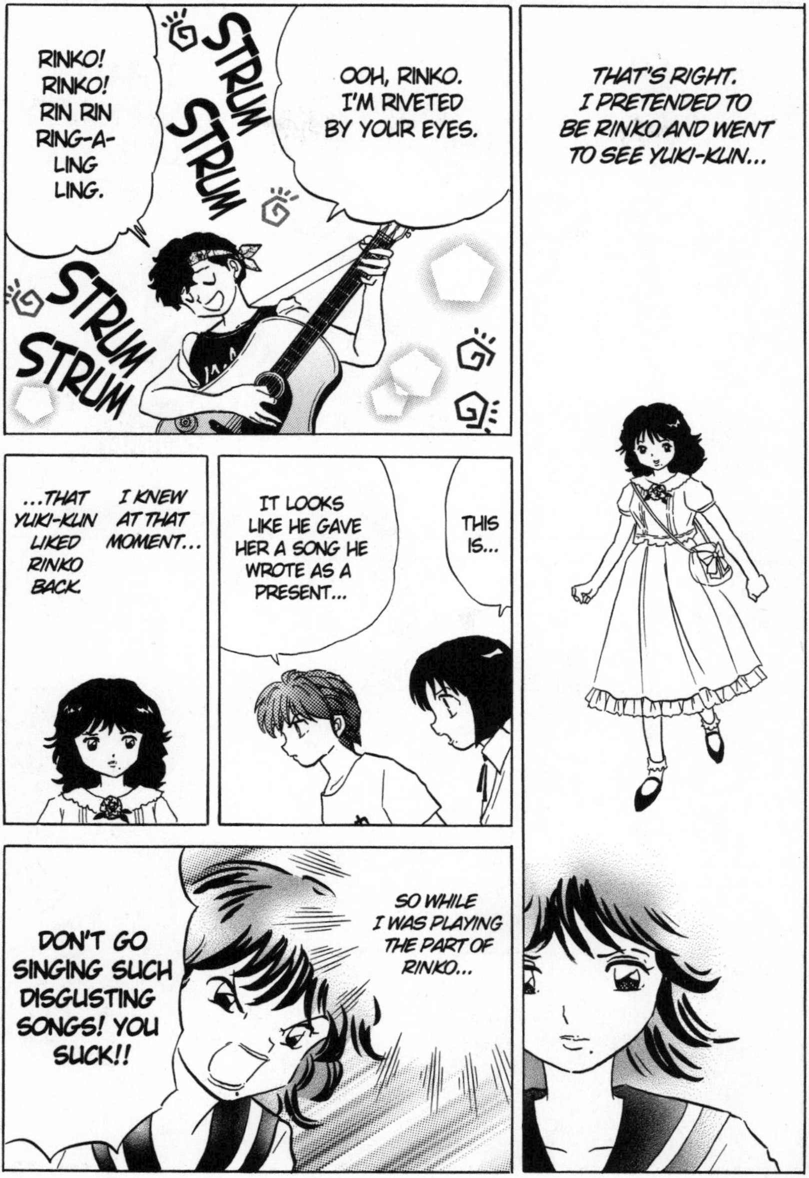
THAT'S RIGHT. I PRETENDED TO BE RINKO AND WENT TO SEE YUKI-KUN...
OOH, RINKO. I'M RIVETED BY YOUR EYES.
STRUM STRUM
RINKO! RINKO! RIN RIN RING-A-LING LING.
STRUM STRUM
THIS IS...
IT LOOKS LIKE HE GAVE HER A SONG HE WROTE AS A PRESENT...
I KNEW AT THAT MOMENT...
...THAT YUKI-KUN LIKED RINKO BACK.
SO WHILE I WAS PLAYING THE PART OF RINKO...
DON'T GO SINGING SUCH DISGUSTING SONGS! YOU SUCK!!

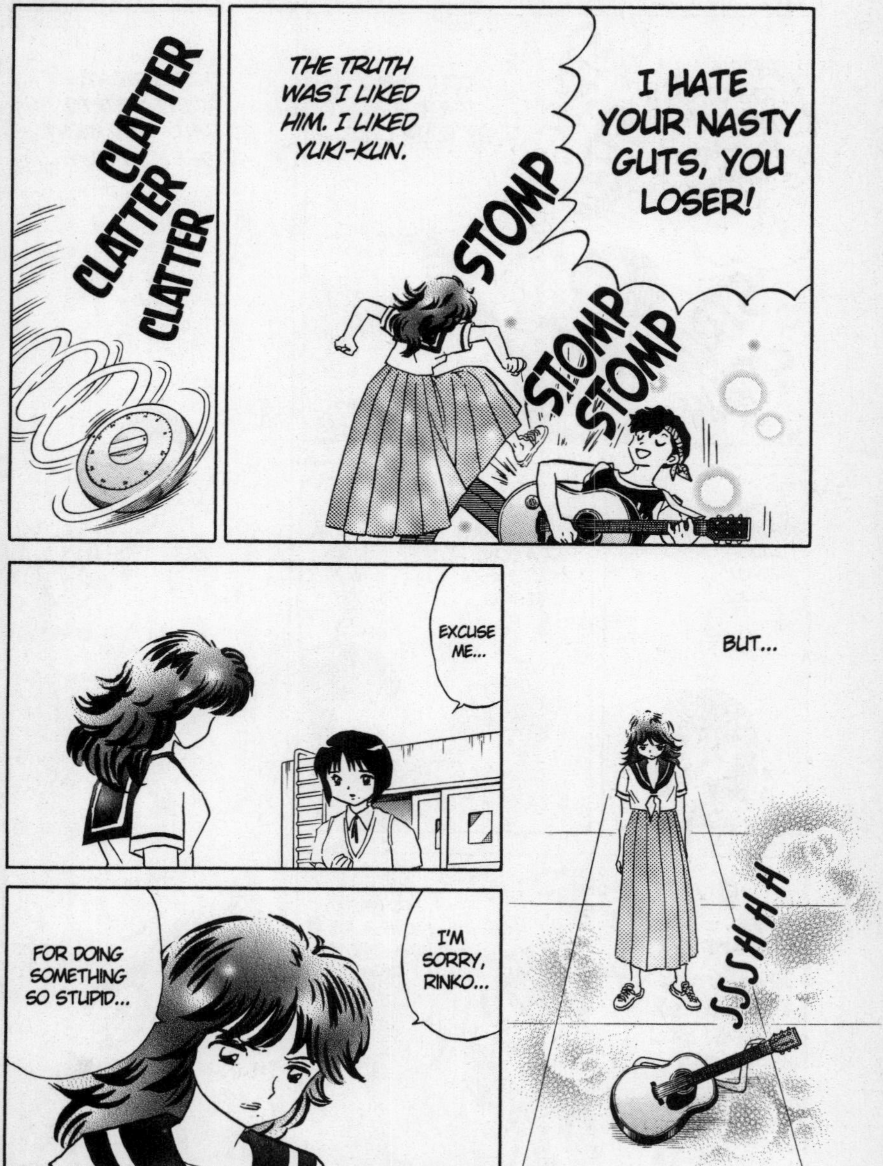
I HATE YOUR NASTY GUTS, YOU LOSER!
THE TRUTH WAS I LIKED HIM. I LIKED YUKI-KUN.
STOMP
STOMP STOMP
CLATTER CLATTER CLATTER
BUT...
SSHHH
EXCUSE ME...
I'M SORRY, RINKO...
FOR DOING SOMETHING SO STUPID...

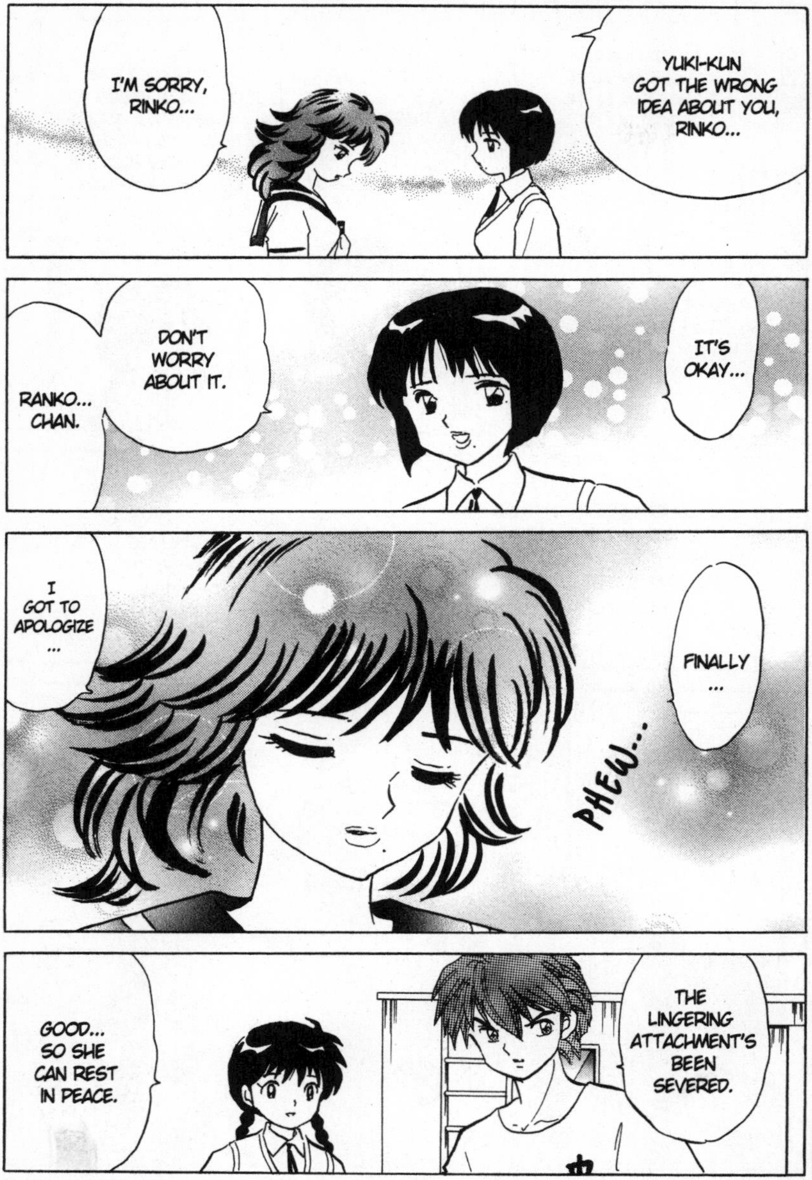
YUKI-KUN GOT THE WRONG IDEA ABOUT YOU, RINKO...
I'M SORRY, RINKO...
IT'S OKAY...
DON'T WORRY ABOUT IT.
RANKO... CHAN.
FINALLY ...
PHEW...
I GOT TO APOLOGIZE ...
THE LINGERING ATTACHMENT'S BEEN SEVERED.
GOOD... SO SHE CAN REST IN PEACE.

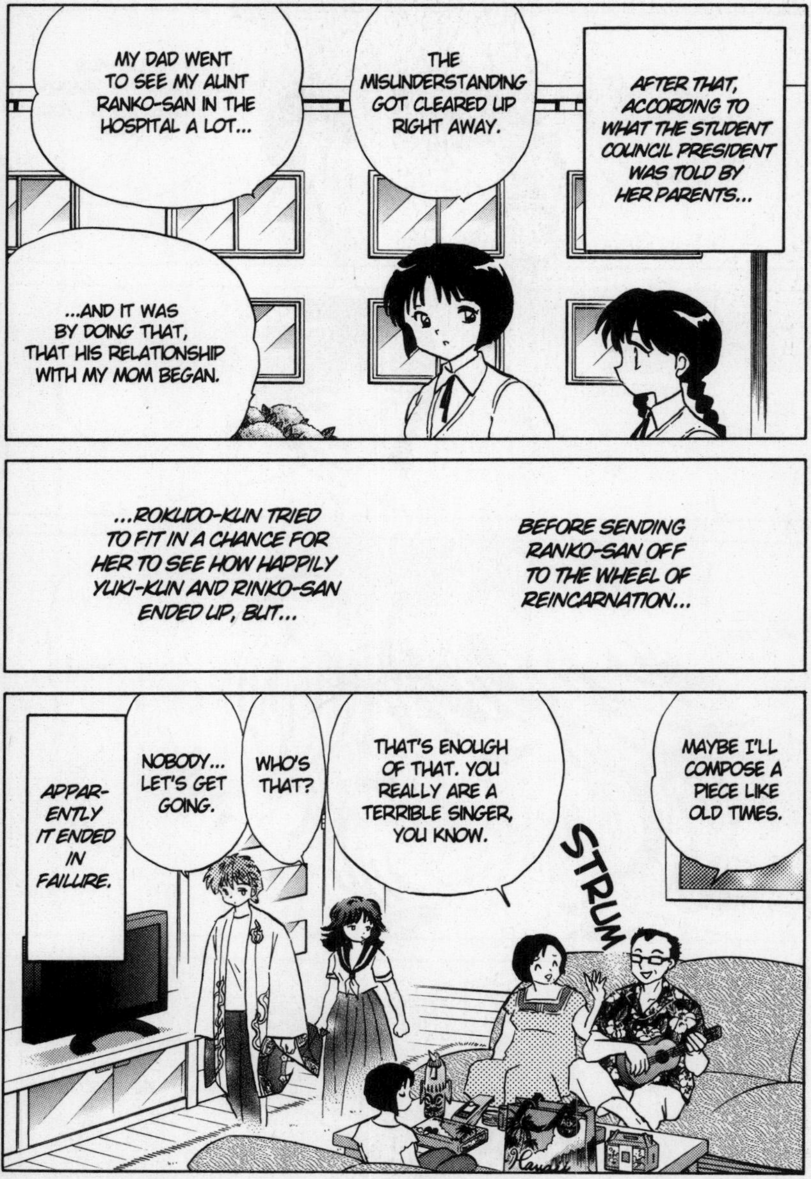
AFTER THAT, ACCORDING TO WHAT THE STUDENT COUNCIL PRESIDENT WAS TOLD BY HER PARENTS...
THE MISUNDERSTANDING GOT CLEARED UP RIGHT AWAY.
MY DAD WENT TO SEE MY AUNT RANKO-SAN IN THE HOSPITAL A LOT...
...AND IT WAS BY DOING THAT, THAT HIS RELATIONSHIP WITH MY MOM BEGAN.
BEFORE SENDING RANKO-SAN OFF TO THE WHEEL OF REINCARNATION...
...ROKUDO-KUN TRIED TO FIT IN A CHANCE FOR HER TO SEE HOW HAPPILY YUKI-KUN AND RINKO-SAN ENDED UP, BUT...
MAYBE I'LL COMPOSE A PIECE LIKE OLD TIMES.
STRUM
THAT'S ENOUGH OF THAT. YOU REALLY ARE A TERRIBLE SINGER, YOU KNOW.
WHO'S THAT?
NOBODY... LET'S GET GOING.
APPAR-ENTLY IT ENDED IN FAILURE.

CHAPTER 54: THE SHINIGAMI CLERK

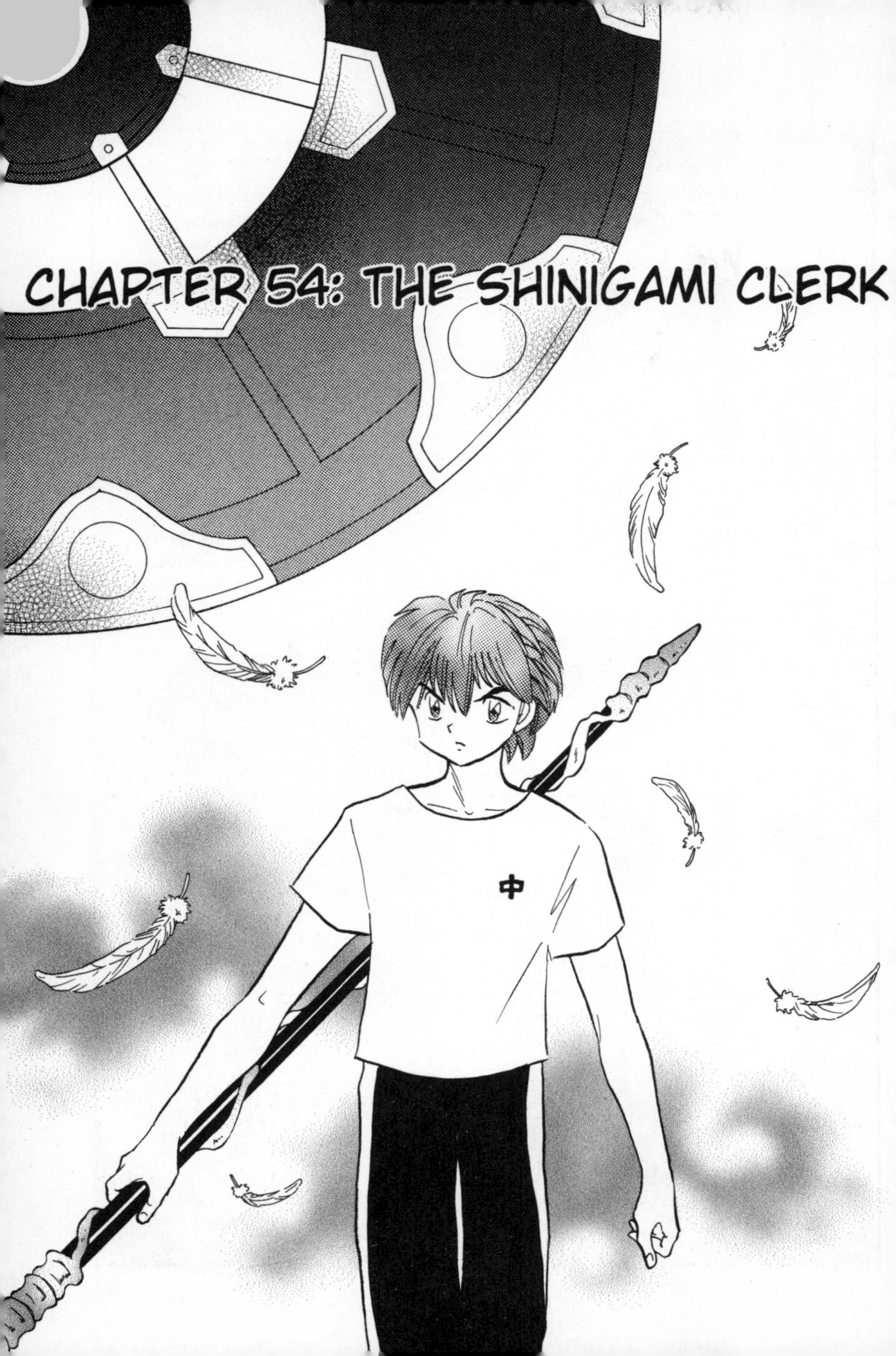
中

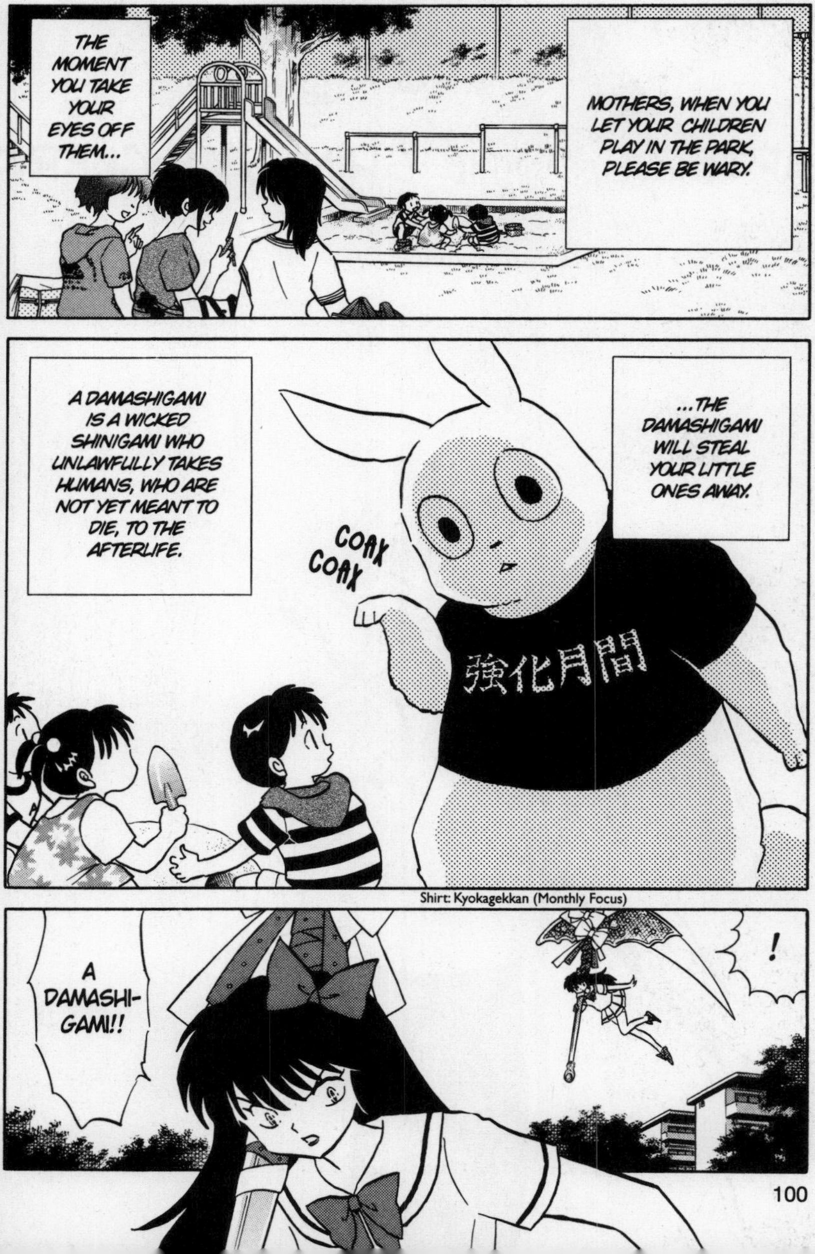
MOTHERS, WHEN YOU LET YOUR CHILDREN PLAY IN THE PARK, PLEASE BE WARY.
THE MOMENT YOU TAKE YOUR EYES OFF THEM...
...THE DAMASHIGAMI WILL STEAL YOUR LITTLE ONES AWAY.
A DAMASHIGAMI IS A WICKED SHINIGAMI WHO UNLAWFULLY TAKES HUMANS, WHO ARE NOT YET MEANT TO DIE, TO THE AFTERLIFE.
COAX COAX
強化月間
!
A DAMASHI-GAMI!!

Shirt: Kyokagekkan (Monthly Focus)

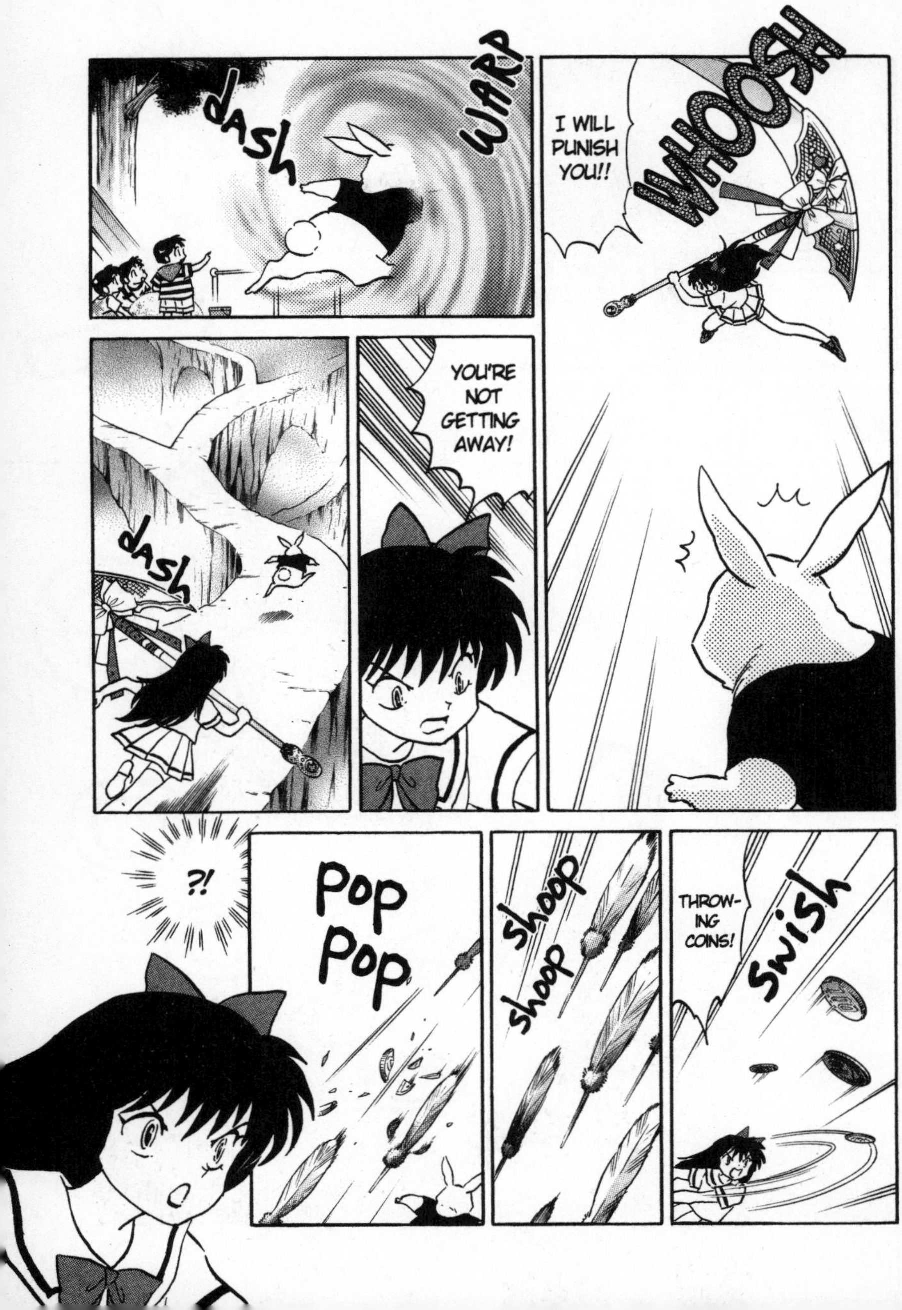
WHOOSH
I WILL PUNISH YOU!!
WARP
dash
YOU'RE NOT GETTING AWAY!
dash
THROW-ING COINS!
swish
shoop shoop
Pop Pop
?!

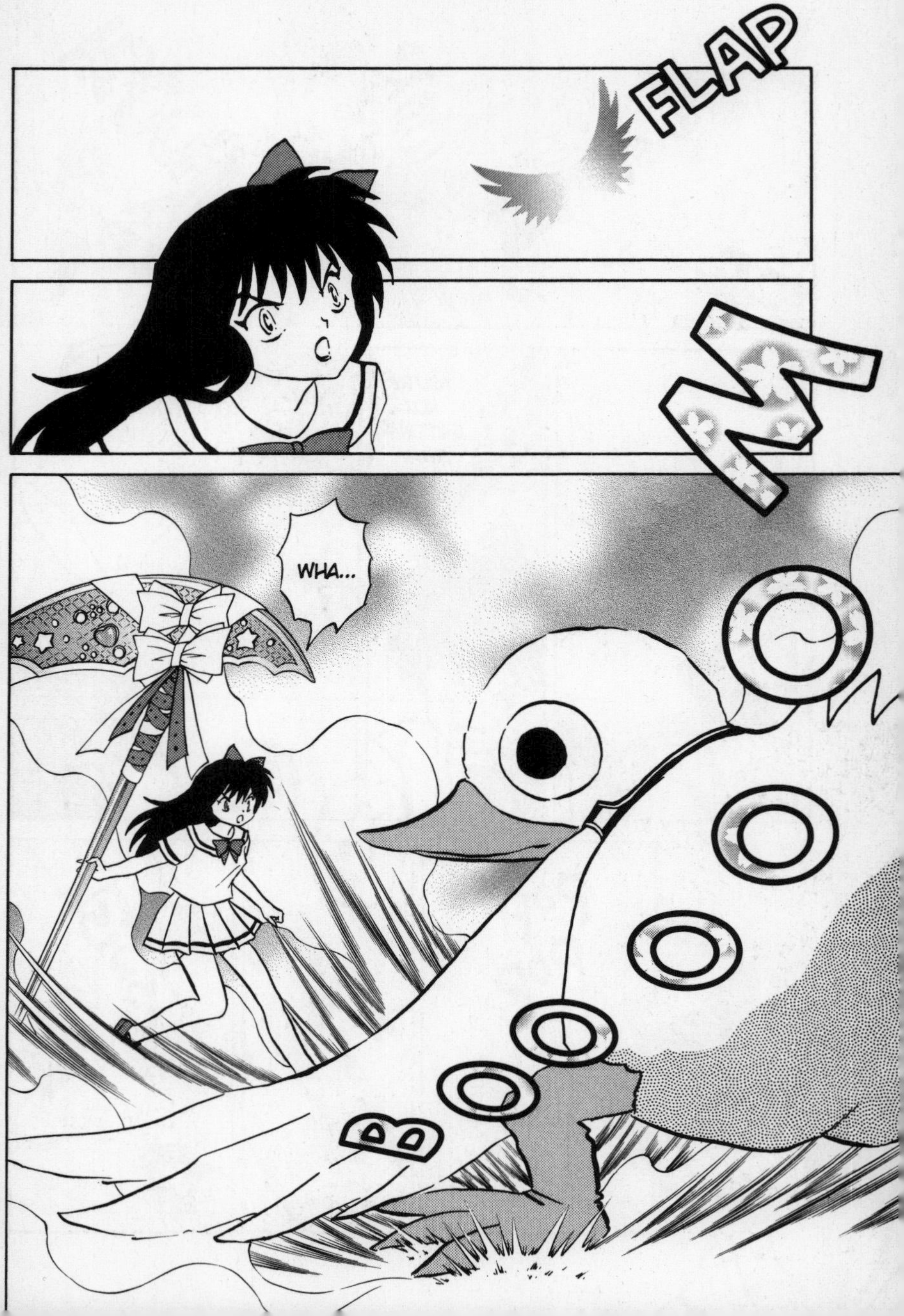
FLAP
WHA...
BOOOOOM

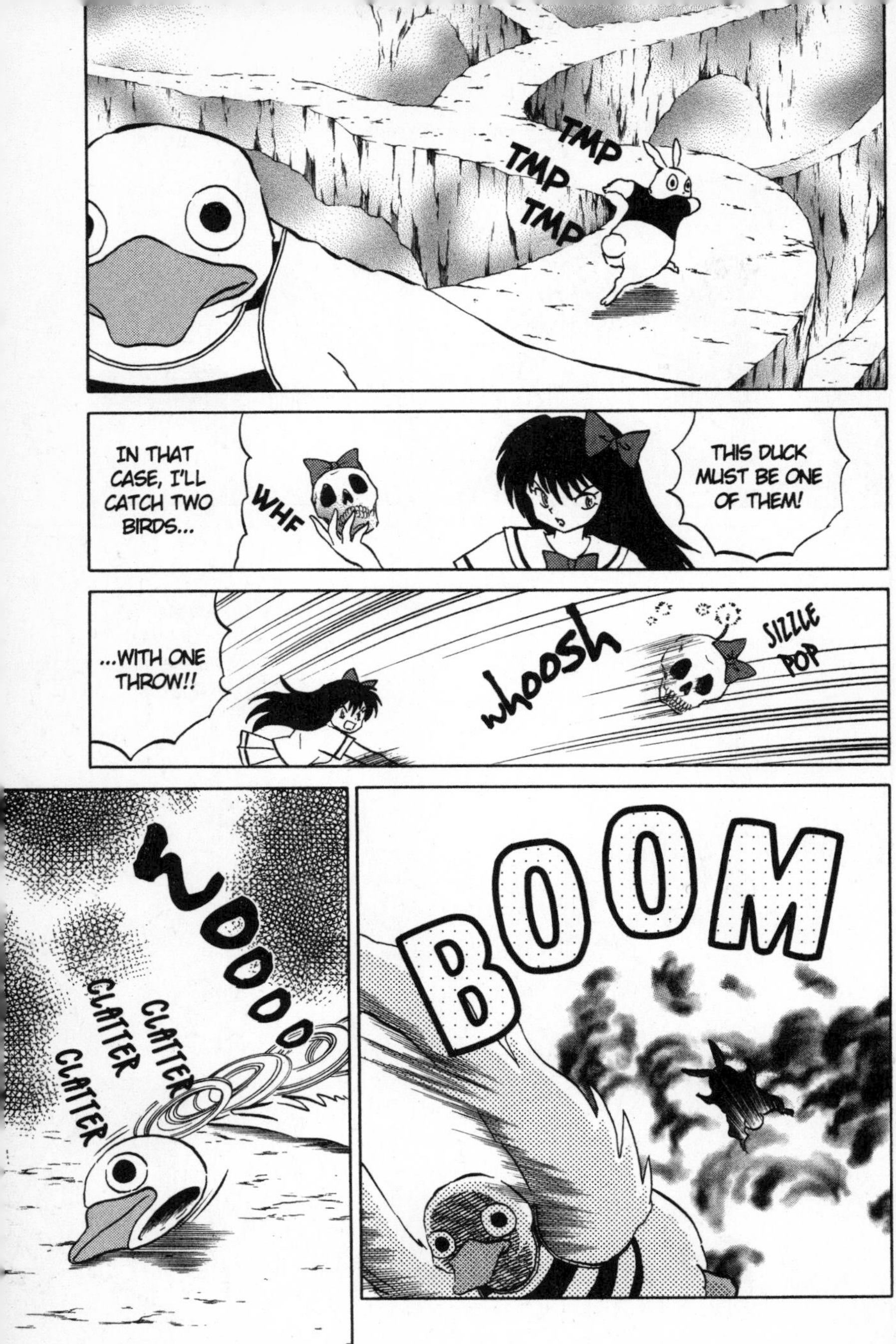
TMP
TMP
TMP
THIS DUCK MUST BE ONE OF THEM!
WHF
IN THAT CASE, I'LL CATCH TWO BIRDS...
SIZZLE POP
whoosh
...WITH ONE THROW!!
BOOM
WOOOOO
CLATTER
CLATTER
CLATTER

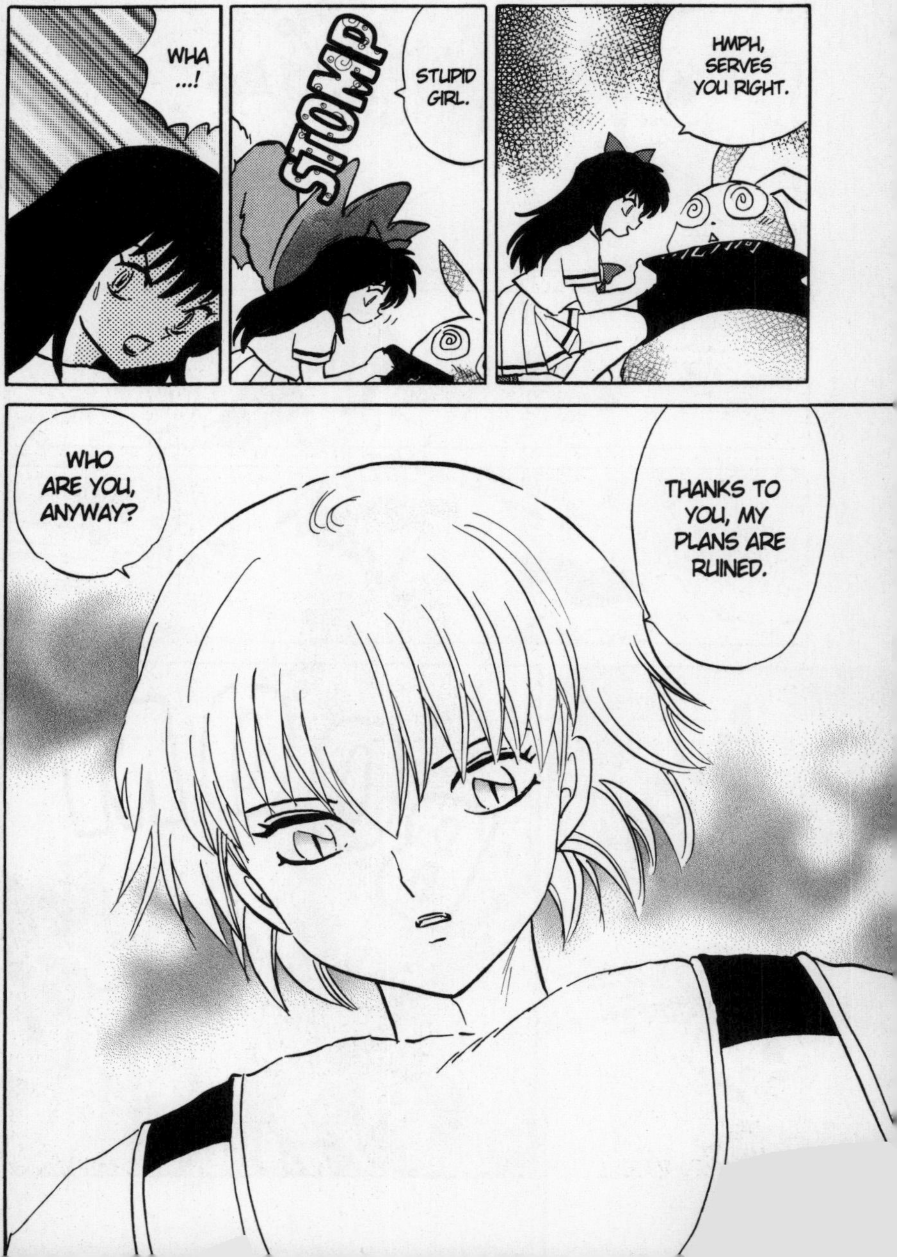
HMPH, SERVES YOU RIGHT.
STOMP
STUPID GIRL.
WHA ...!
THANKS TO YOU, MY PLANS ARE RUINED.
WHO ARE YOU, ANYWAY?

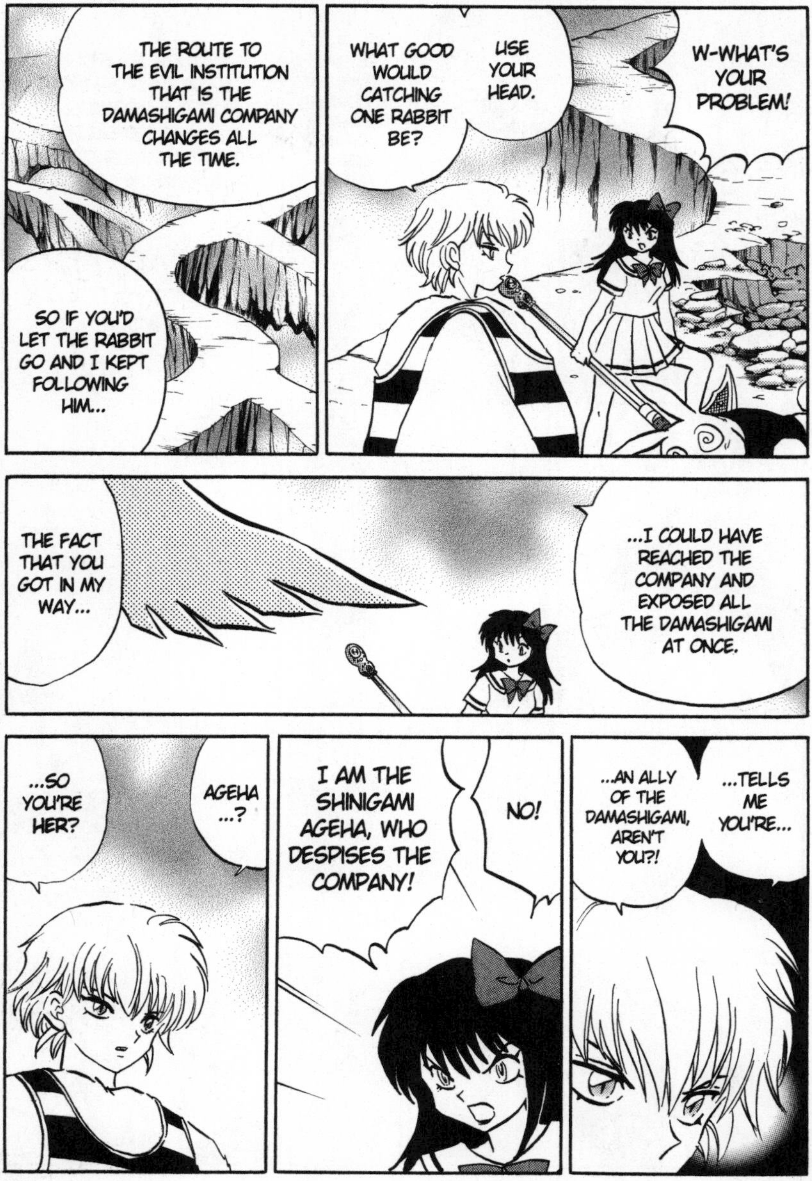
W-WHAT'S YOUR PROBLEM!
USE YOUR HEAD.
WHAT GOOD WOULD CATCHING ONE RABBIT BE?
THE ROUTE TO THE EVIL INSTITUTION THAT IS THE DAMASHIGAMI COMPANY CHANGES ALL THE TIME.
SO IF YOU'D LET THE RABBIT GO AND I KEPT FOLLOWING HIM...
...I COULD HAVE REACHED THE COMPANY AND EXPOSED ALL THE DAMASHIGAMI AT ONCE.
THE FACT THAT YOU GOT IN MY WAY...
...TELLS ME YOU'RE...
...AN ALLY OF THE DAMASHIGAMI, AREN'T YOU?!
NO!
I AM THE SHINIGAMI AGEHA, WHO DESPISES THE COMPANY!
AGEHA ...?
...SO YOU'RE HER?

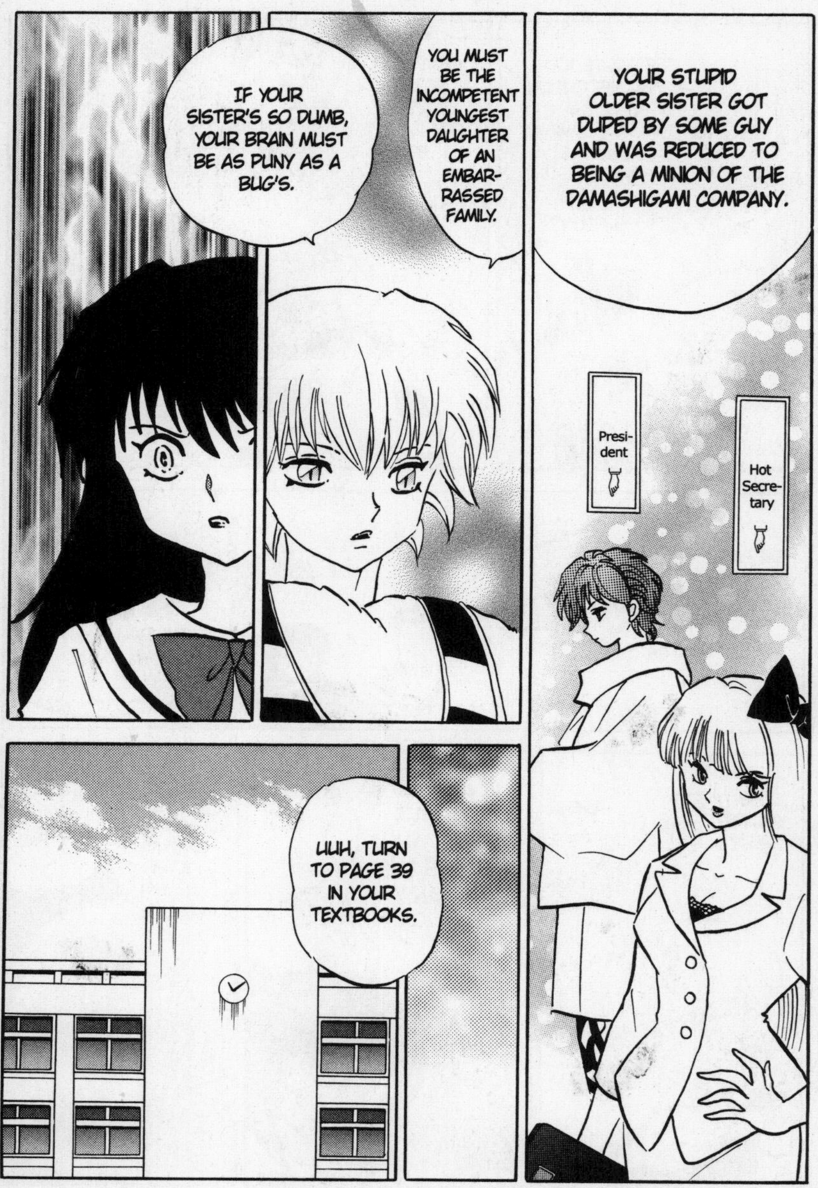
YOUR STUPID OLDER SISTER GOT DUPED BY SOME GUY AND WAS REDUCED TO BEING A MINION OF THE DAMASHIGAMI COMPANY.
President
Hot Secretary
YOU MUST BE THE INCOMPETENT YOUNGEST DAUGHTER OF AN EMBARRASSED FAMILY.
IF YOUR SISTER'S SO DUMB, YOUR BRAIN MUST BE AS PUNY AS A BUG'S.
UUH, TURN TO PAGE 39 IN YOUR TEXTBOOKS.

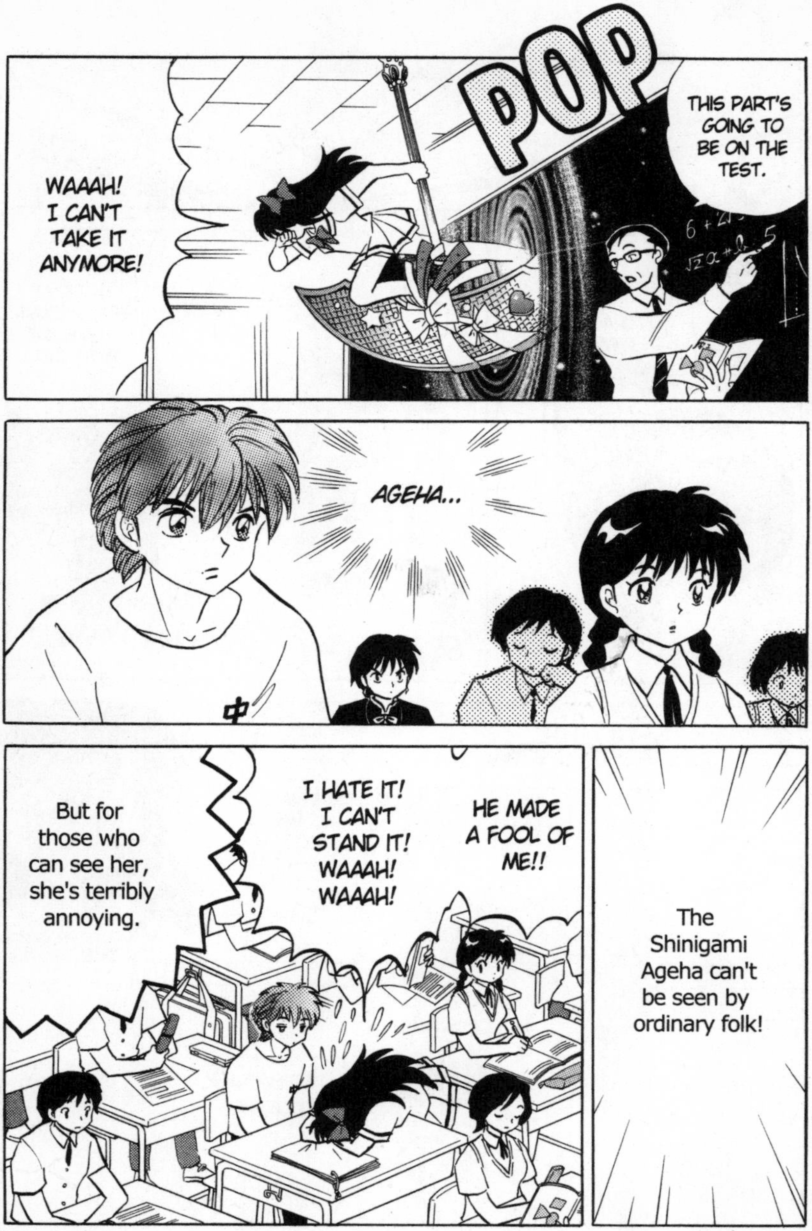

THIS PART'S GOING TO BE ON THE TEST.
POP
WAAAH! I CAN'T TAKE IT ANYMORE!
AGEHA...
The Shinigami Ageha can't be seen by ordinary folk!
HE MADE A FOOL OF ME!!
I HATE IT! I CAN'T STAND IT! WAAAH! WAAAH!
But for those who can see her, she's terribly annoying.

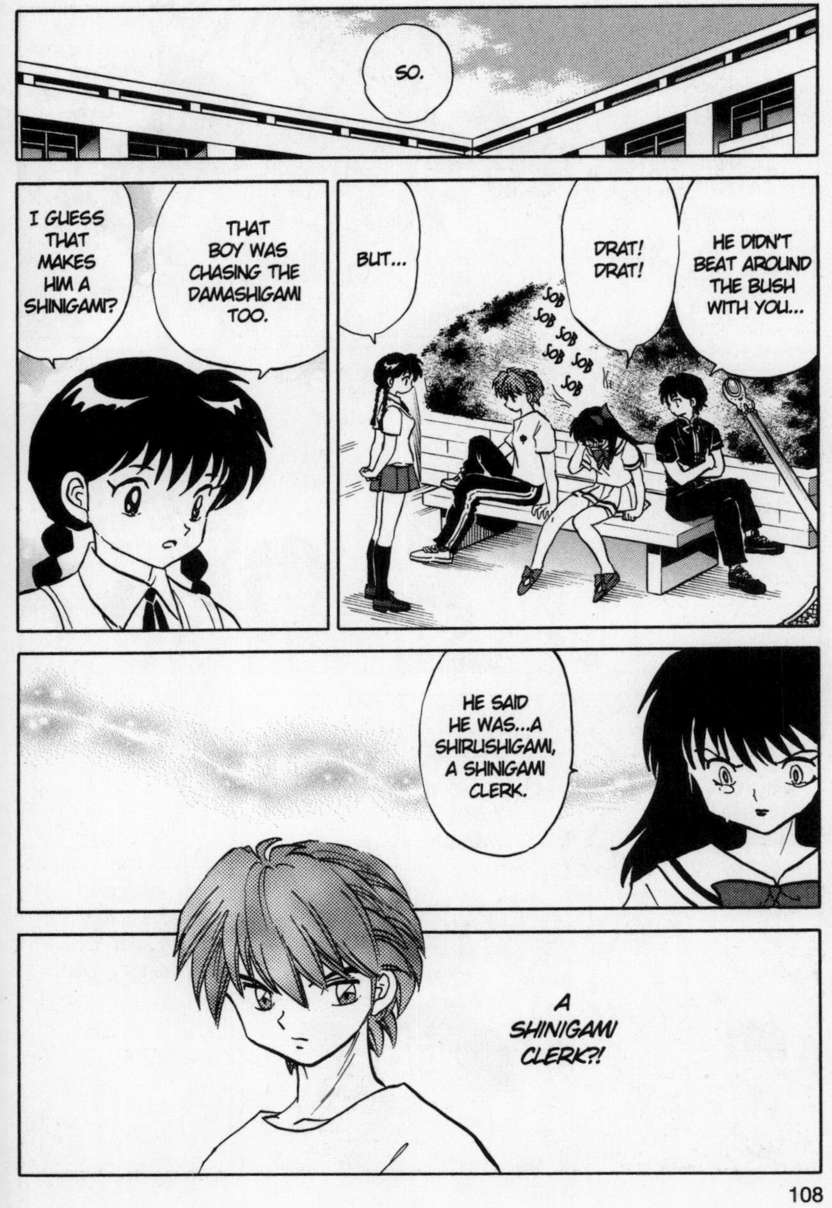
SO.
HE DIDN'T BEAT AROUND THE BUSH WITH YOU...
DRAT! DRAT!
SOB SOB SOB SOB SOB SOB
BUT...
THAT BOY WAS CHASING THE DAMASHIGAMI TOO.
I GUESS THAT MAKES HIM A SHINIGAMI?
HE SAID HE WAS...A SHIRUSHIGAMI, A SHINIGAMI CLERK.
A SHINIGAMI CLERK?!

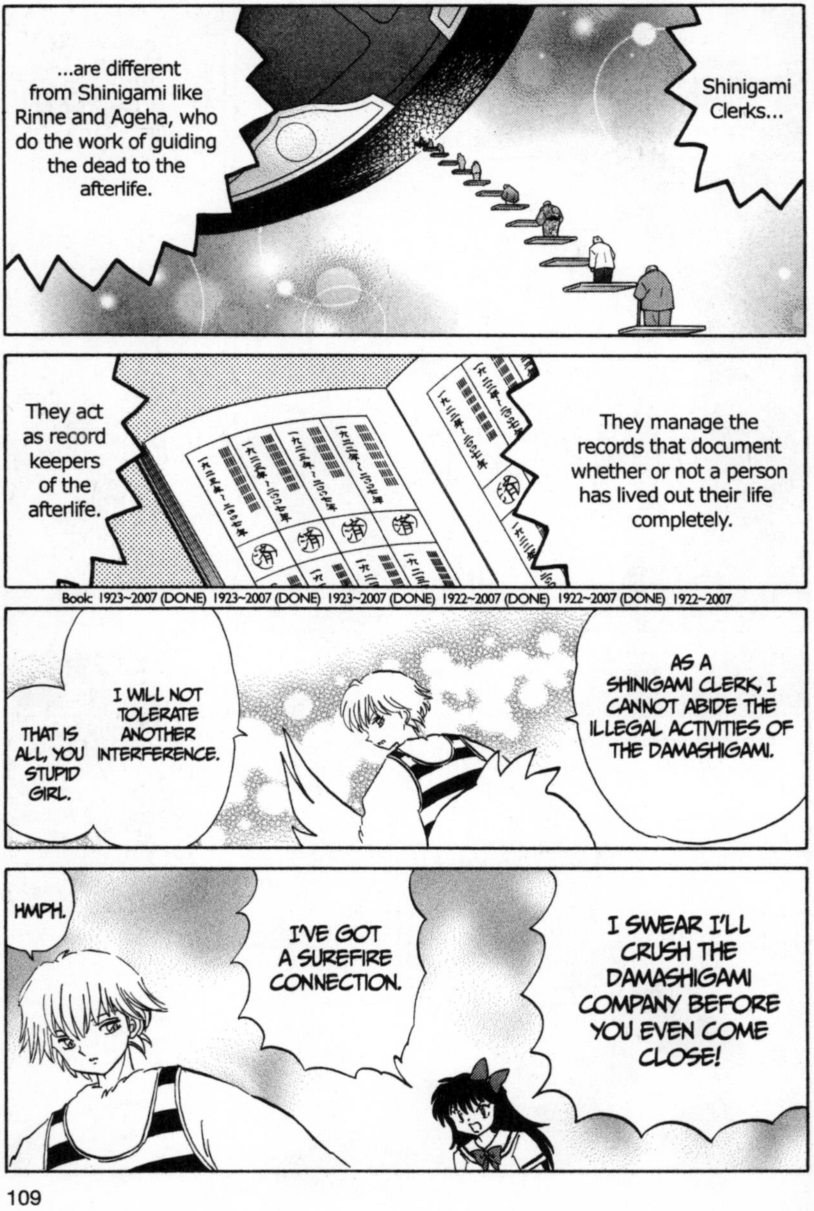
Shinigami Clerks...
...are different from Shinigami like Rinne and Ageha, who do the work of guiding the dead to the afterlife.
They manage the records that document whether or not a person has lived out their life completely.
They act as record keepers of the afterlife.
Book: 1923~2007 (DONE) 1923~2007 (DONE) 1923~2007 (DONE) 1922~2007 (DONE) 1922~2007 (DONE) 1922~2007
AS A SHINIGAMI CLERK, I CANNOT ABIDE THE ILLEGAL ACTIVITIES OF THE DAMASHIGAMI.
I WILL NOT TOLERATE ANOTHER INTERFERENCE.
THAT IS ALL, YOU STUPID GIRL.
I SWEAR I'LL CRUSH THE DAMASHIGAMI COMPANY BEFORE YOU EVEN COME CLOSE!
I'VE GOT A SUREFIRE CONNECTION.
HMPH.

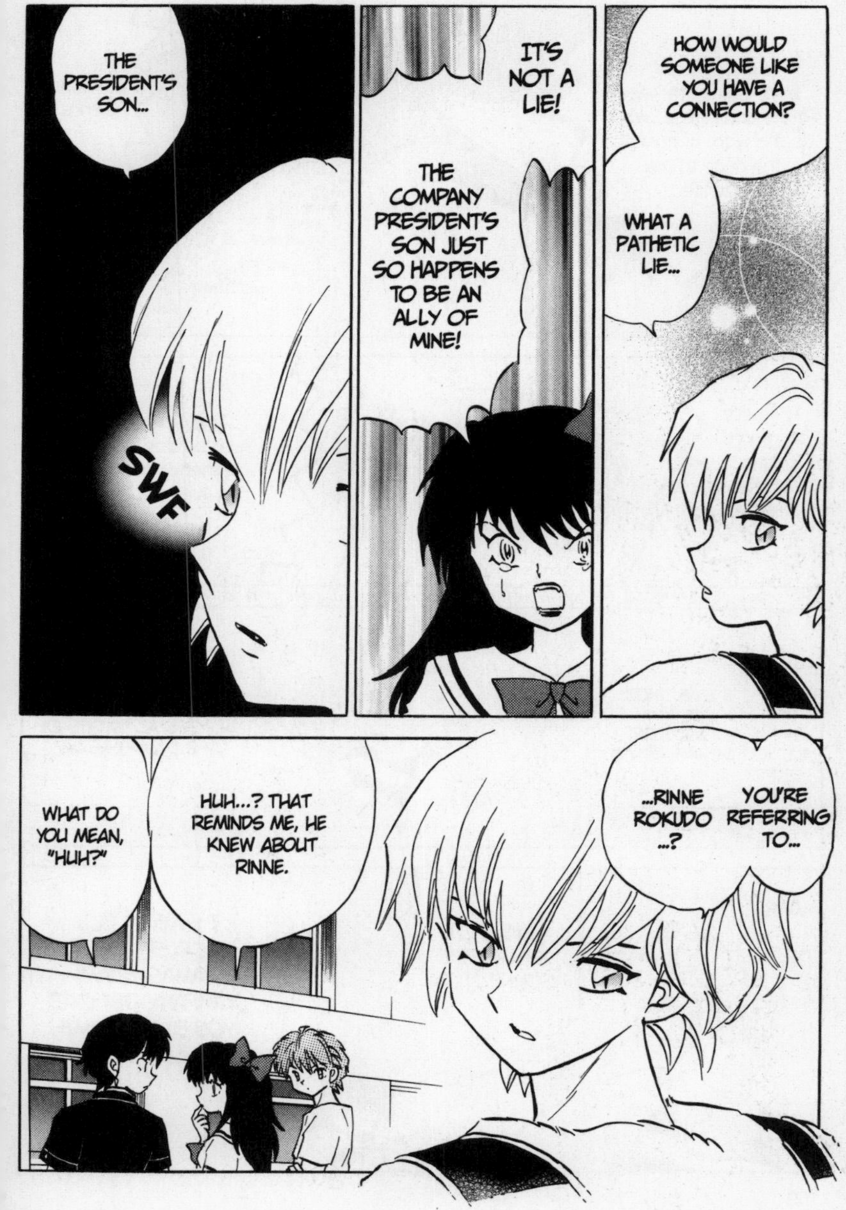

HOW WOULD SOMEONE LIKE YOU HAVE A CONNECTION?
WHAT A PATHETIC LIE...
IT'S NOT A LIE!
THE COMPANY PRESIDENT'S SON JUST SO HAPPENS TO BE AN ALLY OF MINE!
THE PRESIDENT'S SON...
SWF
YOU'RE REFERRING TO... ...RINNE ROKUDO ...?
HUH...? THAT REMINDS ME, HE KNEW ABOUT RINNE.
WHAT DO YOU MEAN, "HUH?"

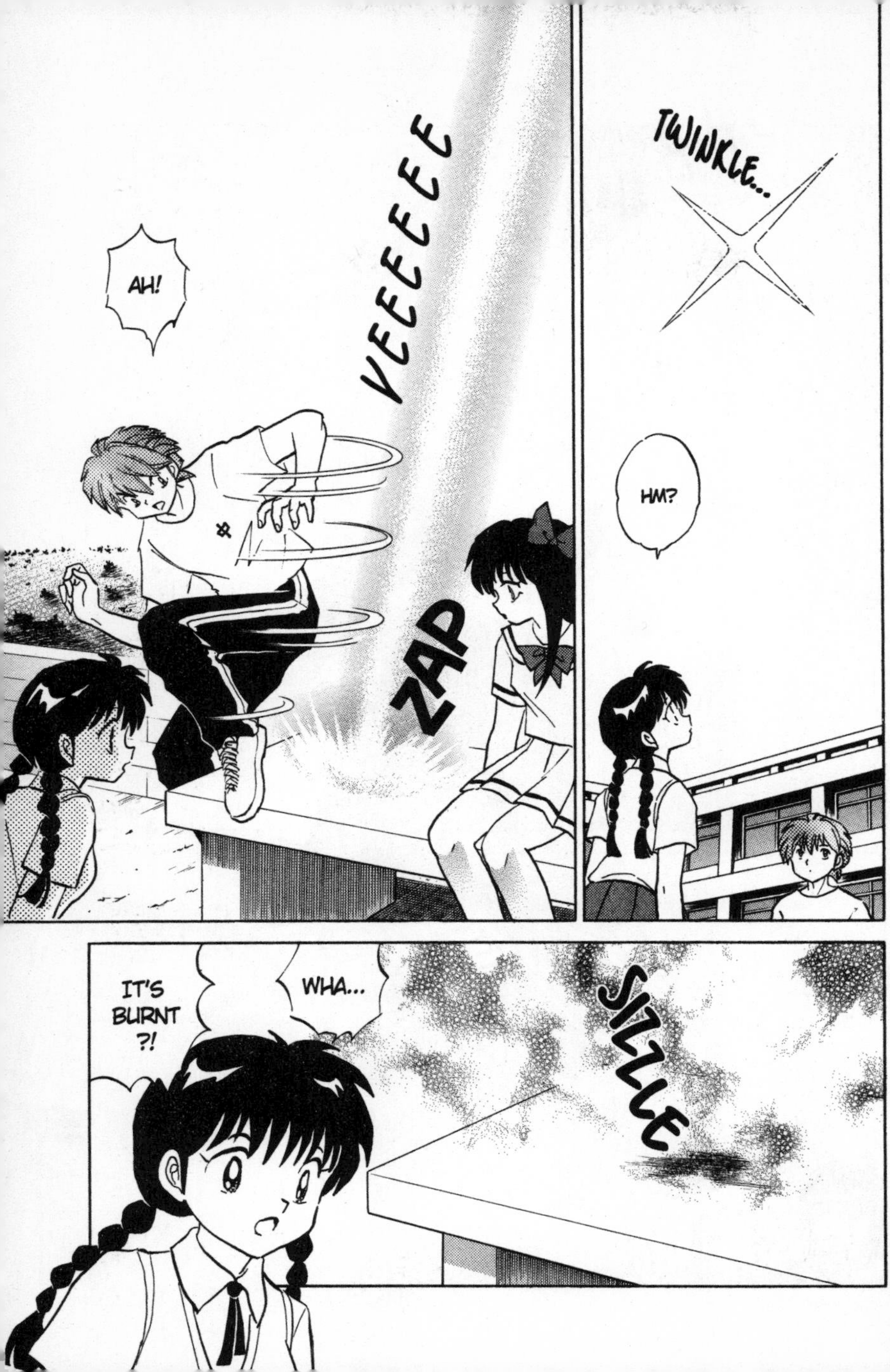
TWINKLE...
HM?
VEEEEEE
AH!
ZAP
SIZZLE
WHA...
IT'S BURNT ?!

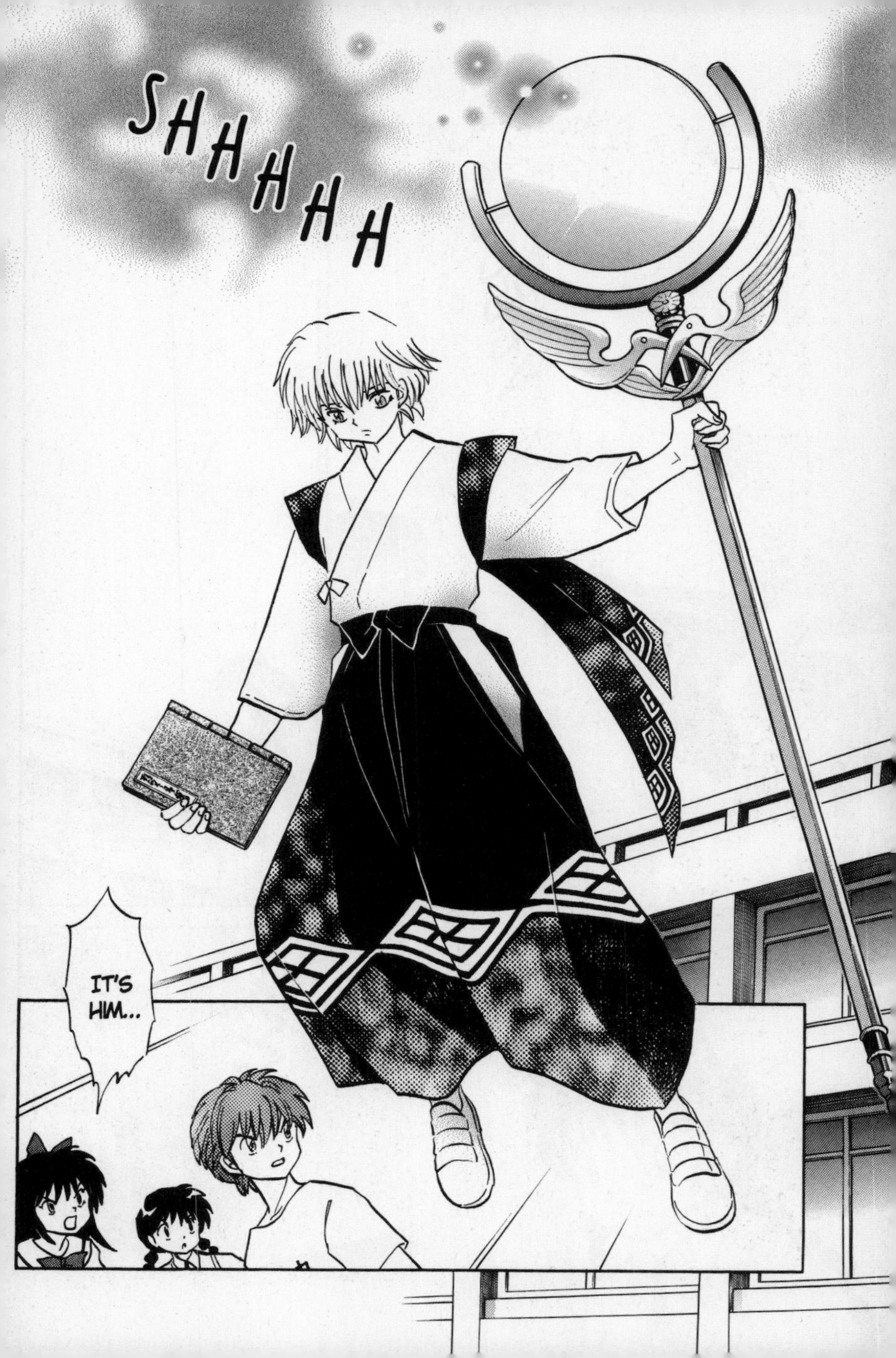
SHHHHHH
IT'S HIM...

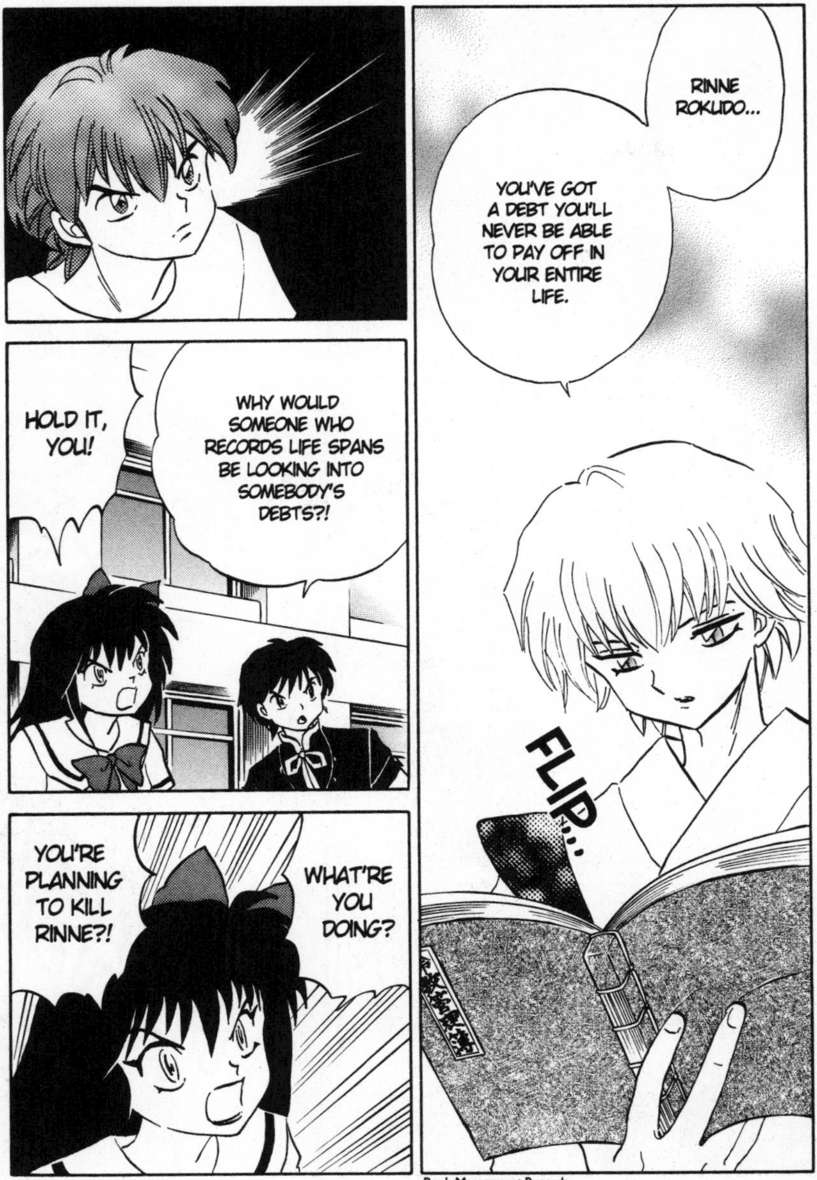
RINNE ROKUDO...
YOU'VE GOT A DEBT YOU'LL NEVER BE ABLE TO PAY OFF IN YOUR ENTIRE LIFE.
FLIP...
WHY WOULD SOMEONE WHO RECORDS LIFE SPANS BE LOOKING INTO SOMEBODY'S DEBTS?!
HOLD IT, YOU!
WHAT'RE YOU DOING?
YOU'RE PLANNING TO KILL RINNE?!
Book Management Records

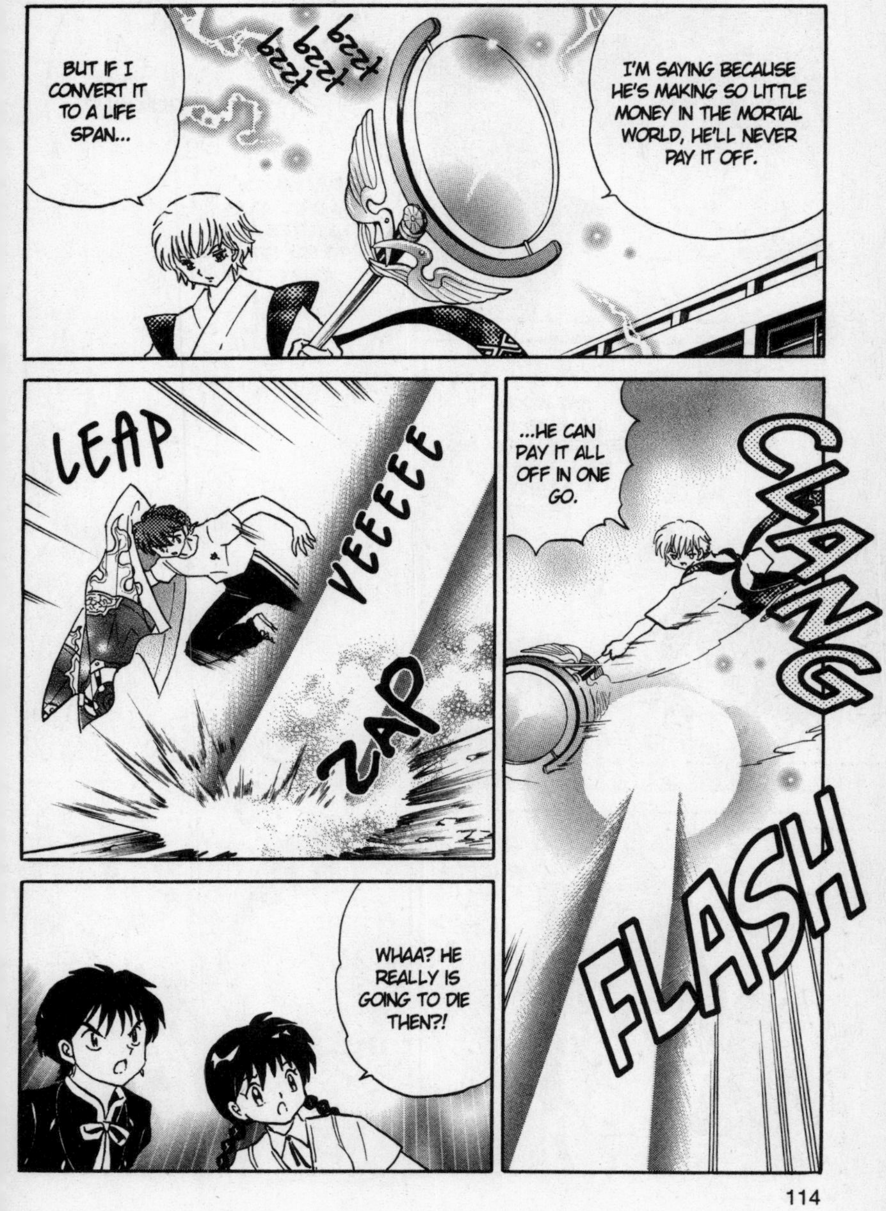
I'M SAYING BECAUSE HE'S MAKING SO LITTLE MONEY IN THE MORTAL WORLD, HE'LL NEVER PAY IT OFF.
BUT IF I CONVERT IT TO A LIFE SPAN...
...HE CAN PAY IT ALL OFF IN ONE GO.
CLANG
FLASH
LEAP
VEEEEE
ZAP
WHAA? HE REALLY IS GOING TO DIE THEN?!

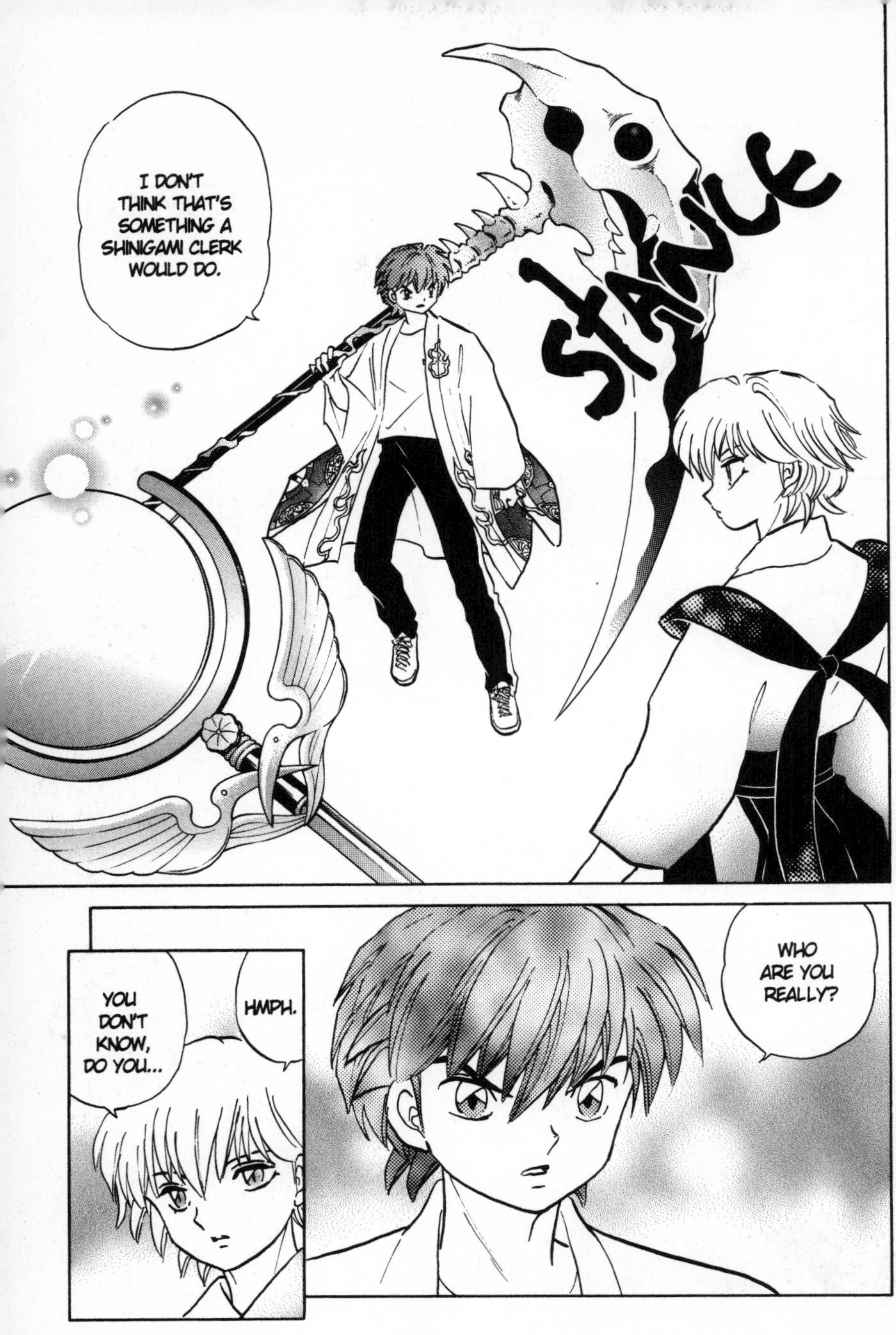
I DON'T THINK THAT'S SOMETHING A SHINIGAMI CLERK WOULD DO.
STANCE
WHO ARE YOU REALLY?
HMPH.
YOU DON'T KNOW, DO YOU...

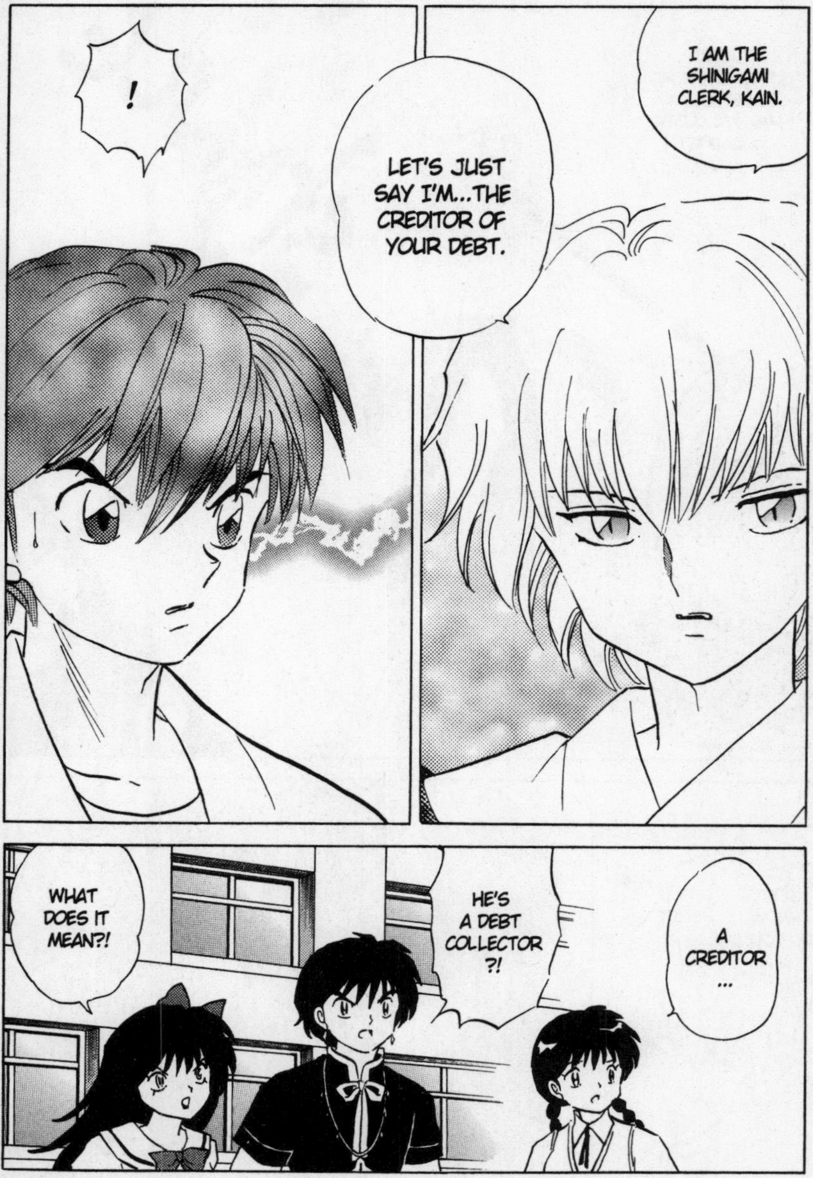
I AM THE SHINIGAMI CLERK, KAIN.
LET'S JUST SAY I'M...THE CREDITOR OF YOUR DEBT.
!
A CREDITOR ...
HE'S A DEBT COLLECTOR ?!
WHAT DOES IT MEAN?!

CHAPTER 55: SEIZURE

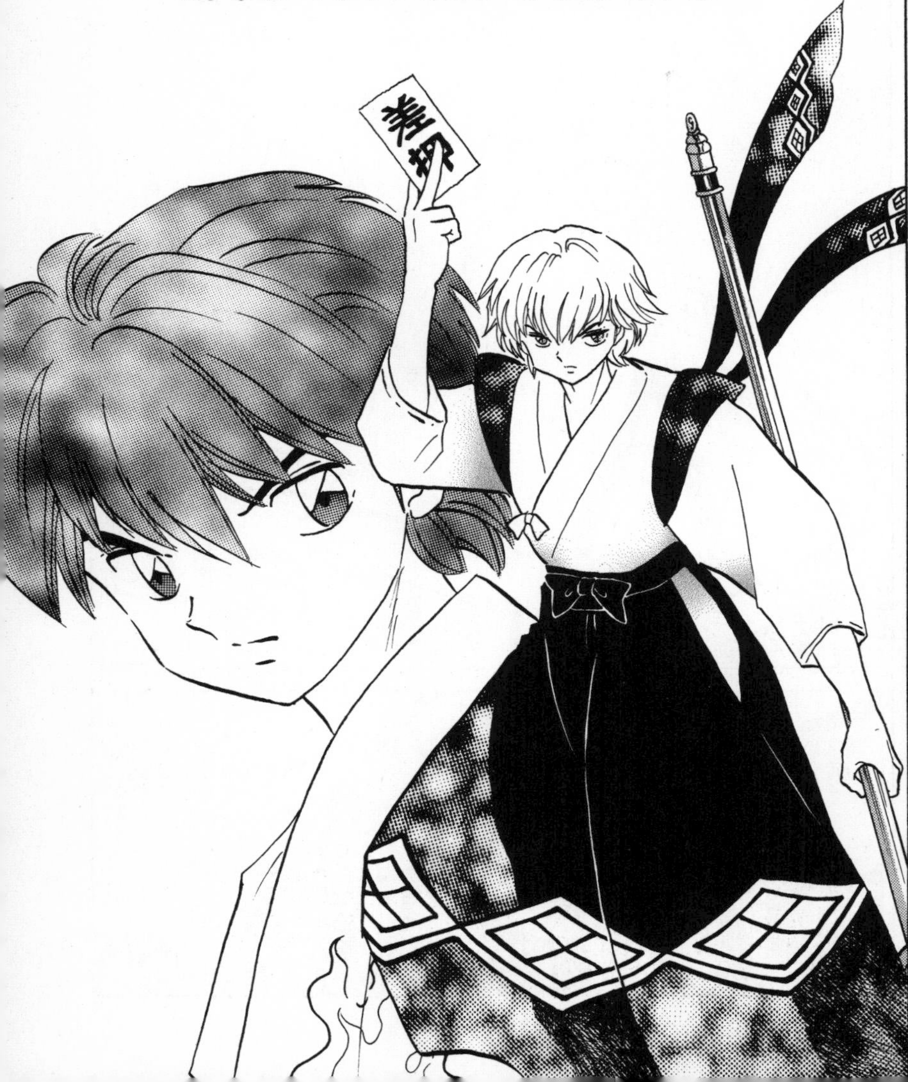
差押

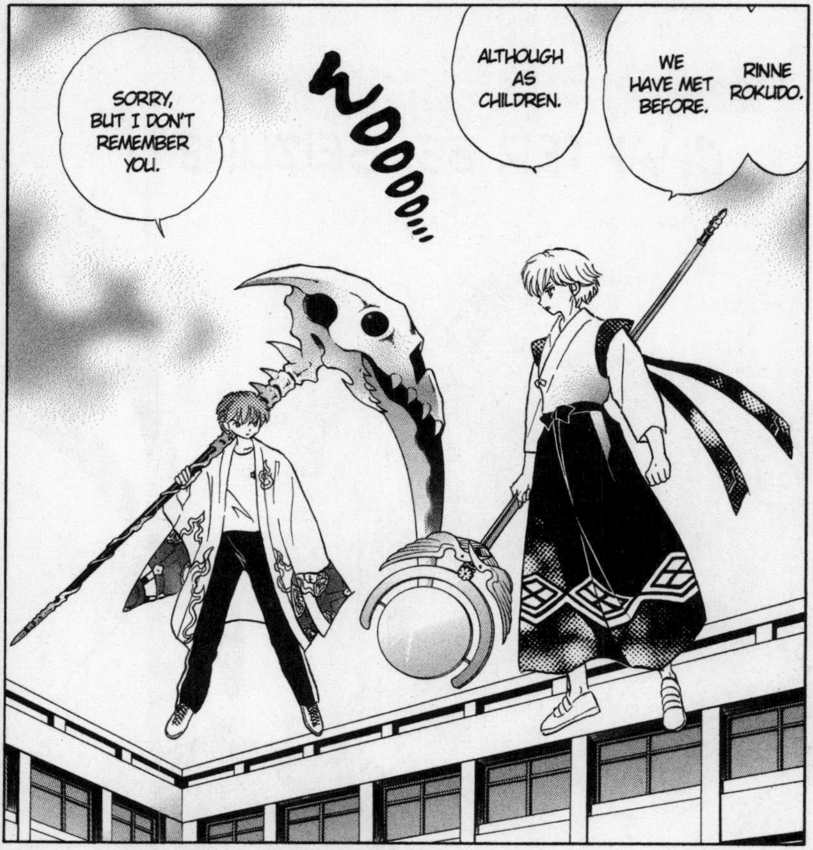
RINNE ROKUDO.
WE HAVE MET BEFORE.
ALTHOUGH AS CHILDREN.
WOOOOO...
SORRY, BUT I DON'T REMEMBER YOU.

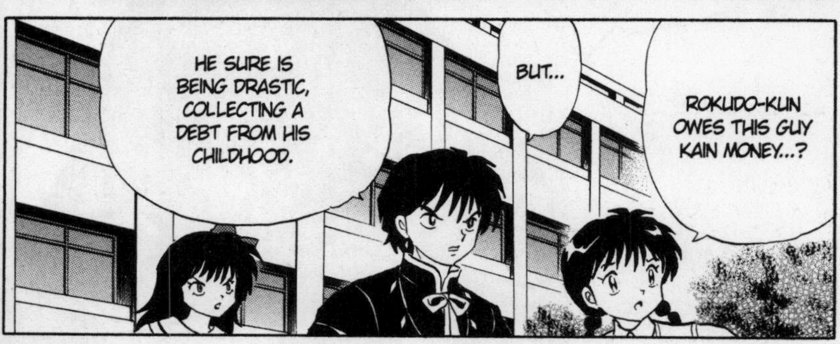
ROKUDO-KUN OWES THIS GUY KAIN MONEY...?
BUT...
HE SURE IS BEING DRASTIC, COLLECTING A DEBT FROM HIS CHILDHOOD.

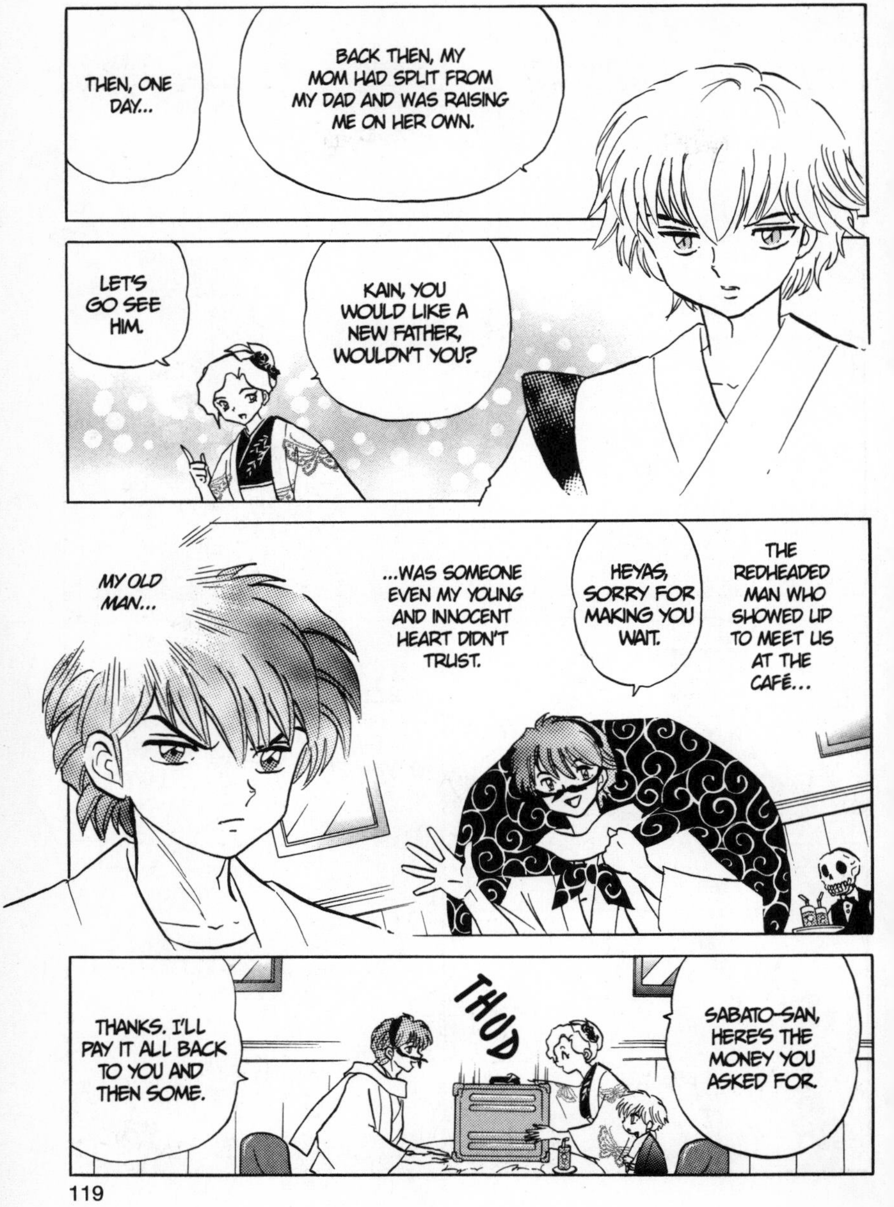
BACK THEN, MY MOM HAD SPLIT FROM MY DAD AND WAS RAISING ME ON HER OWN.
THEN, ONE DAY...
KAIN, YOU WOULD LIKE A NEW FATHER, WOULDN'T YOU?
LET'S GO SEE HIM.
THE REDHEADED MAN WHO SHOWED UP TO MEET US AT THE CAFÉ...
HEYAS, SORRY FOR MAKING YOU WAIT.
...WAS SOMEONE EVEN MY YOUNG AND INNOCENT HEART DIDN'T TRUST.
MY OLD MAN...
SABATO-SAN, HERE'S THE MONEY YOU ASKED FOR.
THUD
THANKS. I'LL PAY IT ALL BACK TO YOU AND THEN SOME.

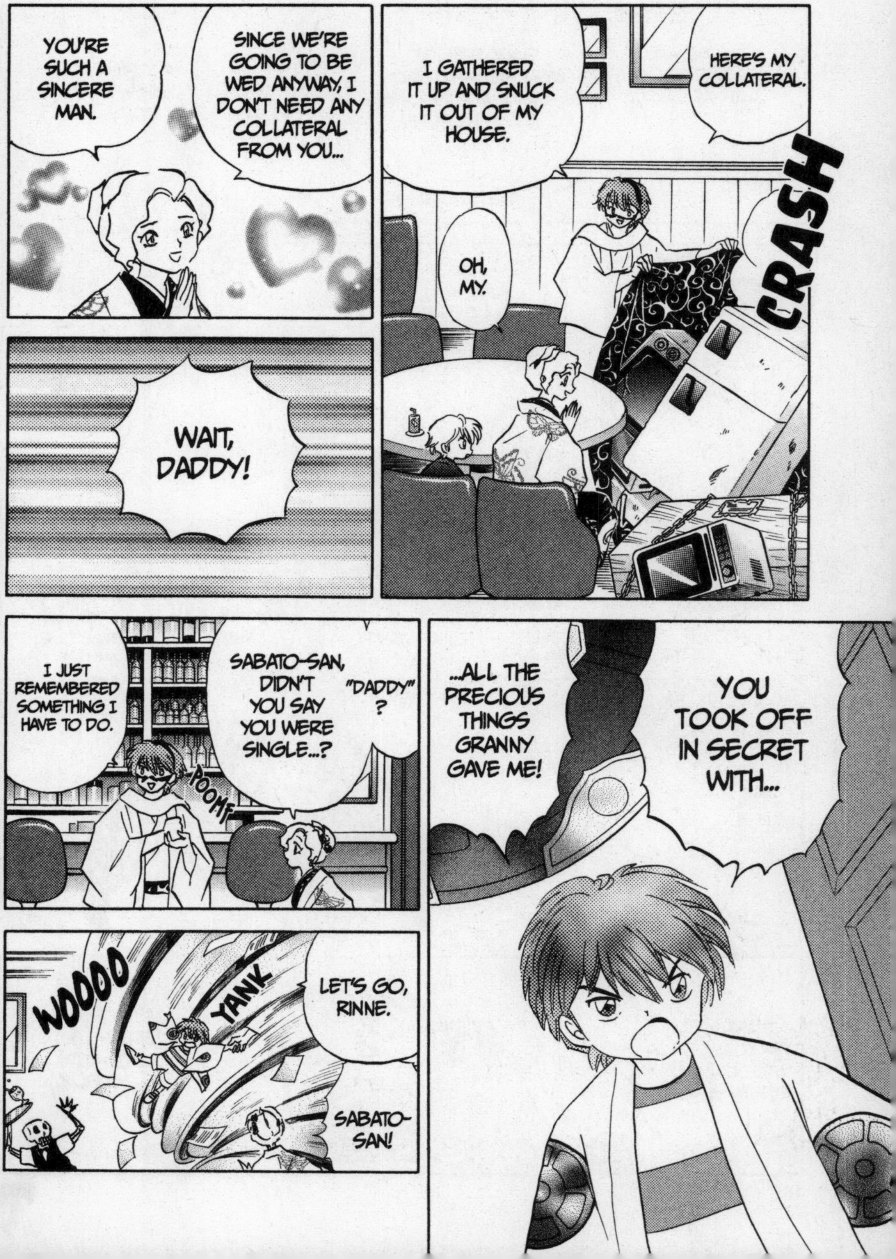
HERE'S MY COLLATERAL.
CRASH
I GATHERED IT UP AND SNUCK IT OUT OF MY HOUSE.
OH, MY.
SINCE WE'RE GOING TO BE WED ANYWAY, I DON'T NEED ANY COLLATERAL FROM YOU...
YOU'RE SUCH A SINCERE MAN.
WAIT, DADDY!
YOU TOOK OFF IN SECRET WITH...
...ALL THE PRECIOUS THINGS GRANNY GAVE ME!
"DADDY"?
SABATO-SAN, DIDN'T YOU SAY YOU WERE SINGLE...?
POOMF
I JUST REMEMBERED SOMETHING I HAVE TO DO.
LET'S GO, RINNE.
YANK
WOOOO
SABATO-SAN!

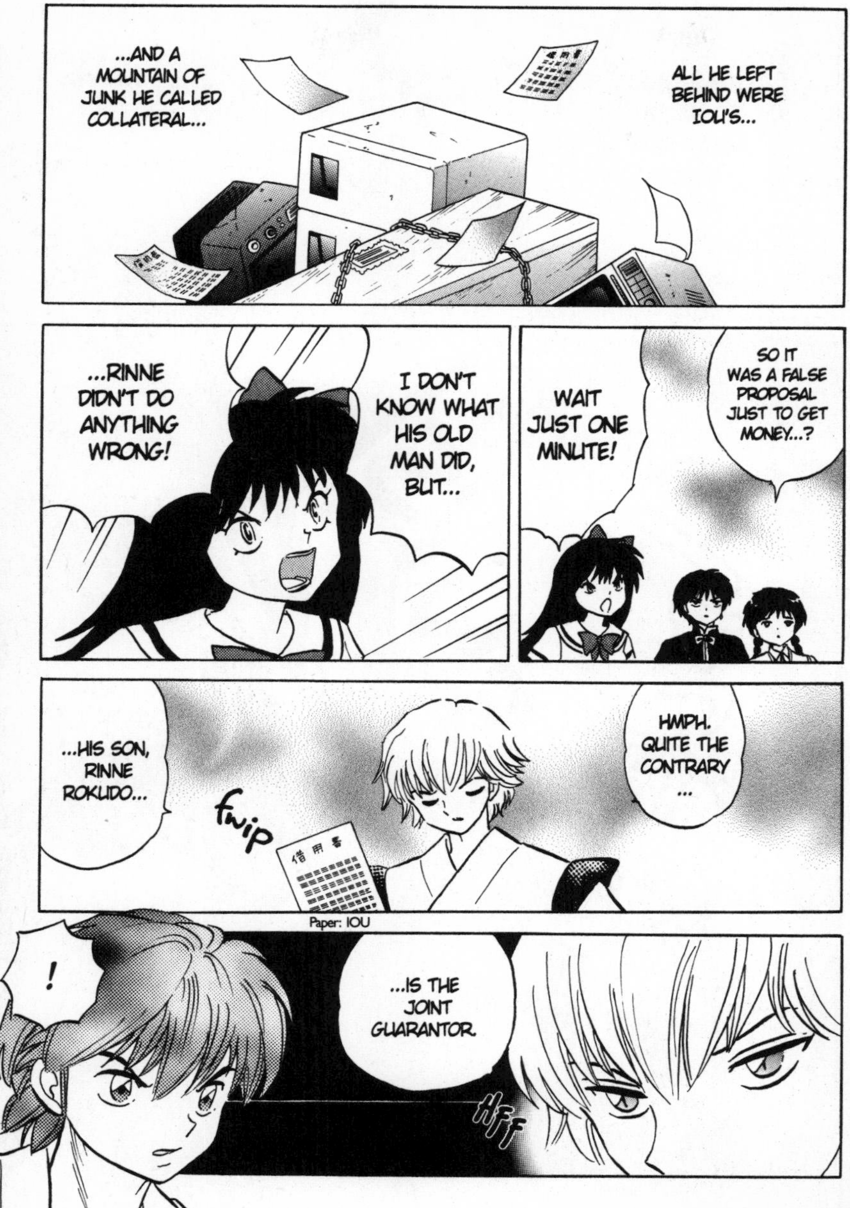
ALL HE LEFT BEHIND WERE IOU'S...
...AND A MOUNTAIN OF JUNK HE CALLED COLLATERAL...
SO IT WAS A FALSE PROPOSAL JUST TO GET MONEY...?
WAIT JUST ONE MINUTE!
I DON'T KNOW WHAT HIS OLD MAN DID, BUT...
...RINNE DIDN'T DO ANYTHING WRONG!
HMPH. QUITE THE CONTRARY ...
fwip
...HIS SON, RINNE ROKUDO...
Paper: IOU
...IS THE JOINT GUARANTOR.
HFF
!

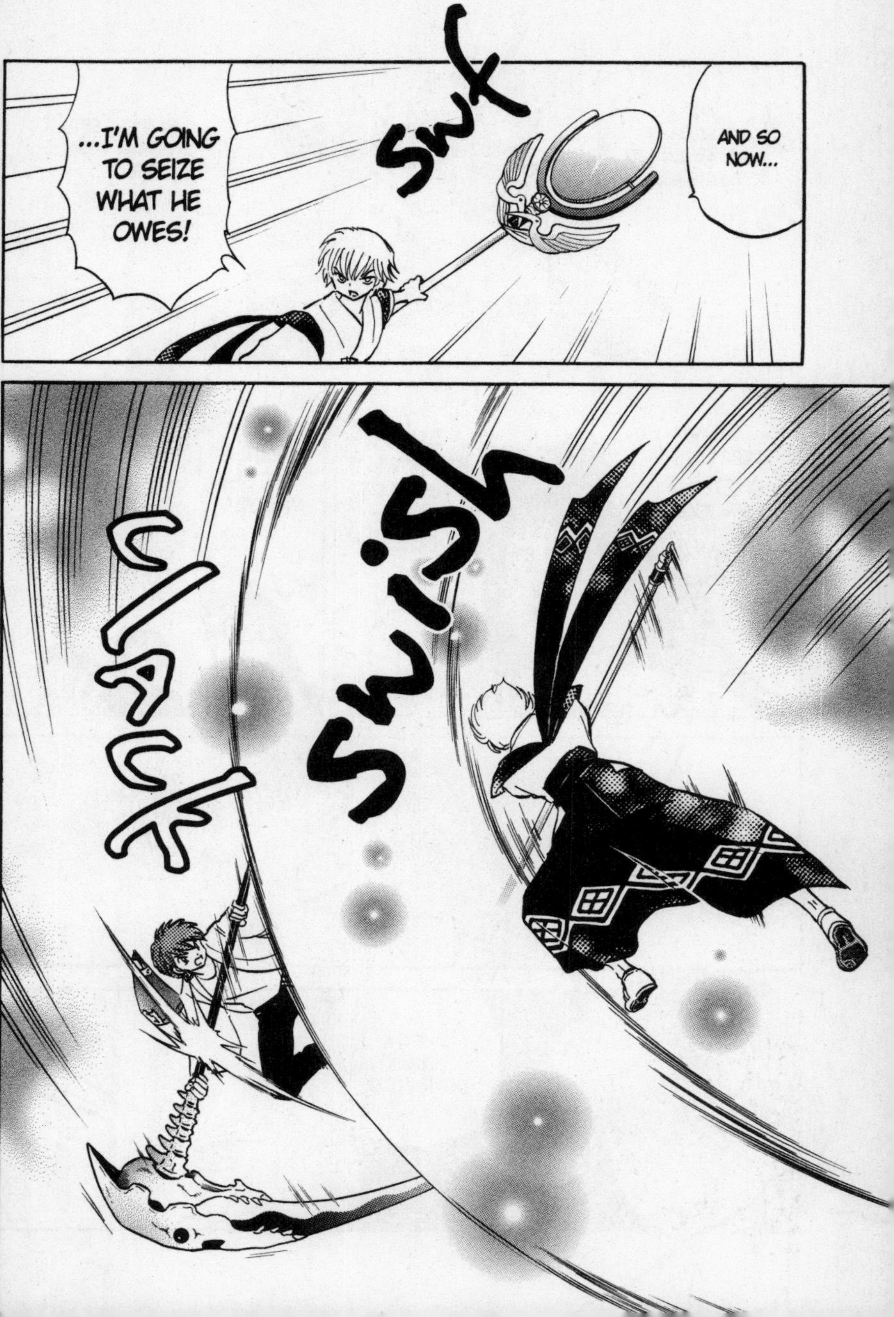
AND SO NOW...
SWF
...I'M GOING TO SEIZE WHAT HE OWES!
SWISH
WHACK

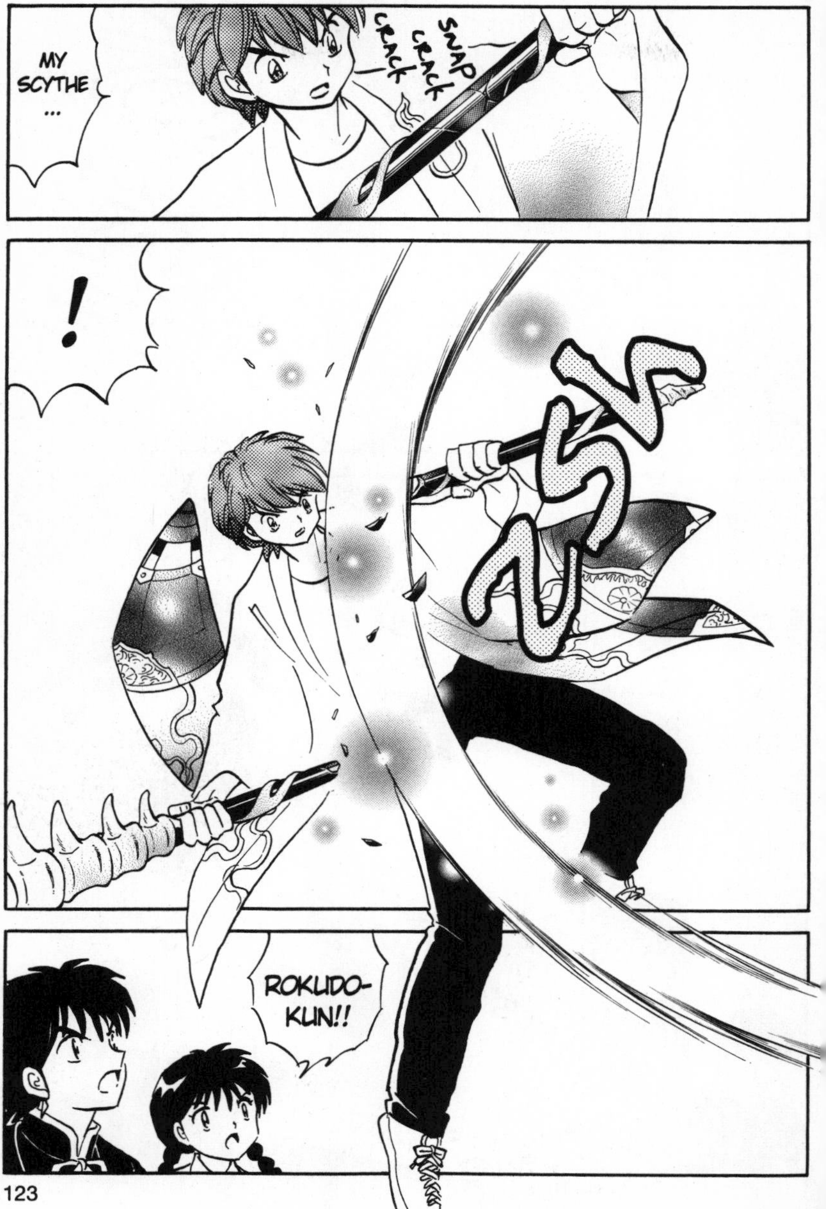
SNAP
CRACK
CRACK
MY SCYTHE ...
!
ROKUDO-KUN!!

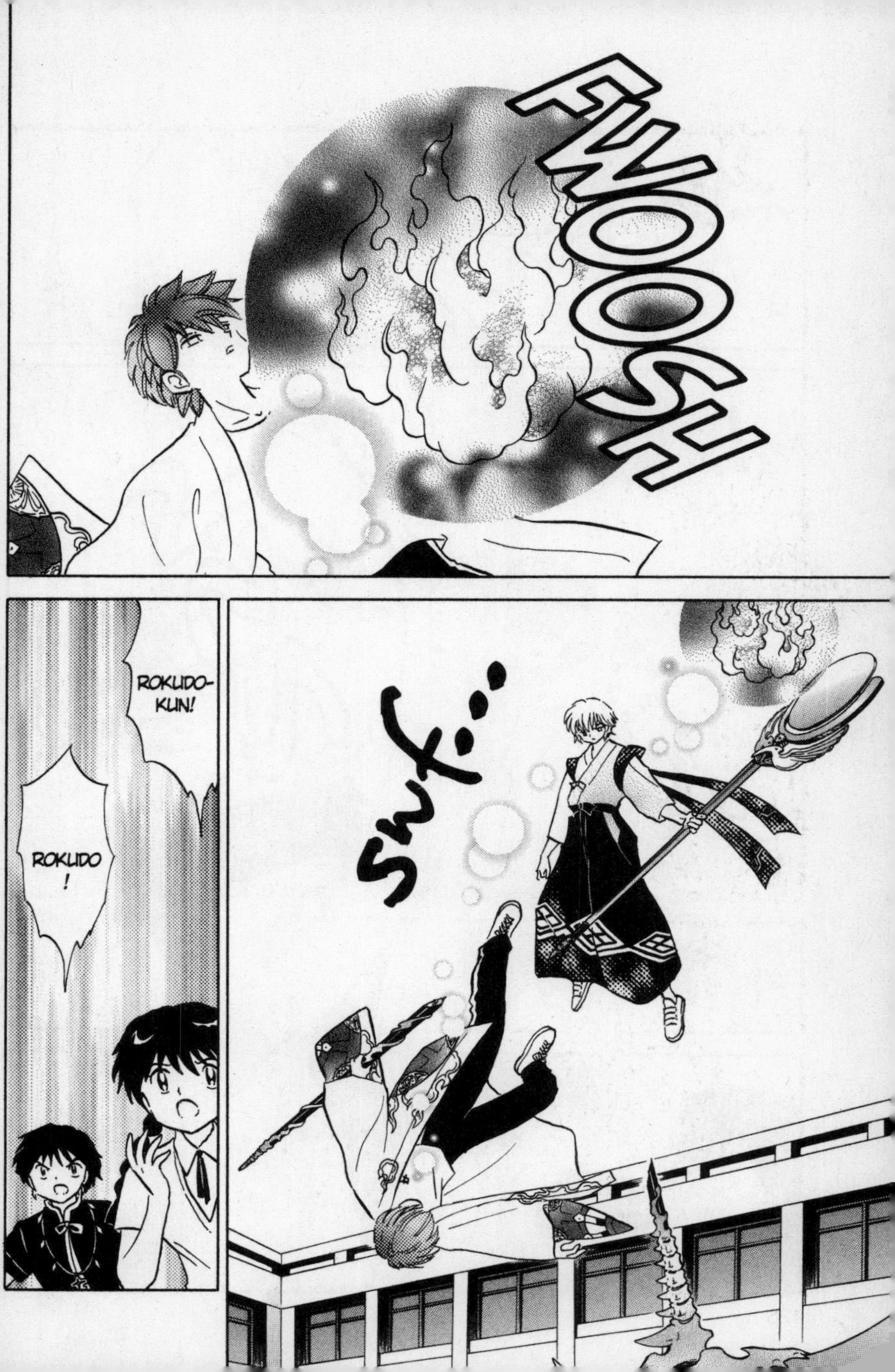
FWOOSH
SWF
ROKUDO-KUN!
ROKUDO!

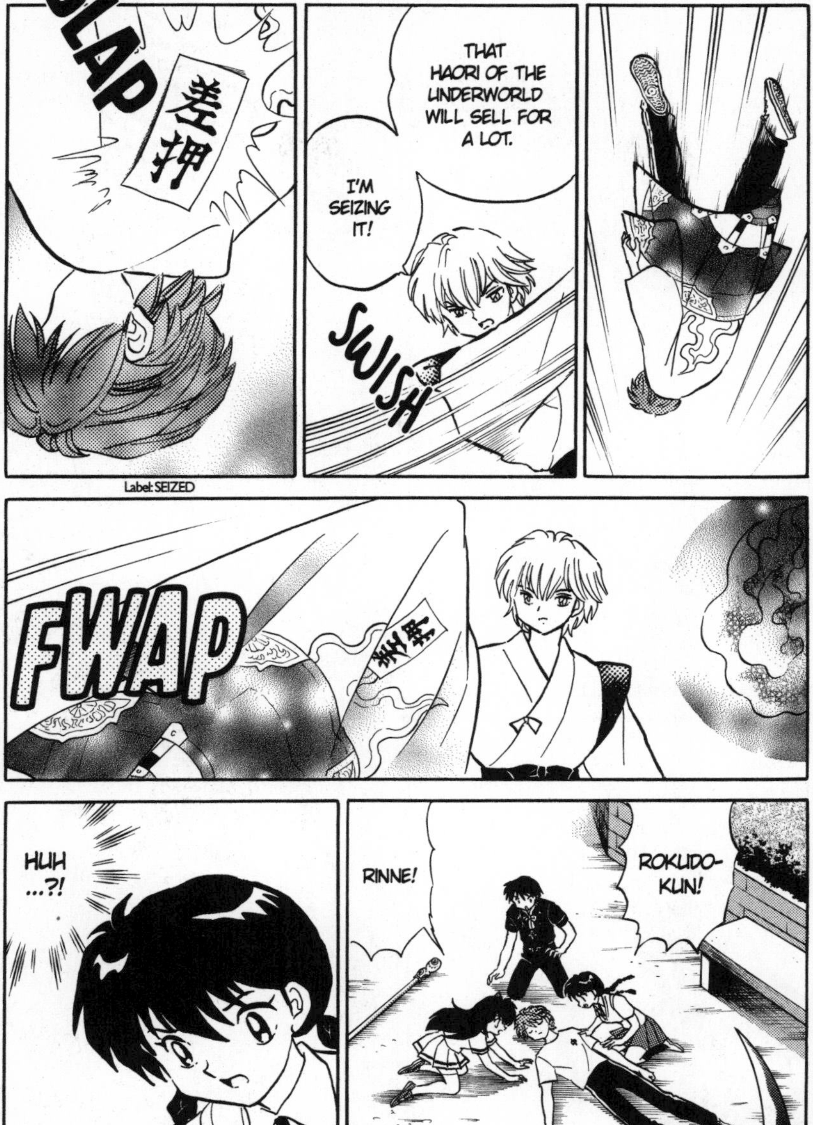
THAT HAORI OF THE UNDERWORLD WILL SELL FOR A LOT.
I'M SEIZING IT!
SWISH
SLAP
差押
FWAP
ROKUDO-KUN!
RINNE!
HUH ...?!
Label: SEIZED

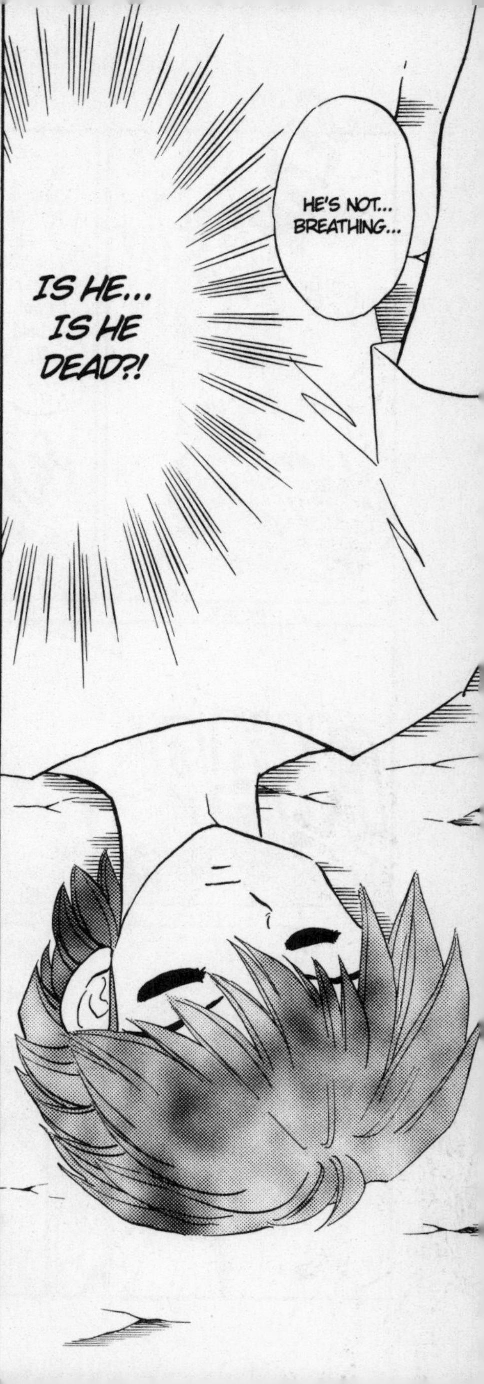
HE'S NOT... BREATHING...
IS HE... IS HE DEAD?!
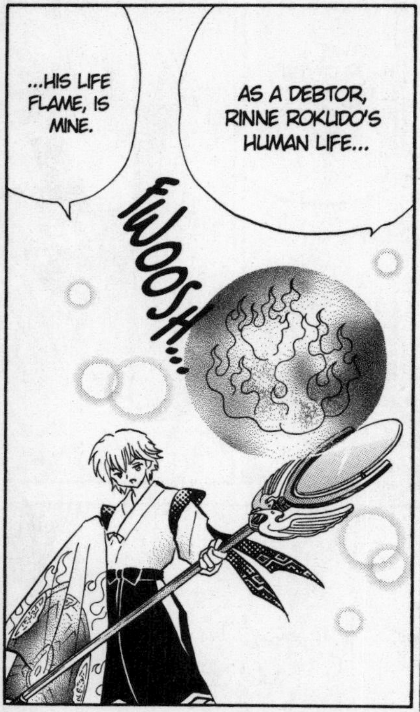
AS A DEBTOR, RINNE ROKUDO'S HUMAN LIFE...
...HIS LIFE FLAME, IS MINE.
FWOOSH...
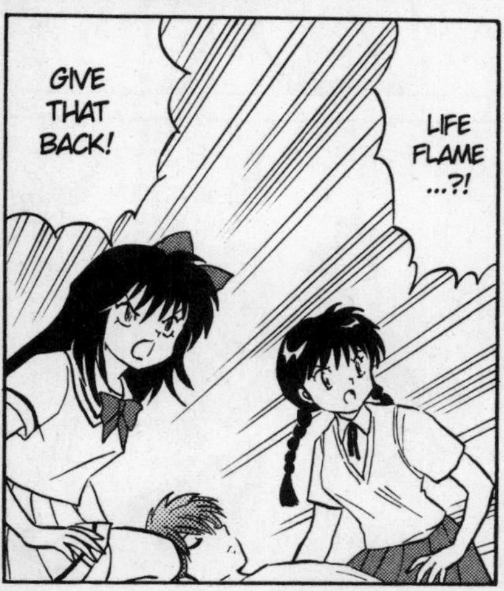
LIFE FLAME ...?!
GIVE THAT BACK!

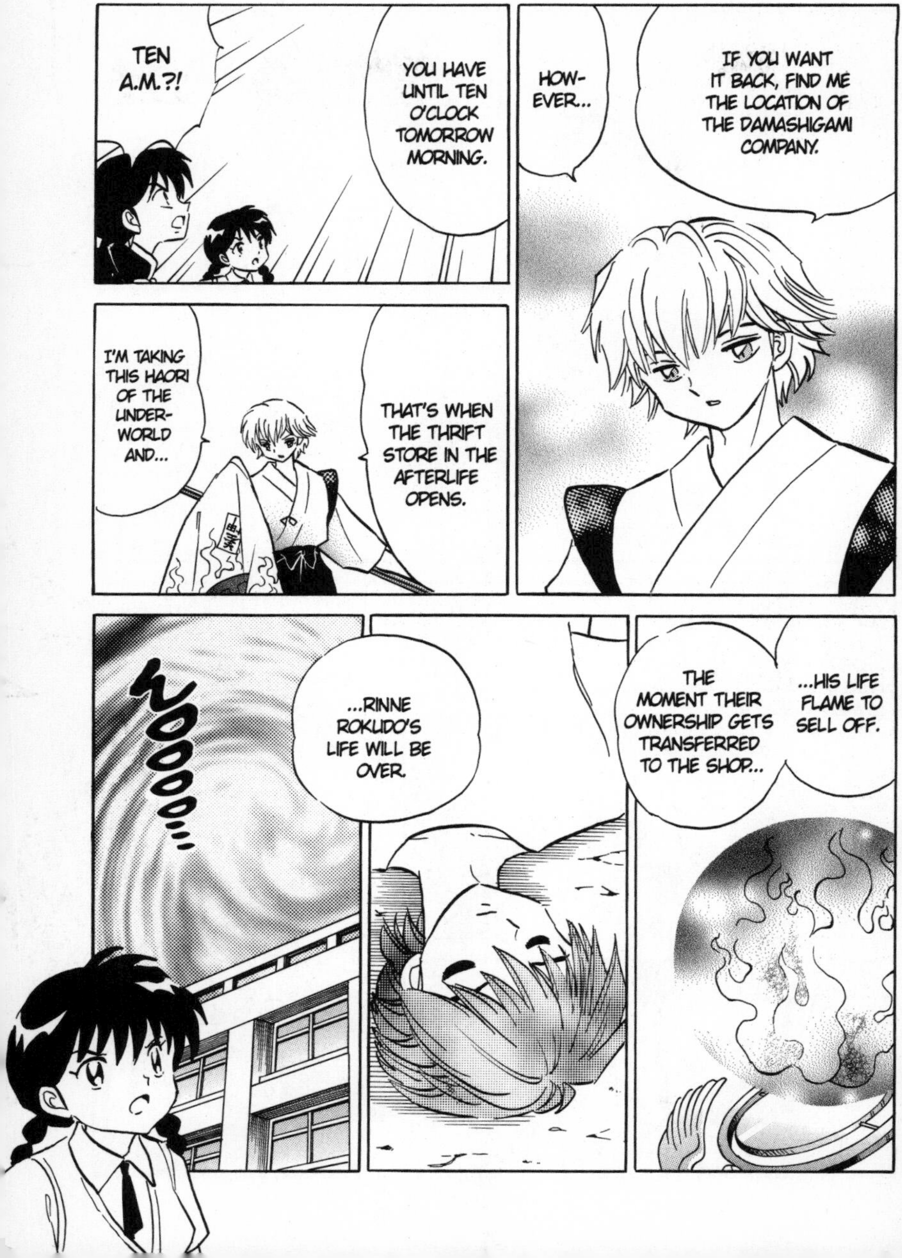
IF YOU WANT IT BACK, FIND ME THE LOCATION OF THE DAMASHIGAMI COMPANY.
HOW-EVER...
YOU HAVE UNTIL TEN O'CLOCK TOMORROW MORNING.
TEN A.M.?!
THAT'S WHEN THE THRIFT STORE IN THE AFTERLIFE OPENS.
I'M TAKING THIS HAORI OF THE UNDER-WORLD AND...
...HIS LIFE FLAME TO SELL OFF.
THE MOMENT THEIR OWNERSHIP GETS TRANSFERRED TO THE SHOP...
...RINNE ROKUDO'S LIFE WILL BE OVER.
WOOOOO...

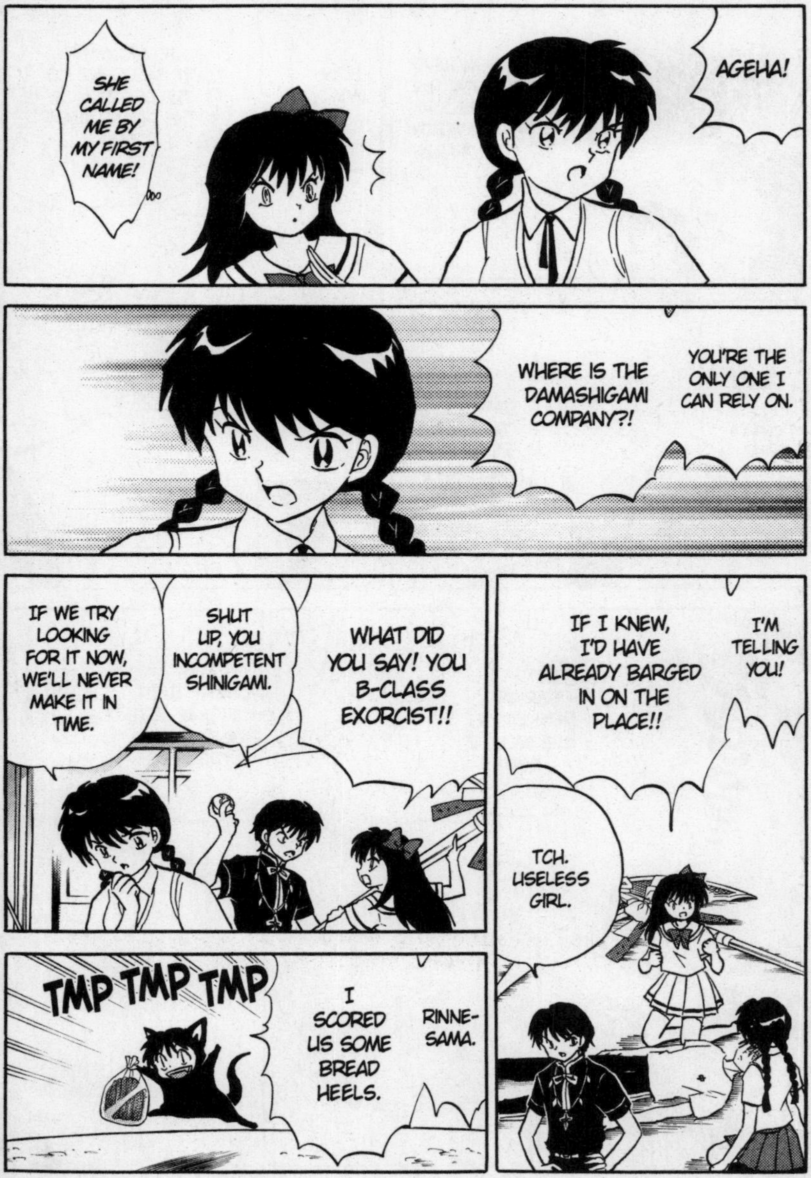
AGEHA!
SHE CALLED ME BY MY FIRST NAME!
YOU'RE THE ONLY ONE I CAN RELY ON.
WHERE IS THE DAMASHIGAMI COMPANY?!
I'M TELLING YOU!
IF I KNEW, I'D HAVE ALREADY BARGED IN ON THE PLACE!!
TCH. USELESS GIRL.
WHAT DID YOU SAY! YOU B-CLASS EXORCIST!!
SHUT UP, YOU INCOMPETENT SHINIGAMI.
IF WE TRY LOOKING FOR IT NOW, WE'LL NEVER MAKE IT IN TIME.
RINNE-SAMA.
I SCORED US SOME BREAD HEELS.
TMP TMP TMP

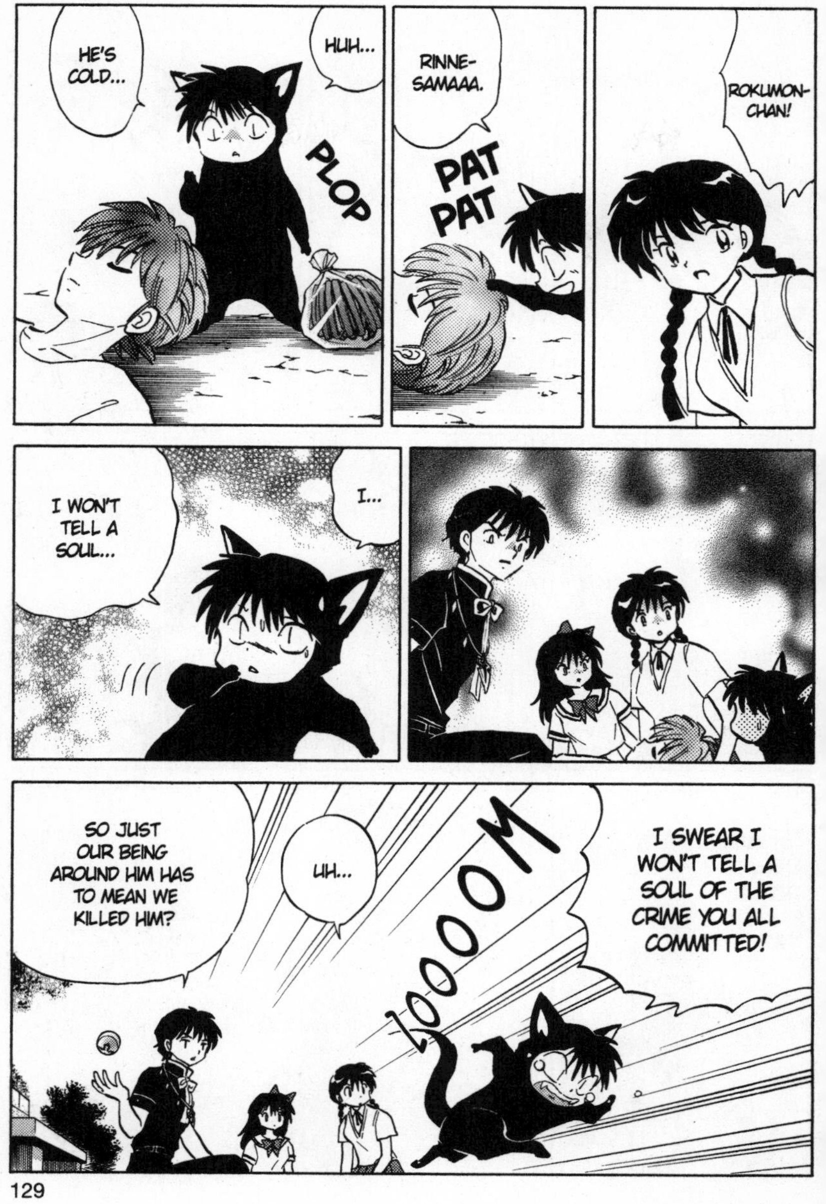
ROKUMON-CHAN!
RINNE-SAMAAA.
PAT PAT
HUH...
HE'S COLD...
PLOP
I...
I WON'T TELL A SOUL...
I SWEAR I WON'T TELL A SOUL OF THE CRIME YOU ALL COMMITTED!
ZOOOOM
UH...
SO JUST OUR BEING AROUND HIM HAS TO MEAN WE KILLED HIM?

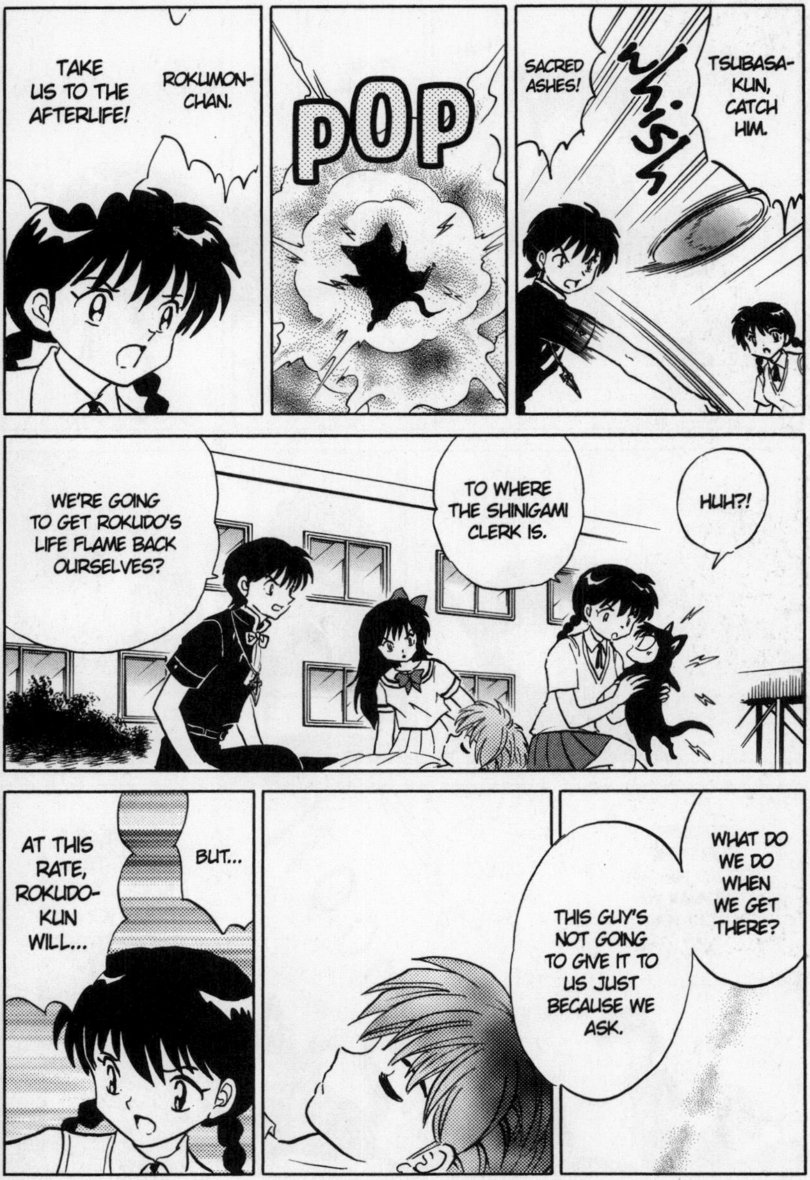
TSUBASA-KUN, CATCH HIM.
whish
SACRED ASHES!
POP
ROKUMON-CHAN.
TAKE US TO THE AFTERLIFE!
HUH?!
TO WHERE THE SHINIGAMI CLERK IS.
WE'RE GOING TO GET ROKUDO'S LIFE FLAME BACK OURSELVES?
WHAT DO WE DO WHEN WE GET THERE?
THIS GUY'S NOT GOING TO GIVE IT TO US JUST BECAUSE WE ASK.
BUT...
AT THIS RATE, ROKUDO-KUN WILL...

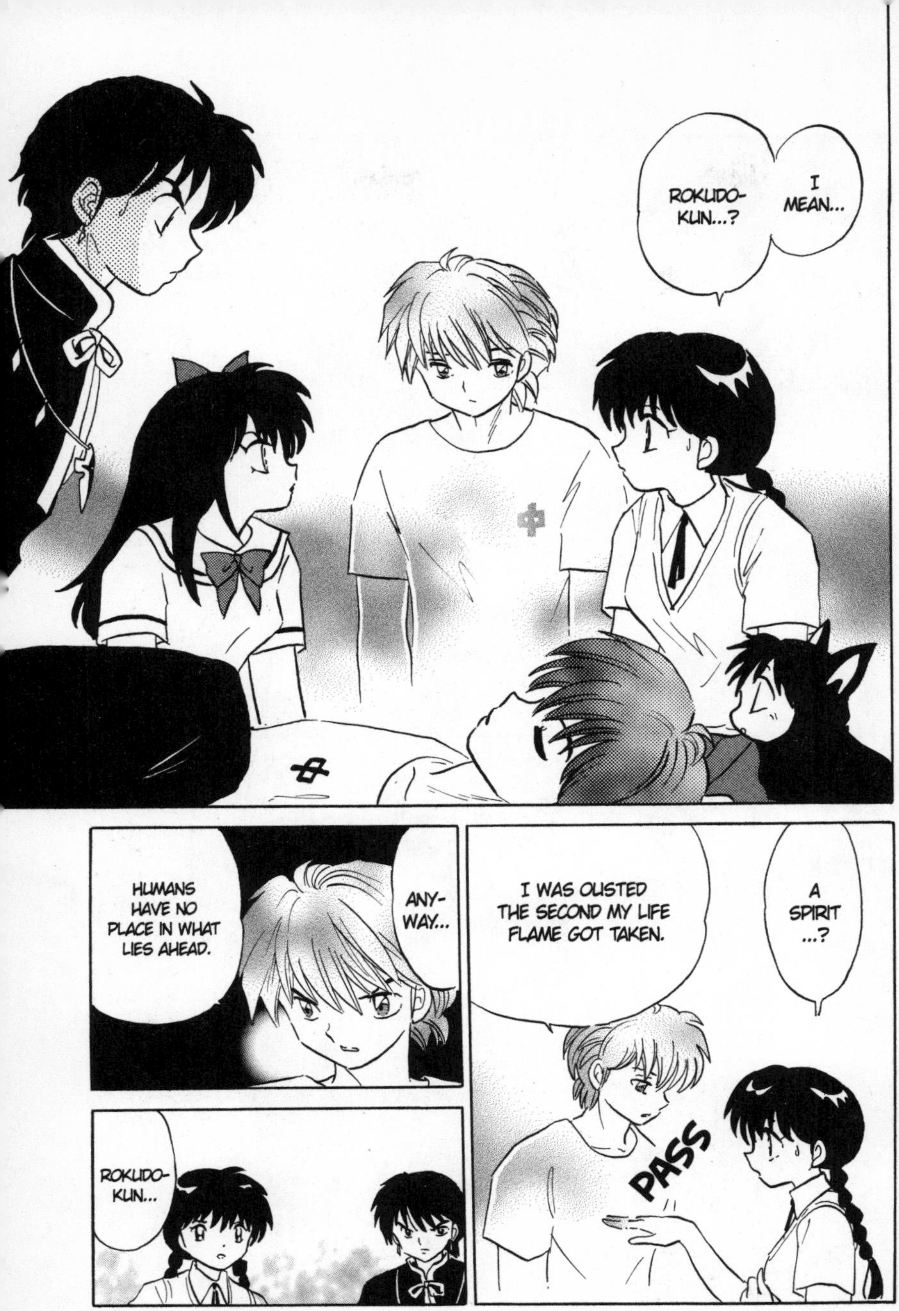
I MEAN...
ROKUDO-KUN...?
A SPIRIT ...?
I WAS OUSTED THE SECOND MY LIFE FLAME GOT TAKEN.
PASS
ANY-WAY...
HUMANS HAVE NO PLACE IN WHAT LIES AHEAD.
ROKUDO-KUN...

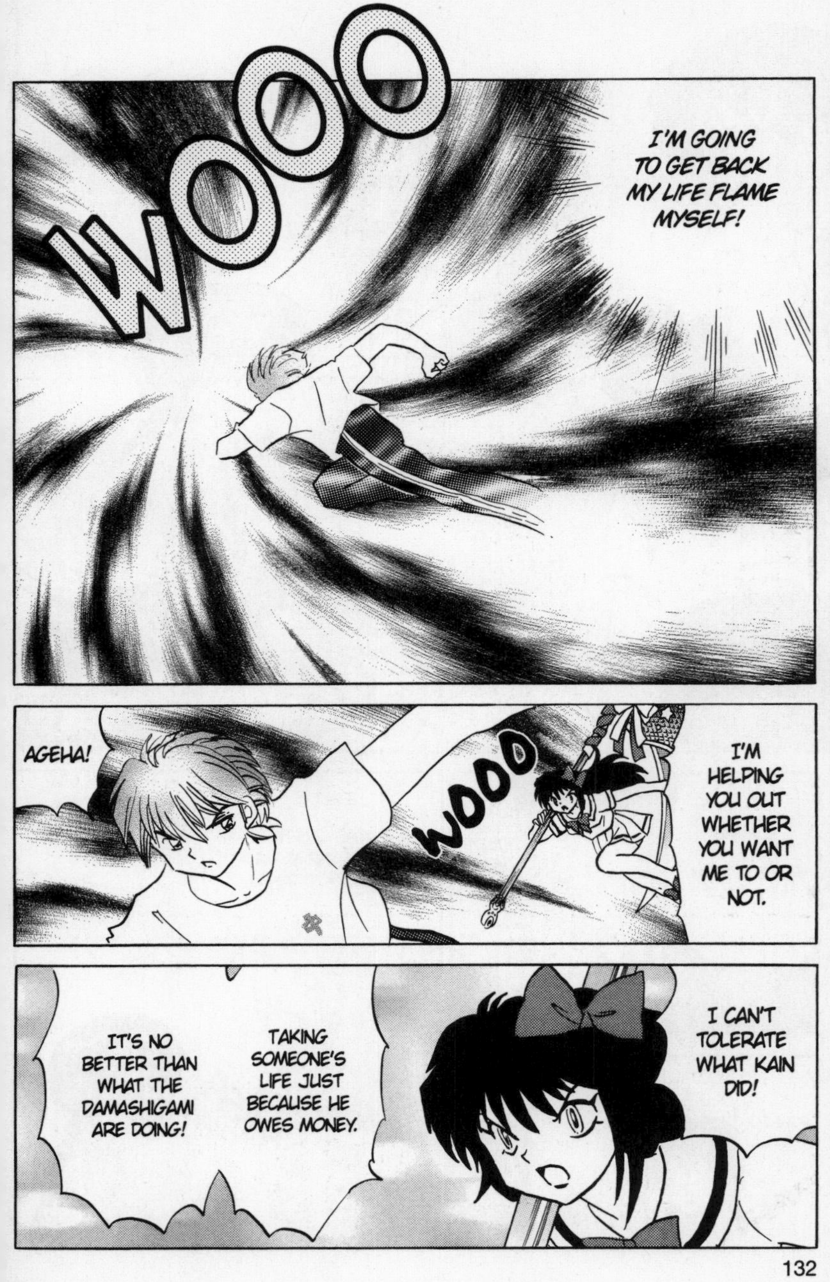
I'M GOING TO GET BACK MY LIFE FLAME MYSELF!
WOOO
I'M HELPING YOU OUT WHETHER YOU WANT ME TO OR NOT.
WOOO
AGEHA!
I CAN'T TOLERATE WHAT KAIN DID!
TAKING SOMEONE'S LIFE JUST BECAUSE HE OWES MONEY.
IT'S NO BETTER THAN WHAT THE DAMASHIGAMI ARE DOING!

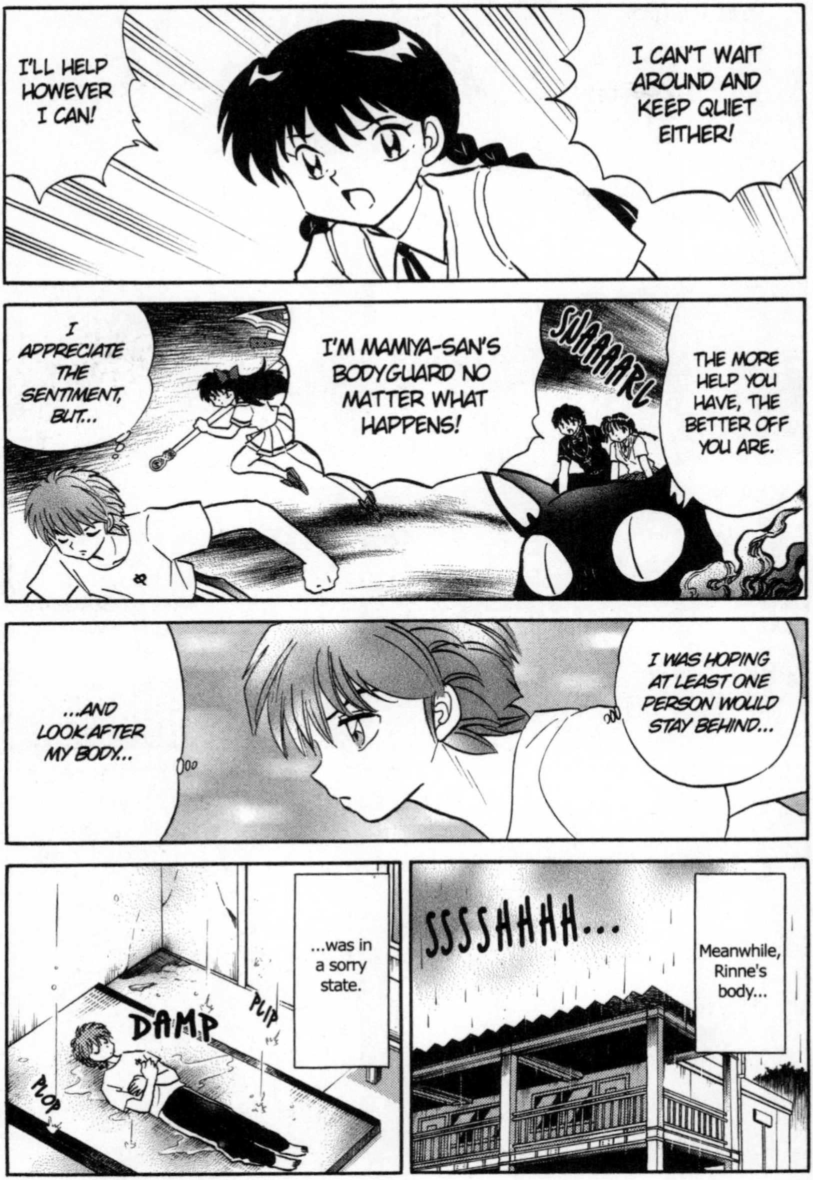
I CAN'T WAIT AROUND AND KEEP QUIET EITHER!
I'LL HELP HOWEVER I CAN!
THE MORE HELP YOU HAVE, THE BETTER OFF YOU ARE.
SWAAAARL
I'M MAMIYA-SAN'S BODYGUARD NO MATTER WHAT HAPPENS!
I APPRECIATE THE SENTIMENT, BUT...
I WAS HOPING AT LEAST ONE PERSON WOULD STAY BEHIND...
...AND LOOK AFTER MY BODY...
Meanwhile, Rinne's body...
SSSSHHHH...
...was in a sorry state.
PLIP
DAMP
PLOP

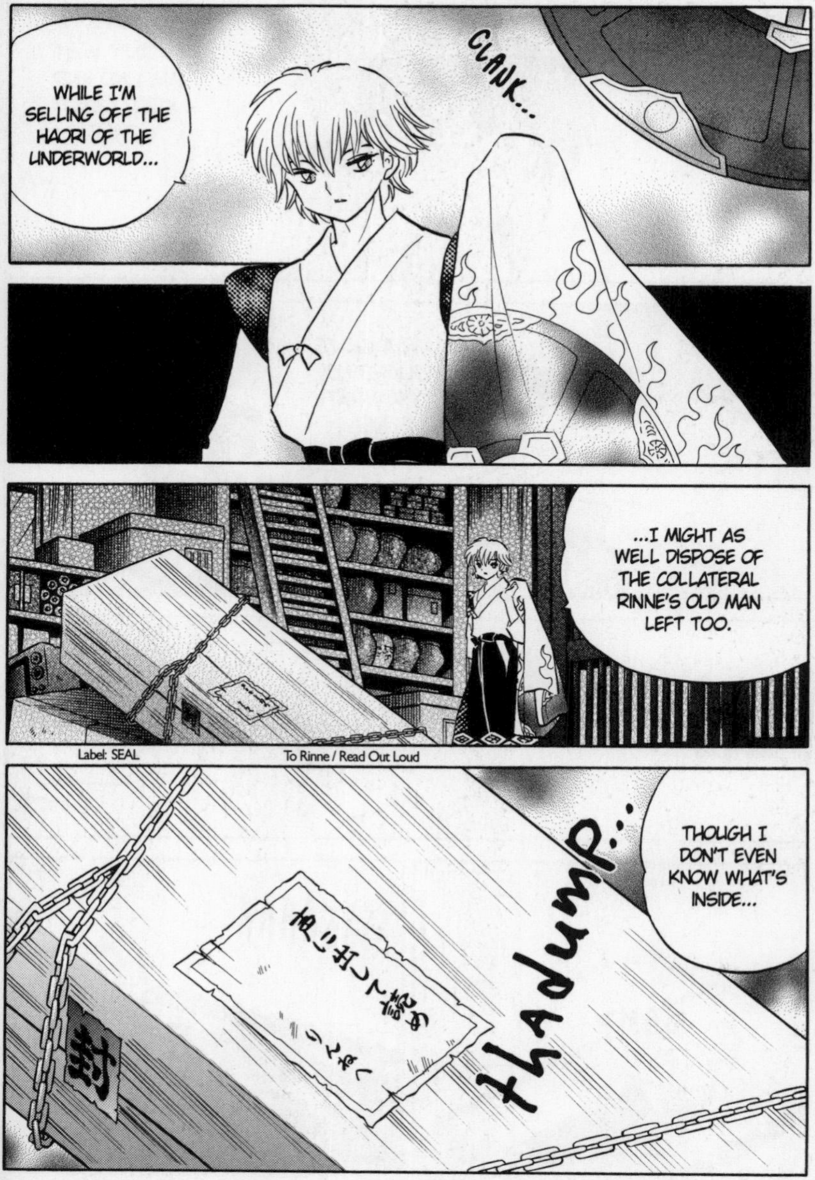
CLANK...
WHILE I'M SELLING OFF THE HAORI OF THE UNDERWORLD...
...I MIGHT AS WELL DISPOSE OF THE COLLATERAL RINNE'S OLD MAN LEFT TOO.
Label: SEAL
To Rinne / Read Out Loud
THOUGH I DON'T EVEN KNOW WHAT'S INSIDE...
THADUMP...

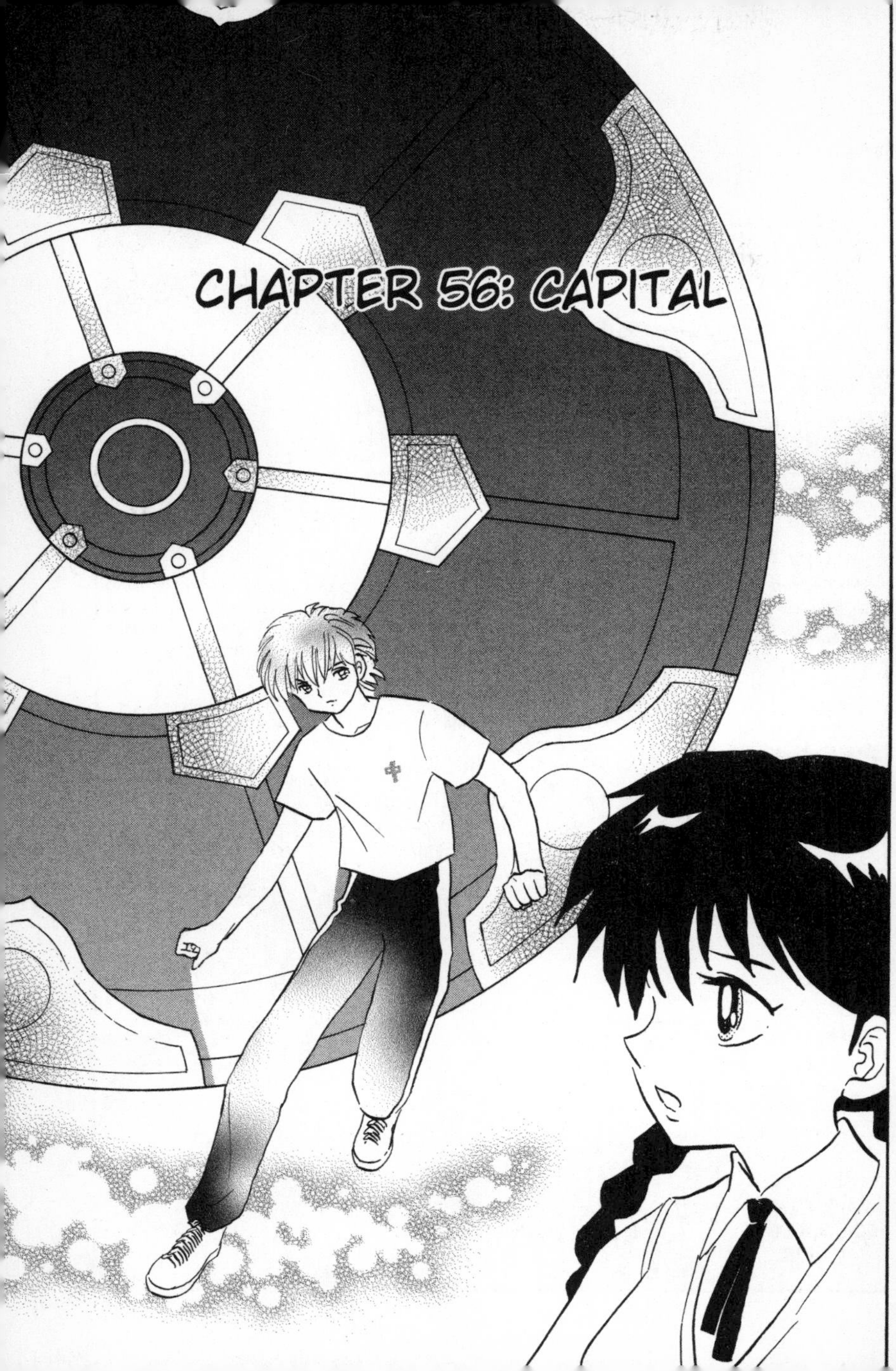
CHAPTER 56: CAPITAL

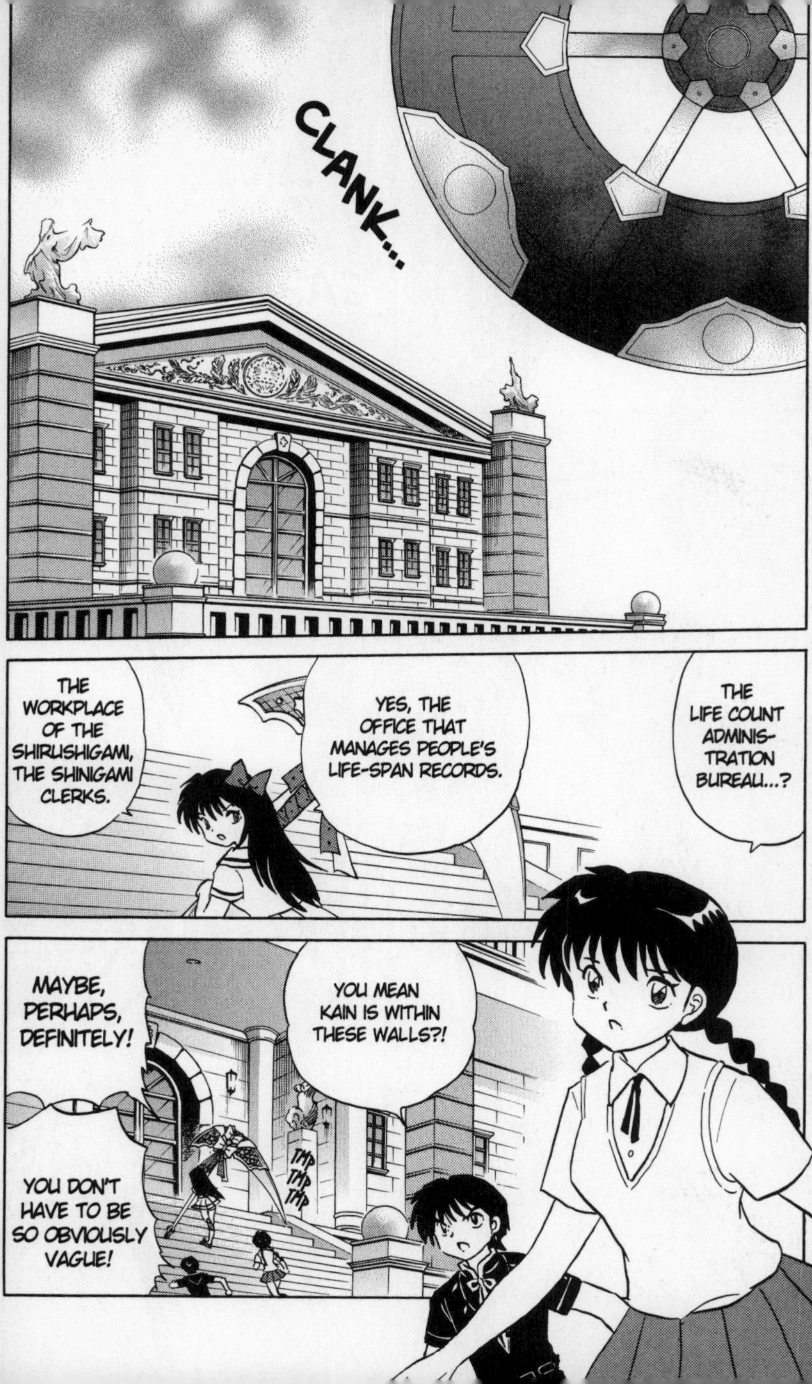
CLANK...
THE LIFE COUNT ADMINIS-TRATION BUREAU...?
YES, THE OFFICE THAT MANAGES PEOPLE'S LIFE-SPAN RECORDS.
THE WORKPLACE OF THE SHIRUSHIGAMI, THE SHINIGAMI CLERKS.
YOU MEAN KAIN IS WITHIN THESE WALLS?!
MAYBE, PERHAPS, DEFINITELY!
TMP TMP TMP
YOU DON'T HAVE TO BE SO OBVIOUSLY VAGUE!

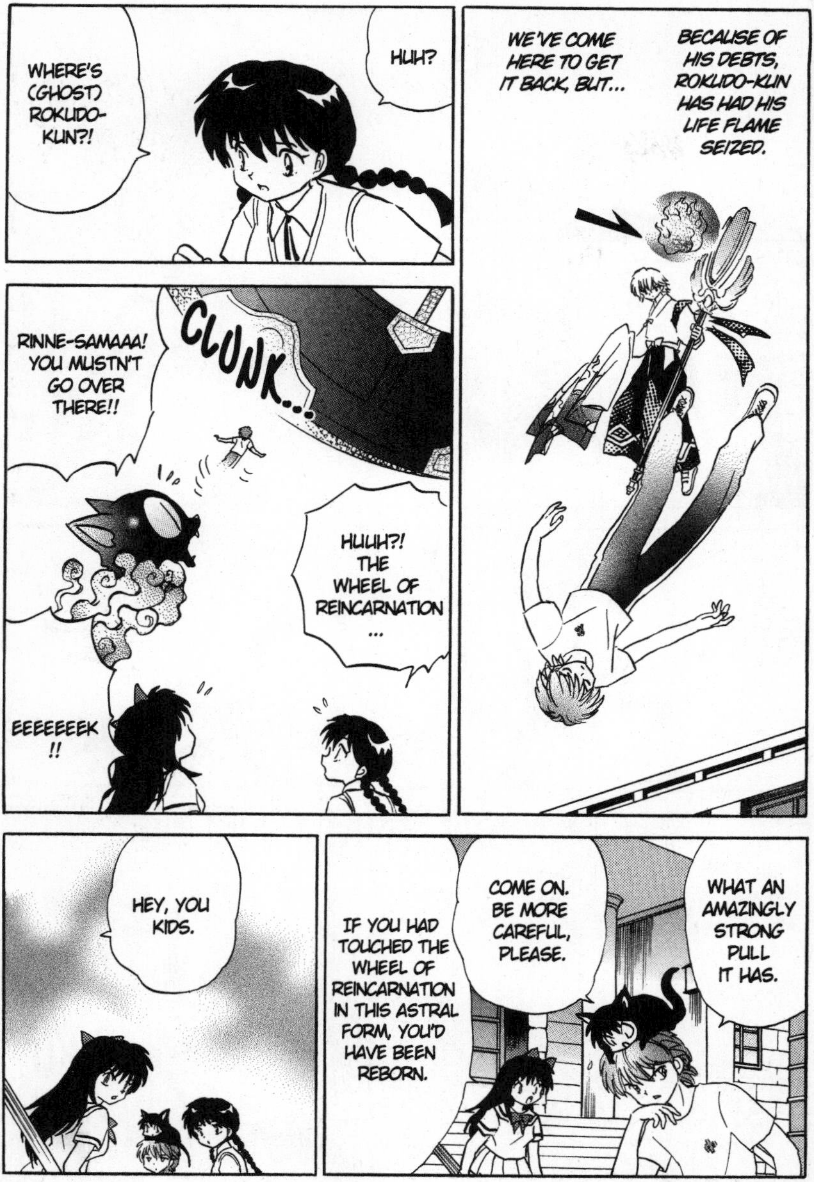
BECAUSE OF HIS DEBTS, ROKUDO-KUN HAS HAD HIS LIFE FLAME SEIZED.
WE'VE COME HERE TO GET IT BACK, BUT...
HUH?
WHERE'S (GHOST) ROKUDO-KUN?!
CLUNK...
RINNE-SAMAAA! YOU MUSTN'T GO OVER THERE!!
HUUH?! THE WHEEL OF REINCARNATION ...
EEEEEEEK !!
WHAT AN AMAZINGLY STRONG PULL IT HAS.
COME ON. BE MORE CAREFUL, PLEASE.
IF YOU HAD TOUCHED THE WHEEL OF REINCARNATION IN THIS ASTRAL FORM, YOU'D HAVE BEEN REBORN.
HEY, YOU KIDS.

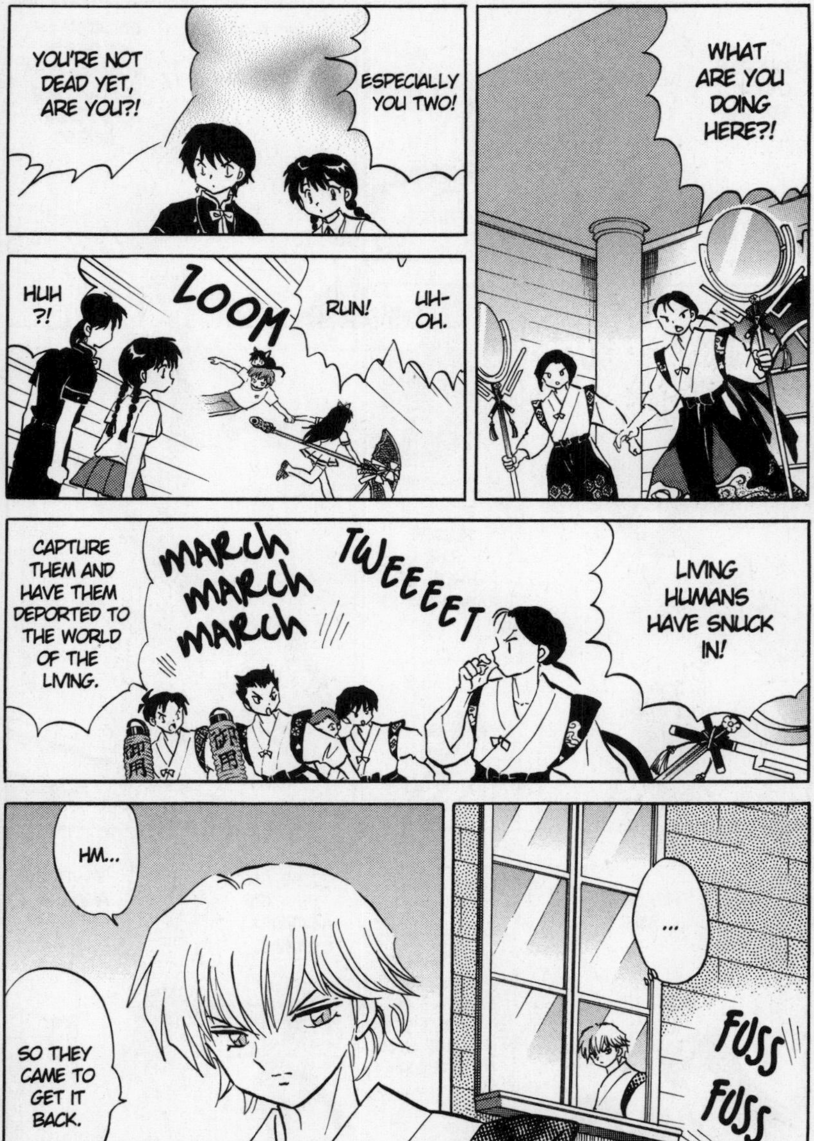
WHAT ARE YOU DOING HERE?!
ESPECIALLY YOU TWO!
YOU'RE NOT DEAD YET, ARE YOU?!
UH-OH.
RUN!
ZOOM
HUH ?!
LIVING HUMANS HAVE SNUCK IN!
TWEEEEET
MARCH MARCH MARCH
CAPTURE THEM AND HAVE THEM DEPORTED TO THE WORLD OF THE LIVING.
...
FUSS FUSS
HM...
SO THEY CAME TO GET IT BACK.

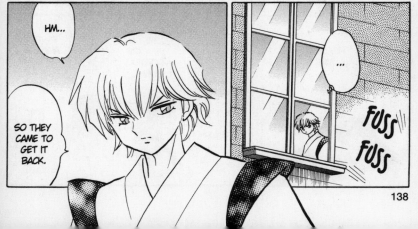

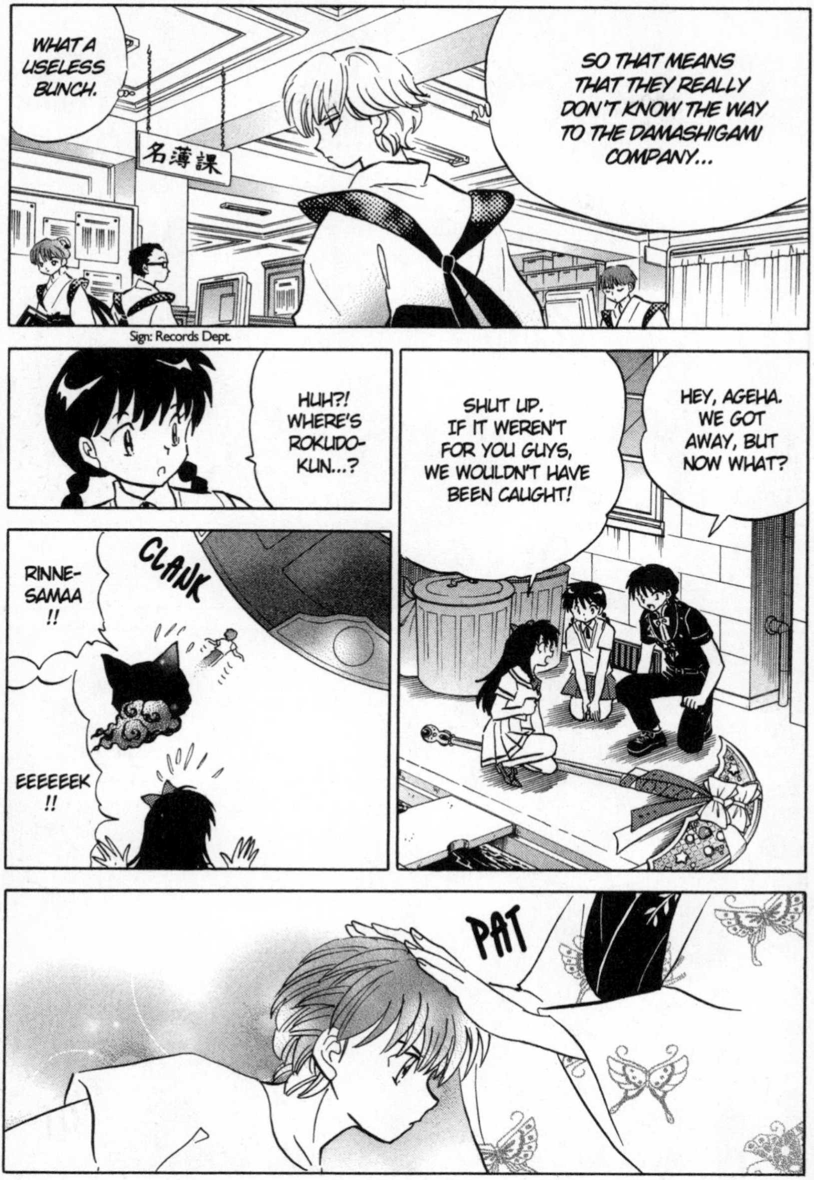
SO THAT MEANS THAT THEY REALLY DON'T KNOW THE WAY TO THE DAMASHIGAMI COMPANY...
WHAT A USELESS BUNCH.
名簿課
HEY, AGEHA. WE GOT AWAY, BUT NOW WHAT?
SHUT UP. IF IT WEREN'T FOR YOU GUYS, WE WOULDN'T HAVE BEEN CAUGHT!
HUH?! WHERE'S ROKUDO-KUN...?
CLANK
RINNE-SAMAA !!
EEEEEEK !!
PAT

Sign: Records Dept.

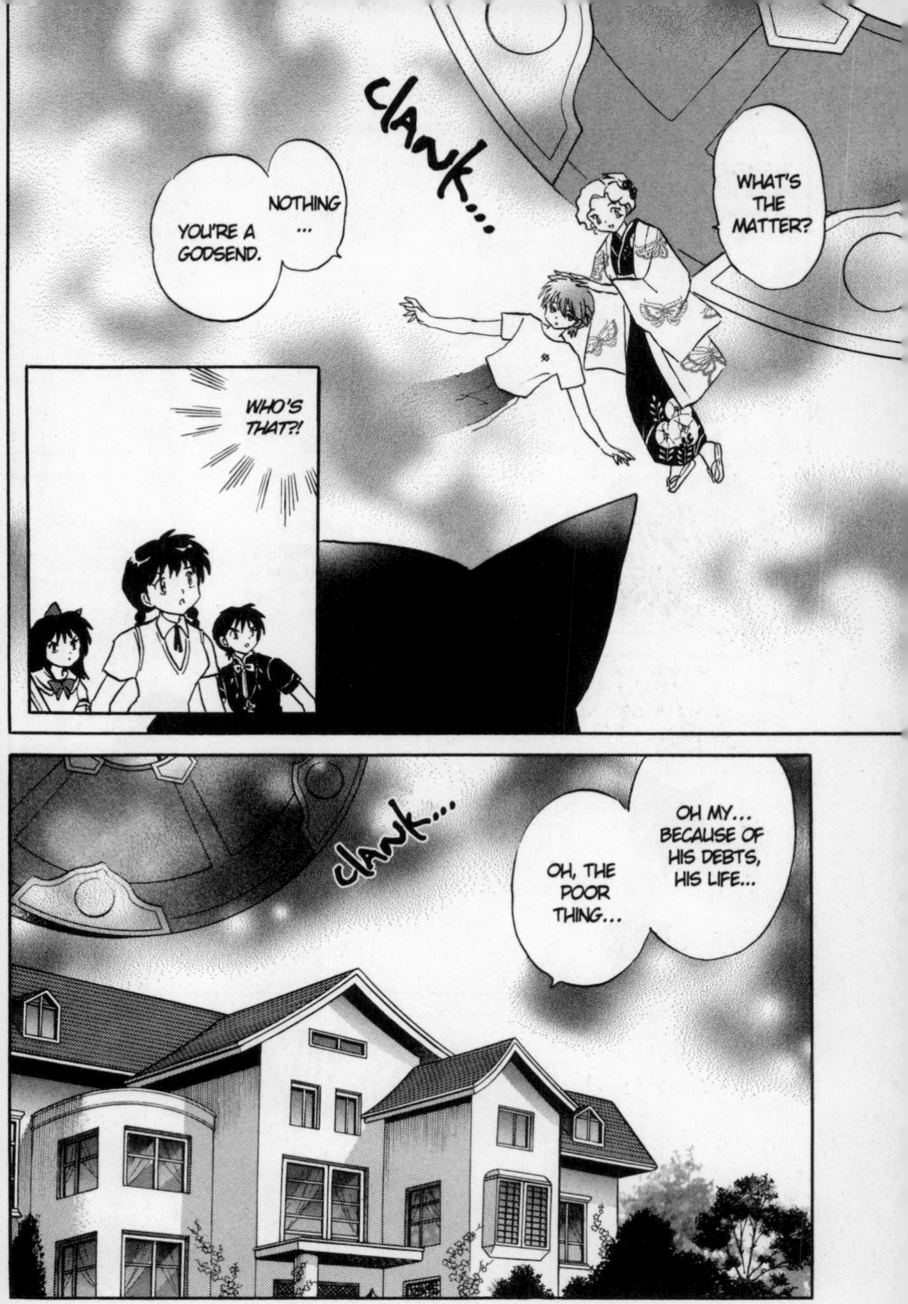
clank...
WHAT'S THE MATTER?
NOTHING ...
YOU'RE A GODSEND.
WHO'S THAT?!
clank...
OH MY... BECAUSE OF HIS DEBTS, HIS LIFE...
OH, THE POOR THING...

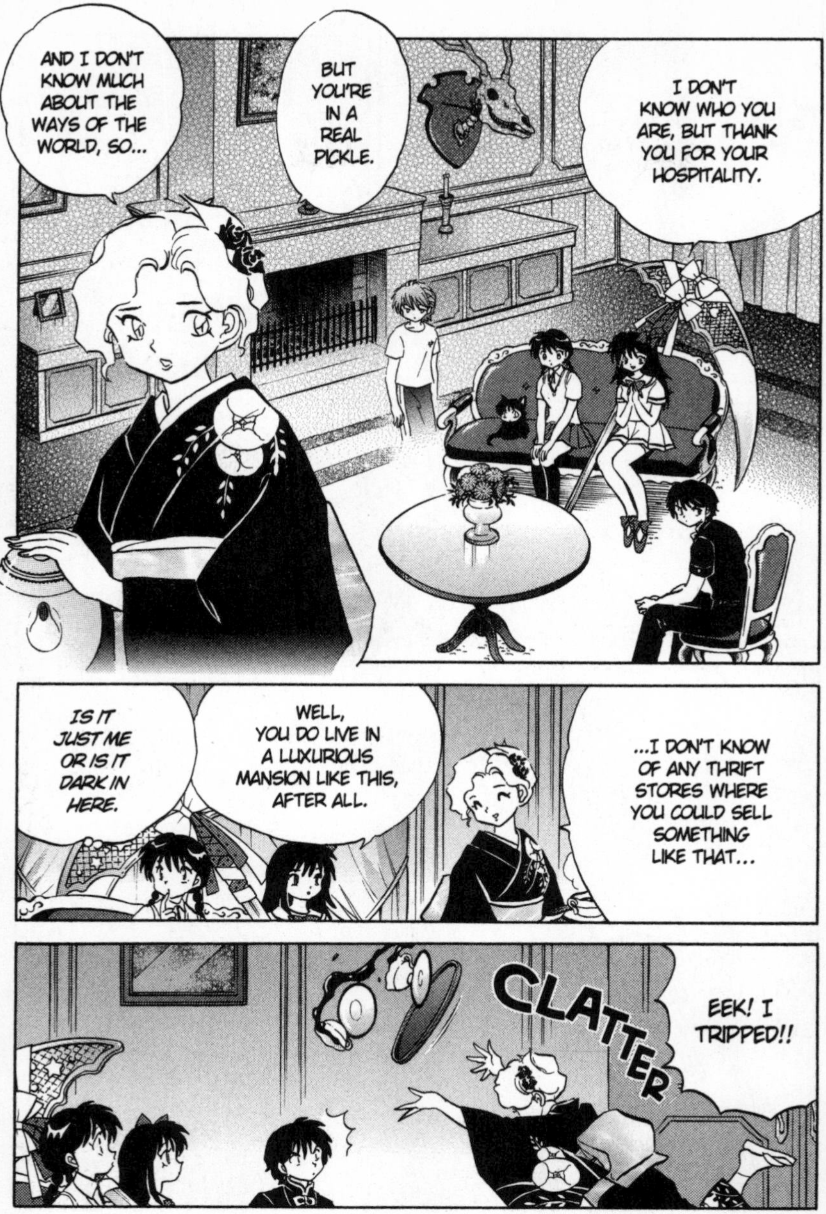
I DON'T KNOW WHO YOU ARE, BUT THANK YOU FOR YOUR HOSPITALITY.
BUT YOU'RE IN A REAL PICKLE.
AND I DON'T KNOW MUCH ABOUT THE WAYS OF THE WORLD, SO...
...I DON'T KNOW OF ANY THRIFT STORES WHERE YOU COULD SELL SOMETHING LIKE THAT...
WELL, YOU DO LIVE IN A LUXURIOUS MANSION LIKE THIS, AFTER ALL.
IS IT JUST ME OR IS IT DARK IN HERE.
EEK! I TRIPPED!!
CLATTER

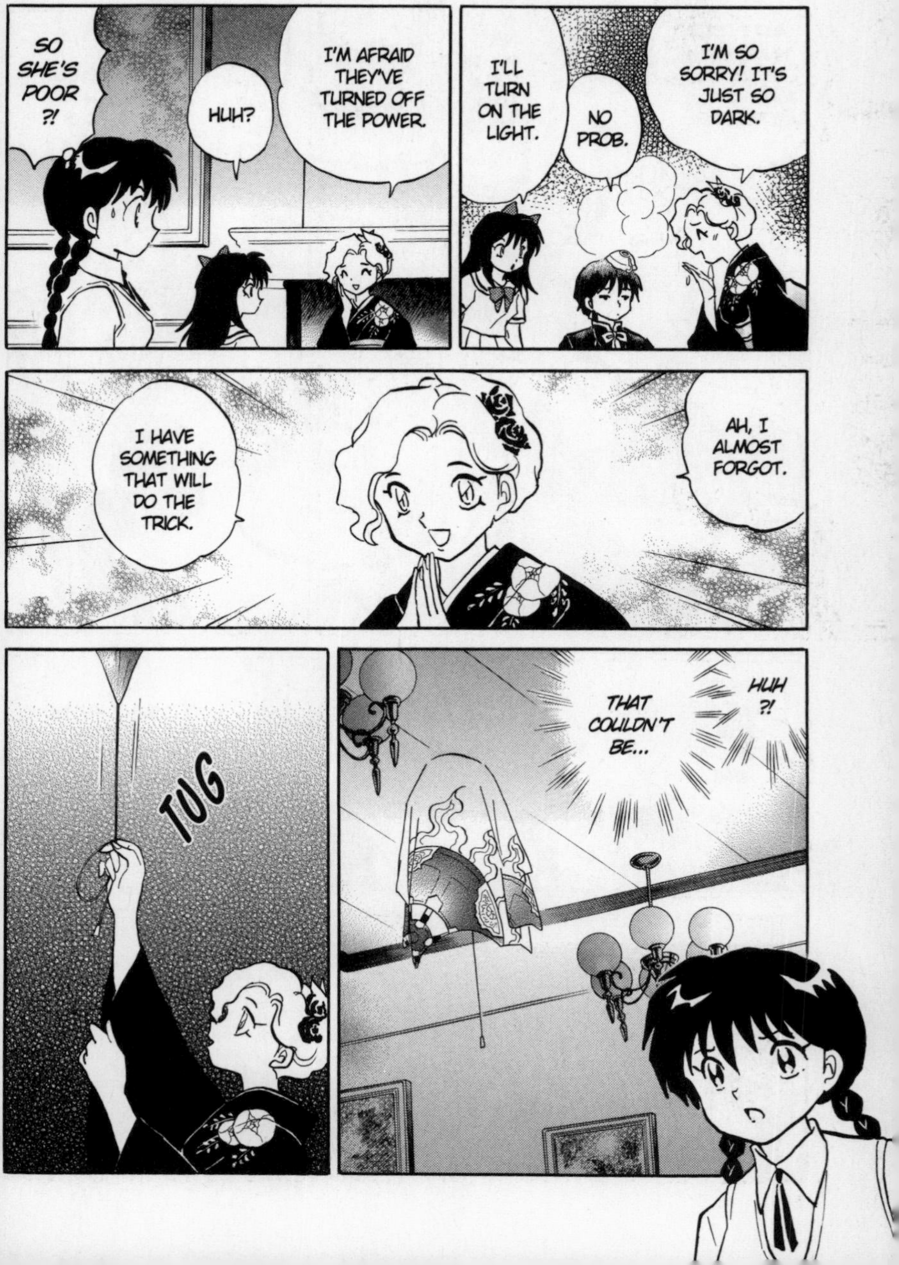
I'M SO SORRY! IT'S JUST SO DARK.
NO PROB.
I'LL TURN ON THE LIGHT.
I'M AFRAID THEY'VE TURNED OFF THE POWER.
HUH?
SO SHE'S POOR ?!
AH, I ALMOST FORGOT.
I HAVE SOMETHING THAT WILL DO THE TRICK.
HUH ?!
THAT COULDN'T BE...
TUG

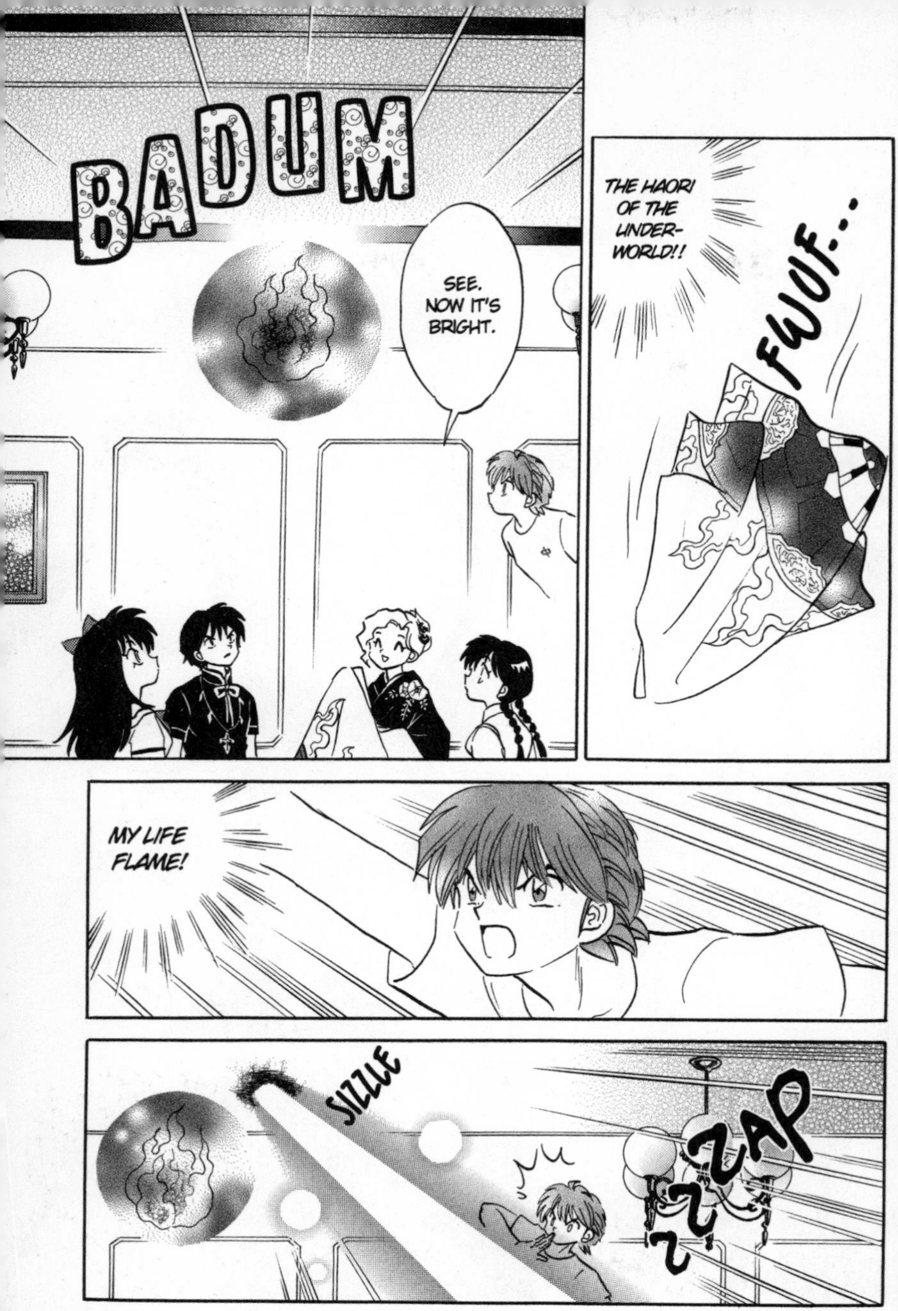

THE HAORI OF THE UNDER-WORLD!!
FWUF...
BADUM
SEE. NOW IT'S BRIGHT.
MY LIFE FLAME!
ZAP
SIZZLE

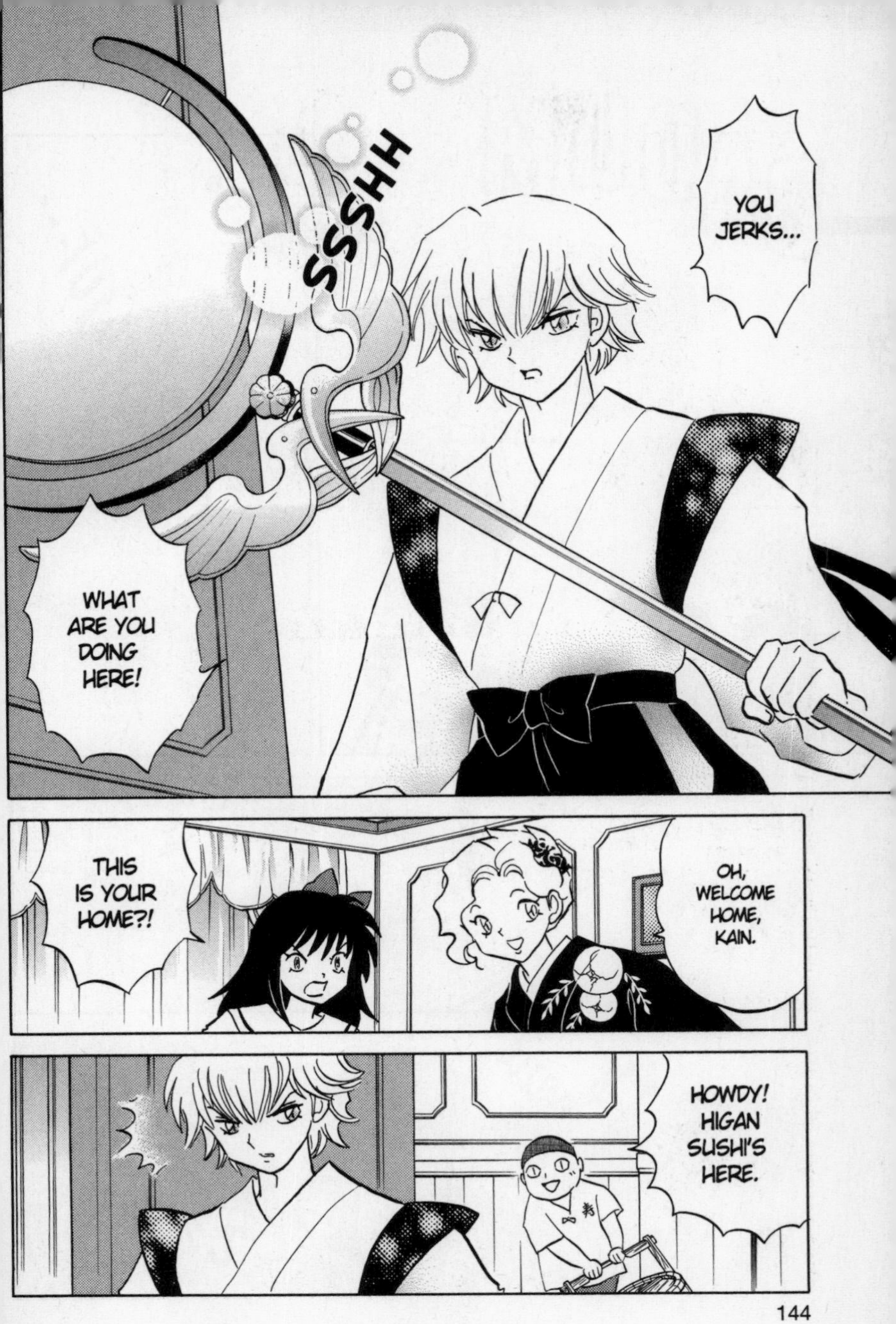
YOU JERKS...
SSSHH
WHAT ARE YOU DOING HERE!
OH, WELCOME HOME, KAIN.
THIS IS YOUR HOME?!
HOWDY! HIGAN SUSHI'S HERE.

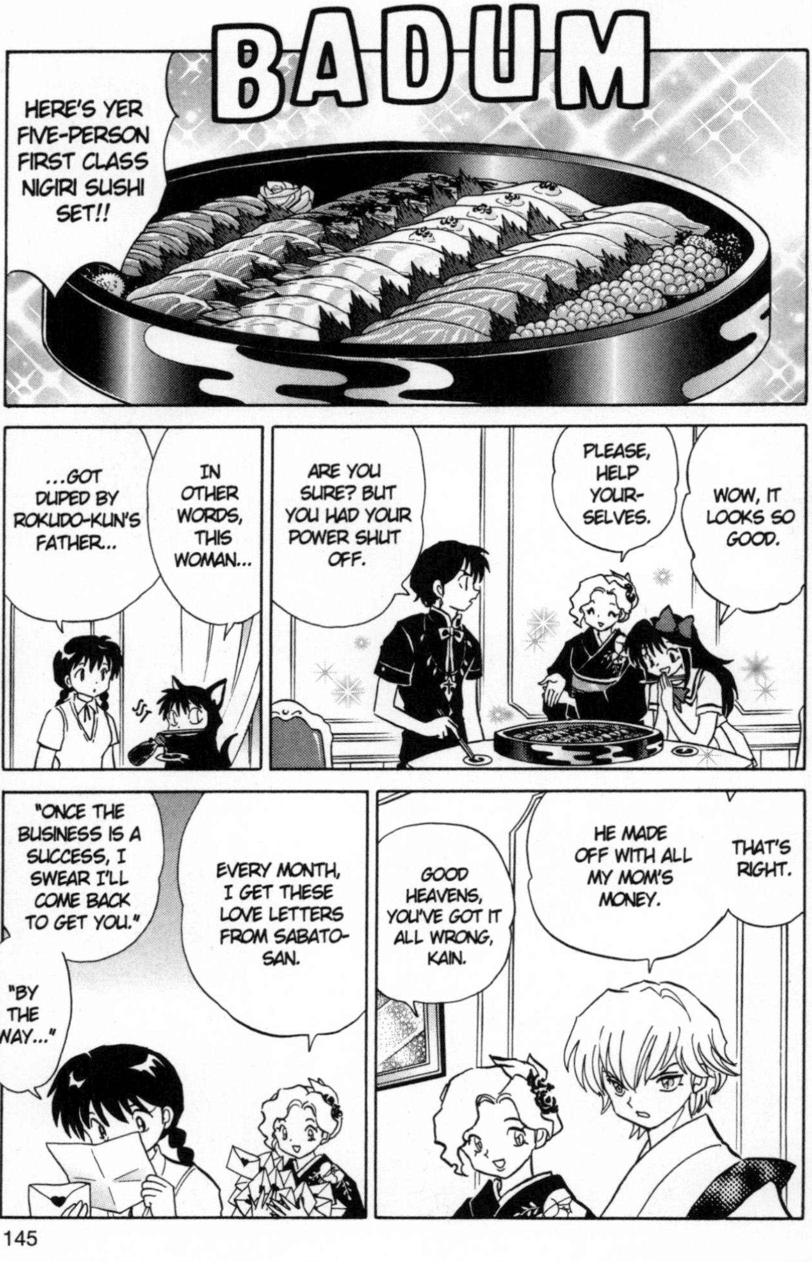
BADUM
HERE'S YER FIVE-PERSON FIRST CLASS NIGIRI SUSHI SET!!
WOW, IT LOOKS SO GOOD.
PLEASE, HELP YOUR-SELVES.
ARE YOU SURE? BUT YOU HAD YOUR POWER SHUT OFF.
IN OTHER WORDS, THIS WOMAN...
...GOT DUPED BY ROKUDO-KUN'S FATHER...
THAT'S RIGHT.
HE MADE OFF WITH ALL MY MOM'S MONEY.
GOOD HEAVENS, YOU'VE GOT IT ALL WRONG, KAIN.
EVERY MONTH, I GET THESE LOVE LETTERS FROM SABATO-SAN.
"ONCE THE BUSINESS IS A SUCCESS, I SWEAR I'LL COME BACK TO GET YOU."
"BY THE WAY..."

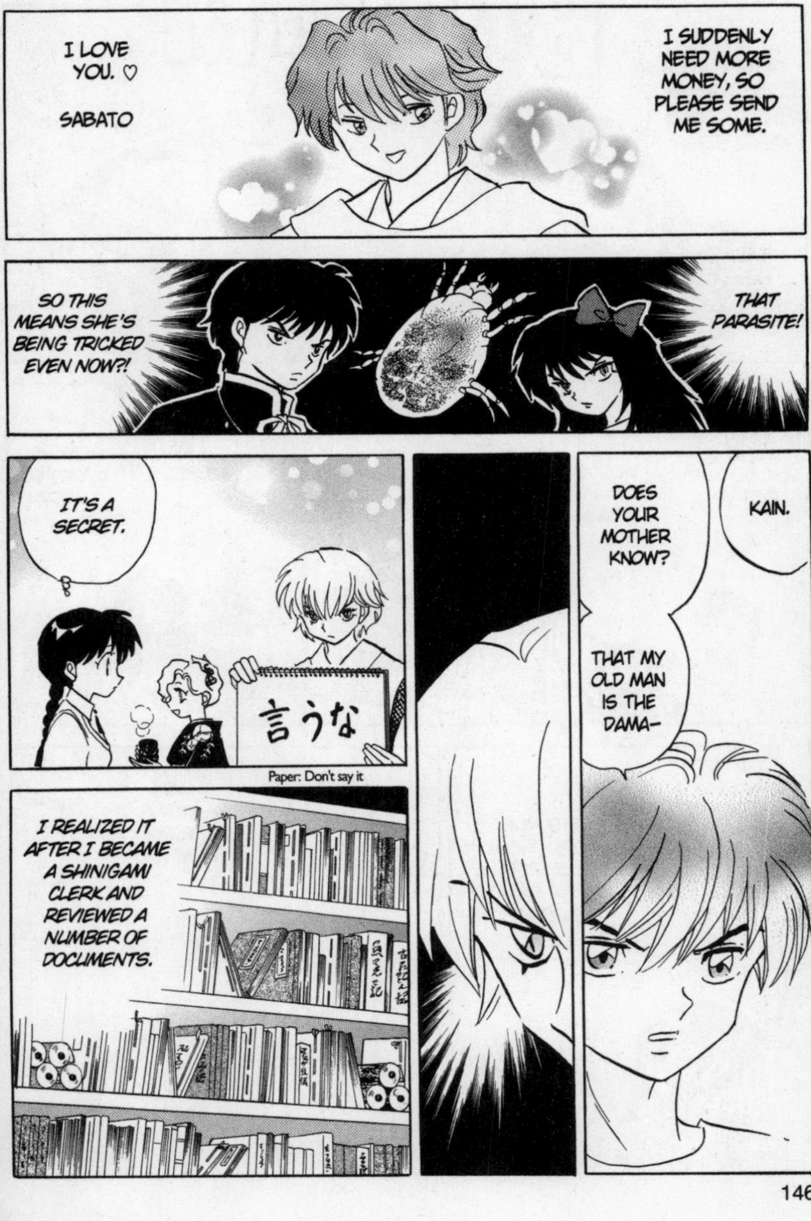
I SUDDENLY NEED MORE MONEY, SO PLEASE SEND ME SOME.
I LOVE YOU. ♡
SABATO
THAT PARASITE!
SO THIS MEANS SHE'S BEING TRICKED EVEN NOW?!
KAIN.
DOES YOUR MOTHER KNOW?
THAT MY OLD MAN IS THE DAMA-
IT'S A SECRET.
言うな
Paper: Don't say it
I REALIZED IT AFTER I BECAME A SHINIGAMI CLERK AND REVIEWED A NUMBER OF DOCUMENTS.

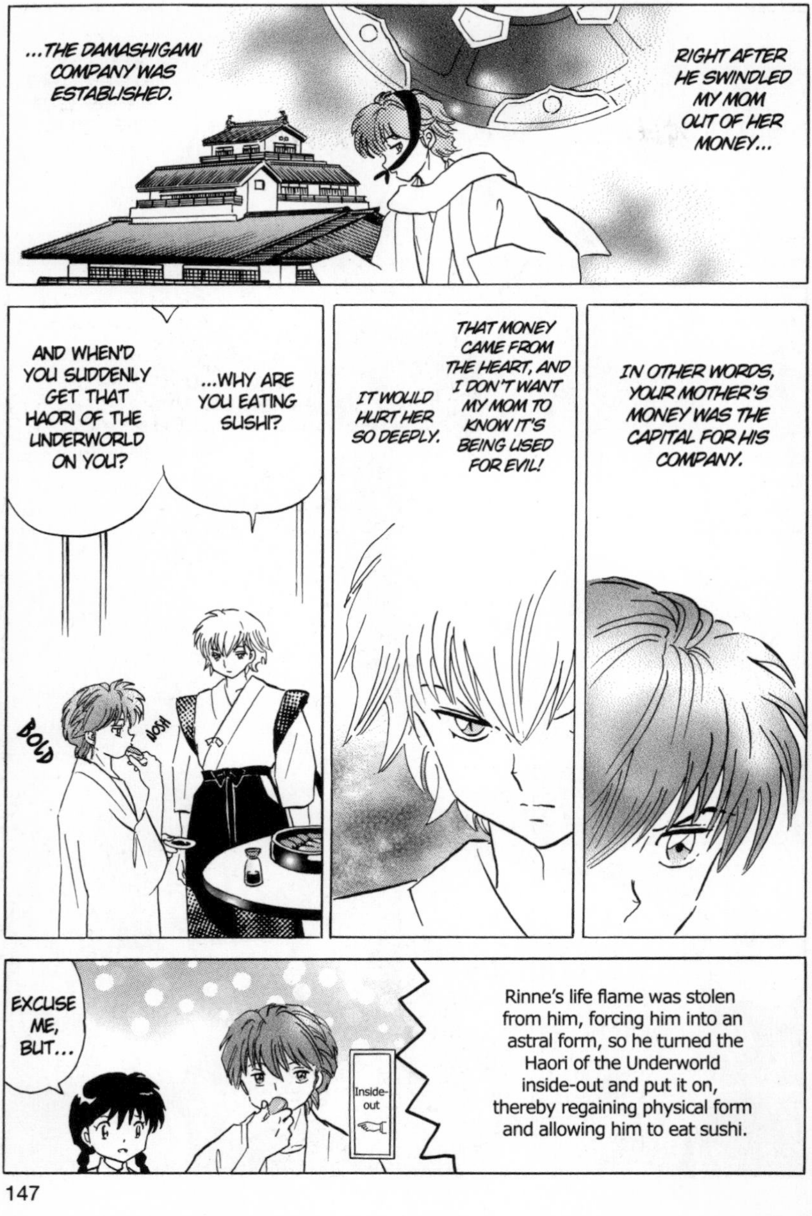
RIGHT AFTER HE SWINDLED MY MOM OUT OF HER MONEY...
...THE DAMASHIGAMI COMPANY WAS ESTABLISHED.
IN OTHER WORDS, YOUR MOTHER'S MONEY WAS THE CAPITAL FOR HIS COMPANY.
THAT MONEY CAME FROM THE HEART, AND I DON'T WANT MY MOM TO KNOW IT'S BEING USED FOR EVIL!
IT WOULD HURT HER SO DEEPLY.
...WHY ARE YOU EATING SUSHI?
AND WHEN'D YOU SUDDENLY GET THAT HAORI OF THE UNDERWORLD ON YOU?
NOSH
BOLD
Rinne's life flame was stolen from him, forcing him into an astral form, so he turned the Haori of the Underworld inside-out and put it on, thereby regaining physical form and allowing him to eat sushi.
Inside-out
EXCUSE ME, BUT...

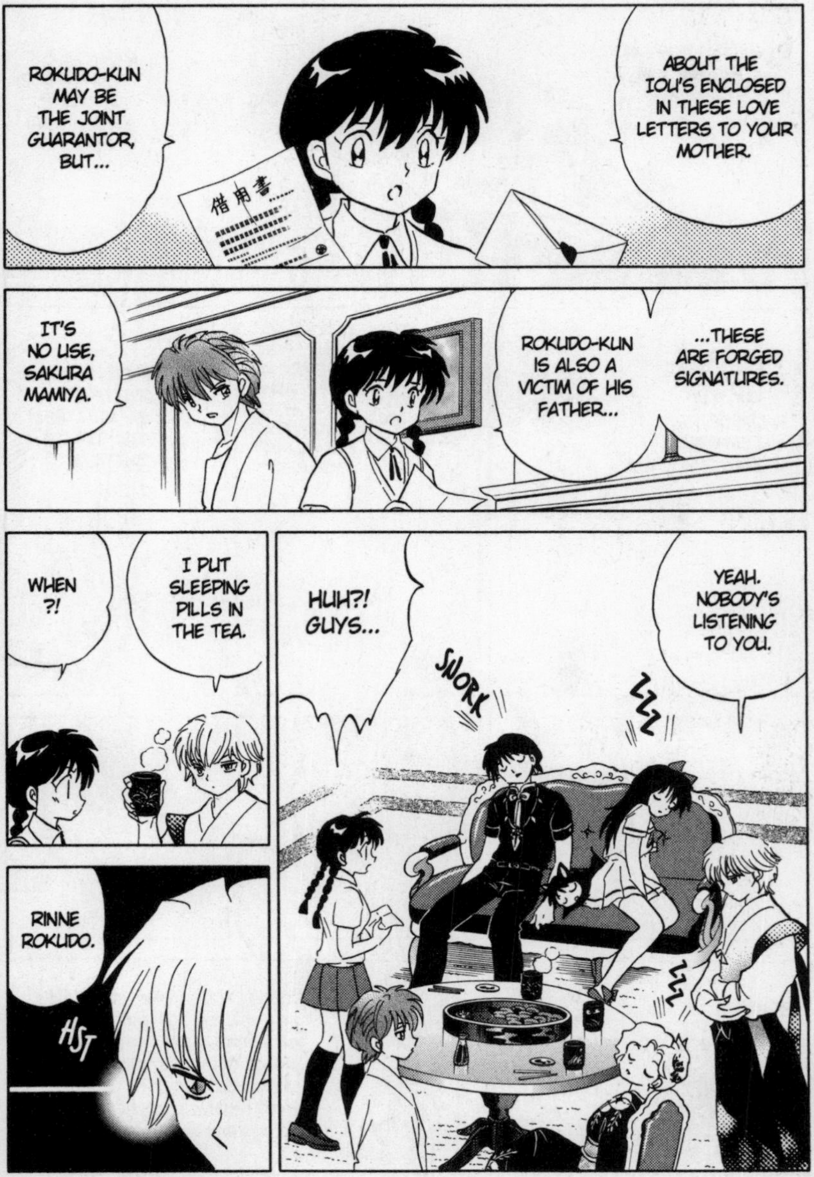
ABOUT THE IOU'S ENCLOSED IN THESE LOVE LETTERS TO YOUR MOTHER.
借用書
ROKUDO-KUN MAY BE THE JOINT GUARANTOR, BUT...
...THESE ARE FORGED SIGNATURES.
ROKUDO-KUN IS ALSO A VICTIM OF HIS FATHER...
IT'S NO USE, SAKURA MAMIYA.
YEAH. NOBODY'S LISTENING TO YOU.
ZZZ
SNORK
HUH?! GUYS...
ZZZ
I PUT SLEEPING PILLS IN THE TEA.
WHEN ?!
RINNE ROKUDO.
HST

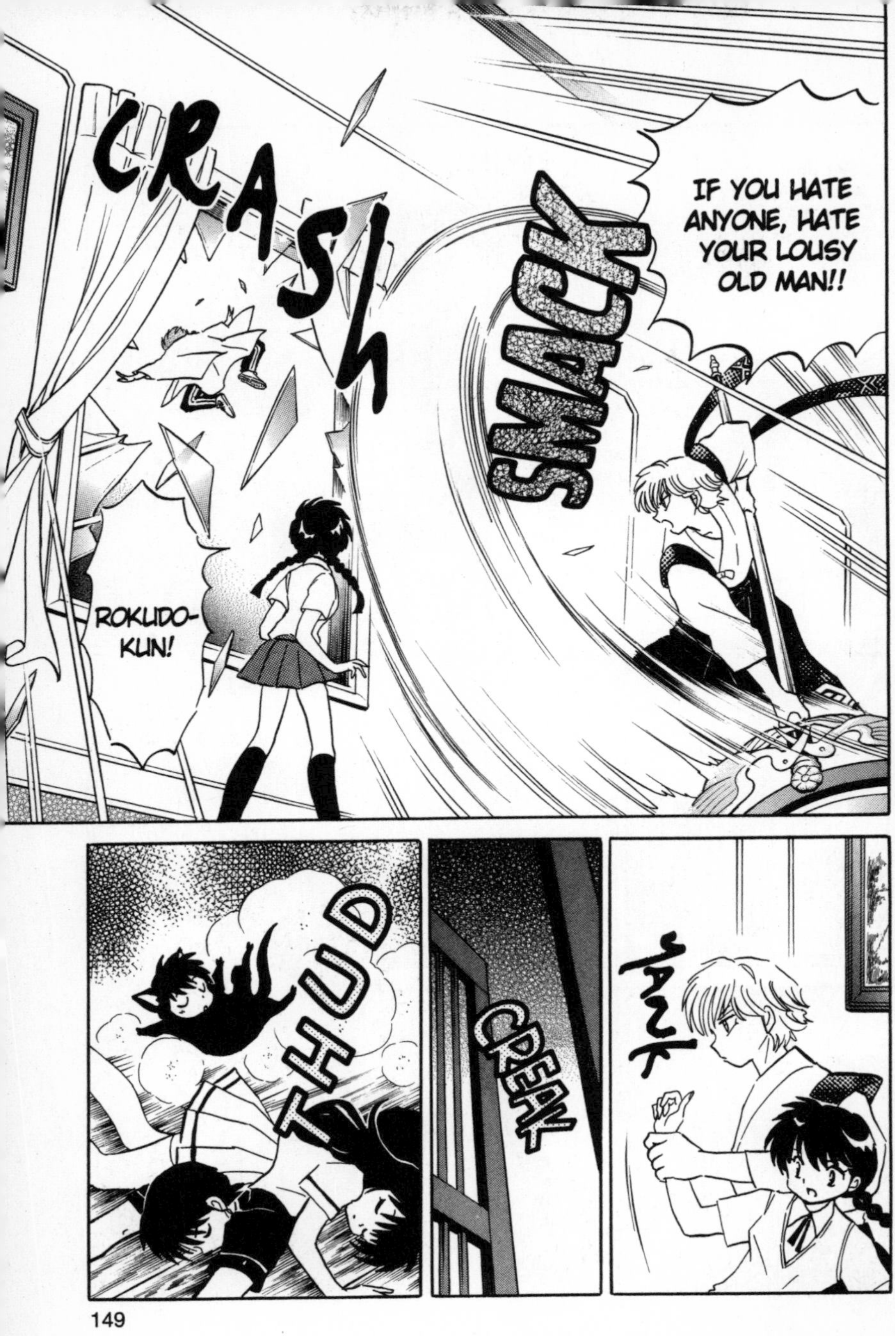
IF YOU HATE ANYONE, HATE YOUR LOUSY OLD MAN!!
SMACK
CRASH
ROKUDO-KUN!
YANK
CREAK
THUD

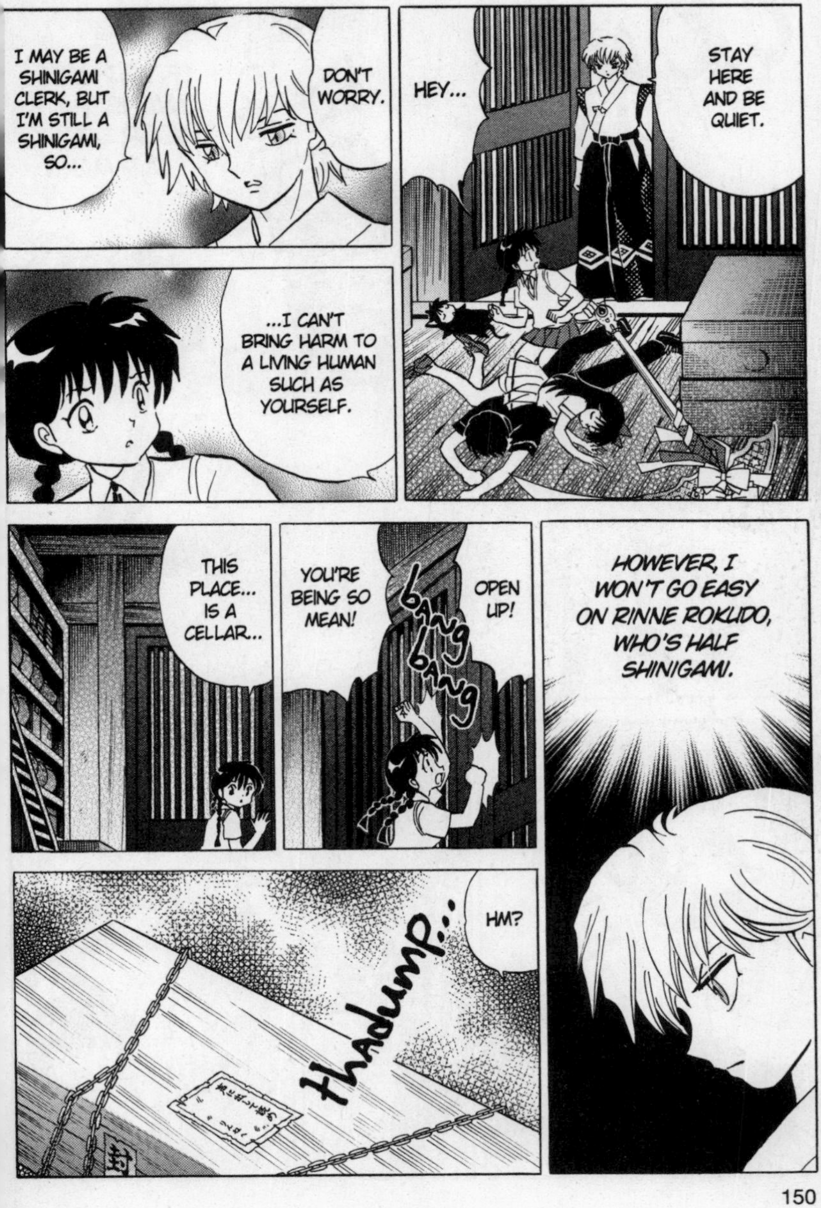
STAY HERE AND BE QUIET.
HEY...
DON'T WORRY.
I MAY BE A SHINIGAMI CLERK, BUT I'M STILL A SHINIGAMI, SO...
...I CAN'T BRING HARM TO A LIVING HUMAN SUCH AS YOURSELF.
HOWEVER, I WON'T GO EASY ON RINNE ROKUDO, WHO'S HALF SHINIGAMI.
OPEN UP!
bang bang
YOU'RE BEING SO MEAN!
THIS PLACE... IS A CELLAR...
HM?
thadump...

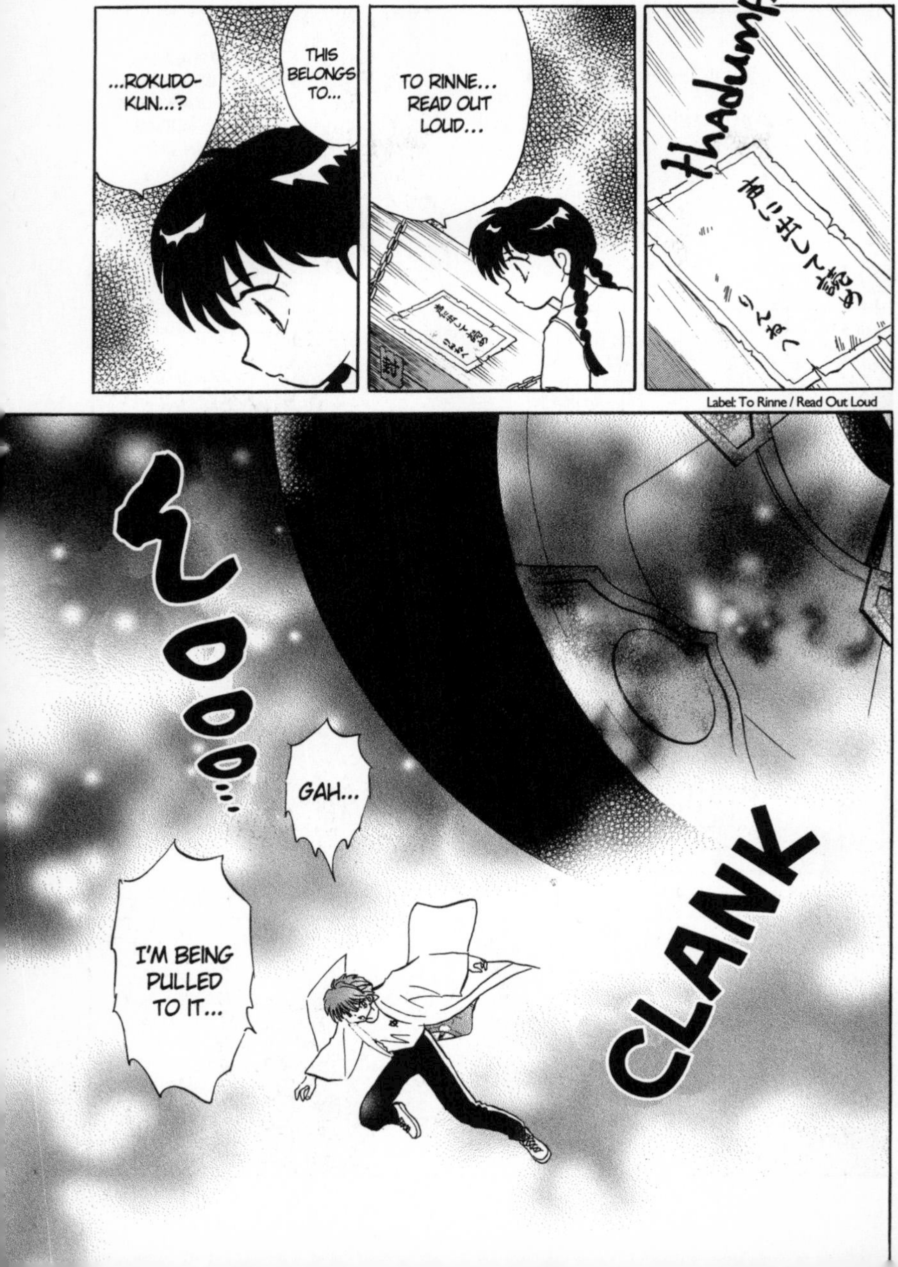
Thadump...
声に出して読め
りんねへ
TO RINNE... READ OUT LOUD...
THIS BELONGS TO...
...ROKUDO-KUN...?
Label: To Rinne / Read Out Loud
CLANK
GAH...
I'M BEING PULLED TO IT...

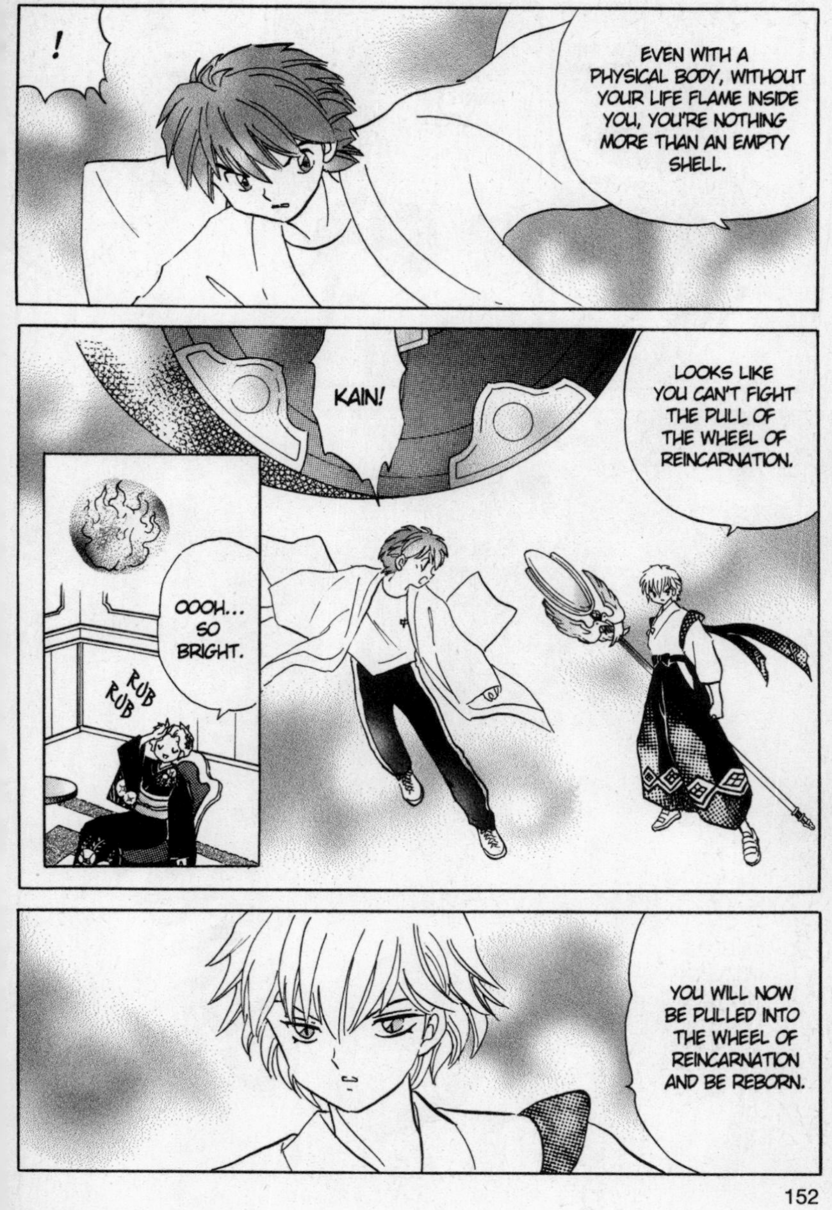
EVEN WITH A PHYSICAL BODY, WITHOUT YOUR LIFE FLAME INSIDE YOU, YOU'RE NOTHING MORE THAN AN EMPTY SHELL.
!
LOOKS LIKE YOU CAN'T FIGHT THE PULL OF THE WHEEL OF REINCARNATION.
KAIN!
OOOH... SO BRIGHT.
RUB RUB
YOU WILL NOW BE PULLED INTO THE WHEEL OF REINCARNATION AND BE REBORN.

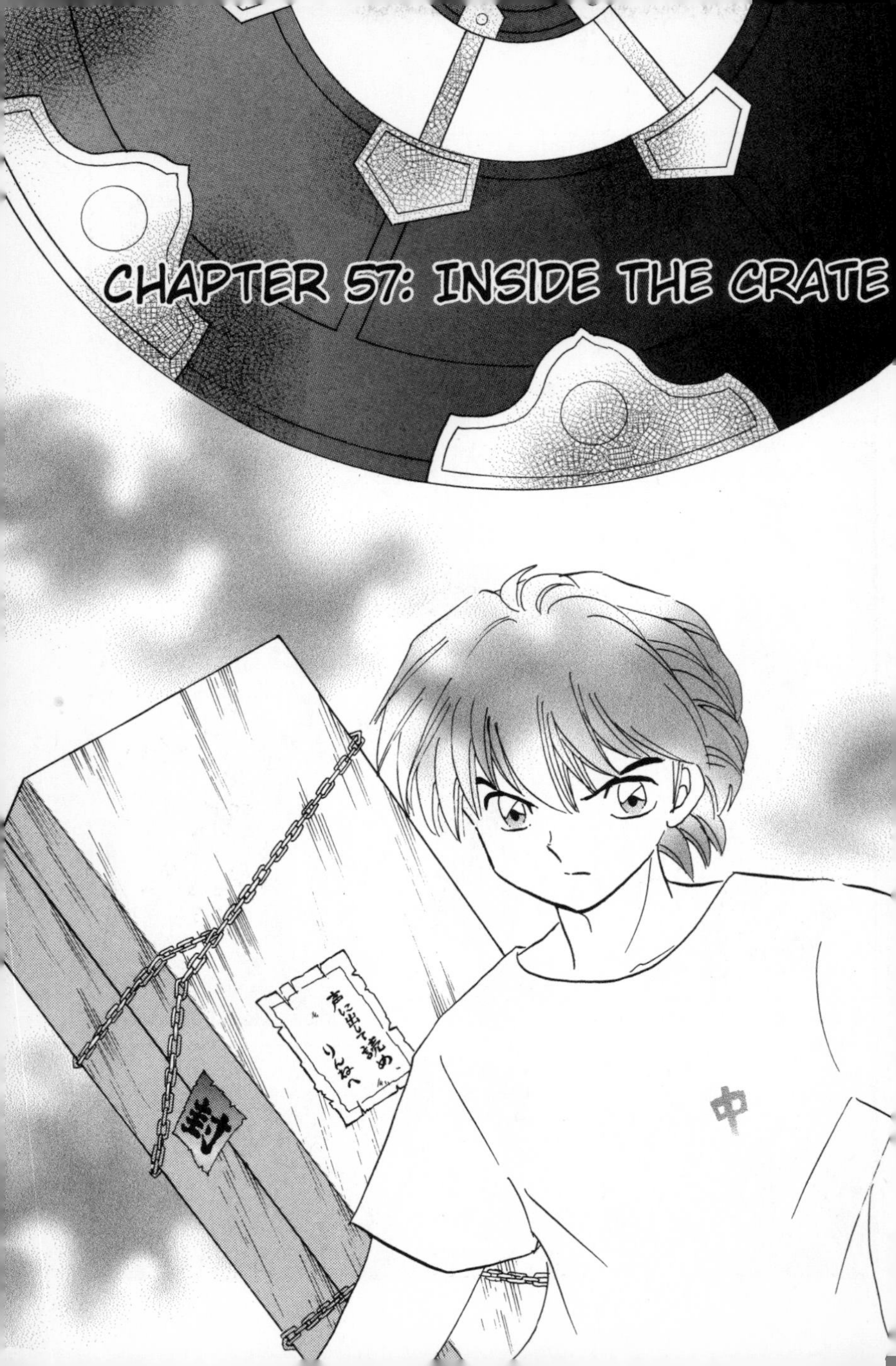
CHAPTER 57: INSIDE THE CRATE
声に出して読め、りんねへ
封
中

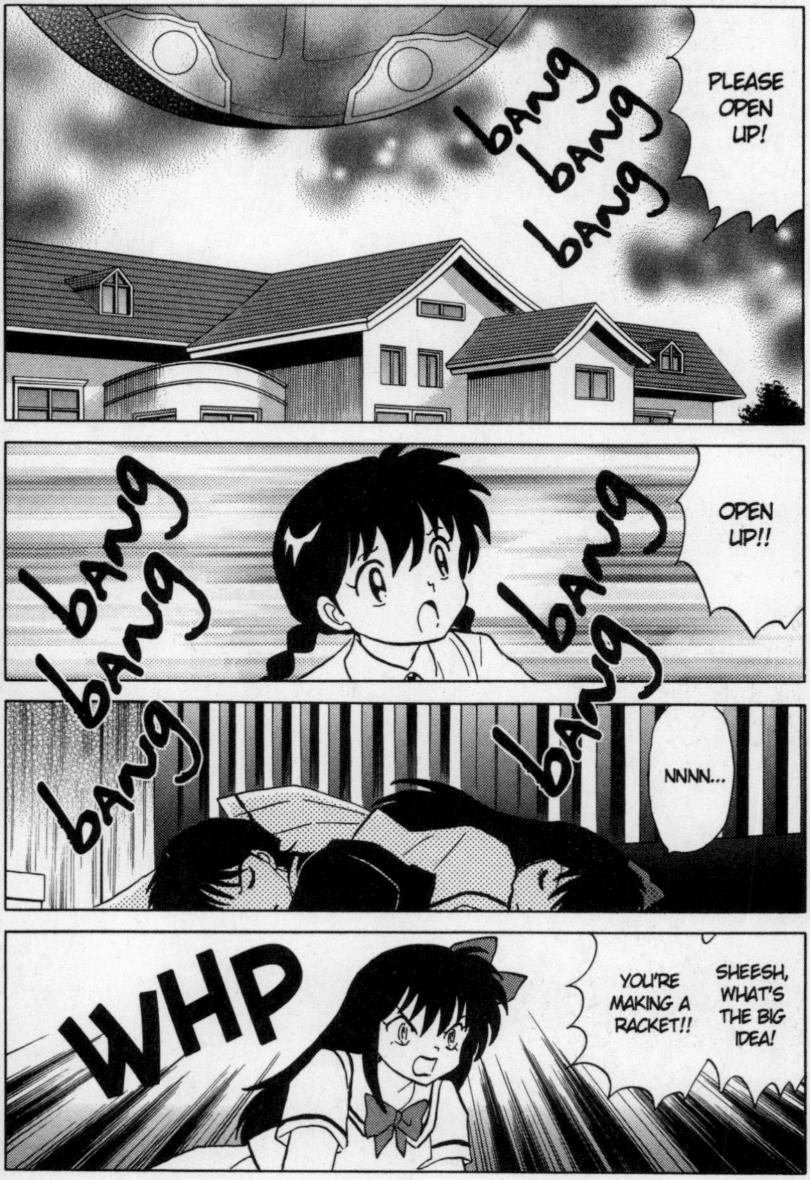
PLEASE OPEN UP!
bang bang bang
OPEN UP!!
bang bang
bang bang bang
NNNN...
SHEESH, WHAT'S THE BIG IDEA!
YOU'RE MAKING A RACKET!!
WHP

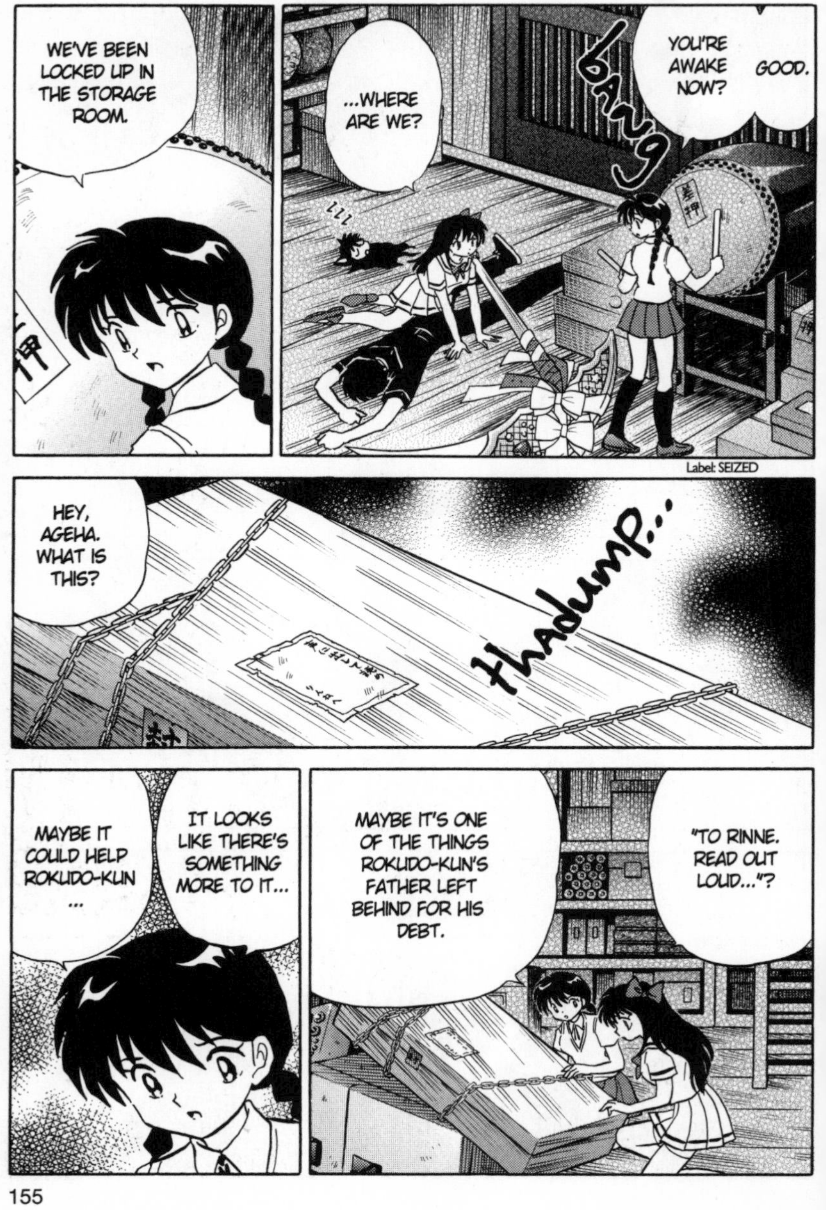
BANG
YOU'RE AWAKE NOW? GOOD.
...WHERE ARE WE?
WE'VE BEEN LOCKED UP IN THE STORAGE ROOM.
Label: SEIZED
HEY, AGEHA. WHAT IS THIS?
Thadump...
"TO RINNE. READ OUT LOUD..."?
MAYBE IT'S ONE OF THE THINGS ROKUDO-KUN'S FATHER LEFT BEHIND FOR HIS DEBT.
IT LOOKS LIKE THERE'S SOMETHING MORE TO IT...
MAYBE IT COULD HELP ROKUDO-KUN ...

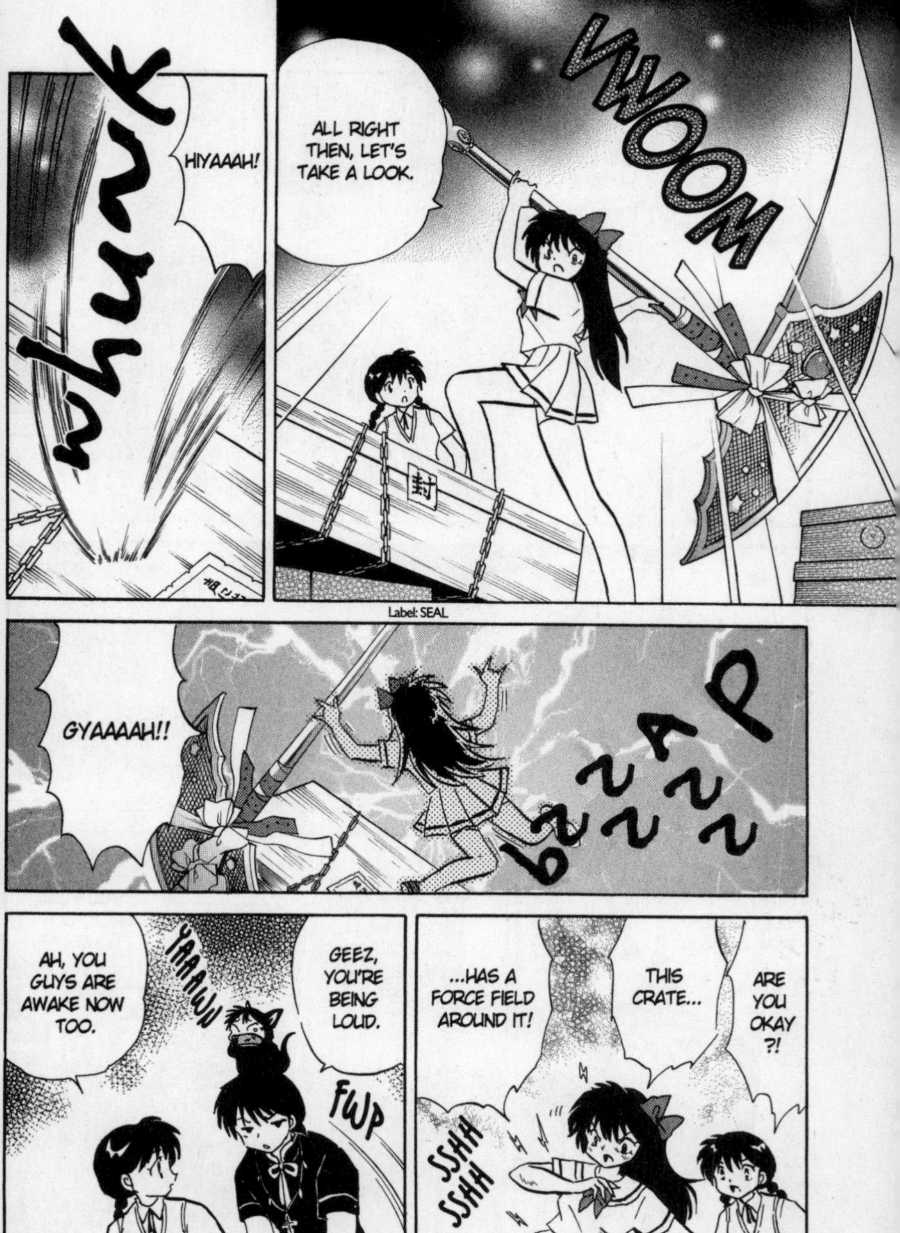
VWOOM
ALL RIGHT THEN, LET'S TAKE A LOOK.
whunk
HIYAAAH!
GYAAAAH!!
ARE YOU OKAY?!
THIS CRATE...
...HAS A FORCE FIELD AROUND IT!
SSHH SSHH
GEEZ, YOU'RE BEING LOUD.
YAAAWN
FWP
AH, YOU GUYS ARE AWAKE NOW TOO.
Label: SEAL

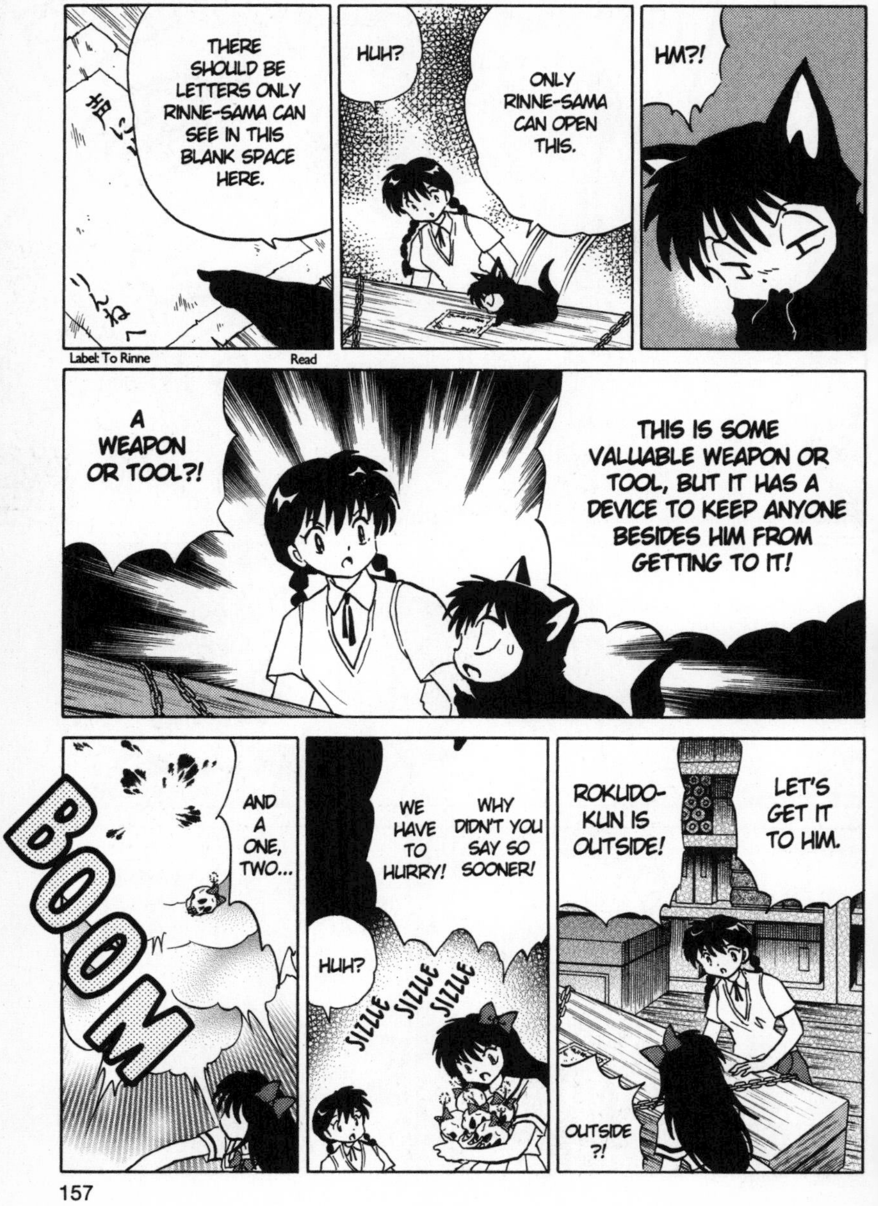
HM?!
ONLY RINNE-SAMA CAN OPEN THIS.
HUH?
Read
THERE SHOULD BE LETTERS ONLY RINNE-SAMA CAN SEE IN THIS BLANK SPACE HERE.
Label: To Rinne
THIS IS SOME VALUABLE WEAPON OR TOOL, BUT IT HAS A DEVICE TO KEEP ANYONE BESIDES HIM FROM GETTING TO IT!
A WEAPON OR TOOL?!
LET'S GET IT TO HIM.
ROKUDO-KUN IS OUTSIDE!
OUTSIDE ?!
WHY DIDN'T YOU SAY SO SOONER!
WE HAVE TO HURRY!
HUH?
SIZZLE SIZZLE SIZZLE
AND A ONE, TWO...
BOOM

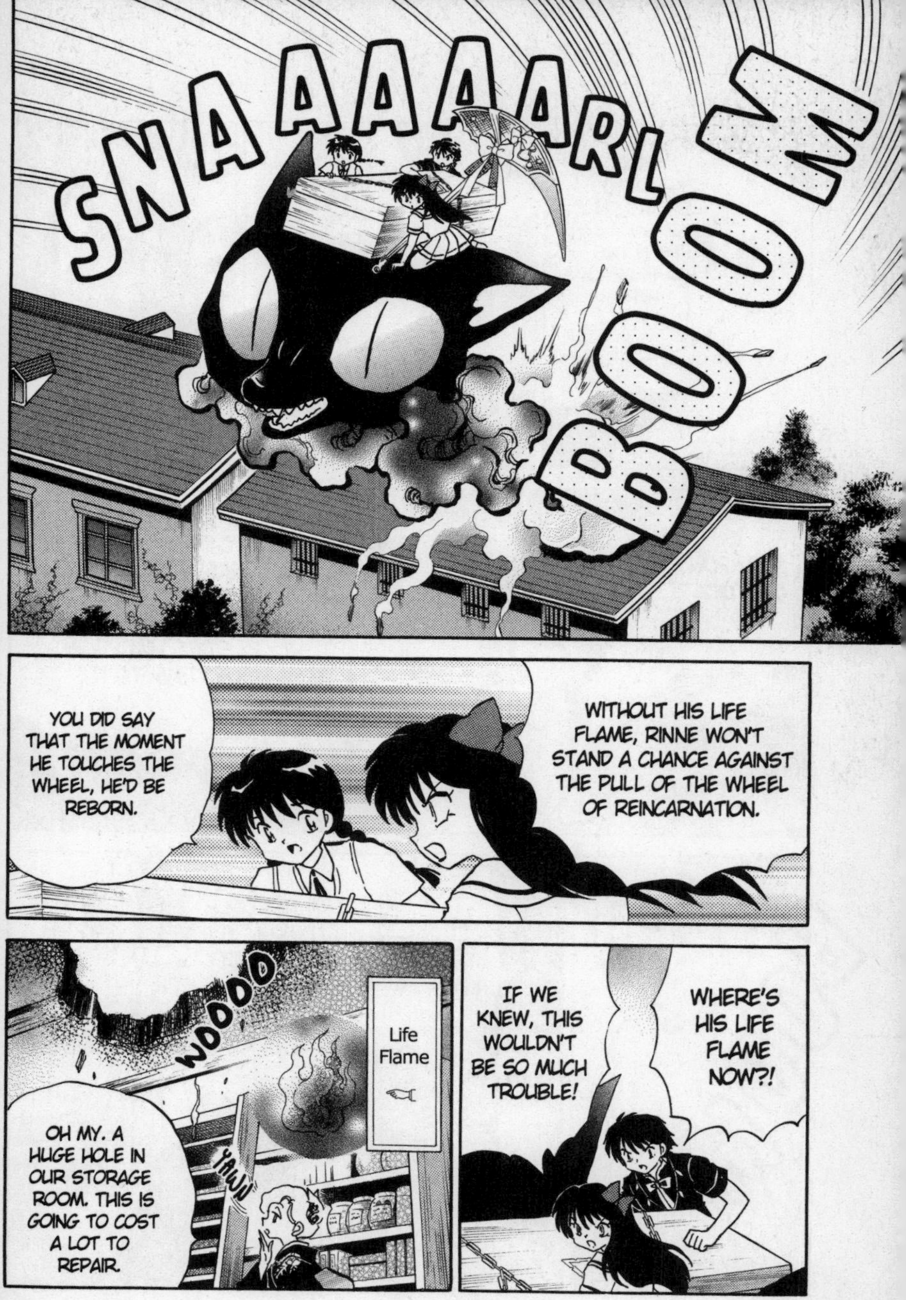
SNAAAAARL
BOOM
WITHOUT HIS LIFE FLAME, RINNE WON'T STAND A CHANCE AGAINST THE PULL OF THE WHEEL OF REINCARNATION.
YOU DID SAY THAT THE MOMENT HE TOUCHES THE WHEEL, HE'D BE REBORN.
WHERE'S HIS LIFE FLAME NOW?!
IF WE KNEW, THIS WOULDN'T BE SO MUCH TROUBLE!
Life Flame
OH MY. A HUGE HOLE IN OUR STORAGE ROOM. THIS IS GOING TO COST A LOT TO REPAIR.

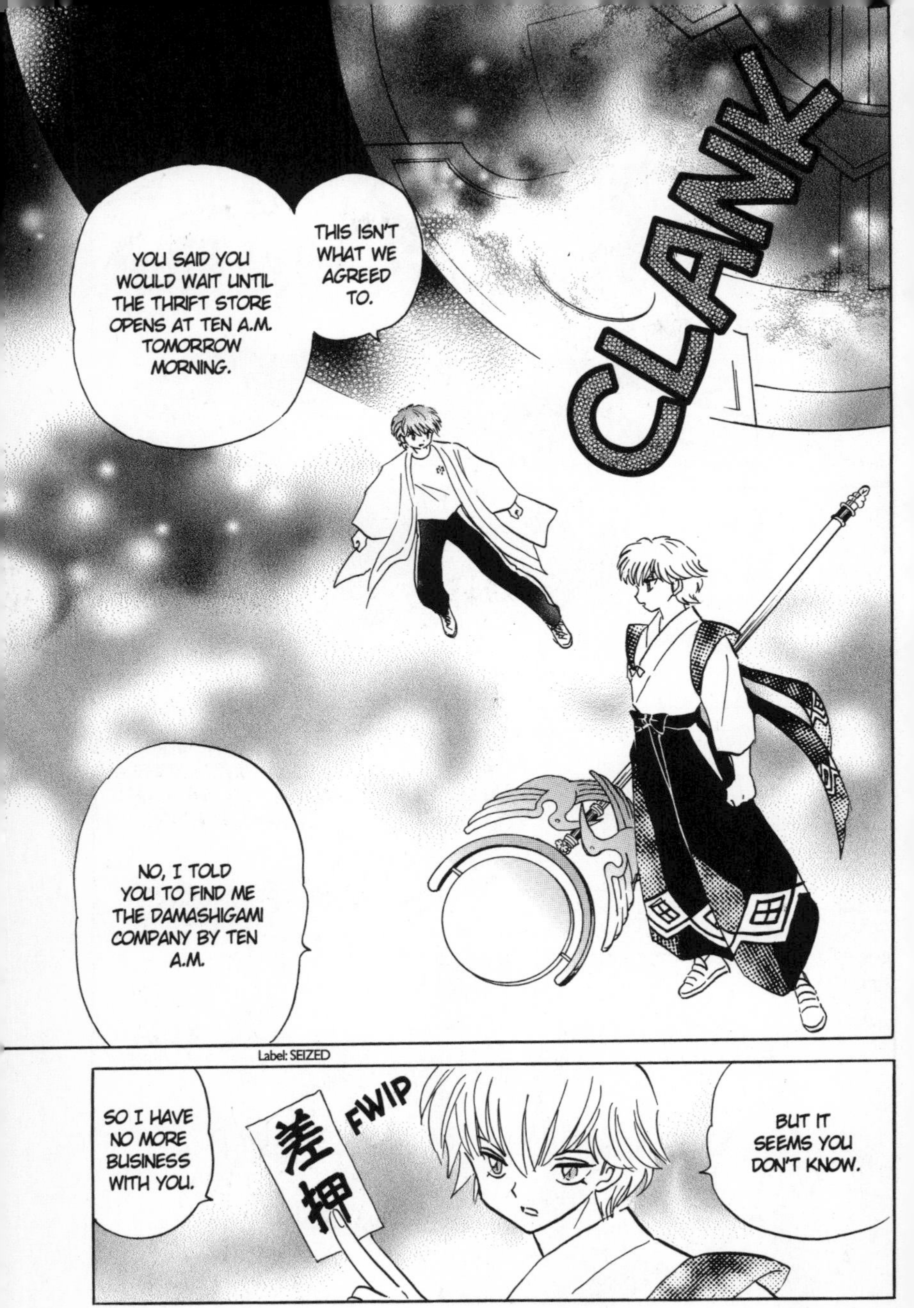
CLANK
THIS ISN'T WHAT WE AGREED TO.
YOU SAID YOU WOULD WAIT UNTIL THE THRIFT STORE OPENS AT TEN A.M. TOMORROW MORNING.
NO, I TOLD YOU TO FIND ME THE DAMASHIGAMI COMPANY BY TEN A.M.
Label: SEIZED
BUT IT SEEMS YOU DON'T KNOW.
FWIP
差押
SO I HAVE NO MORE BUSINESS WITH YOU.

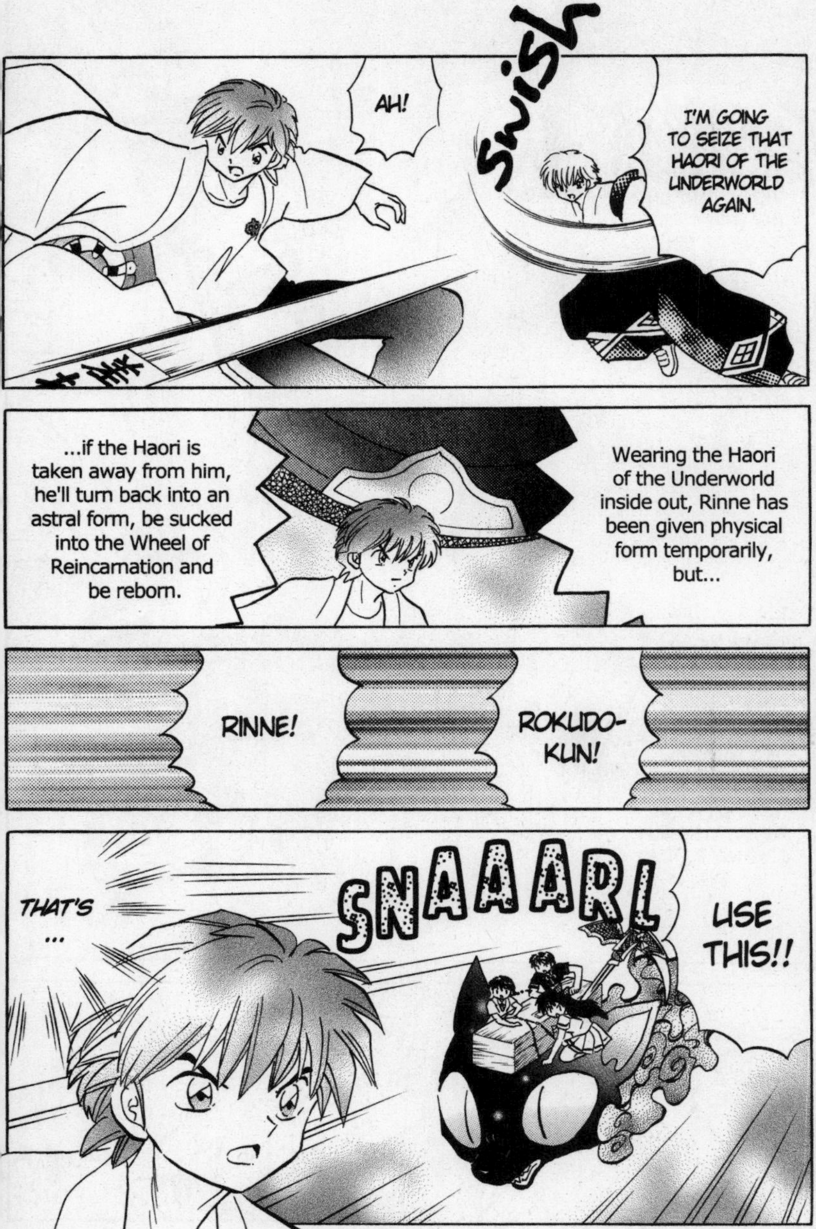
SWISH
I'M GOING TO SEIZE THAT HAORI OF THE UNDERWORLD AGAIN.
AH!
Wearing the Haori of the Underworld inside out, Rinne has been given physical form temporarily, but...
...if the Haori is taken away from him, he'll turn back into an astral form, be sucked into the Wheel of Reincarnation and be reborn.
ROKUDO-KUN!
RINNE!
USE THIS!!
SNAAARL
THAT'S ...

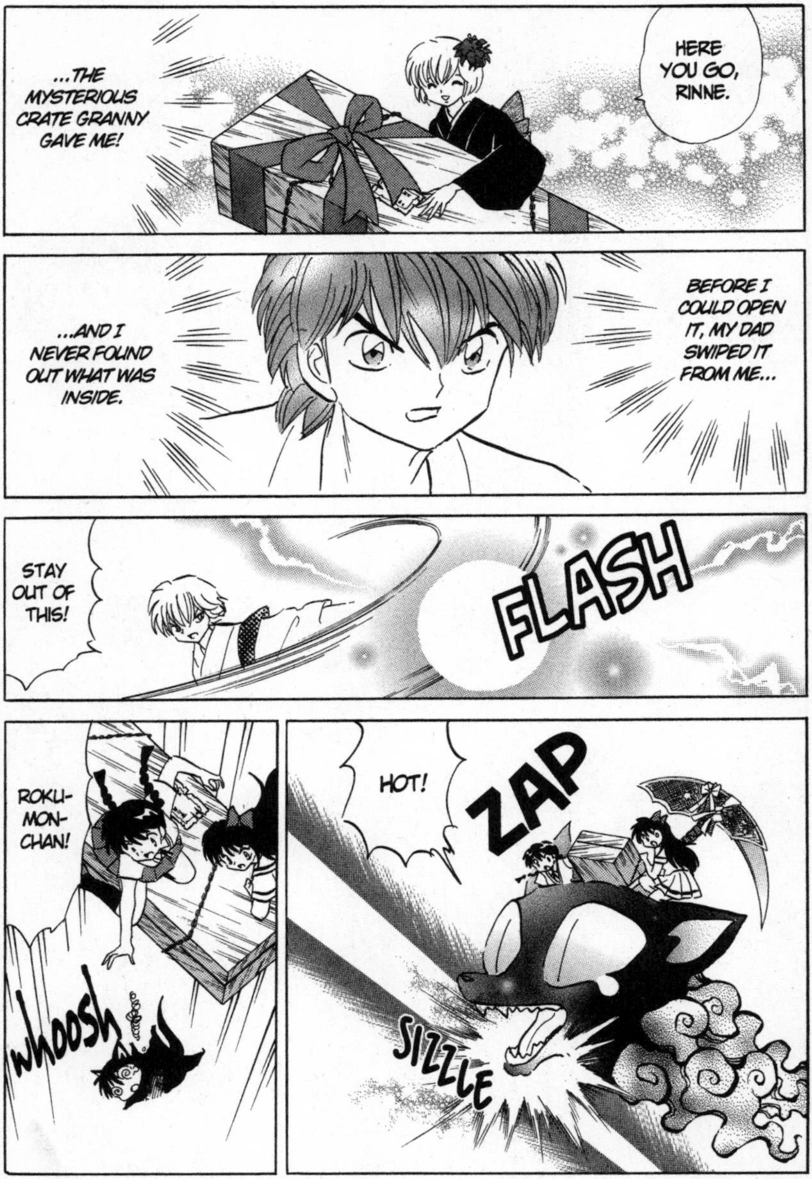
HERE YOU GO, RINNE.
...THE MYSTERIOUS CRATE GRANNY GAVE ME!
BEFORE I COULD OPEN IT, MY DAD SWIPED IT FROM ME...
...AND I NEVER FOUND OUT WHAT WAS INSIDE.
FLASH
STAY OUT OF THIS!
ZAP
HOT!
SIZZLE
ROKU-MON-CHAN!
whoosh

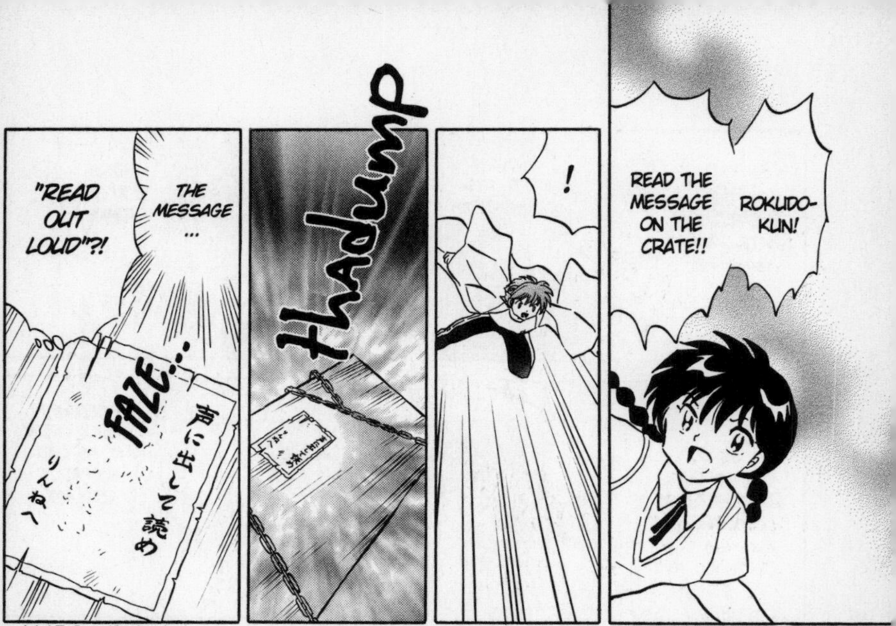
ROKUDO-KUN!
READ THE MESSAGE ON THE CRATE!!
!
thadump
THE MESSAGE...
FAZE...
声に出して読め
りんねへ
"READ OUT LOUD"?!
Label: To Rinne / Read out loud

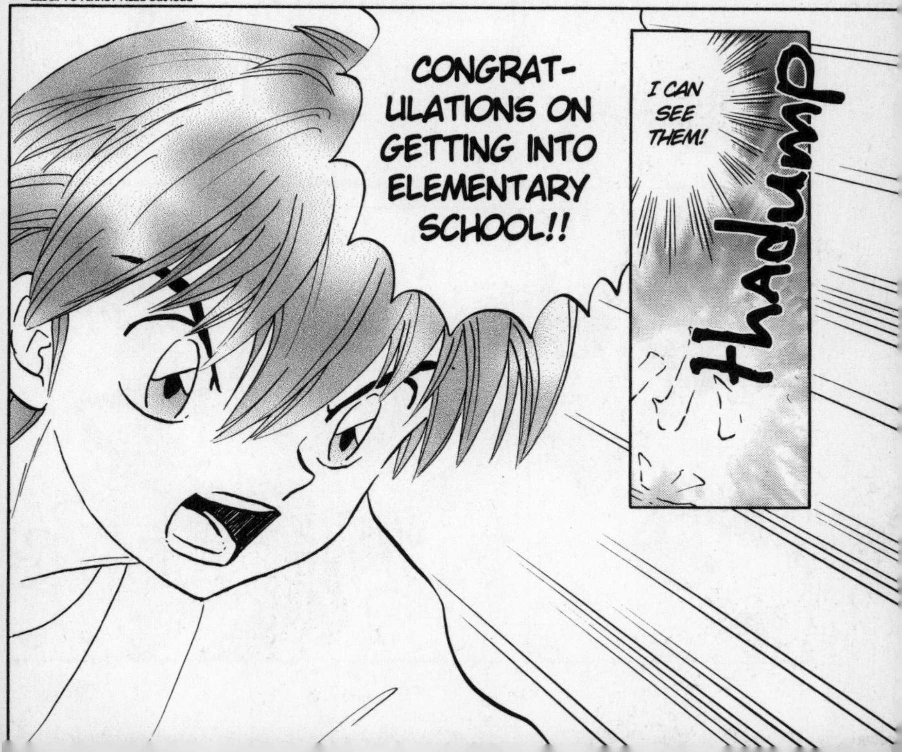
I CAN SEE THEM!
thadump
CONGRAT-ULATIONS ON GETTING INTO ELEMENTARY SCHOOL!!

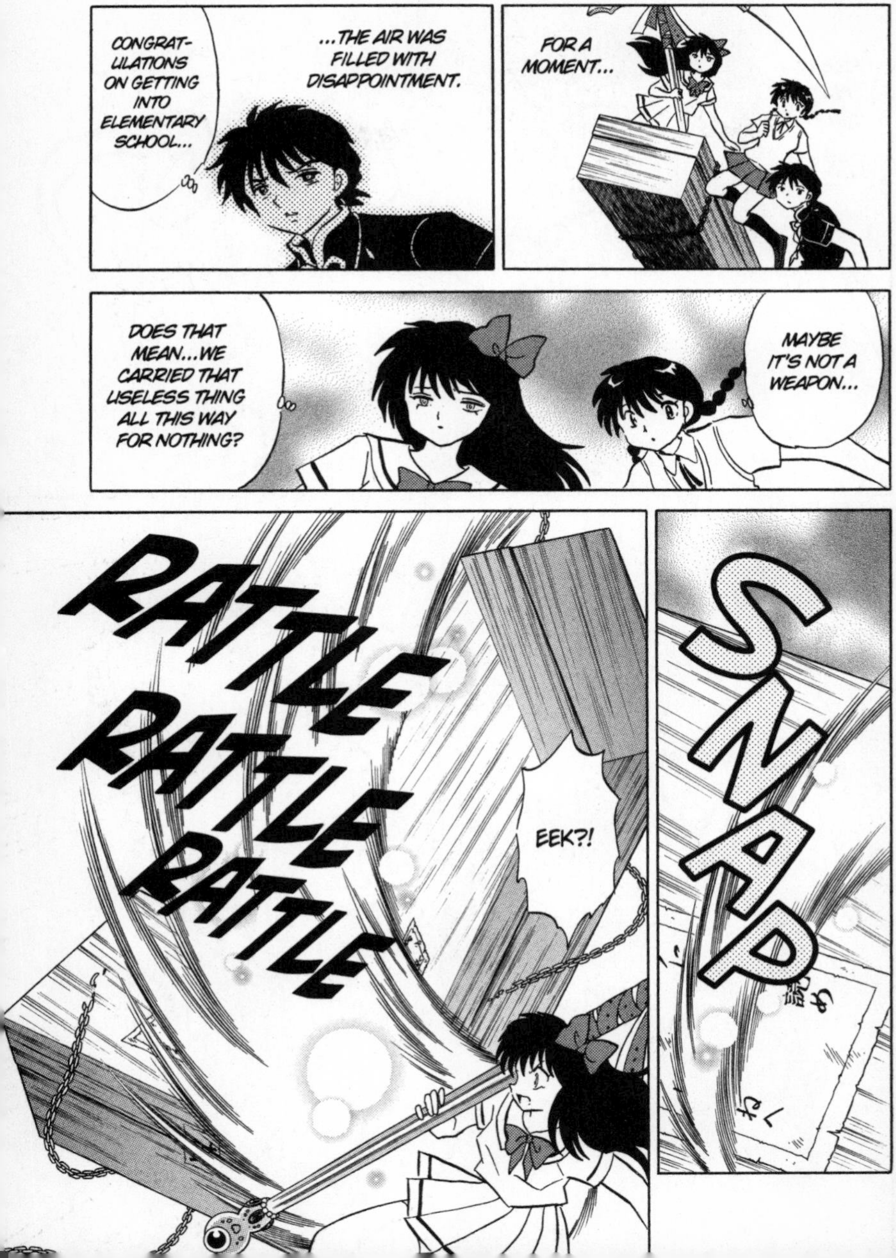
FOR A MOMENT...
...THE AIR WAS FILLED WITH DISAPPOINTMENT.
CONGRAT-ULATIONS ON GETTING INTO ELEMENTARY SCHOOL...
MAYBE IT'S NOT A WEAPON...
DOES THAT MEAN...WE CARRIED THAT USELESS THING ALL THIS WAY FOR NOTHING?
SNAP
RATTLE RATTLE RATTLE
EEK?!

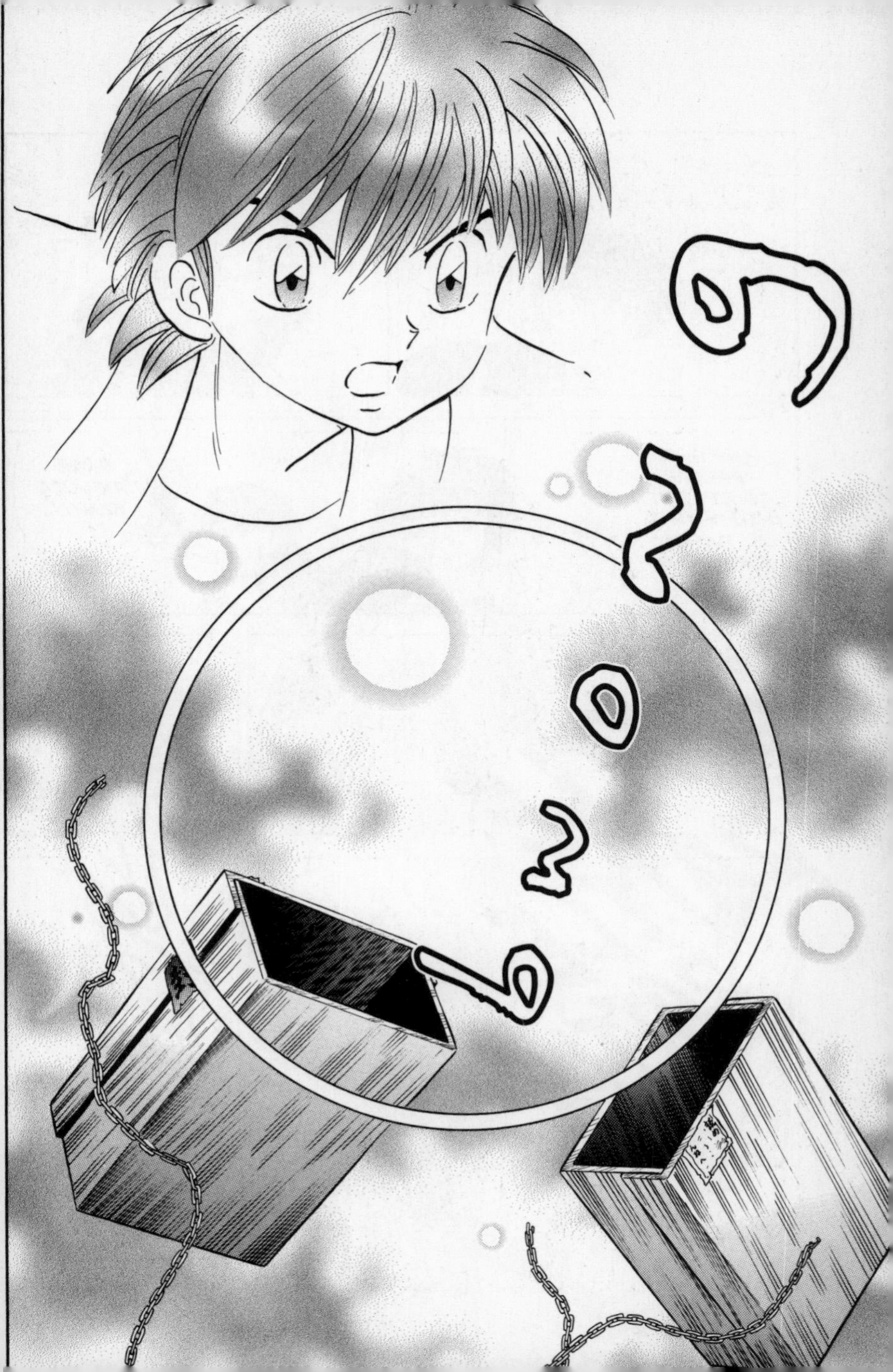

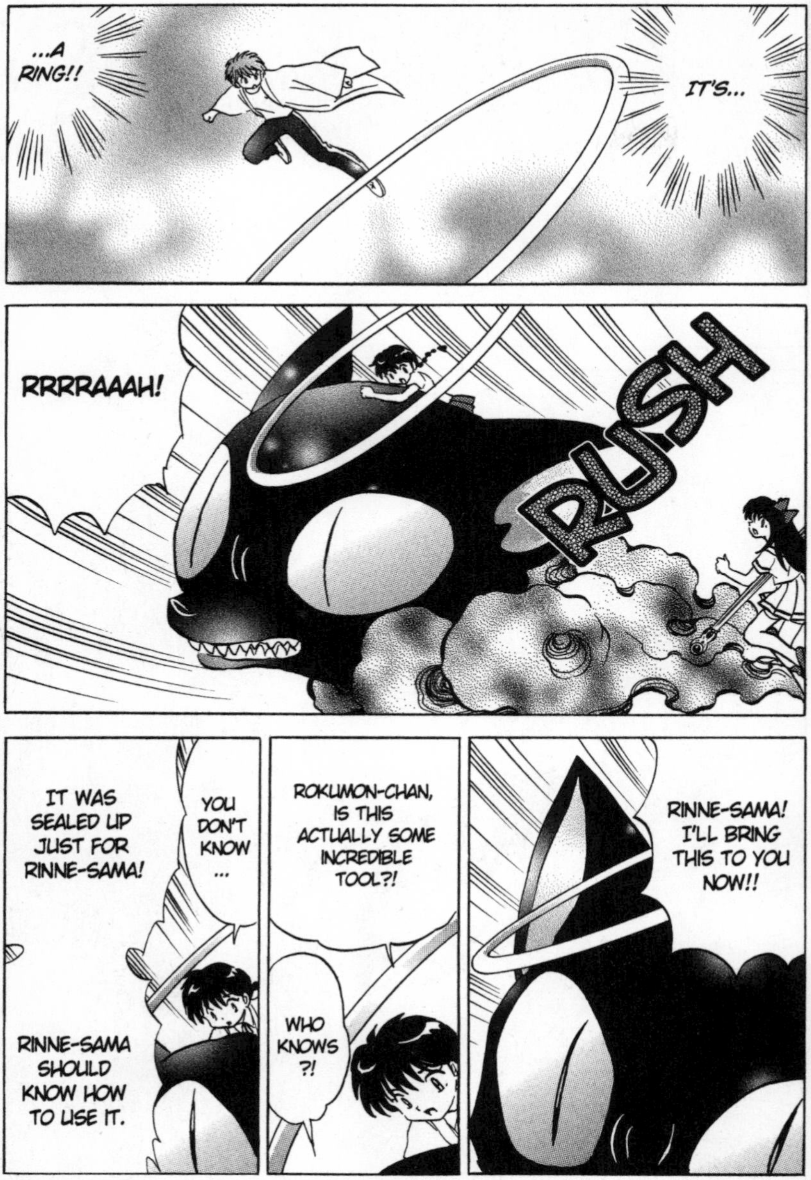
IT'S...
...A RING!!
RUSH
RRRRAAAH!
RINNE-SAMA! I'LL BRING THIS TO YOU NOW!!
ROKUMON-CHAN, IS THIS ACTUALLY SOME INCREDIBLE TOOL?!
WHO KNOWS?!
YOU DON'T KNOW ...
IT WAS SEALED UP JUST FOR RINNE-SAMA!
RINNE-SAMA SHOULD KNOW HOW TO USE IT.

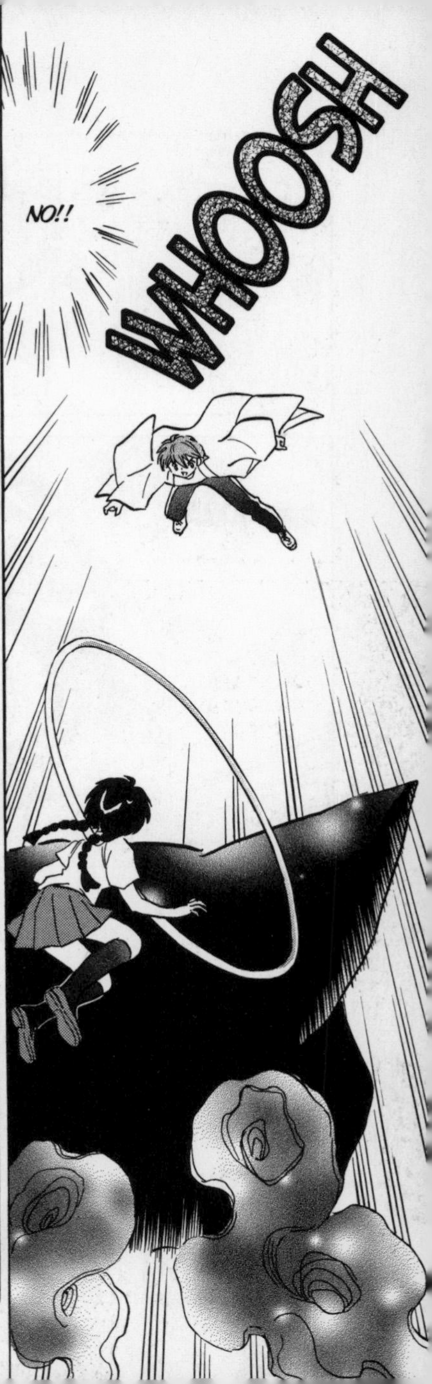
WHOOSH
NO!!

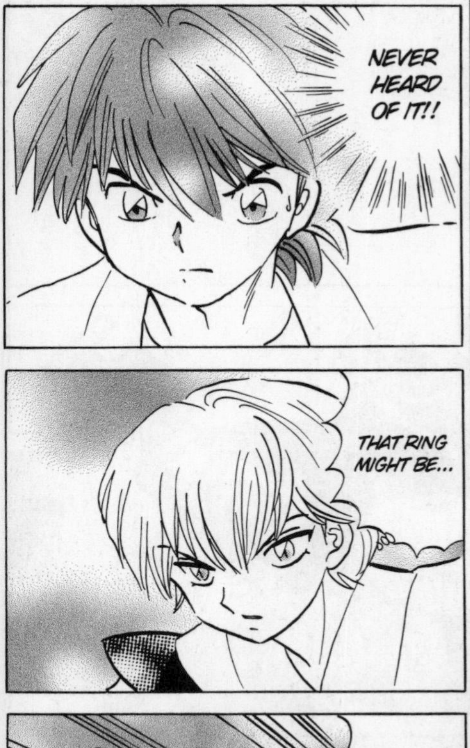
NEVER HEARD OF IT!!
THAT RING MIGHT BE...
Swish
I'LL JUST SEE FOR MYSELF!
差押
Label: SEIZED

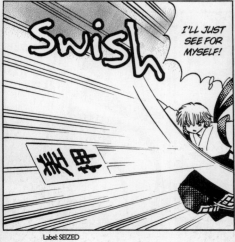

Label: SEIZED

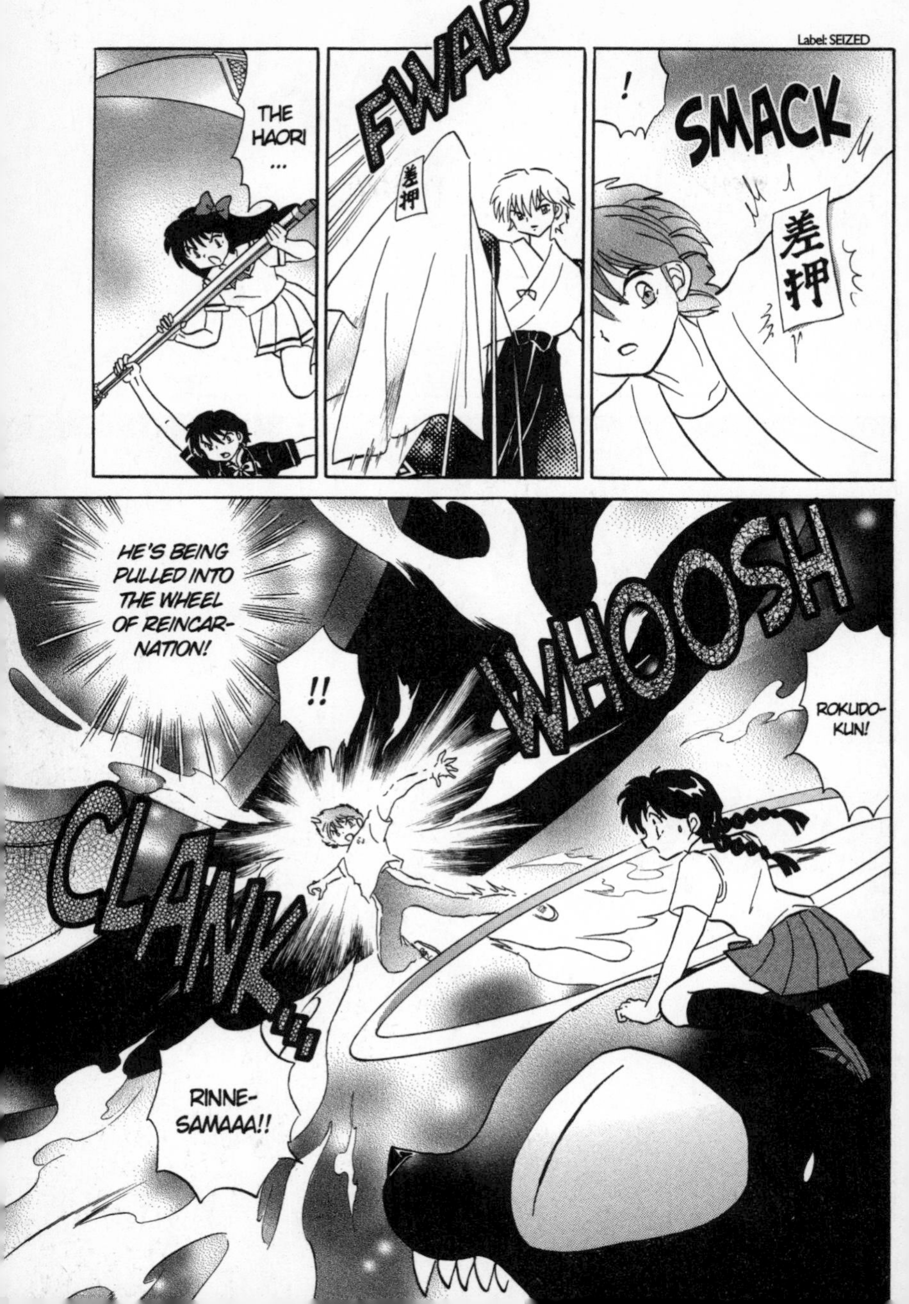

!
SMACK
差押
FWAP
差押
THE HAORI ...
WHOOSH
ROKUDO-KUN!
HE'S BEING PULLED INTO THE WHEEL OF REINCAR-NATION!
!!
CLANK...
RINNE-SAMAAA!!

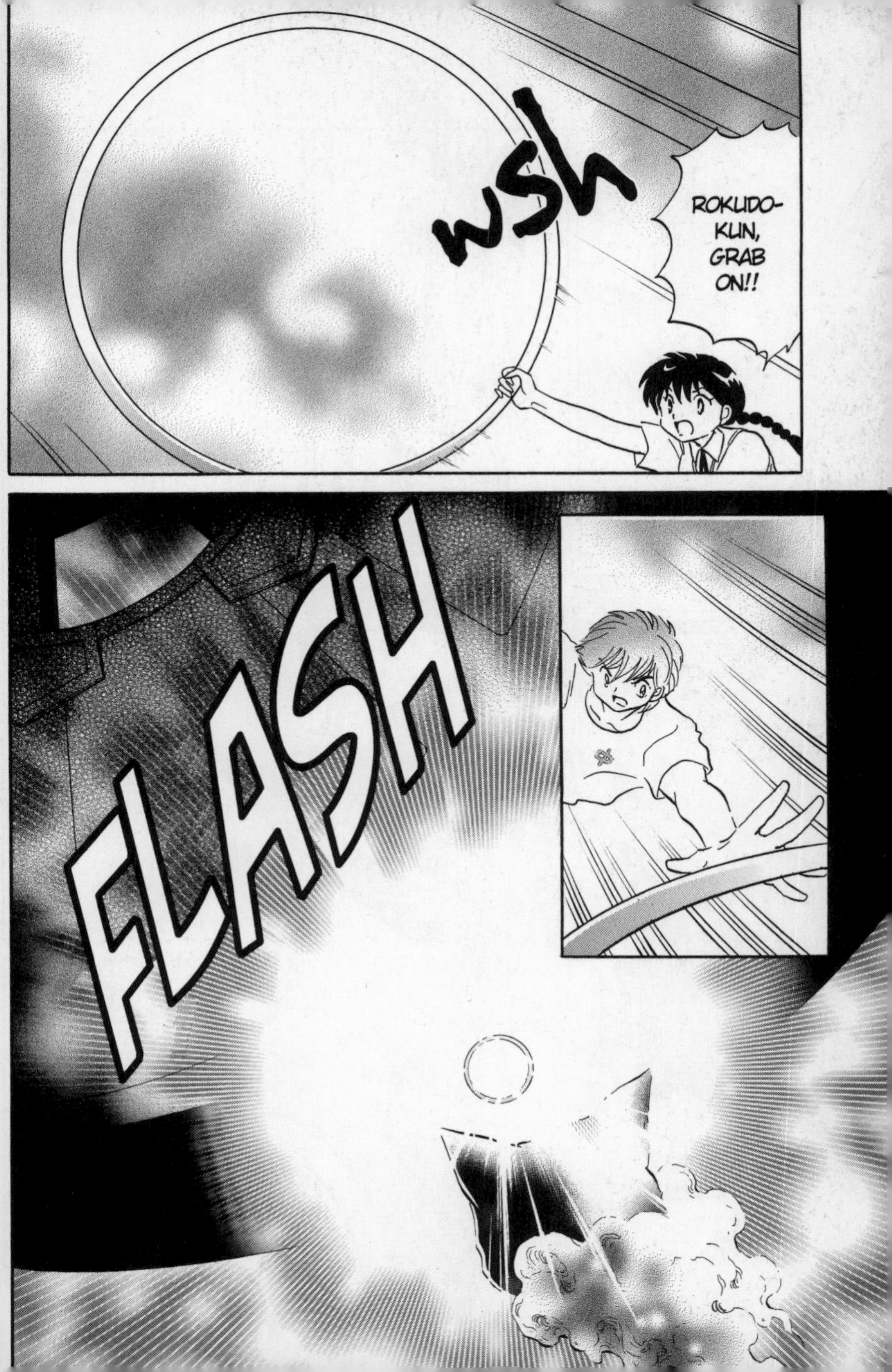
wsh
ROKUDO-KUN, GRAB ON!!
FLASH

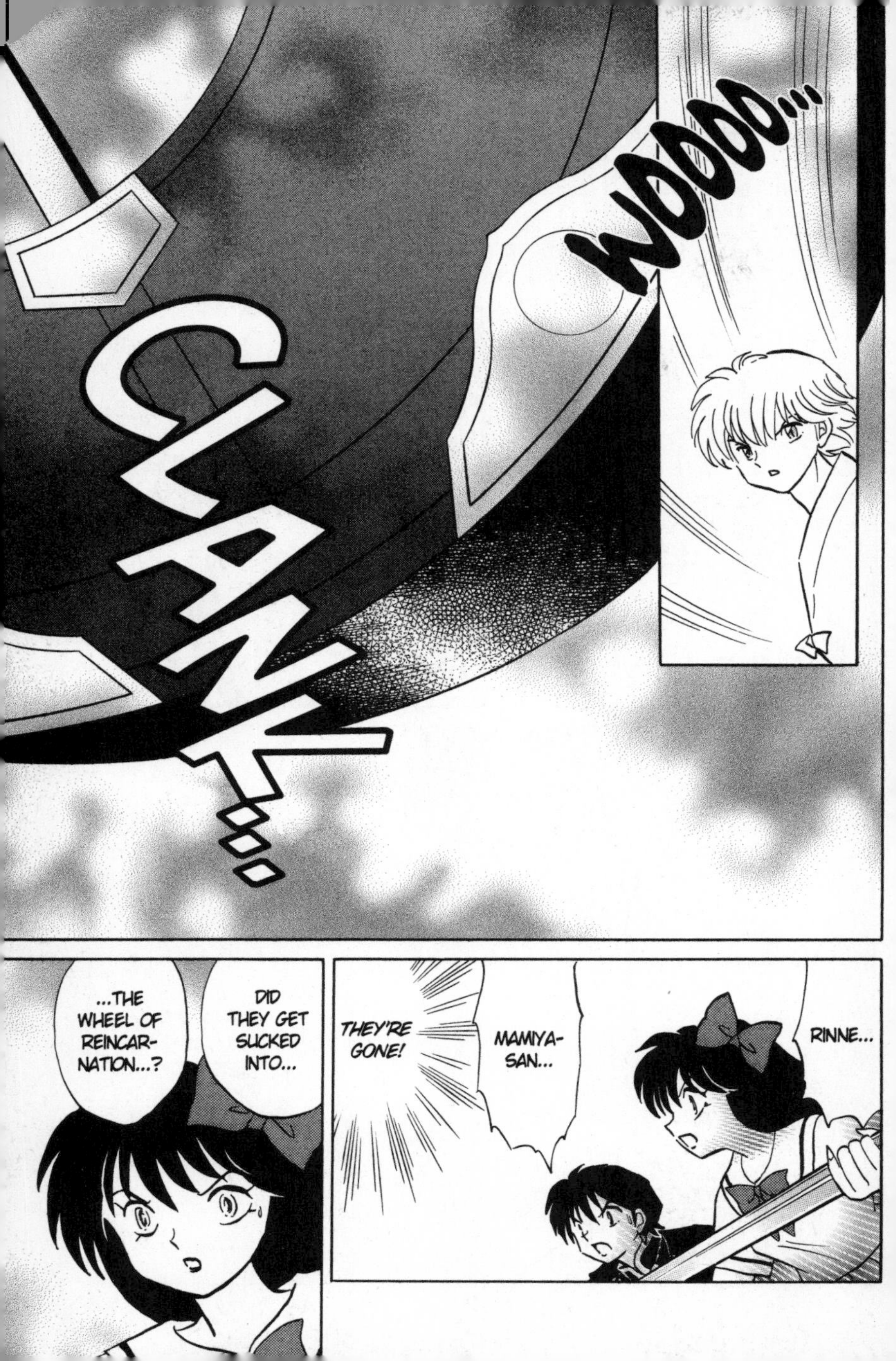
WOOOO...
CLANK...
RINNE...
MAMIYA-SAN...
THEY'RE GONE!
DID THEY GET SUCKED INTO...
...THE WHEEL OF REINCARNATION...?

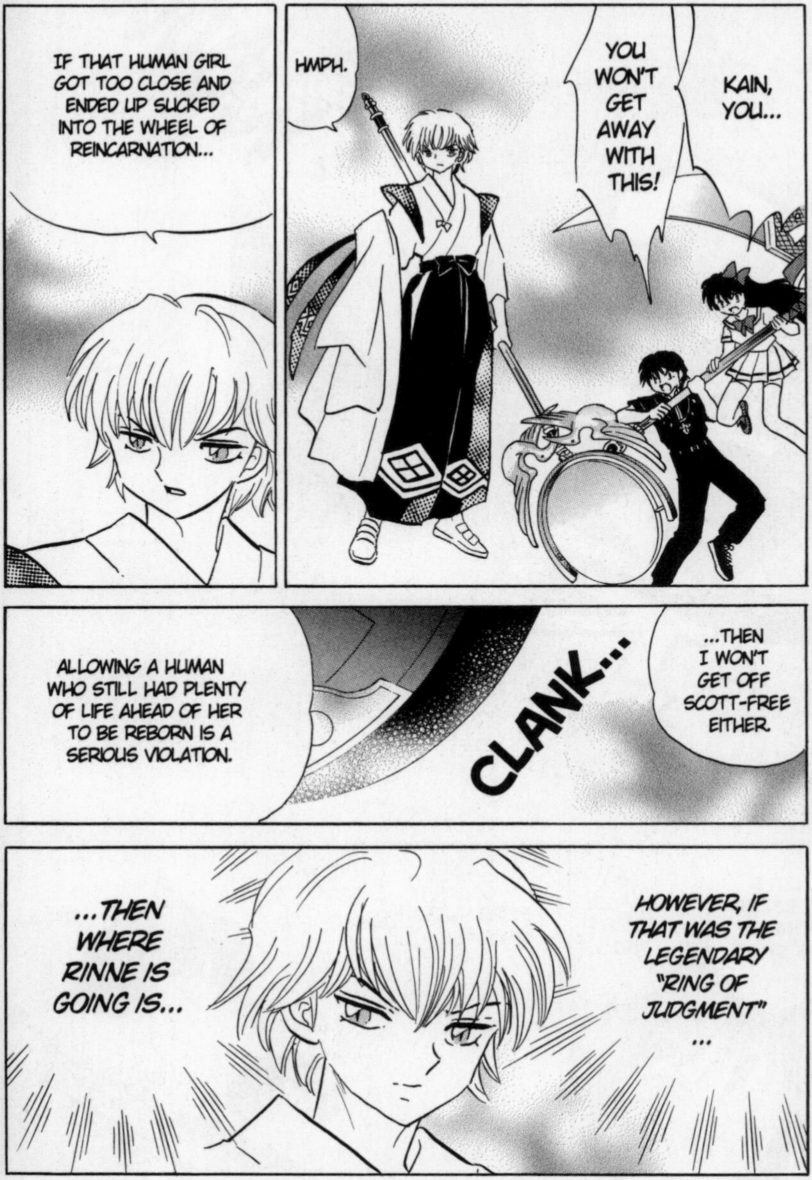

KAIN, YOU...
YOU WON'T GET AWAY WITH THIS!
HMPH.
IF THAT HUMAN GIRL GOT TOO CLOSE AND ENDED UP SUCKED INTO THE WHEEL OF REINCARNATION...
...THEN I WON'T GET OFF SCOTT-FREE EITHER.
CLANK...
ALLOWING A HUMAN WHO STILL HAD PLENTY OF LIFE AHEAD OF HER TO BE REBORN IS A SERIOUS VIOLATION.
HOWEVER, IF THAT WAS THE LEGENDARY "RING OF JUDGMENT" ...
...THEN WHERE RINNE IS GOING IS...

CHAPTER 58: THE RING OF JUDGMENT

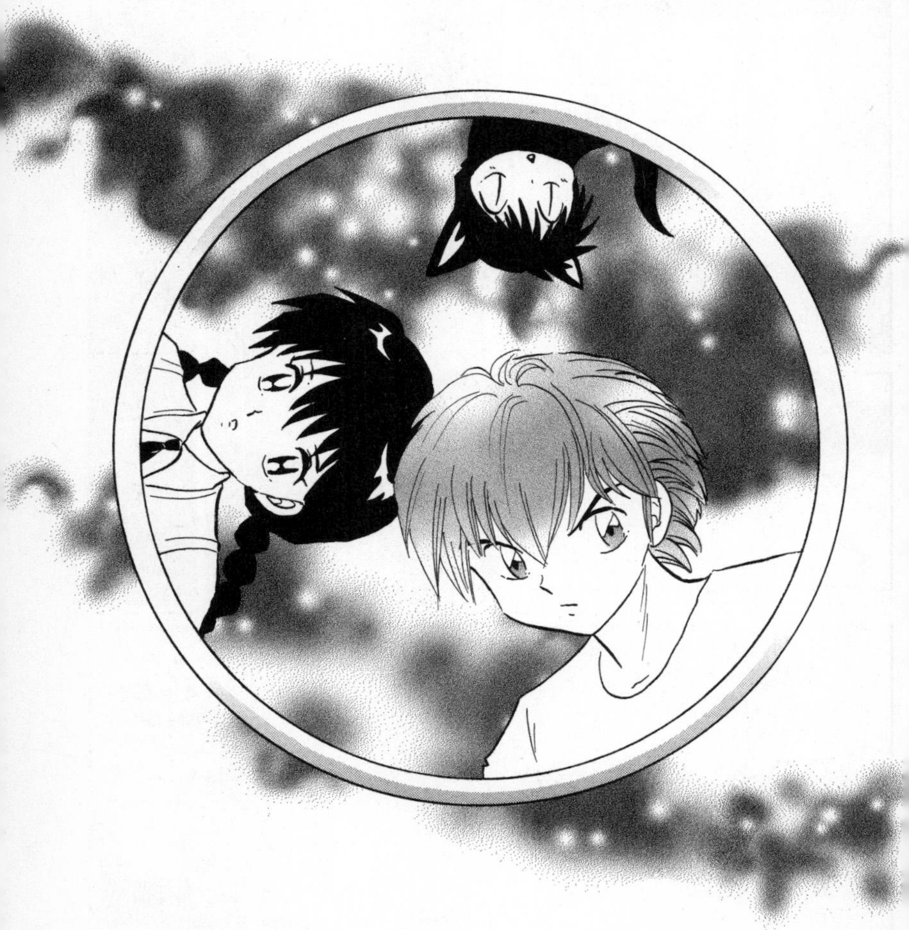

THAT'S RIGHT...

IT'S PITCH BLACK.

WHERE AM I...

...I GOT SUCKED INTO THE WHEEL OF REINCARNATION WHILE IN SPIRIT FORM...

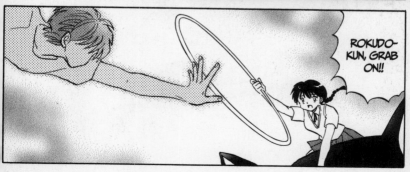

ROKUDO-KUN, GRAB ON!!

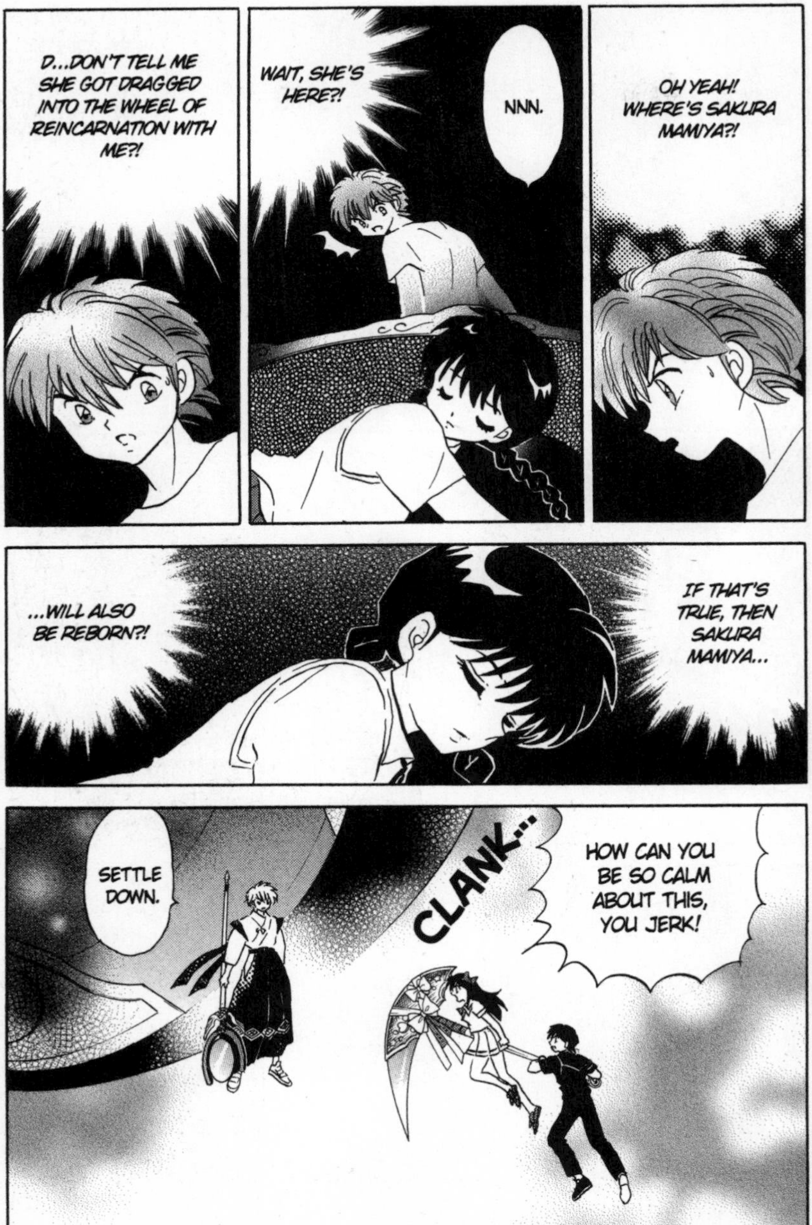
OH YEAH! WHERE'S SAKURA MAMIYA?!
NNN.
WAIT, SHE'S HERE?!
D...DON'T TELL ME SHE GOT DRAGGED INTO THE WHEEL OF REINCARNATION WITH ME?!
IF THAT'S TRUE, THEN SAKURA MAMIYA...
...WILL ALSO BE REBORN?!
HOW CAN YOU BE SO CALM ABOUT THIS, YOU JERK!
CLANK...
SETTLE DOWN.

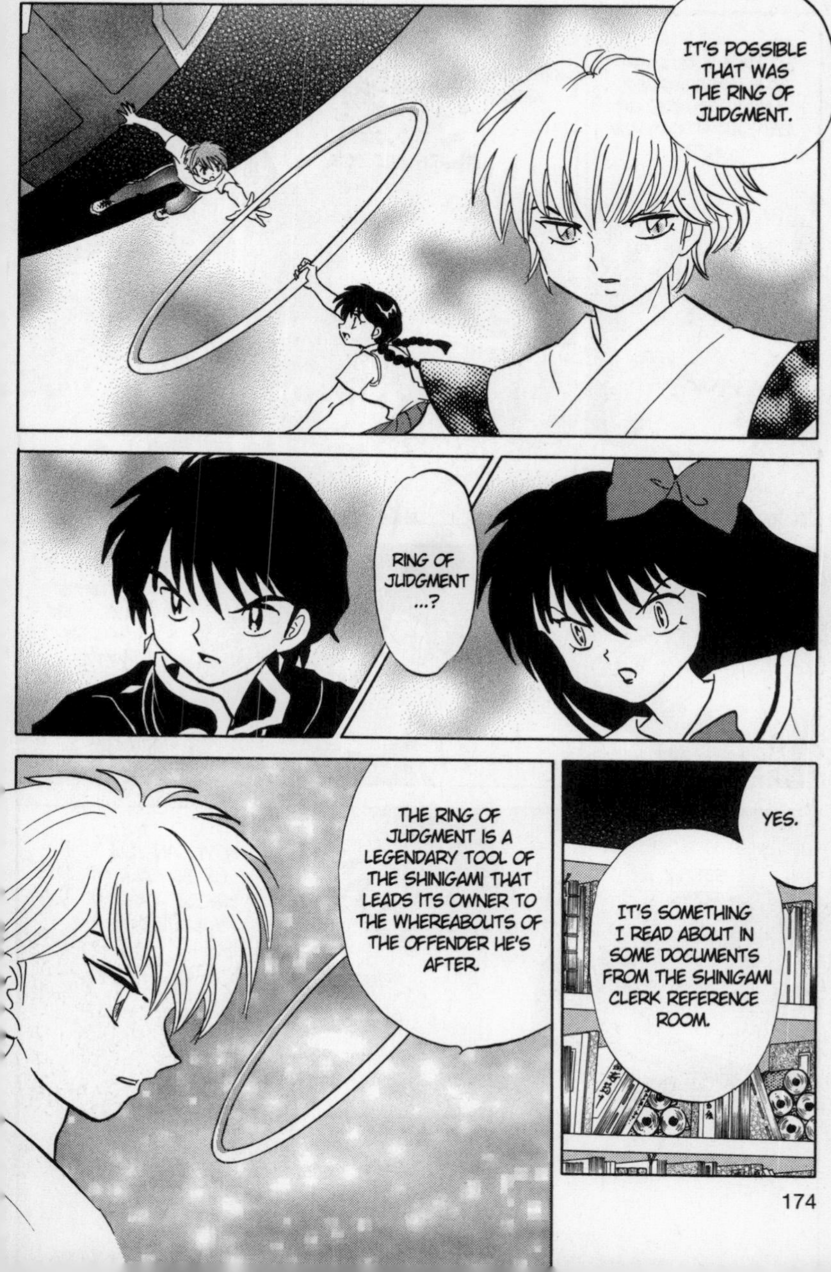
IT'S POSSIBLE THAT WAS THE RING OF JUDGMENT.
RING OF JUDGMENT ...?
YES.
IT'S SOMETHING I READ ABOUT IN SOME DOCUMENTS FROM THE SHINIGAMI CLERK REFERENCE ROOM.
THE RING OF JUDGMENT IS A LEGENDARY TOOL OF THE SHINIGAMI THAT LEADS ITS OWNER TO THE WHEREABOUTS OF THE OFFENDER HE'S AFTER.

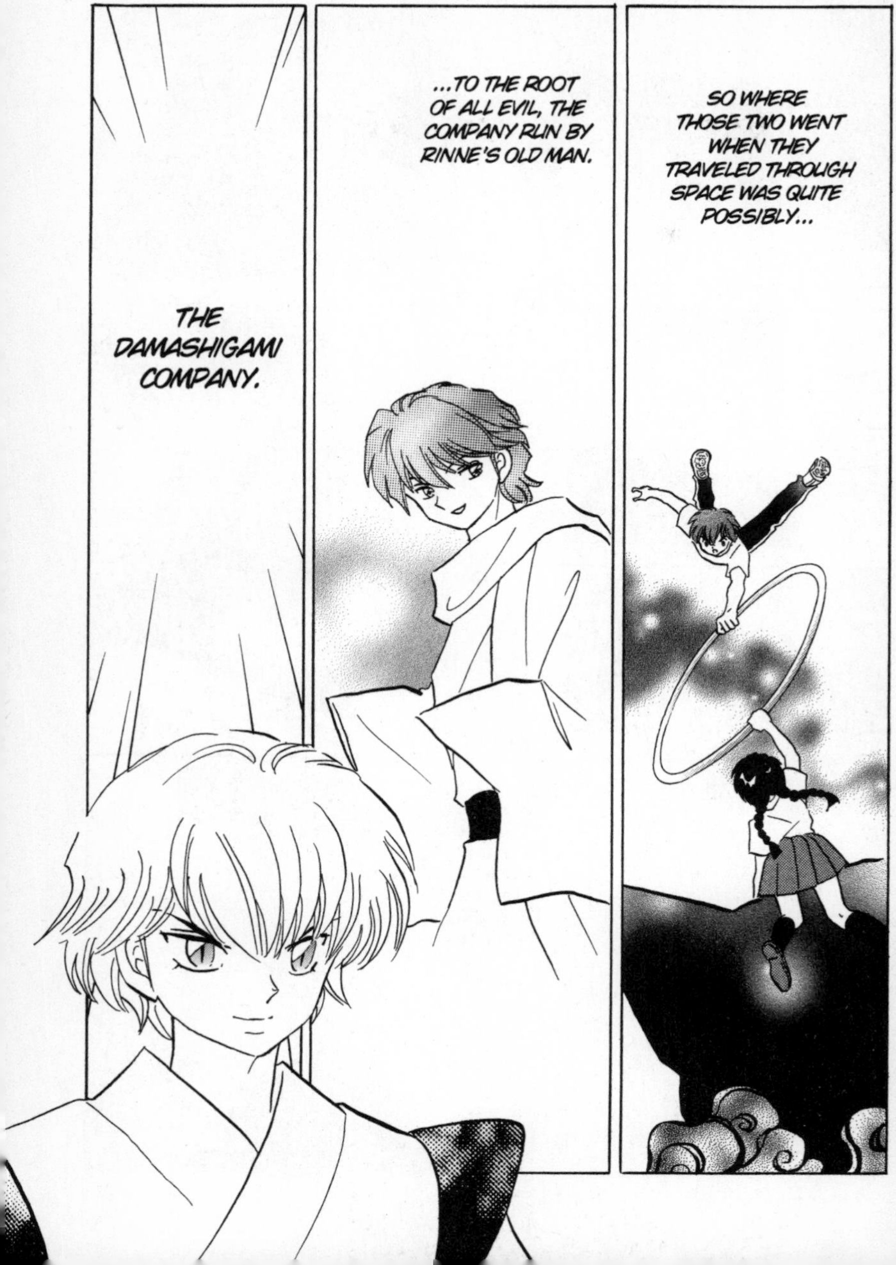
SO WHERE THOSE TWO WENT WHEN THEY TRAVELED THROUGH SPACE WAS QUITE POSSIBLY...
...TO THE ROOT OF ALL EVIL, THE COMPANY RUN BY RINNE'S OLD MAN.
THE DAMASHIGAMI COMPANY.

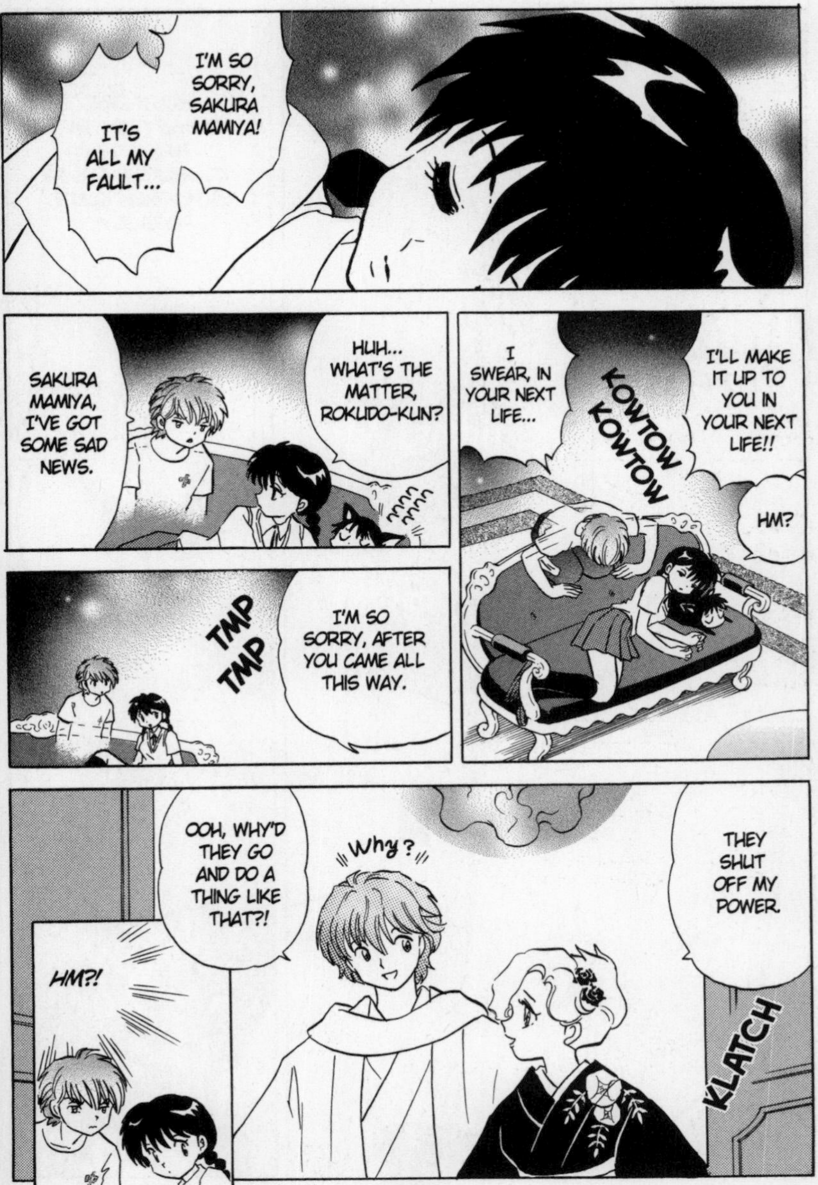

I'M SO SORRY, SAKURA MAMIYA!
IT'S ALL MY FAULT...
I'LL MAKE IT UP TO YOU IN YOUR NEXT LIFE!!
KOWTOW KOWTOW
I SWEAR, IN YOUR NEXT LIFE...
HM?
HUH... WHAT'S THE MATTER, ROKUDO-KUN?
SAKURA MAMIYA, I'VE GOT SOME SAD NEWS.
I'M SO SORRY, AFTER YOU CAME ALL THIS WAY.
TMP TMP
THEY SHUT OFF MY POWER.
KLATCH
Why?
OOH, WHY'D THEY GO AND DO A THING LIKE THAT?!
HM?!

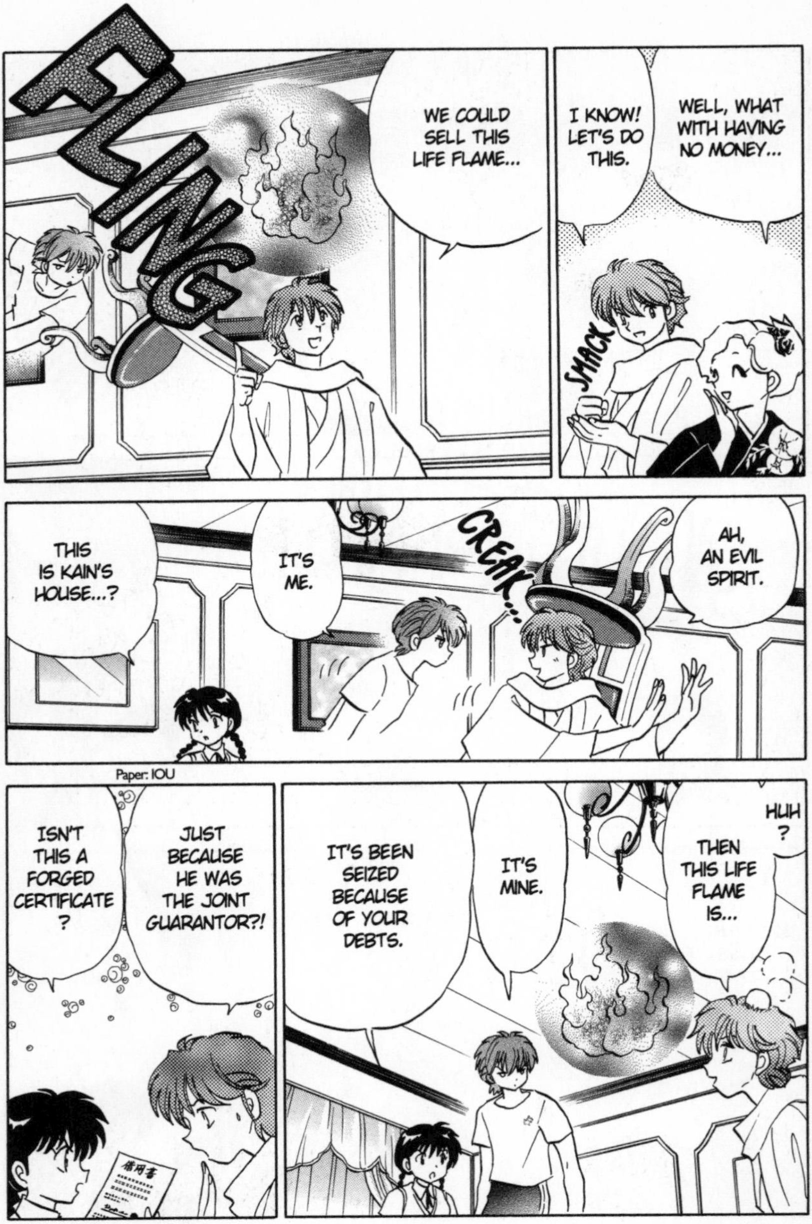
WELL, WHAT WITH HAVING NO MONEY...
I KNOW! LET'S DO THIS.
SMACK
WE COULD SELL THIS LIFE FLAME...
FLING
AH, AN EVIL SPIRIT.
CREAK...
IT'S ME.
THIS IS KAIN'S HOUSE...?
HUH?
THEN THIS LIFE FLAME IS...
IT'S MINE.
IT'S BEEN SEIZED BECAUSE OF YOUR DEBTS.
JUST BECAUSE HE WAS THE JOINT GUARANTOR?!
ISN'T THIS A FORGED CERTIFICATE?

Paper: IOU

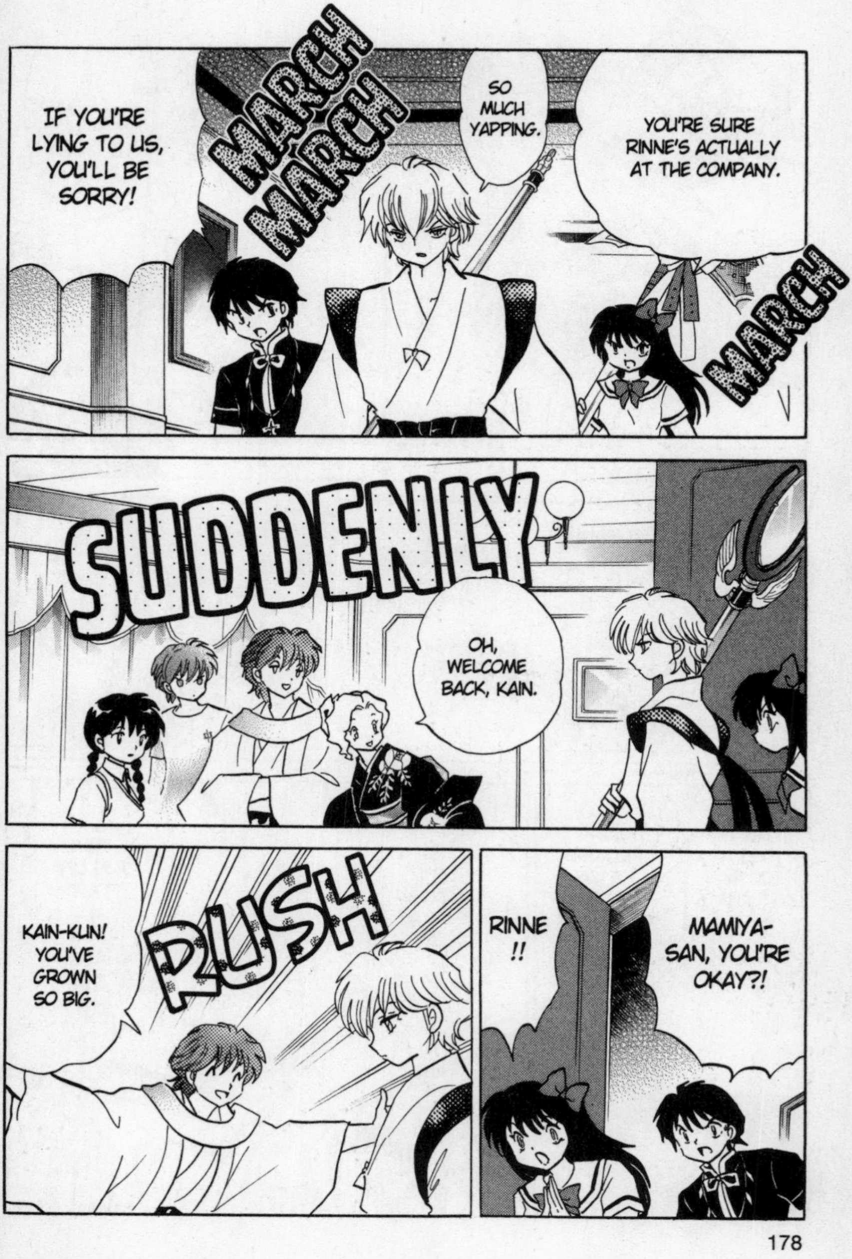

MARCH
YOU'RE SURE RINNE'S ACTUALLY AT THE COMPANY.
SO MUCH YAPPING.
MARCH MARCH
IF YOU'RE LYING TO US, YOU'LL BE SORRY!
SUDDENLY
OH, WELCOME BACK, KAIN.
MAMIYA-SAN, YOU'RE OKAY?!
RINNE !!
RUSH
KAIN-KUN! YOU'VE GROWN SO BIG.

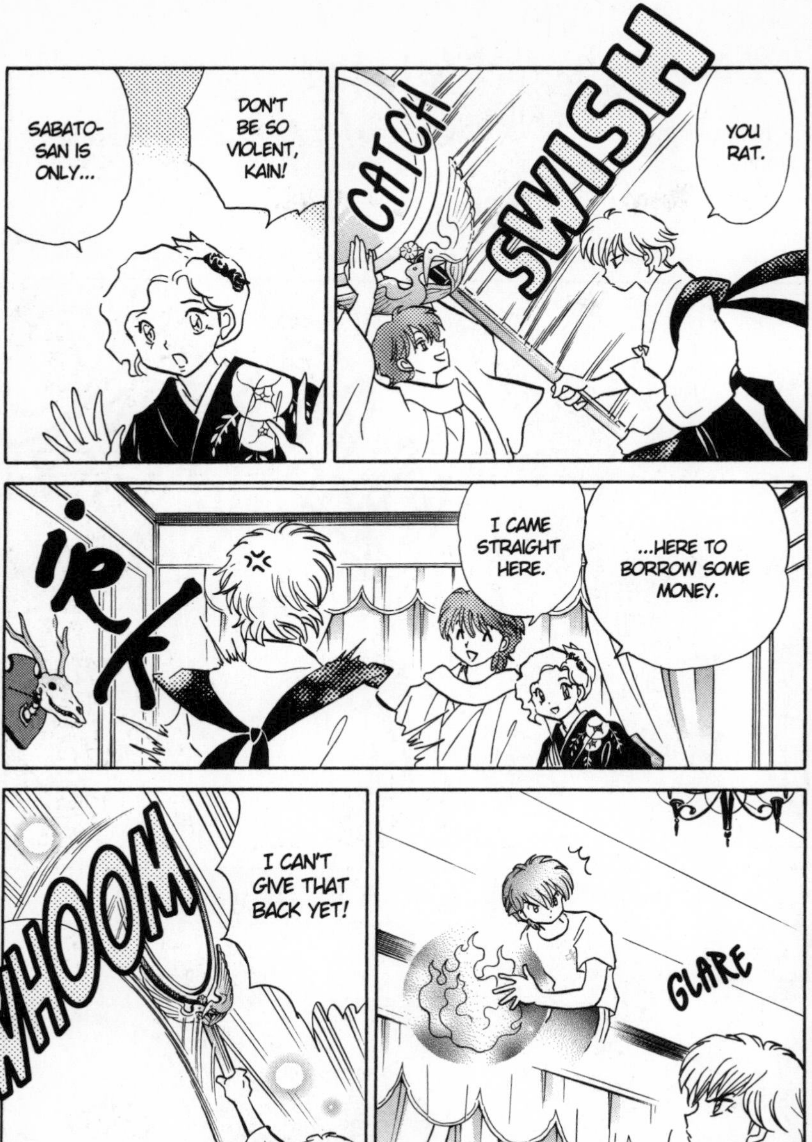
YOU RAT.
SWISH
CATCH
DON'T BE SO VIOLENT, KAIN!
SABATO-SAN IS ONLY...
I CAME STRAIGHT HERE.
...HERE TO BORROW SOME MONEY.
IRK
GLARE
I CAN'T GIVE THAT BACK YET!
WHOOM

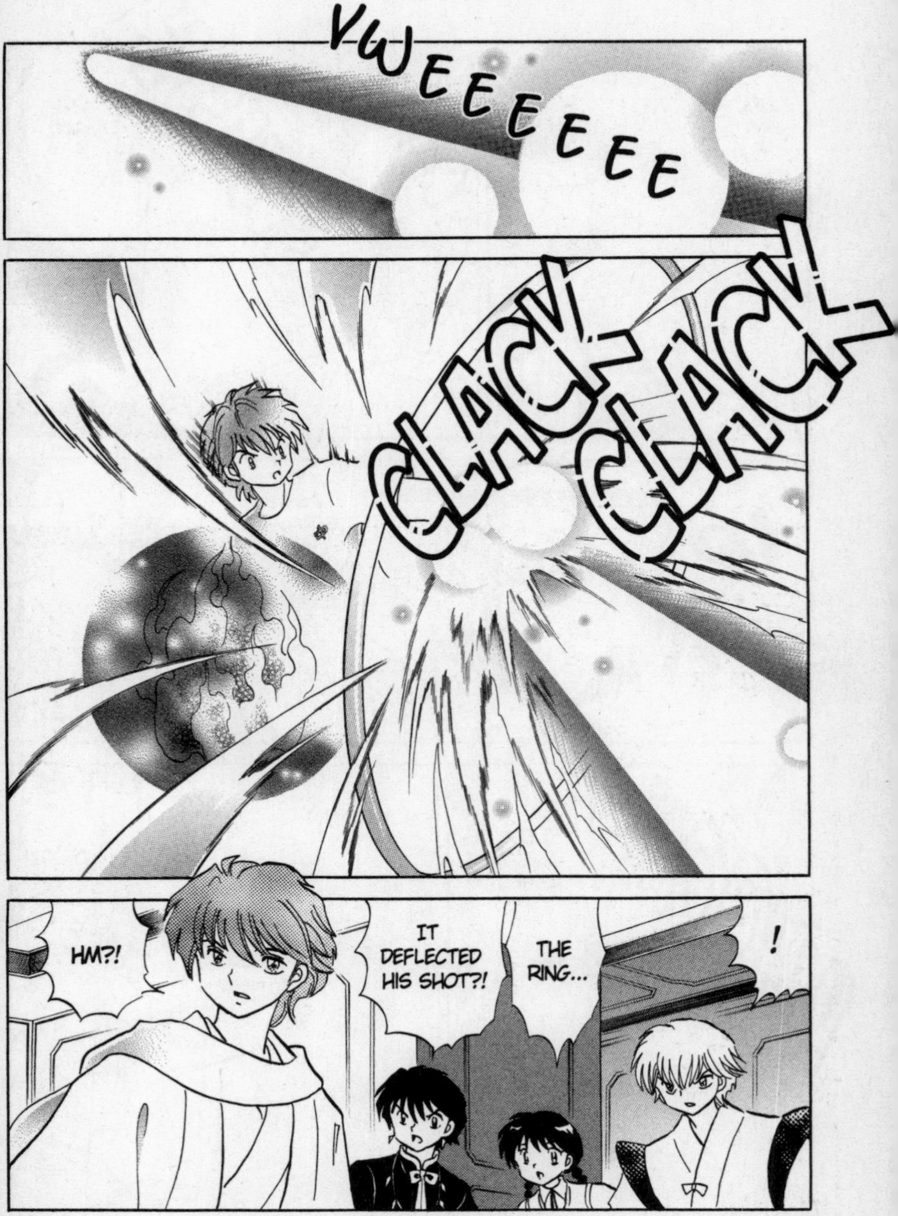
VWEEEEEE
CLACK CLACK
!
THE RING...
IT DEFLECTED HIS SHOT?!
HM?!

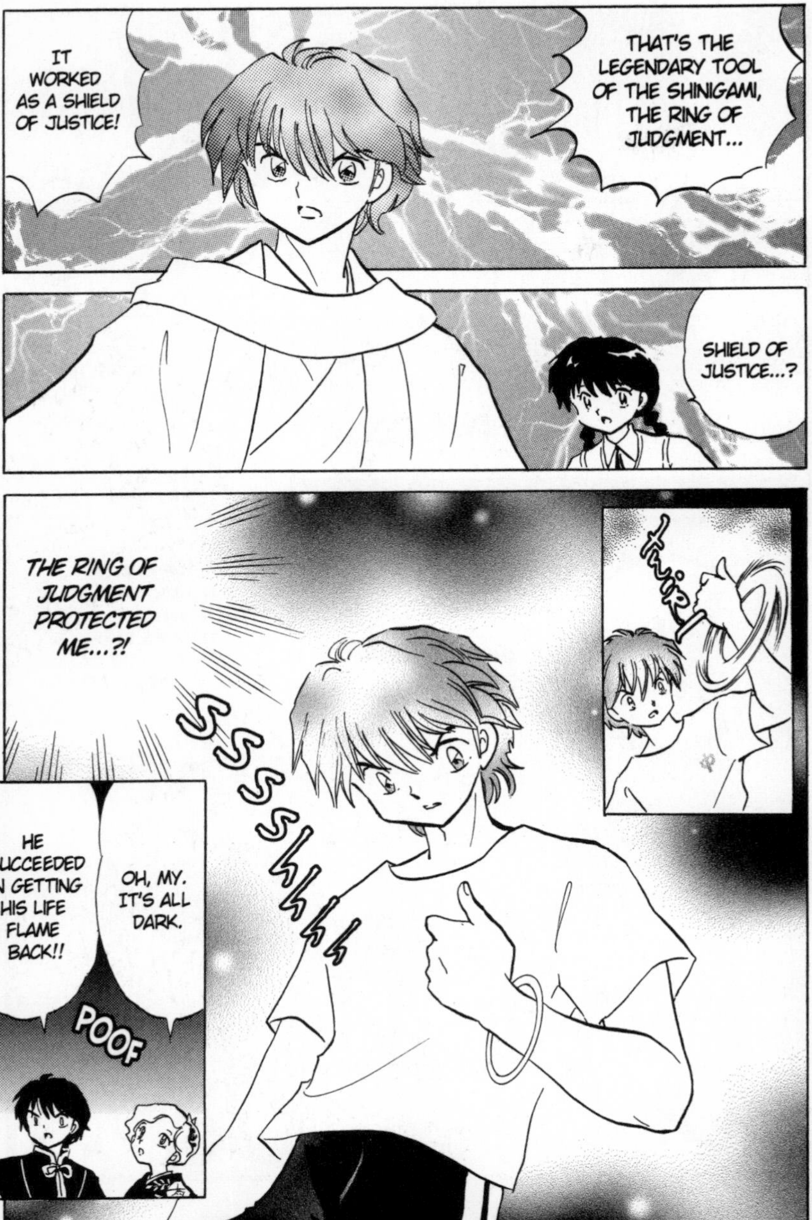
THAT'S THE LEGENDARY TOOL OF THE SHINIGAMI, THE RING OF JUDGMENT...
IT WORKED AS A SHIELD OF JUSTICE!
SHIELD OF JUSTICE...?
twirl
THE RING OF JUDGMENT PROTECTED ME...?!
SSSShhhh
OH, MY. IT'S ALL DARK.
HE SUCCEEDED IN GETTING HIS LIFE FLAME BACK!!
POOF

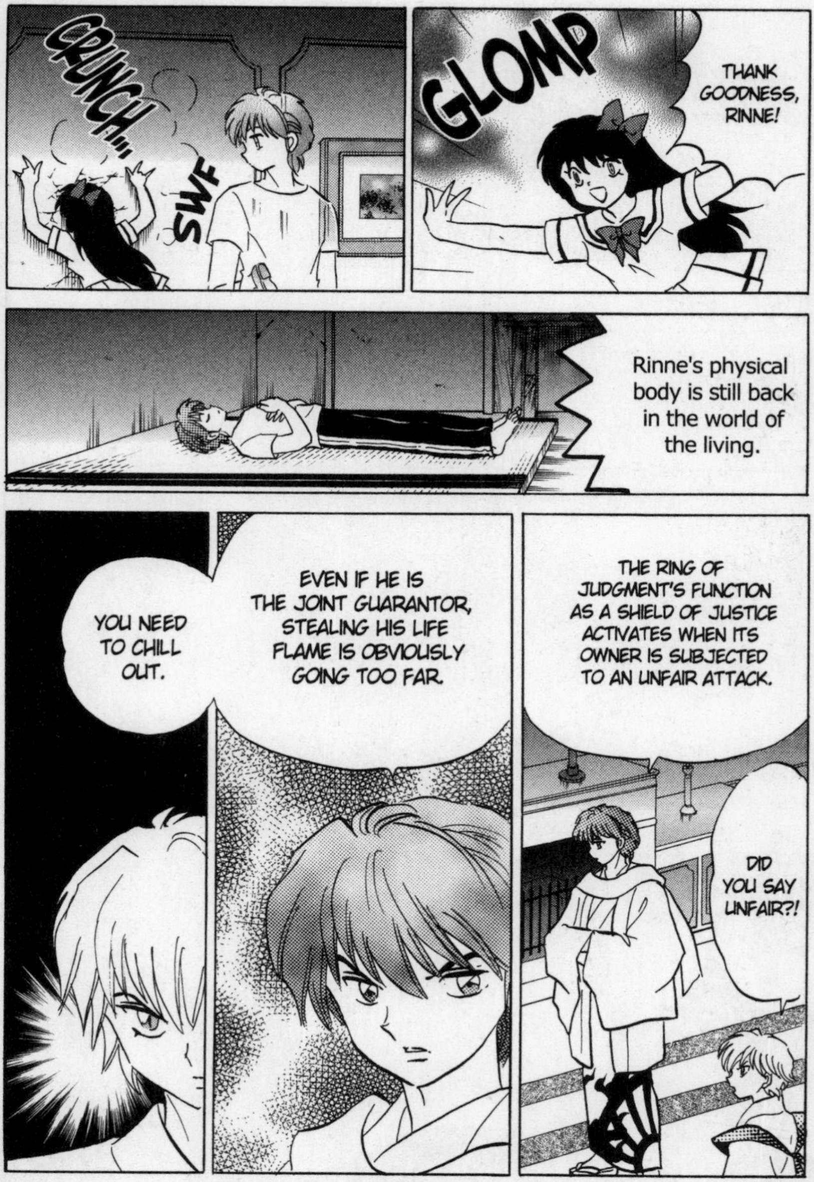
GLOMP
THANK GOODNESS, RINNE!
CRUNCH...
SWF
Rinne's physical body is still back in the world of the living.
THE RING OF JUDGMENT'S FUNCTION AS A SHIELD OF JUSTICE ACTIVATES WHEN ITS OWNER IS SUBJECTED TO AN UNFAIR ATTACK.
DID YOU SAY UNFAIR?!
EVEN IF HE IS THE JOINT GUARANTOR, STEALING HIS LIFE FLAME IS OBVIOUSLY GOING TOO FAR.
YOU NEED TO CHILL OUT.

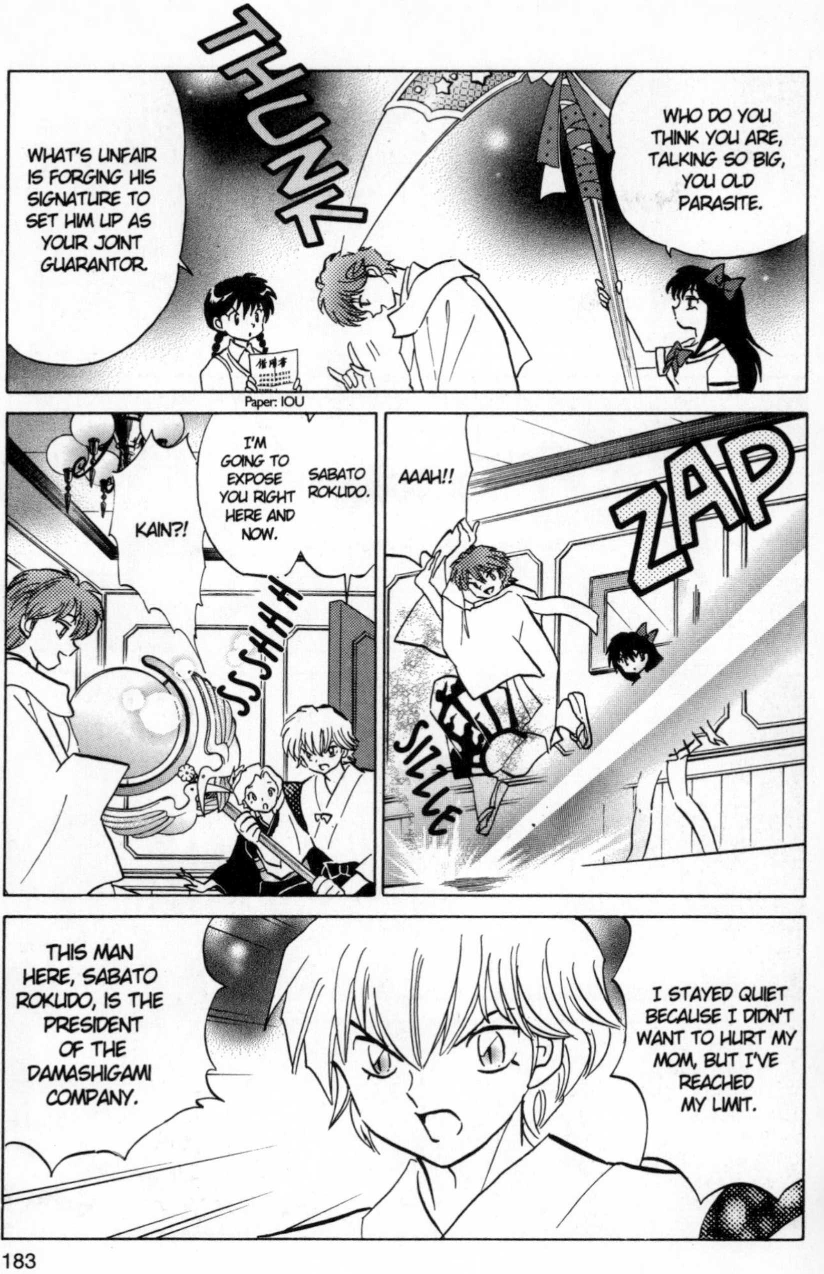
WHO DO YOU THINK YOU ARE, TALKING SO BIG, YOU OLD PARASITE.
THUNK
WHAT'S UNFAIR IS FORGING HIS SIGNATURE TO SET HIM UP AS YOUR JOINT GUARANTOR.
Paper: IOU
ZAP
AAAH!!
SIZZLE
SABATO ROKUDO.
I'M GOING TO EXPOSE YOU RIGHT HERE AND NOW.
KAIN?!
SSHHH
I STAYED QUIET BECAUSE I DIDN'T WANT TO HURT MY MOM, BUT I'VE REACHED MY LIMIT.
THIS MAN HERE, SABATO ROKUDO, IS THE PRESIDENT OF THE DAMASHIGAMI COMPANY.

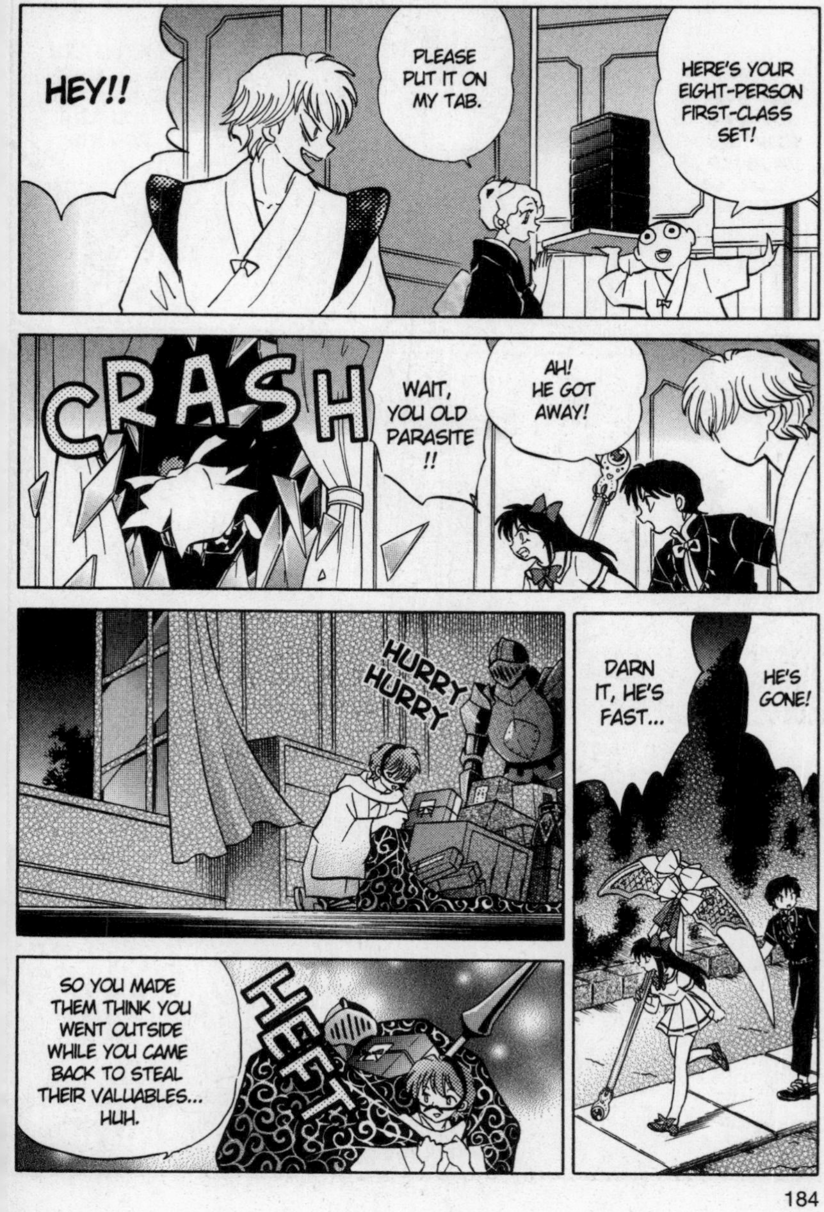
HERE'S YOUR EIGHT-PERSON FIRST-CLASS SET!
PLEASE PUT IT ON MY TAB.
HEY!!
AH! HE GOT AWAY!
WAIT, YOU OLD PARASITE!!
CRASH
HE'S GONE!
DARN IT, HE'S FAST...
HURRY HURRY
HEFT
SO YOU MADE THEM THINK YOU WENT OUTSIDE WHILE YOU CAME BACK TO STEAL THEIR VALUABLES... HUH.

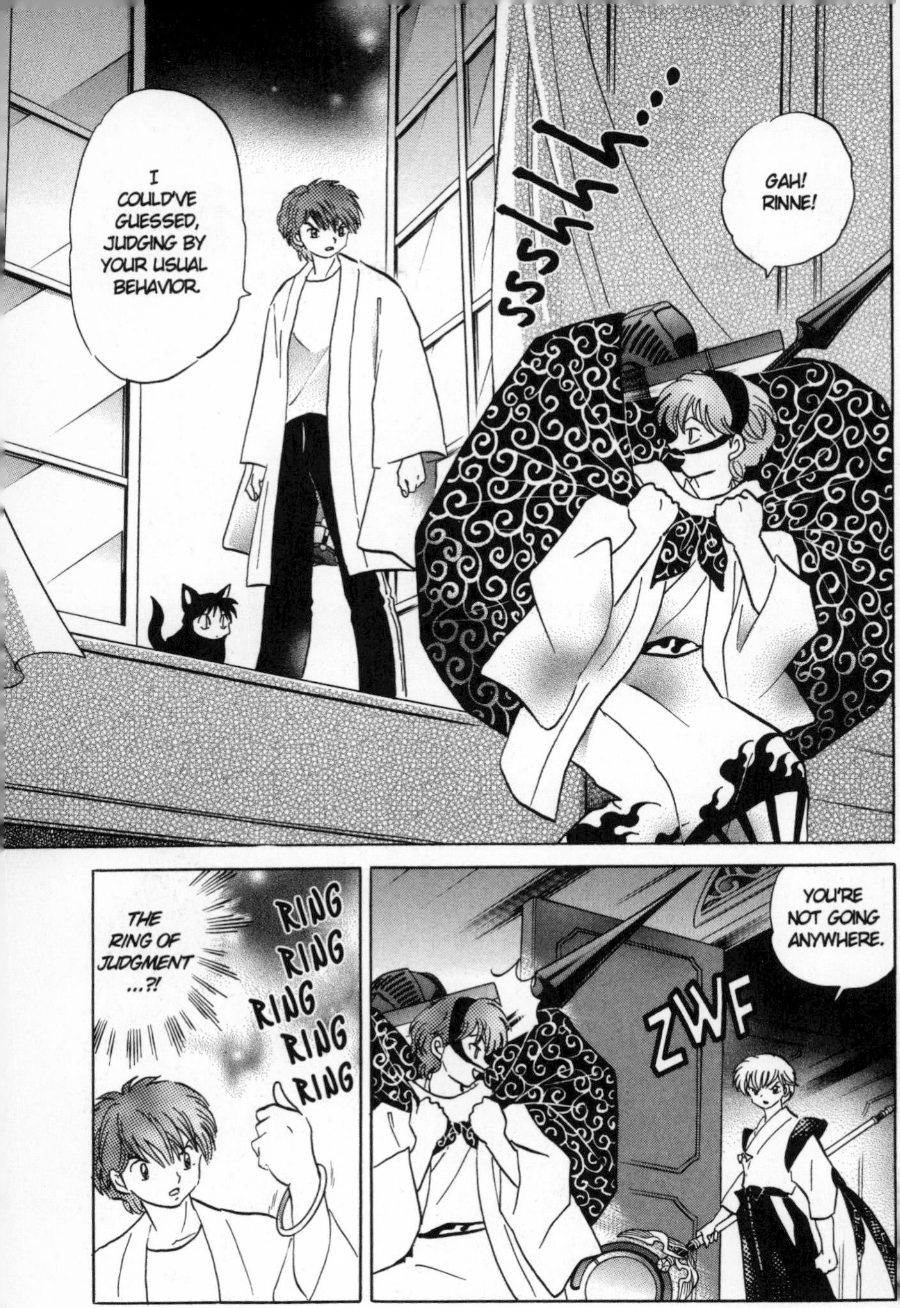
GAH! RINNE!
SSSHHH...
I COULD'VE GUESSED, JUDGING BY YOUR USUAL BEHAVIOR.
YOU'RE NOT GOING ANYWHERE.
ZWF
RING RING RING RING RING
THE RING OF JUDGMENT ...?!

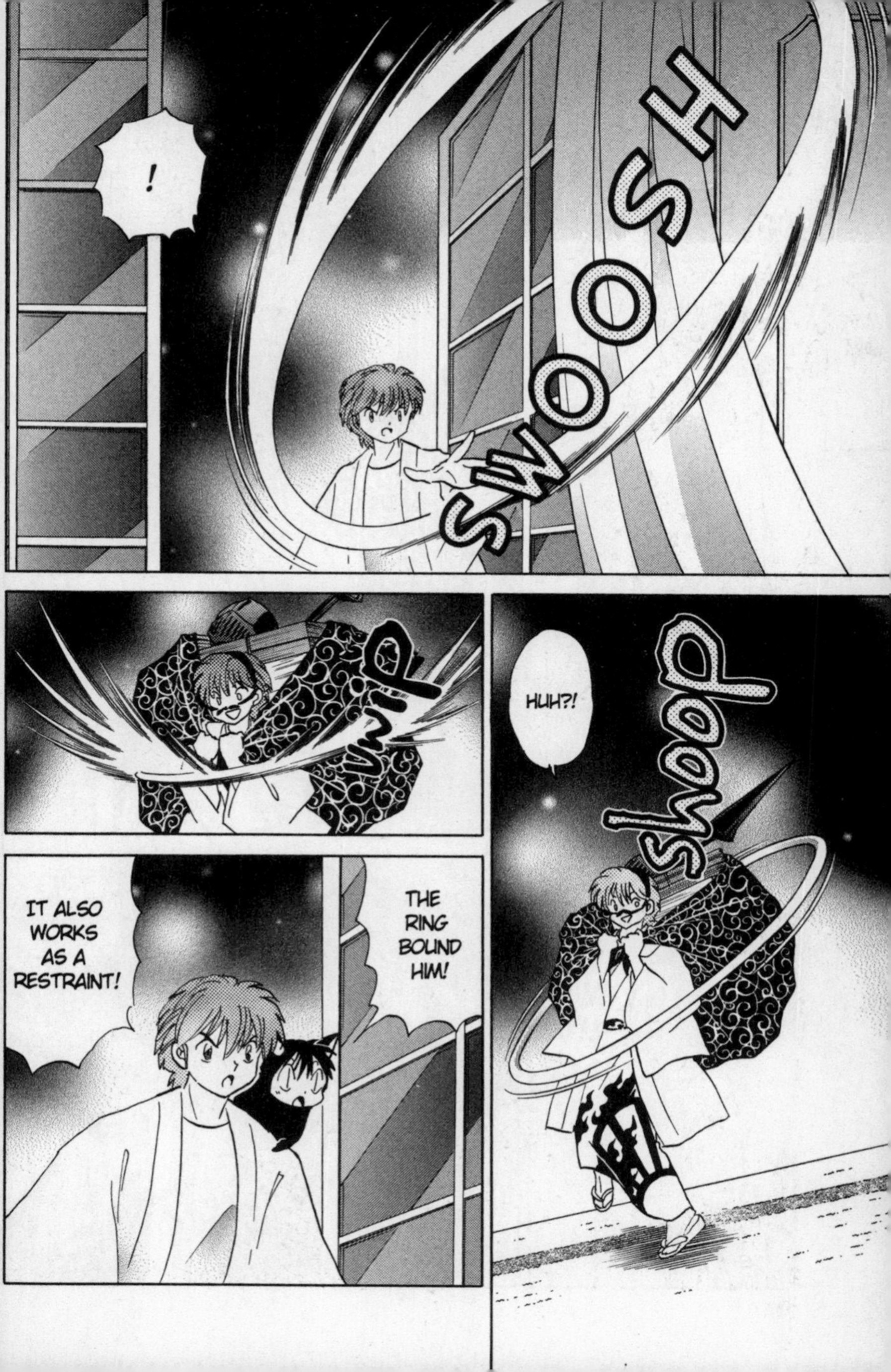
!
SWOOSH
HUH?!
shoop
whip
THE RING BOUND HIM!
IT ALSO WORKS AS A RESTRAINT!

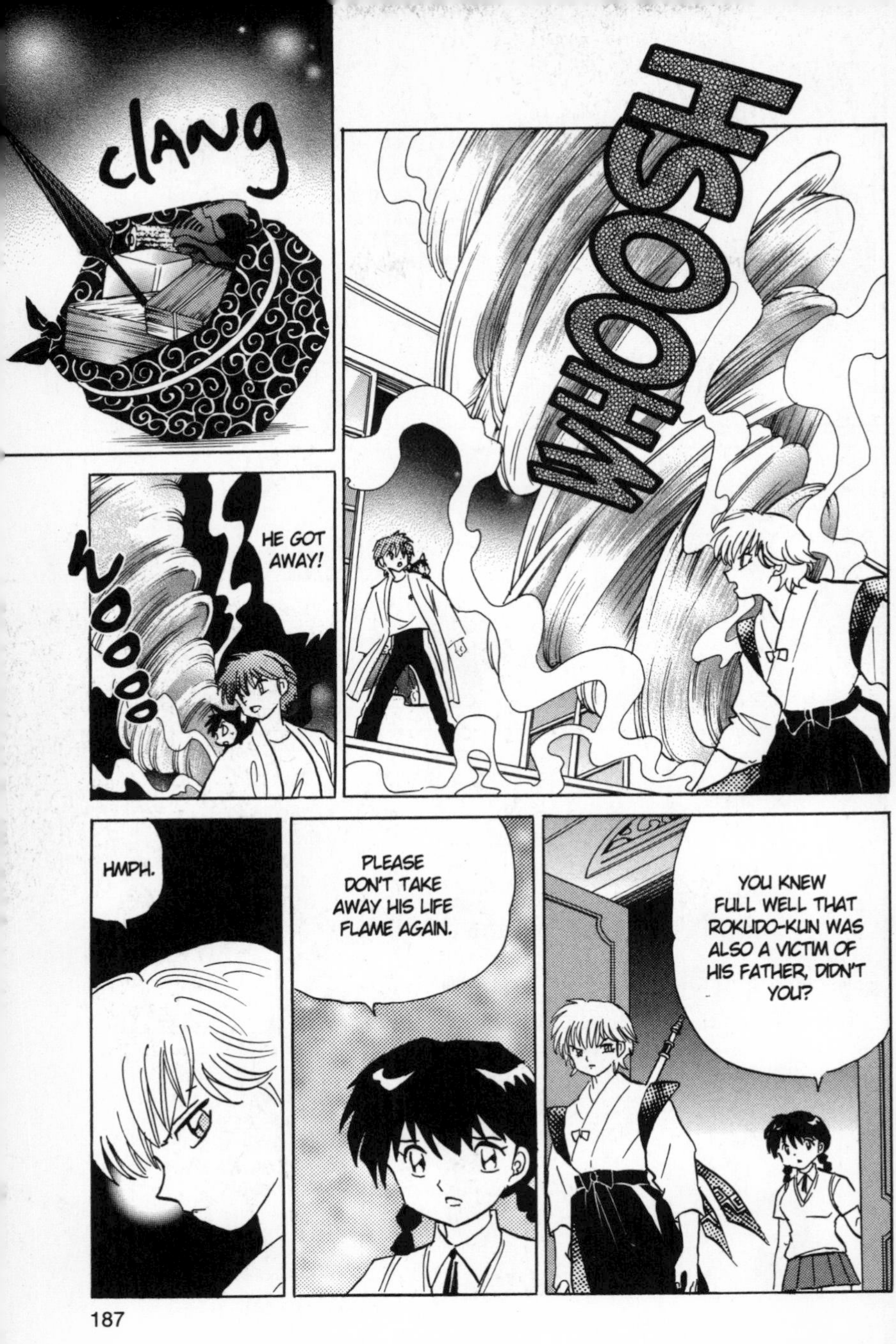
WHOOSH
clang
HE GOT AWAY!
WOOOOO
YOU KNEW FULL WELL THAT ROKUDO-KUN WAS ALSO A VICTIM OF HIS FATHER, DIDN'T YOU?
PLEASE DON'T TAKE AWAY HIS LIFE FLAME AGAIN.
HMPH.

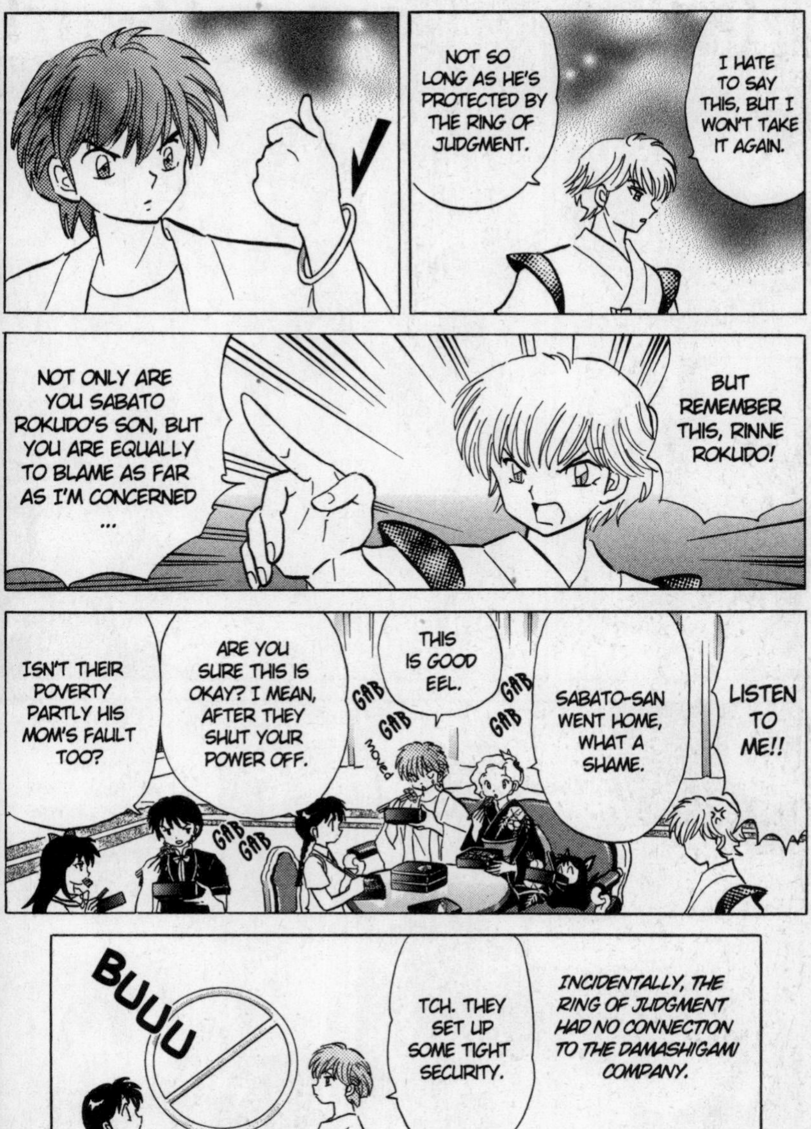
I HATE TO SAY THIS, BUT I WON'T TAKE IT AGAIN.
NOT SO LONG AS HE'S PROTECTED BY THE RING OF JUDGMENT.
BUT REMEMBER THIS, RINNE ROKUDO!
NOT ONLY ARE YOU SABATO ROKUDO'S SON, BUT YOU ARE EQUALLY TO BLAME AS FAR AS I'M CONCERNED ...
LISTEN TO ME!!
SABATO-SAN WENT HOME, WHAT A SHAME.
GAB GAB
THIS IS GOOD EEL.
GAB GAB
moved
ARE YOU SURE THIS IS OKAY? I MEAN, AFTER THEY SHUT YOUR POWER OFF.
GAB GAB
ISN'T THEIR POVERTY PARTLY HIS MOM'S FAULT TOO?
INCIDENTALLY, THE RING OF JUDGMENT HAD NO CONNECTION TO THE DAMASHIGAMI COMPANY.
TCH. THEY SET UP SOME TIGHT SECURITY.
BUUU

RIN-NE VOLUME 6 -END-

STUDENTS BY DAY, DEMON-FIGHTERS BY NIGHT!

KEKKAISHI
【けっかいし】

Teenagers Yoshimori and Tokine are "kekkaishi"—demon-fighters that battle bad beings side-by-side almost every night. They also quarrel with each other, but their biggest fight is the one between their families. Can Yoshimori and Tokine fight together long enough to end their families' ancient rivalry and save the world?

Join this modern-day Romeo and Juliet adventure—graphic novels now available at *store.viz.com*!

ONLY $9.99!

© 2004 Yellow Tanabe/Shogakukan, Inc.

viz
media

www.viz.com
store.viz.com

At Your Indentured Service

Hayate's parents are bad with money, so they sell his organs to pay their debts. Hayate doesn't like this plan, so he comes up with a new one—kidnap and ransom a girl from a wealthy family. Solid plan... so how did he end up as her butler?

Find out in *Hayate the Combat Butler*— buy the manga at store.viz.com!

© 2005 Kenjiro HATA/Shogakukan Inc.

www.viz.com
store.viz.com

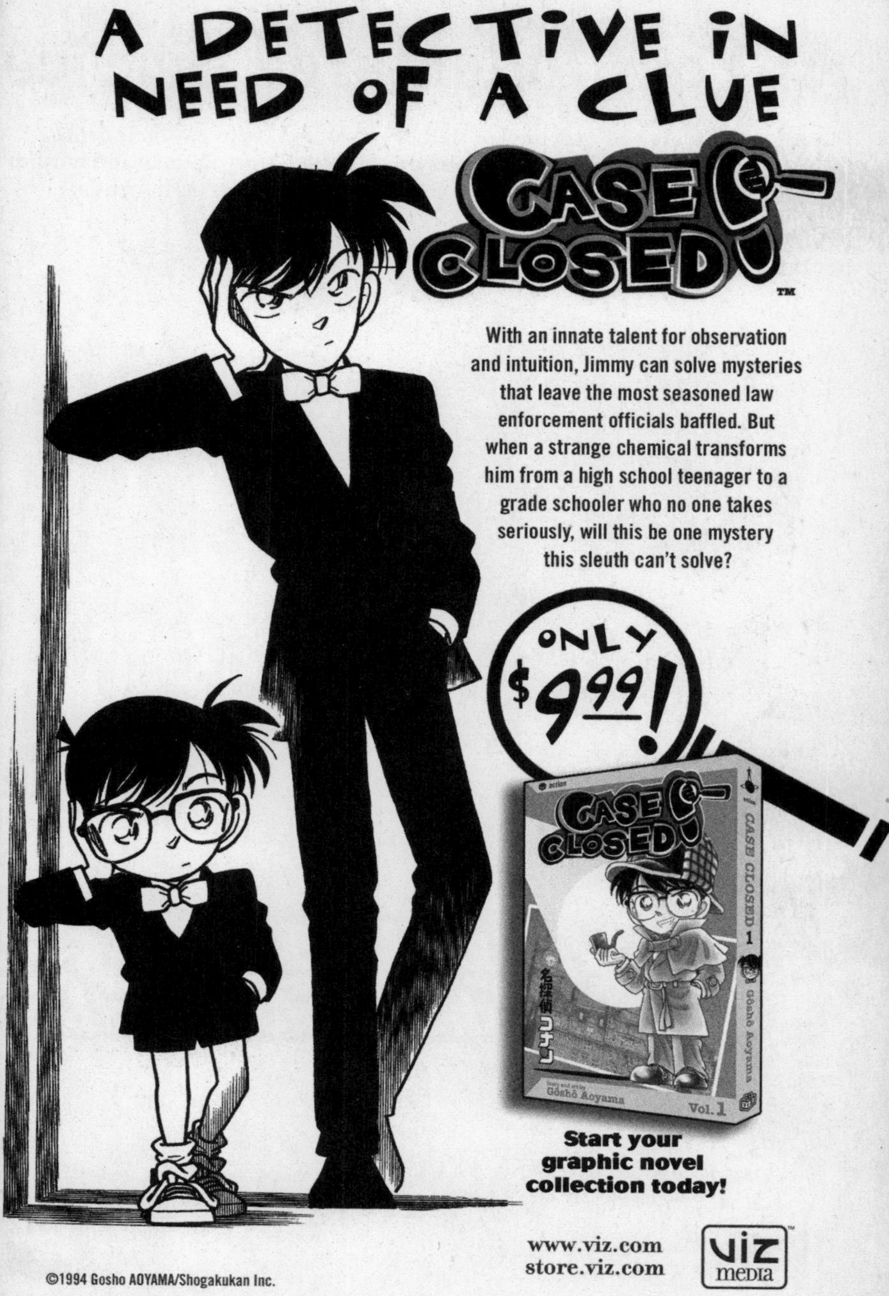
A DETECTIVE IN NEED OF A CLUE
CASE CLOSED™
With an innate talent for observation and intuition, Jimmy can solve mysteries that leave the most seasoned law enforcement officials baffled. But when a strange chemical transforms him from a high school teenager to a grade schooler who no one takes seriously, will this be one mystery this sleuth can't solve?
ONLY $9.99!
CASE CLOSED
名探偵コナン
Gōshō Aoyama
Vol. 1
Start your graphic novel collection today!
www.viz.com
store.viz.com
VIZ MEDIA
©1994 Gosho AOYAMA/Shogakukan Inc.